Joan
with love from
Frank
5 September 2002

POLYBIUS, ROME AND THE
HELLENISTIC WORLD

This volume contains nineteen of the more important of Frank Walbank's recent essays on Polybius and is prefaced by a critical discussion of the main aspects of work done on that author during the last quarter of a century. Several of these essays deal with specific historical problems for which Polybius is a major source. Five deal with Polybius as an historian and three with his attitude towards Rome; one of these raises the question of 'treason' in relation to Polybius and Josephus. Finally, two papers (one now appearing for the first time in English) discuss Polybius' later fortunes – in England up to the time of John Dryden and in twentieth-century Italy in the work of Gaetano de Sanctis. Several of these essays originally appeared in journals and collections not always easily accessible and all students of the ancient Mediterranean world will welcome their assembly within a single volume.

FRANK WALBANK is Professor Emeritus of Ancient History at the University of Liverpool and Honorary Fellow of Peterhouse, Cambridge. He has published continually on Polybius and Hellenistic history since 1933 and is the author of the standard commentary on his work, *A Historical Commentary on Polybius* (1957–1979). His other books include *The Awful Revolution* (1969), *Polybius* (1972), *The Hellenistic World* (1981), *Selected Papers: Studies in Greek and Roman History and Historiography* (1985) and, with N. G. L. Hammond, *A History of Macedonia, Vol. III: 336–167 BC*. He also co-edited both parts of volume VII of *The Cambridge Ancient History* (second edition). He is a Fellow of the British Academy and was awarded the CBE in 1993.

POLYBIUS, ROME AND THE HELLENISTIC WORLD

Essays and Reflections

FRANK W. WALBANK

Emeritus Professor, University of Liverpool
Honorary Fellow of Peterhouse, Cambridge

CAMBRIDGE
UNIVERSITY PRESS

PUBLISHED BY THE PRESS SYNDICATE OF THE UNIVERSITY OF CAMBRIDGE
The Pitt Building, Trumpington Street, Cambridge, United Kingdom

CAMBRIDGE UNIVERSITY PRESS
The Edinburgh Building, Cambridge CB2 2RU, UK
40 West 20th Street, New York, NY 10011-4211, USA
477 Williamstown Road, Port Melbourne, VIC 3207, Australia
Ruiz de Alarcón 13, 28014 Madrid, Spain
Dock House, The Waterfront, Cape Town 8001, South Africa

http://www.cambridge.org

First published 2002

Printed in the United Kingdom at the University Press, Cambridge

Typeface Baskerville Monotype 11/12.5 pt   *System* LaTeX 2ε   [TB]

A catalogue record for this book is available from the British Library

Library of Congress Cataloguing in Publication data
Walbank, F. W. (Frank William), 1909–
Polybius, Rome, and the Hellenistic world : essays and reflections / Frank W. Walbank.
p. cm.
Includes bibliographical references and index.
ISBN 0 521 81208 9
1. Polybius.   2. History, Ancient – Historiography.   3. Hellenism – Historiography.
4. Rome – History – Republic, 510–30 BC – Historiography.   1. Title.

D58.P8 W35   2002
930′.07′2 – dc21   2002020170

ISBN 0 521 81208 9

COLLEGIO DIVI PETRI AC SCHOLAE STUDIA GRAECA
ET ROMANA APUD CANTABRIGIENSES
EXERCENTIUM D D D

Contents

Preface

In 1985 the Cambridge University Press published a score of my *separata* in a volume entitled *Selected Papers*. The present volume contains a further nineteen papers, mostly dealing with Polybius. The majority of these were originally published after 1985, but I have included a few earlier ones, for which there was no room in the earlier volume. I have prefaced them with a newly written chapter, in which I have attempted a survey of the main topics and directions apparent in Polybian studies over the last twenty-five years and have indicated how the papers appearing here fit in with those trends. These papers are arranged in four sections. First, there are nine historical and geographical papers; next, five concerned with Polybius as a historian; then, three on Polybius and Rome; and finally two dealing with the later significance of Polybius, the first in seventeenth-century England at the time of Dryden and the second in twentieth-century Italy, as seen in the writings of the historian Gaetano De Sanctis.

In one or two places, and especially in papers which involve Polybius' views on the Roman constitution, there is some slight repetition; this is unfortunate, but was inevitable if the argument was to be clearly presented in each paper. After full consideration, it seemed better to reprint the articles as they were written and not to abbreviate them in a way likely to cause confusion in any reference to them. There is one partial exception to this, in chapter 4, where I have added a substantial note (in square brackets) giving what now seems to me a more correct and straightforward solution to an old problem in Ptolemaic dating. Elsewhere I have added a few notes in square brackets, giving cross-references and an occasional more recent item of bibliography; but generally I have confined later bibliography to the first chapter. I have of course corrected misprints, false references and the like, where I have detected them. The method of reference adopted is to quote author, date and pagination at the relevant point in the text, but to leave the full details of title and place of publication for the comprehensive bibliography.

Ever since I approached the Press with this project, it has received enthusiastic and constructive support; in particular I am indebted to Michael Sharp, who has done much to improve the book, as indeed have two anonymous referees, who came up with many useful suggestions, including an advantageous change in the choice of papers to be included. Linda Woodward has been a thoughtful and consistently helpful copy-editor. To Dorothy Thompson I am greatly indebted for help with library references and computer problems; and to John Thompson for meticulously reading the whole of chapter 1 and suggesting decided improvements, including a radical change in its construction. My greatest debt, however, is to Pauline Hire, who most generously volunteered to take on the formidable task of bringing all the chapters into line, checking the bibliographical items and reducing the forms of reference, which originally varied from paper to paper, to a single system. To all the above I should like to express my most grateful thanks.

Finally, I should like to say that it is a matter of considerable satisfaction to me that this book continues an association with the Cambridge University Press going back almost seventy years. I have dedicated it to two Cambridge institutions, Peterhouse and the Faculty of Classics, which have meant a great deal to me during the years since I retired here in 1977.

Peterhouse, Cambridge   FRANK W. WALBANK

Acknowledgements

For permission to republish my thanks are due to: Aris and Phillips Ltd, Warminster, Wiltshire (chapter 3); Giorgio Bretschneider, Casella Postale 30011, Rome (chapter 4); Aristide D. Caratzas, Melissa International Publications Inc., Crestwood, NY (chapter 19); J. G. Cotta'sche Buchhandlung Nachfolger GmbH, Stuttgart (chapter 13); The Institute for Balkan Studies, Thessaloniki (chapters 6 and 8); Helena Hurt Pinsent, *Liverpool Classical Monthly*, 4 Wellington Fields, Liverpool L15 0EL (chapter 12); Museum Tusculanum Press, University of Copenhagen (chapter 2); Oxford University Press (chapters 10 and 16); Professors Z. W. Rubinsohn and I. Malkin, Tel Aviv University (chapter 14); Editorial Board, *Scripta Classica Israelica*, Hebrew University, Jerusalem (chapters 5, 11 and 18); Franz Steiner Verlag, Postfach 101061, Stuttgart (chapters 9 and 17); Editorial Board, Studia Hellenistica, KU Leuven (chapter 15); University Press of America, Lanham MD 20760 (chapter 7).

Abbreviations

For classical authors and journals the usual forms, as given in *The Oxford Classical Dictionary*, third edition, ed. S. Hornblower and A. Spawforth (Oxford, 1999) or *L'Année Philologique*, are employed.

ANRW	H. Temporini and W. Haase, eds., *Aufstieg und Niedergang der römischen Welt: Geschichte und Kultur Roms im Spiegel der neueren Forschung*, Berlin–New York 1972–
CAH	*The Cambridge Ancient History*, Cambridge
D–K	H. Diels and W. Kranz, *Die Fragmente der Vorsokratiker*, 6th edn, Berlin 1952
FGH	F. Jacoby, *Die Fragmente der griechischen Historiker*, Berlin–Leiden 1923–
FHG	C. Müller, *Fragmenta Historicorum Graecorum*, Paris, 1841–70
HRR	H. W. E. Peter, *Historicorum Romanorum Reliquiae*, 2 vols., Leipzig, vol. I² 1914, vol. II 1906
IC	M. Guarducci, *Inscriptiones Creticae*, 4 vols., Rome 1935–50
IG	A. Kirchhoff et al., *Inscriptiones Graecae*, Berlin 1873–
ILS	H. Dessau, *Inscriptiones Latinae Selectae*, 3 vols., 1892–1916
ISE	L. Moretti, *Iscrizioni storiche ellenistiche*, 2 vols., Florence, 1967–75
LSJ	H. G. Liddell and R. Scott, *Greek–English Lexicon*, 9th edn rev. H. Stuart Jones, Oxford 1925–40
MRR	T. R. S. Broughton, *The Magistrates of the Roman Republic*, 2 vols., New York 1951; Supplementary volume 1960

OGIS	W. Dittenberger, *Orientis Graeci Inscriptiones Selectae*, 2 vols., Leipzig 1902–5
ORF	H. Malcovati, *Oratorum romanorum fragmenta*, 4th edn, Turin 1976–9
RE	A. Pauly, G. Wissowa and W. Kroll, *Real-Encyclopädie der classischen Altertumswissenschaft*, 83 vols. Stuttgart 1893–1980
SB	F. Preisigke and F. Bilabel, *Sammelbuch griechischer Urkunden aus Aegypten*, Strassburg 1915–
Scott–Saintsbury	Dryden, *Collected Works*, ed. W. Scott, 18 vols., London 1808; revised edn by G. Saintsbury, London 1893
SEG	*Supplementum epigraphicum Graecum*, Leiden 1923–
SGDI	H. Collitz and F. Bechtel, *Sammlung der griechischen Dialekt-Inschriften*, 4 vols., Göttingen 1885–1910
SVA	*Die Staatsverträge des Altertums*: II *Die Verträge der griechisch-römischen Welt von 700 bis 338 v. Chr.* ed. H. Bengtson, Munich 1962; III: *Die Verträge der griechisch-römischen Welt von 338 bis 200 v. Chr.* ed. H. H. Schmitt, Munich 1969
Syll.	W. Dittenberger, *Sylloge inscriptionum Graecarum*, 3rd edn, 4 vols., Leipzig 1915–24
Walbank, *Comm.*	F. W. Walbank, *A Historical Commentary on Polybius*, 3 vols., Oxford, 1957, 1967 and 1979

Note: To give help in following up references, the original pagination of the reprinted articles is indicated at the top of each page on the inner margin, and the original page divisions are marked in the course of the text by a pair of vertical lines, ||.

Polybian studies, c. 1975–2000

During the years following the end of the Second World War there was a remarkable surge of interest in Polybius, which it is hard to dissociate entirely from the contemporary clash of powers and the rise of the United States to preeminence, which were to dominate the next fifty years. For Polybius' central theme was of course the century-long struggle between Rome and Carthage and the rise of Rome to domination in her own world of cities and kingdoms, the *oecumene*. Be that as it may, the publication of a succession of books[1] and articles[2] on Polybius during the sixties – a trend already foreshadowed in the forties and fifties in Ziegler's important *Real-Encyclopädie* article, von Fritz's long study of Polybius' discussion of the mixed constitution and the first volume of my own *Commentary*[3] – has led more than one scholar to speak of a 'Polybian renaissance'.[4]

Some of this work has reflected historians' current interest in such topics as rhetoric and narrative technique, but on the whole older problems have remained uppermost in discussion: on the one hand Polybius' views on his own craft, his methods of composition and the content and purpose of his work and, on the other, his explanation of how and why Rome had been so successful, together with his own attitude towards Rome and her domination since 168 BC. In this introductory chapter I propose to describe and discuss what seem to me to have been the main trends in recent Polybian scholarship, covering roughly the last quarter of a century (though occasionally I shall go back earlier), and to indicate how the papers in this volume relate to these. During this time

[1] See Welwei (1963); Pédech (1964); Roveri (1964); Moore (1965); Eisen (1966); Lehmann (1967); Petzold (1969).
[2] For a selection of important articles and reviews of books on Polybius see Stiewe–Holzberg (1982); and for a detailed survey of work on Polybius between 1950 and 1970 see Musti (1972).
[3] K. Ziegler, *RE* XXI.2, s.v. 'Polybios', cols. 1440–1578; von Fritz (1954) and Walbank, *Comm.* I–III; see also Devroye–Kemp (1956).
[4] The phrase goes back to Schmitthenner (1968) 31; cf. Holzberg in Stiewe–Holzberg (1982) 11 and Nicolet (1983b) 15.

there have been several new books and around 200 articles, contributions to colloquia, collected papers and the like on Polybius. Of these I shall touch only on those which seem to me to be the most significant.[5]

I GENERAL SURVEY

I will begin with some of the basic work on Polybius' text. Here, perhaps the most important development has been the continuation of the excellent Budé edition, with French translation, which has now reached Book XVI under a series of editors.[6] There is still no Oxford text of Polybius and the proposed (and much needed) revision of Paton's Loeb edition seems to have run into the sand. Unfortunately the current pressure in universities for immediate publications makes scholars less inclined to take on work likely to occupy several years. There has been a German translation of Polybius by H. Drexler[7] and in English a Penguin selection translated by Ian Scott-Kilvert.[8] Only a few recent articles have concerned themselves with textual problems. A. Díaz Tejera has suggested new readings in Books II–III[9] and S. L. Radt has critical notes on a score of passages.[10] There have, however, been two important books on Polybius' language and style, one by J. A. Foucault, the other by M. Dubuisson, who investigates Polybius' knowledge of Latin and how far this is reflected in his writing.[11] For all readers of Polybius it is a great boon that, after a long silence, Mauersberger's *Polybios-Lexikon* is once more making progress and has now reached ποιέω; a revision of Volume I.1 (α–γ) has appeared and this is eventually to apply to the whole of Volume I. The new volumes contain many improvements and this important project is warmly to be welcomed.[12]

One problematic aspect of Polybius' text arises out of the odd way it is made up: from Book VI onwards it consists in the main of extracts assembled in the *excerpta antiqua* and the Constantinian selections, supplemented by passages from Athenaeus and the *Suda*. In Volumes II and III of my *Commentary*[13] I have attempted to explain and, where necessary,

---

[5] For a full bibliography see *Année philologique* for the relevant years.
[6] Book I (P. Pédech, 1969), Book II (P. Pédech, 1970), Book III (J. de Foucault, 1971), Book IV (J. de Foucault, 1972), Book V (P. Pédech, 1977), Book VI (R. Weil and C. Nicolet, 1977), Books VII–IX (R. Weil, 1982), Books X–XI (E. Foulon and R. Weil, 1990), Book XII (P. Pédech, 1991) Books XIII–XVI (E. Foulon, R. Weil and P. Cauderlier).
[7] Drexler (1961–3). [8] Scott-Kilvert (1979). [9] Díaz Tejera (1985). [10] Radt (1990).
[11] Foucault (1972); Dubuisson (1985).
[12] For Vol. II.1 see Glockmann and Helms (1998); and for the revision of Vol. I.1 see Collatz, Helms and Schäfer (2000).
[13] Walbank, *Comm.* II, 1–28, III, 1–62.

emend the order in which these passages now stand in Büttner-Wobst's standard text; but that order cannot always be established with certainty. In 1985, for example, I published a proposal to reassign two Polybian passages from the *Suda*: xvi.29 to immediately before ix.40.3, and xvi.38 to immediately before x.25.[14] (For a proposed modification of the order of the fragments in Book XXII see the addition to the last note in chapter 4, below.) I have discussed Athenaeus' contribution to our current text of Polybius elsewhere.[15]

A stimulating essay by Fergus Millar argues that our present text of Polybius, which adds up to less than a third of the original, presents too Roman a flavour.[16] This view can be contested. After all, Polybius' primary, declared purpose was to write, not a simple continuation of Greek history, but an account of the take-over of the 'inhabited world', the *oecumene*, by Rome; and although, especially in the later books, we no longer have access to considerable tracts of the original narrative concerned with Greece and the Near East, it seems unlikely that a full text would have shown a very different emphasis. For one thing, the order in which events throughout the *oecumene* are presented in each Olympiad year, always beginning with *res Italiae*, seems designed to establish a Roman pattern and this continues throughout the *Histories*. The possibility that the way the extracts have survived may have introduced bias was originally suggested by Momigliano in a Vandoeuvres colloquium[17] and was subsequently taken up by W. E. Thompson, who argued, somewhat unconvincingly, that the *excerpta antiqua*, taken only from Books VI–XVIII, represent a working-over of Polybius' text for a military handbook.[18] In its most general form the argument is perhaps still *sub judice* but an important article by P. A. Brunt warns readers of Polybius against possible distortion arising from the selective nature of the Constantinian excerpts.[19] The relevance of fragments both for Polybius' own text and for authors whom he quotes and criticises was the subject of a conference held at Leuven in 2001.

The proceedings of conferences on particular historical or historiographical topics have contributed substantially to Polybian studies in recent years. I have already mentioned the Vandoeuvres conference of 1973. Equally important for Polybian studies were the proceedings of a colloquium held at Leuven in 1988 on the purposes of history,[20] at which

[14] Walbank (1985b).   [15] Walbank (2000).   [16] Millar (1987).
[17] Momigliano (1974b) 35–6.   [18] W. E. Thompson (1985).   [19] Brunt (1980).
[20] Verdin, Schepens and De Keyser (1990). See the separate references, all 1990, to Vercruysse, Schepens, Dubuisson, D'Huys and Wiedemann, and chapter 15 of this volume.

six of the seventeen papers directly concerned Polybius and almost all the others touched on his work. Among other topics dealt with here were Polybius' methodology, his use of *topoi*, his attitude towards Rome and various rhetorical aspects of his writing. A collection of papers on *Greek Historiography*,[21] edited by S. Hornblower, who contributes an important introduction, deals with Polybius at many points and especially in a paper by Peter Derow, who discusses 'historical explanation' as it affects Polybius and his predecessors.[22] Several volumes in a series entitled 'Hellenistic Culture and Society', published by the University of California Press, are important for the study both of Polybius and of the society in which he grew up. I shall mention some of these in the course of this survey. Meanwhile, one should note the inclusion in the series of three volumes devoted to colloquia. Two of these, both published in 1993, contain the proceedings of conferences held at Berkeley[23] and at Austin, Texas[24] in 1988. An important topic, discussed in both volumes, is Hellenistic kingship, for which the evidence of Polybius is indispensable. A third colloquium, held at Cambridge in 1993,[25] contained two papers (by H. Mattingly[26] and A. M. Eckstein[27]) that are relevant to Polybius.

Reference may also be made here to one or two volumes containing the collected papers of scholars whose work has been largely concerned with Polybius. In 1998 Doron Mendels published a collection of his essays, about a dozen of which drew directly on Polybius, especially as a source for social and economic issues in third- and second-century Greece;[28] and in 1985 I published a selection of papers, most of them with a Polybian background.[29] There have also been several important books specifically devoted to Polybius, by K. Meister, H. Tränkle, K. Sacks, D. Golan and A. M. Eckstein;[30] my own Sather Lectures on Polybius were published in 1972.[31] Two studies of Greek historiography, by C. V. Fornara and K. Meister, contain important sections on Polybius.[32] Fornara is interested in him as an example of Greek historiography as contrasted

[21] Hornblower (1994).
[22] Derow (1994). I have criticised Derow's treatment of Polyb. iii.6.7 on ἀρχή, αἰτία and πρόφασις in my review in *Histos*, December 1996; it is the αἰτίαι, the events leading up to a decision to go to war, that constitute 'processes involving several elements' and not the decisions (κρίσεις) themselves, as Derow suggests.
[23] Bulloch, et al. (1993). This book contains a good deal on Polybius, especially in papers by K. Bringmann and L. Koenen on Hellenistic kingship.
[24] Green (1993).   [25] Cartledge, et al. (1997).   [26] Mattingly (1997).
[27] Eckstein (1997).   [28] Mendels (1998).   [29] Walbank (1985a).
[30] Meister (1975); Tränkle (1978); Sacks (1981); Golan (1995); Eckstein (1995).
[31] Walbank (1972a).   [32] Fornara (1983); Meister (1990) 153–66.

with other literary genres and Meister's general handbook has a special section on Polybius.

Finally, the volume of work devoted to Polybius has been considerably augmented as a result of the growing interest in the Hellenistic world and in the rise of Rome in recent decades. This has led to several important publications, many of which, though not directly concerned with Polybius, necessarily draw on and discuss his work. For the Hellenistic world generally I will mention only the indispensable political survey by Ed. Will, Claire Préaux's outstanding study of the Hellenistic world (though it has little on Polybius), the histories by Peter Green, Graham Shipley and myself, and Volume VII.1 of the new edition of *The Cambridge Ancient History.* Volume VIII deals with Roman events from 220 to 133 BC, which includes most of the period covered by Polybius' *Histories*; Volume VII.2 covers the First Punic War.[33] Also relevant here are Volume III of the *History of Macedonia* by N. G. L. Hammond and myself, which covers most of the period treated by Polybius,[34] and R. M. Errington's *History of Macedonia.*[35] On Roman expansion and Polybius' treatment of this see also the recent works of W. V. Harris, E. S. Gruen, W. Huss (a notable history of Carthage), and J. Seibert (on Hannibal).[36]

Chapters 3–10 of the present volume concern incidents and institutions figuring in Polybius' account of the Greek and Hellenistic world. Chapters 3 and 4 deal with aspects of Hellenistic Egypt, chapter 5 compares two well-recorded processions, one in Ptolemaic Alexandria under Ptolemy II and the other in Daphne near Antioch in the Seleucid kingdom under Antiochus IV, as examples of image-creation in the two main Hellenistic kingdoms. Chapter 6 discusses Polybius' picture of Hellenistic Macedonia, chapter 7 the rôle of sea-power in the Antigonid monarchy and chapter 8 demonstrates the logic behind Polybius' apparently improbable claim (v.102.1) that the Macedonian royal house (under the Antigonids) had always aimed at universal power. In chapter 9 I trace the importance of the Achaean League and its shrine at the Homarion, aided by the Homeric echoes of the name Achaea, down to AD 67 and defend Polybius' account of the early development of the League; and in chapter 10 I offer a solution to the old problem concerning the constitution of the Achaean assemblies.

---

[33] Will (1979), (1982); Préaux (1978); Green (1990) especially 269–85; Shipley (2000); Walbank (1981); *CAH*, 2nd edn, VII.1 (1984), VII.2 and VIII (1989).

[34] Hammond and Walbank (1988).   [35] Errington (1986).

[36] Harris (1979); Gruen (1984); Huss (1985); Seibert (1993).

II POLYBIUS' VIEWS ON THE CONTENT AND PURPOSE OF HISTORY: METHODOLOGY AND ASPECTS OF COMPOSITION

Polybius stands out among ancient historians in his anxiety to define the sort of history he wrote. In ix.1.1–5 he distinguishes three kinds of history: the 'genealogical kind', which is attractive to the casual reader (τὸν φιλήκοον), 'accounts of colonies, city foundations and kinship ties', which appeal to the reader with antiquarian interests, literally 'the man with curiosity and subtle learning' (τὸν πολυπράγμονα καὶ περιττόν) and, finally, 'affairs (πράξεις) of peoples (ἔθνη), cities and rulers'. His own work, he tells us, falls into the third category and he describes it as of interest to the politician (ὁ πολιτικός). Probably because it dealt with πράξεις,[37] he calls it 'pragmatic history' (πραγματικὴ ἱστορία), an expression not found earlier and probably his own formulation. It is a phrase which has provoked much controversy; indeed, scarcely anyone discussing Polybius as a historian can have failed to come up with his own translation of this.[38]

Two main issues arise in relation to Polybius' use of the expression 'pragmatic history': what it implied in terms of content and whether Polybius regarded it as restricted to a particular historical period. Petzold has argued for a didactic element in 'pragmatic history'[39] and this view has been taken up and developed in a long and important article by his pupil B. Meissner,[40] who claims that any definition of 'pragmatic history' must take into account all aspects of Polybius' work. This paper contains some excellent observations, for example that Polybius' extensive criticism of other historians is intended in part to furnish negative examples of what is to be avoided, and it offers a good characterisation of Polybius as a historian. But its definition of 'pragmatic history' seems to me to rest on the fallacy that this phrase must embrace in its meaning everything that Polybius chooses to include in his *Histories*.[41]

A more recent study of the phrase, that of H. Beister,[42] is particularly concerned with the question whether 'pragmatic history' is supposed to apply only to the period covered in Polybius' *Histories*. On this there have been several views. Meister,[43] pointing to the passage referred to above (ix.1.1–5), argues that, although in practice Polybius is dealing only

---

[37] Cf. xxxix.8.6: Polybius will write τὰς κοινὰς τῆς οἰκουμένης πράξεις, the common events of the inhabited world.

[38] See Walbank (1972a), 66–96. For a bibliography of recent suggested meanings of the phrase see Beister (1995) 329 n.1.

[39] Petzold (1969).   [40] Meissner (1986).   [41] Cf. Walbank (1972a) 56 n. 148.

[42] See n. 38.   [43] Meister (1990) 160.

with contemporary and near-contemporary events, 'pragmatic history' covers the whole of the period following the 'age of colonisation', which indeed means the colonisation of the eighth to the sixth centuries and excludes the expansion into Asia after Alexander. This view in effect defines 'pragmatic history' more as the description of a historical period than as a kind of historiography. Beister, however, argues convincingly that 'pragmatic history' need not essentially contain any chronological component: it is simply, as Polybius says, 'the events of peoples, cities and rulers'. It is also history useful to the πολιτικός who, Beister thinks, can be either a politician or a student of politics.

It is true that Polybius nowhere specifically restricts 'pragmatic history' to any particular period; but in his own work, obviously, it is with the period he is covering, namely from where Timaeus' *Histories* ended to 146 BC, that it is concerned. The phrase 'peoples, cities and rulers' is one often to be found in inscriptions and elsewhere as a piece of official Hellenistic jargon.[44] This seems to stamp 'pragmatic history' as primarily political and military, although in Polybius' sixth book and elsewhere it clearly does not preclude the discussion of other matters; for, as Meissner shows, the *Histories* contain much that is not purely military or political, for example the drawing of moral lessons.[45] But these elements are not to be regarded as included in the definition of 'pragmatic history'. Polybius also touches on events which took place earlier than his own chosen period, where his narrative or comments on his narrative render that necessary;[46] such events are neither included under 'pragmatic history' nor are they excluded by any chronological aspect attached to the phrase. How in fact Polybius saw the remote past is a subject on its own and one discussed both in chapter 12 below and in an interesting article by G. A. Lehmann.[47]

If 'pragmatic history' refers basically to history with a political and military content, another phrase used by Polybius, 'apodeictic history' (ἀποδεικτικὴ ἱστορία), seems rather to describe a method of composition.[48] This expression has also been the subject of much controversy. In a well-argued exposition, K. Sacks has shown that the word ἀποδεικτική (or the phrase 'with *apodeixis*', μετ' ἀποδείξεως) simply relates to a fuller narrative in contrast to a summary (κεφαλαιώδης)

---

[44] Cf. Walbank (1972a) 56 n. 145.   [45] See Eckstein (1995).
[46] E.g. i.12.7–9 (general statement), ii.18–20 (early Celtic invasions), 38–40 (early Achaean history), iii.22–7 (Punic–Roman treaties).
[47] Lehmann (1989/90). In chapter 11, I discuss Timaeus' views on the past.
[48] Polyb. ii.37.3, iv.40.1 (with διήγησις); cf. x.21.8 (ὁ μετ' ἀποδείξεως ἀπολογισμός), contrasting the *Histories* with Polybius' biography of Philopoemen.

account.[49] It does not describe a special kind of historical treatment; nor does it in itself mean 'history which investigates causes' – though in practice it is difficult to see how an extended historical narrative could exclude such an investigation.

Polybius also claims that his history is 'universal', not in Ephorus' sense of covering the whole of the past,[50] but in embracing the whole *oecumene* at a time when its history has itself become a single whole. This claim, as I have explained elsewhere,[51] implies a certain sleight of hand, inasmuch as it involves Polybius in projecting the concept of the unity of a historical composition (in contrast to a 'continuous history' like that of Xenophon) onto the events it describes. Polybius' notion of 'universal history' has come to the fore in recent years. In particular, J. M. Alonso-Nuñez has taken up this theme,[52] stressing the geographical limitations implied in Polybius' concept of the *oecumene* and attaching importance to the idea of the 'four world-empires', leading up to that of Rome, which, he argues, played an important part in Polybius' thought.[53] In contrast, Doron Mendels has contended[54] that the *topos* of the 'four – or four-plus-one – world-empires' (i.e. Assyria, Media, Persia, Macedonia plus Rome) had not yet crystallised at the time Polybius was writing. More recently Katherine Clarke has discussed the same question, emphasising the spatial aspect of Polybius' unified *oecumene* in contrast to Derow and Millar, both of whom point rather to Roman *imperium* and the universal enforcement of Roman orders as an expression of power.[55] Clarke sees the unified *oecumene* as σωματοειδής, 'like a corporeal whole'; the biological metaphor used here is one which, she claims, is significant for Polybius' interpretation of the development of historical institutions, including states and empires.[56]

Another aspect of Polybius' view of historiography which has attracted recent attention is the antithesis which he draws between utility and pleasure and the rôle he proposes for these two concepts in the composition of his *Histories*. I have discussed this in chapter 15 below and it is also the subject of an article by V. D'Huys,[57] who in an analysis of Polybius'

---

[49] Sacks (1981) 171–5.   [50] Cf. Polyb. v.53.2 for Ephorus' universal history.
[51] See Walbank (1972a), 67; this sleight of hand is facilitated by Polybius' emphasis on the rôle of Fortune, *Tyche*, in bringing about this unity. On 'continuous history' see Cicero, *Ad fam.* v.12.2, 12.6.
[52] Alonso-Nuñez (1990) especially 186 n. 32 for a bibliography of earlier discussion of this topic in some of the works mentioned above in n. 1.
[53] Alonso-Nuñez (1983).   [54] Mendels (1981).   [55] Derow (1979) 4–6; Millar (1987) 1.
[56] Clarke (1999a) 124; see also (1999b) 278–9, with useful bibliography.
[57] D'Huys (1990) with bibliography at 267 n. 1.

account of the battle of Zama (xv.9–14) shows how particular *topoi*, which
are to be found in accounts of battles in earlier historians as well as in
Homer and the tragedians, also occur in Polybius, but only to a limited
extent and at points where they help to clarify the narrative. Polybius,
in short, does not sacrifice truth in order to create an effect. Others who
have touched on this problem are S. Mohm, K. Sacks, J. Boncquet and
H. Labuske.[58] Polybius' contrasting of utility and pleasure is only one of
the themes in his work that look back to some of his predecessors and it
raises the question whether his place in a historical tradition should be
regarded as an important element in any assessment of his work.

The study of tradition in historical writing is discussed at length in
an important recent book by J. Marincola.[59] In this study Marincola
assesses the literary and moral traditions inherited by a succession of
Greek historians, including Polybius, which help to shape their writing.
He isolates the various rhetorical and compositional devices they employ,
in order, for instance, to establish their *bona fides* and their competence
as historians, and he identifies the precepts, examples and modes of
operation, which they hand down from one to another for adoption (with
or without modification) in order to support their claims. This approach
is new in so far as it treats historical texts, not least that of Polybius, more
as a form of self-definition than as an unprejudiced factual narrative. It
sees historical texts as a means of negotiation between the historian and
his readers. It involves studying Polybius in his social context, especially
in his relationship to a reading public and a tradition of historical writing;
and it leads to a consideration of his purpose in writing *in that particular
context* rather than simply accepting his historical statements as if they
were all objectively determined. When, for example, Polybius remarks
that the Rhodian historians Zeno and Antisthenes were moved by the
desire for glory and renown, he is formulating an aspect of motivation
carrying implications for other writers, including himself, which must be
taken into account in assessing anything he and others write. From this
perspective historiography can be seen as a form of self-projection.

I have summarised this argument at some length as it seems a good
illustration of a new approach to be found increasingly in writers on
historiography. One should perhaps note, however, that it is basically less
novel than it might appear to be. The good critic has always known that
behind a historian's account lie assumptions and aims directly related
to his predecessors, to his contemporary situation and (if he is a public

---

58 Mohm (1977) 250–61; Sacks (1981) 122–70; Boncquet (1982–3); Labuske (1984).
59 Marincola (1997); I have reviewed this work in *Histos* (1997), 1–9.

figure like Polybius) to his own political career, his present stance and his future ambitions; also that literary presentation can affect the emphasis of his narrative.

I will close this section with a look at several further methodologi-cal questions which have attracted the attention of Polybian scholars. The first of these is a query: did Polybius set out to construct a consis-tent account of how historical research should be conducted and history written? The question arises particularly in relation to two chapters in the twelfth book (xii.25e and 27). In the first of these, which introduces an elaborate comparison between practitioners of medicine and historians, Polybius identifies three fields in which the 'pragmatic historian' may work. First, in a library, studying and comparing memoirs and other documents; secondly, by investigating geographical features of all kinds, which of course involves travel; and, thirdly, by acquiring political expe-rience. Discussing these, he asserts that it is folly to think that one can write satisfactory history by applying oneself (as Timaeus did) to only the first of these. In xii.27, however, he introduces a quite different distinc-tion, based on whether the historian uses his eyes or his ears. Here the ears are the organs employed both in reading (presumably aloud) and in interrogating eye-witnesses of historical events; reading – Timaeus' method – is easy, but interrogating witnesses is very difficult, though in fact it constitutes 'the most important part of history'. A few lines ear-lier, however, Polybius has told us that information conveyed through the eyes is superior to what we learn through the ears. The different approach adopted in these two chapters and the apparent contradiction in xii.27 (where the eyes are superior to the ears but the interrogation of eye-witnesses through the ears is the most important thing of all) present problems on the assumption that they are part of a developed and coher-ent guide to writing history. The likelihood, as Schepens has observed,[60] is that Polybius' remarks in the two passages are independent of each other and have simply grown out of his primary purpose at this point, that of demolishing all Timaeus' pretensions. They are not, therefore, to be reconciled as elements in a comprehensive and internally consistent exposition of how history should be written.

A second issue which is basic for our view of Polybius as a historian is that of truthfulness and how far he was committed to this in principle and in practice. Polybius, of course, repeatedly asserts the importance of truth, which, he insists, is essential if history is to be of any use – though in his criticism of other writers he distinguishes between deliberate and

---

[60] Schepens (1974) and (1990) 50 n. 39; see also Sacks (1981) 26 n. 10.

unintentional falsehood and in consequence how the two should be judged.[61] Important objections to taking this distinction simply at face-value have, however, been raised by M. Vercruysse,[62] who points out that in his many criticisms of other historians Polybius invokes no single, clearly defined criterion for distinguishing between 'true' and 'false' and for evaluating sources on that basis, but that he adduces a variety of grounds on which to question their veracity, the one constant element in these criticisms being Polybius' purpose, which is to confirm his own status and reliability. Such passages Vercruysse would read primarily as a means towards self-definition and so demote the issue of truth *per se* to a secondary level. How far Polybius himself satisfied his own demand for truth is a question implicit in Schepens' work on such compositional devices as emphasis and vivid description (ἐνάργεια), which can result, if not in falsehood, at any rate in a distortion of the actual narrative of events.[63]

A third and important aspect of Polybius' compositional method is his insertion of speeches, a traditional feature in ancient historiography, which served more than one purpose and in itself raises the question of truth and falsehood, depending on the accuracy with which the original speech (if it was ever made) is reproduced. Several scholars have discussed the rhetorical aspect of this convention. Mogens Hansen has written on the 'battle-exhortations', which both in Polybius and traditionally account for many such speeches; and C. Wooten has drawn attention to the influence of Demosthenes on Polybius' speeches. Some aspects of Wooten's argument have been queried by T. Wiedemann, in a paper which discusses the impact of rhetoric on Polybius' composition generally. In particular he mentions the battle-scene and the character-sketch as areas where rhetoric is employed and he furnishes a useful analysis of the various situations which Polybius chooses to emphasise by the insertion of speeches.[64] In a lecture already mentioned above,[65] Fergus Millar suggests that Polybius uses speeches as a way of exercising criticism without revealing his own views; this, as we shall see later, is relevant to some passages directly concerned with Roman policy in the Third Punic War. A rhetorical device not without some similarity to the use of speeches (if Millar's point is accepted) is discussed by J. Davidson, in a stimulating discussion of what he calls 'the gaze in Polybius',[66] by which he means Polybius' habit of presenting events not directly but

[61] See especially Polyb. xvi.14.3 (Zeno and Antisthenes). See on this Luce (1989).
[62] Vercruysse (1984) and (1990).   [63] Schepens (1975); see also Gill (1984).
[64] Hansen (1993); Wooten (1974); Wiedemann (1990).   [65] Millar (1987) 15–16; see above, n. 16.
[66] Davidson (1991).

rather as seen through the eyes of several characters in the narrative, a device which diverts the reader from the historian.

A fourth aspect of Polybius' compositional technique has, on the contrary, the result of drawing the reader's attention rather towards the author. I refer to his constant indulgence in polemic against other writers, including his predecessors, those whom he has used as sources and his contemporaries. This is a topic dealt with in most books on Polybius' method, for example those of Meister and Sacks.[67] A more recent study of the question, particularly as it concerns Timaeus, is Guido Schepens' contribution to the Leuven conference on ancient historiography frequently mentioned above, in which he discusses the purpose behind Polybius' polemic. In an earlier paper on this subject I had stressed some of the personal motives behind Polybius' attacks on other historians – political in the case of Phylarchus, social prejudice in that of Pytheas, jealousy in that of Timaeus and so on.[68] Schepens rightly emphasises Polybius' genuine concern for methodology, as an element in his polemic, and the importance of his anxiety to correct what he regarded as faults springing from a wrong conception of what history was about. This is, I think, correct and demonstrates how a critical historian like Polybius is often moved by more than one sort of motivation. More recently, Marincola has emphasised Polybius' use of polemic as a means of self-definition and has shown how this often reveals not merely his critical spirit and his concern for the nature of historical writing, but also a liking for rhetorical display (ἐπίδειξις) and some indulgence in Alexandrian pedantry. This subject is also discussed by J. Boncquet and by H. Verdin, who in the course of discussion at the Leuven conference of 1988 commented that Polybius' most methodologically directed criticism is to be found in his most polemical passages. This is a useful warning against trying to set up too rigid a separation between the various concerns by which he was motivated[69].

A final point which seems in place here is one raised by Marincola about the rôle of the historian,[70] when, as is true for Polybius, he is himself a statesman or military man who played a part in events which he was subsequently to describe. Whether, and in what circumstances, he should use the first or third person to refer to himself in this situation may seem a trivial or even pedantic point, but it has several implications for the

[67] Meister (1975); Sacks (1981) 66–78.   [68] Walbank (1962).

[69] Schepens (1990); Marincola (1997) especially 222–34; Boncquet (1982–3); Verdin in Verdin, Schepens and De Keyser (1990) 71.

[70] Marincola (1997) 188–92.

Histories. Marincola has shown that up to Book XXXVI Polybius follows the norm introduced by Thucydides, which was to use the third person to describe his participation in actual events and the first person when he wrote as a historian. From xxxvi.11–12 onwards, however, Polybius ceases to make this distinction in describing his own part in historical events and comments on this fact (in xxxvi.12): it is done, he explains, because of his close personal involvement in the events from 150 onwards and because he wishes to avoid the tedious repetition which would arise if he stuck closely to the accepted convention. Marincola observes that the change in rôle and mode of reference make what follows appear 'to lose the perspective of history and become suspiciously like memoirs'. This is true and significant, and perhaps indicates the point at which this account should turn to a related aspect of Polybius' work that has especially occupied scholarship.

III POLYBIUS AND ROME

Since Rome lies at the centre of the *Histories*, it is not surprising that much recent work on Polybius has been on issues related to Rome. In particular, the causes of her successful rise to world domination, and the various factors which he sees as contributing to it, have continued to evoke controversy. These factors include such matters as the relevance of early Roman history, dealt with in some form in the lost *archaeologia* in Book VI, to his general theme, the superiority of the Roman army and problems connected with its composition, organisation and functioning, other aspects of Roman life and culture, the ἔθη καὶ νόμιμα (vi.11.4) which shaped the way Romans lived and, not least, the part played by Fortune, *Tyche*, in the rise of Rome. Another aspect of Polybius' concern with Rome is his attitude towards the ruling power, whether he began by being critical of her conduct and came over in due course to a full acceptance of her supremacy or, indeed, whether he was favourable to Rome from the time he decided to write his history or was, on the contrary, critical (and how critical?) of her policy throughout his life. Closely linked with this are the reasons for his decision to extend his *Histories* to cover the years 167 to 145 in a further ten books (XXXI–XL). There has also been a study by Arthur Eckstein of Polybius' use of moral criteria, not only in relation to Rome but also in his judgemental remarks on other historical situations.[71] This book is important in drawing attention to an aspect

---

[71] Eckstein (1995).

of Polybius' thought which some scholars (including myself) have been liable to underestimate.

In a separate article[72] Eckstein has also examined Polybius' views on the Romans generally and has argued that he did not see them as basically different from others or as in any way extraordinary or specially favoured by fortune, but simply as a people who enjoyed the advantages of outstanding military skill and moral superiority. M. Roux explains their undoubted military skill as lying especially in the effectiveness of Roman generalship – though he also points out that Polybius describes several battles in which fortune played an important part in the Roman victory.[73] There is a very full discussion of the rôle of fortune (however defined) in the wider context of Rome's rise to ecumenical power in J.-L. Ferrary's important study of the ideological background of that rise;[74] and I deal with one aspect of the place of *Tyche* in the *Histories* in chapter 16 below. Recently Andrew Erskine has argued that there is an element of the stereotyped picture of the barbarian in Polybius' description of the Romans, although (like other Greek writers) he never calls them barbarians in his own voice.[75]

On Polybius as a specifically military historian there is a general critique by E. W. Marsden.[76] Peter Connolly discusses (with impressive illustrations) the character of Polybius' manipular army and his comparison of it with the phalanx; and P. Sabin tries to make sense of what exactly went on at the battle-face at the time of Polybius (with useful bibliography).[77] The most important work on Polybius' account of the Roman army in the middle republic is that of Peter Brunt,[78] who shows convincingly that Polybius is not invariably content to rely on his own knowledge of Roman army organisation acquired as an eyewitness during his years in Rome, but that his description of the annual levy of troops (the *dilectus*) on the Capitol, for instance, must derive from an earlier, somewhat antiquated, account, since the procedures described could not possibly have been carried out there with the numbers available in the late third and early second centuries. Brunt's book is also indispensable for its discussion of Polybius' analysis of the number of troops available to Rome against the Gauls in 225 (ii.24) and so a few years later against Hannibal.

At the very outset of his first book Polybius makes it clear that an important factor in Rome's success was her 'mixed constitution';[79] and an account of this occupies much of Book VI. The unitary view of that

---

[72] Eckstein (1997).   [73] Roux (1993).   [74] Ferrary (1988) 265–76.

[75] Erskine (2000).   [76] Marsden (1974).   [77] Connolly (1981) 64–207; Sabin (2000).

[78] Brunt (1971) especially 625–34 on the Roman levy.   [79] i.1.5 with Walbank, *Comm.* i ad loc.

book as having been written as a single whole, was advocated in 1954 by C. O. Brink and myself,[80] and this seems now to be generally accepted.[81] But a good deal has been written on how the various elements contained in the book mesh together in Polybius' exposition. These are, first, the cycle of seven good and corrupt constitutional forms, which alternate in the so-called *anacyclosis*; secondly, the 'mixed', or, more correctly, the 'balanced', constitution of the Hannibalic period, with its combination of kingly, aristocratic and popular elements; and, finally, the biological concept of a constitution which has its 'natural' beginnings, growth, perfection, decline and end. In addition, there is the basic problem raised by any historical 'pattern' which depends for its fulfilment on the actions of individuals exercising their free will. Recent discussion of this area in Polybius' thought is to be found in articles by A. Díaz Tejera, E. Braun, J. M. Alonso-Nuñez and S. Podes.[82] In particular Podes compares the account of the cycle of constitutions contained in vi.4.7–19 with the fuller version in vi.5.4–9.9 and discusses the relationship between the actions of individuals and the social forces which, in Polybius' account of the *anacyclosis*, appear to bring about a predetermined sequence. This same contrast between personal action and social forces is also emphasised in a stimulating essay by David Halm,[83] who distinguishes those elements in the constitutional cycle which are attributable to 'nature' (φύσις) from those arising out of the freely taken decisions of men, between the degenerative factors which produce decay in the good constitutions and the unconstrained actions of individuals which bring about the overthrow of the corrupt forms. Halm argues that Polybius' cycle of social change nevertheless derives ultimately from patterns of behaviour rooted in human nature, which has within it contradictory impulses towards voluntary cooperation and towards personal aggrandisement, both of which play a rôle in the cycle. Halm would interpret Polybius' cyclical scheme rather more flexibly than the text of Polybius suggests. But the order in which the constitutions appear in that sequence is fairly inflexible, since it is only by keeping some residual kingly and aristocratic powers in the

---

[80] Brink and Walbank (1954).   [81] See for example Eisenberger (1982).

[82] Díaz Tejera (1975); Braun (1983) (querying whether Polybius was influenced at all by Aristotle); Alonso-Nuñez (1986); Podes (1991a) and (1991b). How Polybius saw constitutional 'decline' is discussed in chapter 13 in this volume.

[83] Halm (1995). Halm convincingly corrects my interpretation (in *Comm.* I) of vi.5.2–3. Polybius there states that if there are any omissions in his general exposition of the *anacyclosis*, they will be clarified in what follows (τῶν ἑξῆς ῥηθησομένων). I took the 'general exposition' to refer to the account in 4.7–10 and 'what follows' to the fuller account in 5.4–9.14. Halm points out that the words τῶν μετὰ ταῦτα ῥηθησομένων (9.14) refer to the rest of the book, and that this makes it more likely that the 'general exposition' of 5.3 refers to 5.4–9.14 and the clarification mentioned there also indicates the rest of the book.

successive changes that Rome is able, eventually, to step out of the cycle and embrace a 'mixed' constitution.

Polybius' 'mixed constitution' clearly springs out of Greek political theory and a basic question, which has led to considerable discussion, is whether it really offers a valid account of the Roman constitution at the time of the Hannibalic War (or indeed in the second century, when Polybius was writing). Momigliano thought it had no validity at all; in his book *Alien Wisdom* he dubs it 'Polybius' non-existent mixed constitution'.[84] That is because he thought that Polybius had simply missed out some of the most important elements in the Roman state. He did not, for example, understand the nature of the Roman confederacy and he ignored the Latin allies. More recently the pendulum has swung the other way. In his recent book on the constitution of the Roman republic[85] Andrew Lintott argues that, though perhaps inadequate in its description of the functioning of various political and constitutional organs, Polybius has given us a very fair analysis of where power at Rome resided. He credits him with originality as the author of a critique which goes beyond general theory in its appreciation of the part played by internal conflict in the development of a constitution rightly seen by Polybius as 'the product of history'. In a series of controversial papers (and one book) Millar has also argued in favour of the reality of Polybius' 'mixed constitution' and especially of the rôle he assigns to the people.[86] Rejecting Gelzer's long popular model of a state run essentially by the *nobiles*,[87] Millar argues that Polybius is right in assigning real power to the people. He is supported in this interpretation by A. Yacobson[88] (who, however, deals mainly with a period somewhat later than Polybius), but is sharply criticised by K.-J. Hölkeskamp.[89] The debate seems likely to continue.

There have been many other contributions to the discussion of the constitutional section of Book VI, several of them relating Polybius' views to those of later writers who propose cyclical historical models or theories involving mixed constitutions. Two books which merit mention here are those of G. Trompf and W. Nippel;[90] L. Canfora also sets Polybius' account in a wider context.[91] How far the cyclical concept inherent in the *anacyclosis* can be reconciled with a linear view of history is the subject of a paper by K. E. Petzold.[92] Chr. Schubert draws attention to

---

[84] Momigliano (1975) 44.   [85] Lintott (1999).
[86] Millar (1984), (1986), (1987), (1989), (1995), (1998).
[87] Gelzer (1912).   [88] Yacobson (1999).   [89] Hölkeskamp (2000).
[90] Trompf (1979) especially 4–115; Nippel (1980).   [91] Canfora (1993).   [92] Petzold (1977).

Polybius' use of medical terminology and the existence of a theory of 'checks and balances' within the Hippocratic corpus.[93] There are also two important papers by Claude Nicolet, one discussing Book VI and the other Roman institutions generally.[94] A recent study by W. Blösel[95] takes up the old problem of how far Cicero's *De re publica* can be employed to throw light on the possible contents of Polybius' lost *archaeologia*. This topic is touched on in chapter 14 below, where there is also discussion of Polybius' distinction between the path taken by a state declining from democracy into mob-rule and that of an unnamed state (actually Rome) which eventually slides back onto the wheel of the *anacyclosis* after enjoying a period under a mixed constitution. This distinction is more closely analysed in chapter 18.

Polybius is not exclusively concerned with political issues in his account of Rome. His interest in customs and traditions (ἔθη καὶ νόμιμα) is discussed by R. Martínez Lacy;[96] and one important aspect of this side of Roman life which did not escape Polybius' attention, the relationship of clients and patrons, has been dealt with in a paper by I. E. M. Edlund.[97] The importance of religion in Roman life was fully recognised by Polybius and this subject has received considerable attention from Polybian scholars. His sources for what he has to say on religion – some of them contradictory – are discussed by G. J. D. Aalders.[98] For Paul Pédech Polybius was virtually without belief in the gods;[99] and K. Doering includes Polybius in a general discussion of religion as a means of social control, with particular reference to vi.56.6–15.[100] M. G. Morgan, however, points out that the real purpose of this passage in Polybius is to emphasise the piety of the Roman upper class, though he admits that the reference there to the manipulation of the masses does not quite fit that picture.[101] On this subject there is more in Eckstein's book;[102] and there is also a relevant article by van Hooff.[103] An article by G. Schepens on Timaeus' (and Polybius') account of Phalaris' bull contains a useful bibliography on the theme of religion in Polybius;[104] but the most recent relevant study of this topic is by J. E. Vaahtera.[105]

I have left to the end of this section consideration of Polybius' views on Roman imperial expansion and work on that topic. Three questions have dominated discussion: first, how far Polybius is consistent in his picture of Roman aims and Roman actions leading to the wars which eventually

---

[93] Schubert (1995).   [94] Nicolet (1974), (1983b).   [95] Blösel (1998).
[96] Martínez Lacy (1991).   [97] Edlund (1977).   [98] Aalders (1987).   [99] Pédech (1965).
[100] Doering (1978).   [101] M. G. Morgan (1990).   [102] Eckstein (1995) 140 n. 88.
[103] Van Hooff (1977).   [104] Schepens (1978).   [105] Vaahtera (2000).

secured ecumenical domination; secondly his own attitude towards Rome as a dominant power; and, thirdly, why he decided to extend his *Histories* to cover the years 167–145 in Books XXXI–XL. It was Polybius' belief (i.3.6) that the Roman decision to aim at universal dominion was taken at the end of the Hannibalic War. Nearly forty years ago,[106] I published a paper arguing that Polybius' detailed account of how the major wars broke out was inconsistent with his general thesis and more in accord with what at that time was the widely accepted view of Maurice Holleaux,[107] that the Romans acquired their empire more or less piecemeal in a succession of wars characterised by Holleaux as 'defensive imperialism'. Today, and not least as a result of a study by W. Harris,[108] that view is no longer tenable. My own position was seriously undermined by Peter Derow,[109] who showed convincingly that Polybius' account of Rome's behaviour in her major wars and in the events leading up to these was quite consistent with his overall view of Roman policy. One particular merit of Derow's paper is to have demonstrated that for the Romans and for Polybius 'ecumenical domination' did not necessarily imply direct political control, but simply characterised a situation in which the conquered peoples were henceforth obliged to do what Rome commanded.

Polybius' views on the character of Roman expansion, therefore, no longer present a serious problem. But his attitude towards Rome as the dominant power continues to be controversial. In several articles and a book[110] I have in the past argued that, in the years following his removal to Rome in 167, Polybius was critical of Rome and expressed that attitude in several anti-Roman comments on Roman policy in Books XXX–XXXIII, covering the years 167 to 152, but that after then, and during the Third Punic War, the Macedonian rising and the Achaean War, he swung over to support of Rome and approval of her use of *Realpolitik*. This view has provoked considerable criticism, especially in an article by B. Shimron, in which he concludes that Polybius never came round to supporting Rome.[111] Dubuisson was inclined to follow my view that Polybius did indeed swing over to a pro-Roman position;[112] but Millar has argued that he took an adverse view of Rome from 168 onwards and never changed this.[113] Nowhere, he points out, does Polybius express positive approval of Roman policy. Ferrary is exceptional in arguing that

---

[106] Walbank (1963).   [107] Holleaux (1921).
[108] Harris (1979); see especially 107–17 on Polybius' evidence. For a useful critique of Harris see North (1981).
[109] Derow (1979).   [110] Walbank (1963); (1965b); (1972a) 157–83; (1974); (1981/2).
[111] Shimron (1979/80).   [112] Dubuisson (1990).   [113] Millar (1987).

Polybius was basically pro-Roman from 167 onwards, despite his series of critical remarks on Roman policy in the books covering the years 167 to 152.[114] These, he claims, do not reflect basically anti-Roman feeling and his readers were expected to give at least two cheers for Rome.

Most other recent writers accept that there is some degree of anti-Roman feeling in Books XXX–XXXIII, or at least some divergence from Roman criteria. Yet these were of course the years in which Polybius must have resolved to write his *Histories*. In a book entirely concerned with the problem of Polybius' attitude towards Rome, Domenico Musti argues that throughout his life Polybius remained devoted to the ideals and the institutions of the Hellenistic world and in particular his own Achaean Confederacy, but that this did not necessarily make him an enemy of Rome.[115] Musti also lays stress on some economic motives for Roman warfare, evidence for which he claims to find in Polybius. However, such motives hardly obtrude in Polybius' analysis of the rise of Rome to world dominion.

An important passage for this controversy has been Polybius' account (xxxvi.9) of views held in Greece concerning the rights and wrongs of the Third Punic War. There were, he tells us, four views. The first was that the Romans were wise and statesmanlike to destroy Carthage, their secular enemy. A second view claimed that their action illustrated a growth of moral corruption in Rome, which was fast becoming a tyrant city. A third view was that Rome had shown impiety and treachery towards Carthage, and that this revealed a decline from earlier Roman claims to fight wars straightforwardly; and a fourth view defended Rome against this charge, pointing out that it was the Carthaginians who had behaved treacherously by making an act of surrender (*deditio*) and then going back on it. There is no agreement about which, if any, of these views are those of Polybius himself. Harris thinks he accepted the second and the fourth;[116] but Eckstein, who discusses the problem in detail in his study of 'moral vision' in the *Histories*,[117] takes the view (shared by J. W. Rich)[118] that Polybius was ambivalent about the Third Punic War, but too closely involved on the Roman side to speak out critically. Many years ago, in a chapter in his book on *Alien Wisdom*,[119] Momigliano declared that it was a waste of time asking whether Polybius supported Rome or not; clearly he did. 'Polybius', he coldly remarks elsewhere,[120] 'studied the West under Roman auspices and according to Roman needs, if not by

[114] Ferrary (1988) 265–91.   [115] Musti (1978).   [116] Harris (1979) 271–2.
[117] Eckstein (1995) 217.   [118] Rich, reviewing Eckstein's book in *CR* 49 (1999) 26.
[119] Momigliano (1975) 22–49.   [120] Momigliano (1974a) 4.

Roman order.' But equally clearly Polybius was to some degree uneasy at the recent resort to terror and repression. Because he did not choose to give us his own explicit views on this matter, we can never reach complete certainty how he stood. But I am now inclined to think that something like Momigliano's assessment of Polybius' position is right – though I see him as a little less subservient than Momigliano suggests. I would only add that, besides paying attention to the constraints exercised on him by a Roman environment between 167 and 145, we should perhaps also bear in mind his mainly Achaean environment from 145 onwards.

The question of Polybius' attitude towards Rome is closely linked to the problem presented by his decision to extend the *Histories* to take in the years 167 to 145, and the reasons he offers for so doing (iii.4–5); and this in turn is affected by our uncertainty about the dates at which the various parts of the *Histories* were written and published. In 1957 I argued that five or six books had appeared by 150/49 and that a final revision appeared posthumously.[121] Various scholars have since suggested modifications of this view. G. A. Lehmann puts the publication of the first six books soon after 145/4, but also argues for a posthumous edition of the whole. R. Weil is completely sceptical about the possibility of ascertaining the dates of composition and publication and does not even accept that Polybius adopted a revised plan.[122] Ferrary, however, believes that Books I and II appeared in 150/49, III–IV in 145 or 144 and the rest at later intervals. This avoids the assumption of a second edition of Book III, since on its first appearance it can, on this dating, have included the chapter containing the plan for the proposed extension. This is very neat, but runs up against one problem: how could Polybius, in a book published in 145 or 144, seriously speak of possible 'reversals of fortune' (iii.4.5) for the defeated states in the situation after the Achaean War? (Shimron assumes this remark to be a mere general maxim, which can be ignored.[123]) However, this brings us to the final problem, why Polybius chose to extend his *Histories* to 145.

In iii.4.12 Polybius tells us that the extension will enable the reader to ascertain the condition of each people after the struggle was over and all had come under Roman domination 'until the disturbed and troubled times that afterwards ensued'. When did these 'troubled times' begin? Shimron thinks it was in 158, as some of the events mentioned as belonging to them suggest;[124] but this seems hard to sustain, for in iii.4.12 Polybius speaks of making what is virtually a new start with the 'troubled

[121] Walbank, *Comm.* I, 292–7.   [122] Weil (1988).
[123] Shimron (1979/80) 104–5.   [124] Shimron (1979/80) 109–10.

times' and that hardly applies to his narrative from 158 onwards. Despite Polybius' vagueness, it seems most likely that he envisages the 'break' as occurring around 151, when his own rôle 'as an eye-witness, participant and even controller of events' (iii.4.13) began. For indeed any discussion of Polybius' reasons for his extension must take account of his statement here that his main reason (τὸ μέγιστον) for extending his work was his personal rôle in those events. In 1977 I argued that this personal story was Polybius' real reason for the extension and that the alleged reasons – to assess Roman rule and ascertain the conditions among the conquered peoples – were little more than a smoke-screen.[125] I would no longer press that case in its extreme form, though it surely contains some truth. Indeed it gains some support from Marincola's observation (cited earlier)[126] that in xxxvi.11–12 Polybius draws attention to his abandonment of the usual literary convention in referring to oneself in a historical narrative and adopting one more suited to memoirs. In iii.9.4–6 Polybius claims that his extension will show how the Romans used their power after 167 and how the non-Roman world judged them. This claim must be taken seriously; yet the ambiguities in iii.4–5 and the failure of scholars to reach unanimity about what conclusions Polybius would expect us to draw suggests that, as in the debate about the rights and wrongs of the Third Punic War, he prefers to leave the matter to his readers. Unanimity is likely to remain elusive. Incidentally this problem raises the more general question of whether Polybius himself should in any way be regarded as a traitor to his fellow-Greeks; this is a topic touched on in this volume in chapter 17 and also in chapter 20, dealing with De Sanctis' very negative view of the Achaean historian.

IV CONTRIBUTIONS TO HISTORY AND GEOGRAPHY

Many of the publications which we are considering here relate to historical events and situations for which Polybius is a source. I cannot here deal with more than a selection of these but I will try to comment primarily on those which are of historical importance or raise problems. Since Polybius' history was largely concerned with military and political issues many of these publications refer to the causes of wars, events leading up to these and incidents arising in the course of them.

A particularly intractable passage is Polyb. i.11.1f., which is important because it describes events preceding the first Roman decision to operate

---

[125] Walbank (1977).   [126] Marincola (1997) 188–92; see above, n. 70.

overseas. In it Polybius records the Senate's failure to reach a decision whether or not to respond to an appeal for help from Campanian merceⁿaries, the Mamertini, who had seized Messana by violence. This appeal raised moral issues, since only recently the Romans had severely punⁱished a similar band of mercenaries who had seized the Italian town of Rhegium. Eventually, however, oἱ πολλοί 'favoured consenting' and this led to a positive answer. Are oἱ πολλοί a majority of the Senate, or are they 'the many' expressing their view in a popular assembly or in some other way? This problem, originally raised by R. Develin in a Michigan dissertⁱation of 1973,[127] is discussed at length in the proceedings of two successive seminars held by S. Calderone in the University of Messina in 1976 and 1981, which include the comments of a dozen scholars from Italy, France, Germany, England and the U.S.A., whose views had been canvassed.[128] Their answers divided almost equally between the two views (with some hedging!), but at the second meeting the participants agreed unanimously with Professor Calderone's view that oἱ πολλοί were a majority of the Senate. This was also the view taken in 1987 by A. M. Eckstein;[129] but some very substantial arguments against it had already been raised in 1984 by D. B. Hoyos.[130] Either view leaves residual problems, with the possibility of some telescoping of procedures in Polybius' account. But on the whole it seems to me more likely that it was the people and not 'a majority' of the Senate who forced the decision to help the Mamertini against first Syracuse, but very soon against Carthage.

Polybius' narrative is rarely so ambiguous as it is here. There has, however, been discussion and disagreement in connection with his acⁿcounts of the lead-up to both the Second and Third Punic Wars and the Third Macedonian War. In 1983[131] I queried A. Momigliano's argument that Polybius did not regard the Roman seizure of Sardinia as relevant to the origins of the Second Punic War.[132] On the Third Macedonian War D. Golan has assembled material from Polybius pointing to some sympathy expressed by the historian for Perseus;[133] and H. Nottmeyer has discussed Achaean relations with Rome between 180 and 146 and

[127] Develin (1973) 121–2.
[128] See Calderone (1981). A preliminary publication of the results of the first seminar had been published and privately circulated by the Istituto di Storia Antica dell' Università di Messina, entitled 'Seminario di ricerca'.
[129] Eckstein (1987a) 315–17, 335–40, and (1980); reviewing the former in *CR* 38 (1988) 315–17, J. W. Rich came down against this view.
[130] Hoyos (1984a).   [131] Walbank (1983).
[132] Momigliano (1975) 28; cf. (1980). On Sardinia see also Dubuisson (1979) and Schwarte (1993).
[133] Golan (1989).

criticised Polybius for failing to understand the causes of the disaster, which were, he thinks, due largely to the failure of the Lycortas group to appreciate the need for full collaboration with Rome.[134] Callicrates, he contends, had the right idea about relations with Rome. In an article of 1995 D. W. Baronowski analyses the events leading to the Third Punic War, distinguishing 'cause' and 'pretext' in the sense indicated in Polyb. iii.6. Not only the causes of wars but also their conclusions, as set out by Polybius, can raise problems, particularly where there is a Livian version of the same events. Polybius' account of the territorial clauses of the Treaty of Apamea (188) contains a lacuna, which has to be filled from Livy xxxviii.38.4. The reference here to a river 'Tanais' is something of a puzzle. A. H. McDonald identified it with some probability as the upper waters of the Calycadnus;[135] A. Giovannini's claim that it is the well-known Tanais, the River Don in the Ukraine, can hardly be right.[136] On the naval clauses of this treaty, McDonald and the present writer proposed readings of both Polybius (xxi.43.13) and Livy (xxxviii.38.8),[137] which have won the approval of R. M. Errington in *The Cambridge Ancient History*[138] and P. G. Walsh in his new Oxford text of Livy XXXVI–XL.[139]

Among the Polybian topics of Roman history which have continued to arouse controversy have been the treaties between Rome and Carthage (iii.22.1–27.10), Hannibal's march across the Alps (iii.33.5–56.6) and Scipio's capture of New Carthage (x.2.1–20.8) – all ancient *cruces*. The treaties receive full attention in W. Huss' *Geschichte der Karthager*.[140] He dates the first treaty to the first half of the fifth century, the second to 348, a third (only in Livy) to 343 and the Polybian third treaty to 279; he accepts the reality of the so-called treaty of Philinus, dating it to 306, and puts the 'Ebro-treaty' in 226/5. Others have also discussed these treaties, both before and after the publication of Huss' book. E. Badian[141] rejects the Philinus treaty. S. Calderone[142] rejects the identification of Polybius' second treaty with that mentioned in Livy vii.27.2 and so the date for it of 348. A. M. Eckstein argues that friendship between Rome and Saguntum was established before Hamilcar's death and so before the Ebro Treaty, which was therefore irrelevant to that friendship.[143] B. D. Hoyos has discussed the treaty of 279.[144] And more recently B. Scardigli has published a comprehensive study of all the treaties, with Italian translation and commentary.[145]

[134] Nottmeyer (1995).   [135] McDonald (1967).   [136] Giovannini (1982).
[137] McDonald and Walbank (1969).   [138] Errington (1989) 289.   [139] Walsh (1999).
[140] Huss (1985); see also *SVA* 121, 326, 438, 466, 493, 497 and 503.   [141] Badian (1980).
[142] Calderone (1980).   [143] Eckstein (1984).   [144] Hoyos (1984b).   [145] Scardigli (1991).

Another ancient problem which still crops up is the location of Hannibal's Alpine crossing (iii.49.5–56.4). In 1971 a lively account of the many proposed solutions was published by Dennis Proctor,[146] who hesitatingly came down in favour of the Col du Clapier (which was also Huss' choice[147]). A slight variant on this, leading to the Col de Savine-Cloche, has the approval of H. Wallinga.[148] More recently J. Seibert has boldly suggested[149] that Hannibal divided his army into two parts, which crossed by the Mt Genèvre and Little St Bernard passes – a somewhat drastic solution to a source problem. The general balance of the evidence seems to me to favour one of the passes in the Mt Cenis group; but doubts still subsist.

The main problem presented by the account of Scipio's capture of New Carthage in 209 is to explain the regular evening fall in the level of the water in the lagoon, which Scipio exploited to take the city. Attributing this to wind action, E. Foulon mounts a defence of Polybius' account.[150] Antonio and Martin Lillo, however, have argued that the θαλαττουργοί of x.10.12 were 'fish-trappers', who controlled the water-level with a sluice.[151] Another example of a problem which turns on the meaning of a word in Polybius is an article by S. L. Ager on Cretan juridical arrangements;[152] the word κοινοδίκιον, restored in Polyb. xx.15.4, is central to an argument on the nature of this institution, which Ager takes to be a body settling private disputes between citizens of Cretan cities, not a federal court of arbitration, as some have argued. Battles too have attracted attention: the battle of the Bagradas, Ecnomus, Hannibal's battle on the Tagus, Caphyae,[153] Cannae,[154] Mantinea (207),[155] Cynoscephalae[156] and Pydna.[157] Non-Roman battles dealt with include Issus (xii.17–18 for Callisthenes' account),[158] Sellasia[159]

---

[146] Proctor (1971).   [147] Huss (1985) 300–6.   [148] Wallinga (1986).
[149] Seibert (1993) 106–13.   [150] Foulon (1984).   [151] Lillo (1988).   [152] Ager (1994).
[153] See W. E. Thompson (1986) (Bagradas); Tipps (1985) (Ecnomus: a defence of Polybius' account); Hine (1979) (Tagus: emending Polybius' text to conform with Livy xxi.5); Pritchett (1969) 120–32 (Caphyae).
[154] See Huss (1985) 328–30 with n. 255 for bibliography on Cannae to that date. Kussmaul (1978) draws on tactics in later times (1520–1870) to throw light on Polybius' account of Cannae.
[155] Pritchett (1969) 66–72.
[156] Pritchett (1969) 133–44 and Hammond (1988), who locates the battle at Zoodokhos Pege, about 7 km north of Pharsalus.
[157] Pritchett (1969) 145–76 and Hammond (1984).
[158] Hammond (1994c) identifies the Polybian river Pinarus with the modern Pajas, not, as I argued in *Comm.* ii, 364–76, with the Deli Chai.
[159] Pritchett (1965) 59–70, locates Troules further north than in Kromayer's site, accepted in my *Comm.* i, 634, and identifies Olympus with the modern Provatares; this looks convincing. Pritchett (1984) supplements this account with a discussion of two sites relevant to the battle (Polyb. ii. 65–9); see also Le Bohec (1993) 404–46.

and Raphia.[160] Most of these battles involve studies of topography. Polybius' interest in this subject is pursued in several publications by Kendrick Pritchett. Examples relevant to Polybius are his studies of Philip V's campaign in north-west Greece in 219, his Peloponnesian campaign of 219/18 and his march on Thermum in 218;[161] Pritchett also studies several sites mentioned by Polybius in Acarnania.[162]

Following a tradition which goes back to Herodotus, Polybius devotes a good deal of attention to both ethnography and geography. An example of work on the former is R. Urban's detailed discussion in 1991 of Polybius' account of the Celts,[163] a topic taken up a year later by P. Berger, who elsewhere argues for Polybius' unreliability when dealing with peripheral peoples.[164] On the importance of geography in Polybius' *Histories* there is now an excellent book by Katherine Clarke,[165] which covers a wide range of issues and sets Polybius in a long tradition. In particular she argues that geography and the consideration of spatial relations are not something Polybius relegates to Book XXXIV, but that they penetrate the whole of the *Histories* in such a way that geography is closely linked with history and historiography throughout. This work seems to me to bring out the importance of geography to Polybius in a manner not hitherto attempted. Chapter 2 below also deals with geography in Polybius.

During the period we are considering there has been a good deal of interest in economic and social questions, particularly in Sparta, as they appear in Polybius. This was a topic especially to the fore in Israel during the years 1962–82. D. Mendels in particular published a series of articles written between 1977 and 1981, which are now reprinted in the volume of his collected papers already referred to.[166] Why Polybius did not mention Cleomenes' economic and social reforms is a matter of disagreement between Mendels and Shimron.[167] Against Shimron, who explains Polybius' silence on this important reform of Cleomenes as caused by its being alien to his idea of the Lycurgan constitution, Mendels

---

[160] Galili (1976–7) is a well thought out discussion of the whole Raphia campaign, based on a good knowledge of the terrain. For discussion of the Ptolemaic troop numbers, see Winnicki (1989).

[161] Pritchett (1989) 1–83 (Peloponnese), 126–40 (Thermum); (1991) 1–39 (north-west Greece), 41–5 (Thermum).

[162] Pritchett (1991) 83–100; (1992) 79–114.   [163] Urban (1991).

[164] Berger (1992) (Celts), (1995) (peripheral peoples).

[165] See Clarke (1999a) 1–128, for her discussion of Polybius.

[166] See above n. 28. This work contains papers dealing with Cleomenes III and with social and economic problems in third- and second-century Greece, in all of which Polybius' evidence is of prime importance.

[167] Shimron (1972).

suggests a combination of reasons, chief among them being Polybius' embarrassment at the virtual disintegration of the Achaean League, when attacked by the army of Cleomenes' reorganised Sparta. The same subject is also discussed by P. Oliva and by Z. Papastyliou-Philiou.[168]

The majority of the papers referred to in this section are concerned with the traditional problems which arise when we turn to Polybius as a source for historical events; they do not adopt new approaches to the same extent as those dealing with his methodology or indeed his rôle as a geographer.

V THE TRANSMISSION AND INFLUENCE OF POLYBIUS SINCE ANTIQUITY

For Polybius' 'after-life' we are mainly indebted to Arnaldo Momigliano, who, in his posthumously published Sather lectures (delivered originally in 1961–2),[169] sets him in the general context of a study of the separate strands of ancient historiography – Persian, Greek, Jewish, Roman and ecclesiastical – which have in various ways shaped the interests and the manner of writing prevalent among modern historians. This long-awaited volume contains a series of penetrating comments on Polybius from perhaps the most outstanding ancient historian of his generation. Momigliano here reminds us that, although Polybius never enjoyed the popularity of Thucydides in antiquity, he came into his own during the renaissance, following his reappearance in Florence around 1418 in Leonardo Bruni's Latin account of the First Punic War and of events down to the Roman seizure of Milan, based firmly on Polybius (i–ii.35). From this time onwards Polybius was the 'master of political, diplomatic and military wisdom', dominating the thought of rulers throughout the sixteenth and seventeenth centuries and (along with Livy and Tacitus) shaping the writing of history in a political and military mould.

For a detailed examination of this re-birth there are two outstanding publications by Momigliano, both scintillating in their wit and lightly worn learning.[170] It is perhaps the brilliance of Momigliano's writing that has deterred most recent scholars from tackling this branch of Poly-bian studies. There has, however, been something on the translations of Perotti (1454) and Casaubon (1609) by M. Milne and N. Pace;[171] Pace compares Perotti's translation with Bruni's Livianising Latin version and

---

[168] Oliva (1971); Papastyliou-Philiou (1995).   [169] Momigliano (1990) especially 49.
[170] Momigliano (1974a) and (1974b).   [171] Milne (1989); Pace (1988) and (1989).

discusses the manuscripts used by Perotti. E. Garin writes on Polybius and Machiavelli and attributes the latter's pessimism partly to Polybius;[172] and A. Dionisotti has discussed Polybius' rôle in the curriculum of Jean Strazel, who taught François I Greek in the early sixteenth century.[173]

Another burst of interest in Polybius occurred at the time of the American revolution, when his sixth book came up in discussion among the founding fathers of the republic – though, as Momigliano points out,[174] his work was adduced chiefly to illustrate rather than to determine current thinking. In this context Emilio Gabba has discussed the classical inheritance in the thought of John Adams, especially in relation to Polybius' remarks on the mixed constitution and on federalism. But Paul Rahe, in a comprehensive study of the influence of classical republicanism in the American revolution, while referring briefly to the resemblance between the Roman mixed constitution in Polybius and the institutional checks introduced into the American constitution, stresses rather the different assumptions of the two societies about the purpose of the state; for whereas John Adams saw this as promoting the ease, comfort and security of its citizens, Polybius (vi.47.1–4, 48.2–5) – like Plato, Aristotle, Isocrates and Demosthenes before him and , later, Augustine – thought its task was to make them noble and good.[175]

In chapter 19 below I discuss early editions and translations of Polybius into English and the background of Dryden's introduction to Sheeres' translation of Books I–V; and in chapter 20 I deal with the work of a distinguished modern historian of Rome, Gaetano De Sanctis, for whom Polybius was both an indispensable source and an object of contempt – in short, an author whom it is impossible to ignore and from whom it is hard to remain detached.

---

[172] Garin (1990).   [173] Dionisotti (1983).
[174] Momigliano (1974a) 10.   [175] Gabba (1996); Rahe (1992) 352 and 602.

Historical and geographical papers

2

The geography of Polybius*

I

In the year 59 BC Cicero found the shape of Roman politics both dis-
tasteful and alarming, and he therefore retired to his villa at Antium
and resolved to follow Atticus' advice and write a Geography. For this
purpose Atticus furnished him with copies of the best works of the
most outstanding Greek authors. But Cicero soon wearied of the task.
'Γεωγραφικὰ *quae constitueram magnum opus est*' he writes.[1] There is no
unanimity among the experts. Eratosthenes, who was to have been his
model, is criticised, he finds, by Hipparchus and Serapio; the subject is
difficult, monotonous, not adapted to literary embellishment. Presumably Cicero abandoned his project, for we hear no more of it; and four
years later, when he was writing the *De oratore*, geography was still an
obscurior scientia.[2]

The phrase has its justification. Alexandrian geography was in fact an
obscure science, and a highly specialised one, both abstruse and uncon-
genial to anyone with Cicero's lively preference for popularisation rather
than original thought. But Greek geography had not begun as a science.
Between Herodotus and Eratosthenes lies a deep gulf, of method as well
as time, and any consideration of Polybius' contribution to geography
must take these two traditions into account. It will therefore be appropriate to consider how Greek geographical writing began, and what factors
led to its modification. ||

When Herodotus set down the account of his enquiry – his ἱστορίη –
what he wrote and published was a history; but it was also our earliest extant work of descriptive geography. It is significant for the later
development of the study of geography, and altogether typical of their humanistic outlook, that the Greeks originally drew no distinction between

* [[*Classica et Mediaevalia* 9 (1948) 155–82]]
[1] *Ad Att.* ii.6.1; cf. ii.4.3; 7.1.   [2] *De oratore* i.59.

geography, ethnology and history.[3] Their historians make geographical digressions; their geographers stray into the field of history. Down to the age of Polybius and Poseidonius it is the usual practice to combine history and geography in a single work; and Strabo, though we think of him as a geographer, was also a historian. In fact, from the time of Hecataeus, Greek geography is a subject distinguished not by any clearly defined frontiers, but by its primarily humanistic content.[4]

In Herodotus the intermingling of geography and history is the natural result of a technique which proceeds by means of digressions, which rejoices in the elaboration of excursuses, sometimes set one inside another like a Chinese puzzle box. This is the method of the popular story-teller,[5] developed into high art by the consummate skill of the historian. It established the digression, and especially the geographical digression, as a normal feature of historical writing, which subsequent historians turned to their own various purposes. There is little geographical discussion in Thucydides. But later historians, Ephorus, Theopompus, Duris, and, among the Romans who drew upon the same tradition, Sallust, Caesar, Livy, Tacitus and Ammianus, all have their digressions describing the lands with which they are – often only superficially – concerned. Sensational writers like Duris and Phylarchus were mainly interested in producing startling effects, and they employed geographical digressions to that end, in a manner recognised by rhetorical theory.[6] Others were seriously || interested in the relationship between human history and the stage on which it was enacted. But in either case humanistic geography developed largely as an aspect of history, or at most as an appendage to it. It was a development which by no means ruled out progress, and it offered no hindrance to the emergence of geography, in other hands, as an independent study. What it did was to lay down a 'style' of treatment which historians found it difficult to evade: and Polybius' interest in geography and the various geographical excursuses in his work must be considered partly from this formal aspect.

II

It must not, however, be overstressed. Polybius' digressions, however much they may follow the traditional style of composition established by previous historians, arise essentially out of the needs of his own work.

[3] Cf. Müllenhoff (1890) 351.   [4] Cf. Ninck (1945) 33ff.   [5] Cf. Howald (1944) 42–3.
[6] Cf. Theon *prog.* 119.27 for the use of ἐκφράσεις of a country as a means of producing ἐνάργεια: cf. Burck (1934) 199.

'Es gibt keine Polybiosfrage' – 'Polybius presents no problems' writes Professor Ernst Howald,[7] perhaps a little over-confidently: but he is to this extent right, that there was never a historian so anxious to display all the tools of his trade, to tell us not only on the basis of what evidence he makes his statements, but also with what object. To Polybius geography is an essential part of the background of his history. Serious political and military history – πραγματικὴ ἱστορία – he tells us,[8] consists of three parts: first (and least important) there is the critical study of memoirs and documents; secondly the survey of cities, places, rivers, lakes, and in general all the peculiar features of land and sea, and the distances of one place from another; and thirdly political experience (πολιτικαὶ πράξεις).[9] Of these three || activities the most important is the personal research and enquiry by the eyewitness on the spot,[10] the αὐτοπάθεια,[11] which will give his work the vivid and convincing atmosphere which lies outside the scope of the bookish writer. This vivid background is not, however, to serve – as in Duris or Phylarchus – merely to titillate the reader. 'No one' writes Polybius elsewhere[12] 'need be surprised when in the course of my history I reach such localities – [he refers to Spain and Africa] – if I avoid any description of them. But if there be any who insist on such descriptions of each place that may be mentioned, they are perhaps unaware that they are much in the case of gourmands at a supper party, who taste everything on the table and neither truly enjoy any dish at the moment nor digest any enough to derive beneficial nourishment from it in the future.'

This rather severe and practical attitude towards geography inevitably limited its field; indeed, as we shall see, it closed Polybius' eyes or at any rate his interests against the more scientific developments which had been taking place in the preceding century. But within his own limits he was exacting, and insisted on making full use of the new facilities which now existed for extending the scope of geographical research. 'In olden times,' he writes[13] 'we find very few of the Greeks who attempted to enquire into the outlying parts of the world, owing to the practical impossibility

---

[7] Howald (1944) 87ff.   [8] xii.25e.1; cf. Cuntz (1902) 3–4.

[9] τοῦ περὶ τὰς πράξεις τὰς πολιτικάς. In view of 25 g.1; 28.1–5; and also of the comparison with the doctor's training (25 d), the third part of which is surgery and pharmaceutics (i.e. actual experience), the sense of this phrase seems to be 'political experience' rather than 'the review of political events' (Paton), 'die Beschäftigung mit den πολιτικαὶ πράξεις' (Cuntz (1902) 4). The three parts of history-writing are not to be undertaken in the order Polybius lists them (as Cuntz suggests); they are merely three aspects of the historian's activity, which obviously in practice would be carried on simultaneously.

[10] xii.4c.3.   [11] xii.25h.4ff.   [12] iii.57.6. I follow W. R. Paton's translation (Loeb edition).

[13] iii.57.5ff.; cf. iv.40.2.

of doing so . . . But in our own times since owing to Alexander's empire in Asia, and that of the Romans in other parts of the world, nearly all regions have become approachable by sea or land, and since our men of action in Greece are relieved from the ambitions of a military or political career, and have therefore ample means for enquiry and study, we ought to be able to arrive at a better knowledge and something more like the truth about lands which were formerly little known.' In an age in which all parts of the world had become accessible, it was || incumbent on the historian to go and see for himself; and this precept Polybius put conscientiously into practice, thereby playing a considerable part in the Greek discovery of western Europe.

Moved mainly by intellectual curiosity, Polybius undertook a number of journeys, the chronology of which is a controversial topic[14] into which it would be inappropriate to enter in this chapter. From 167 until 150 he was a political prisoner at Rome; but we are not, I believe, justified in assuming that for a close friend of the Scipios this necessarily implied strict internment within the frontiers of Latium, as some scholars have argued.[15] As Professor De Sanctis has pointed out, the important services which Polybius claims to have rendered the Epizephyrian Locrians[16] are to be connected with the Dalmatian Wars of 156/5, and those frequent visits to their town of which he speaks must therefore have taken place during his forced stay in Italy. We have Polybius' own testimony to the fact that at some time he made a journey 'through Africa, Spain, Gaul, and on the ocean that lies beyond'[17] and he claims the right to speak with confidence about Hannibal's crossing of the Alps because he has not only questioned eye-witnesses, but has also personally inspected the country and made the passage of the Alps 'to learn for myself and see' (γνώσεως ἕνεκα καὶ θέας).[18] Nissen made the reasonable suggestion[19] that Polybius accompanied Scipio Aemilianus to Spain in 151 BC, when he served there under L. Licinius Lucullus, and that his acquaintance with Gaul, the Alps and the Po Valley, dates to his return overland from Spain in 150. Shortly afterwards, in spring 149, when Polybius, now released from exile, had barely had time to return to his home in Arcadia, he received a request to proceed to Lilybaeum: he went as far as Corcyra, but then, on the basis of information which suggested that the Carthaginians had accepted the Roman terms, he returned || home.[20] A little later, when the war after all flared up, he appeared at Carthage and, probably in 146, after the fall of

[14] See e.g. Cuntz (1902); De Sanctis (1916) 209ff.   [15] So Cuntz (1902) 55ff.
[16] xii.5.1–3; cf. De Sanctis (1916) 210.   [17] iii.59.7.   [18] iii.48.12; cf. xii.28a.4.
[19] Nissen (1871) 271.   [20] xxxvi.11.

the city, at Scipio's instigation, underlook a voyage of discovery through the Pillars of Hercules and along the African coast[21] as far as Lixos, the modern Wādī Dar'a,[22] in an attempt to localise the Atlas mountains more accurately than had previously been done.[23] In this voyage, in the course of which he also penetrated some distance up the coast of Portugal,[24] we see the first-fruits of the breaking-down of the Punic ban on free voyaging in the west, and the gathering of reliable knowledge about lands which popular fancy had previously peopled with Amazons, Gorgons, Pans and Satyrs. Later, at some uncertain date, Polybius visited Asia Minor and met that remarkable woman Chiomara at Sardes.[25] He was at Alexandria sometime during the reign of Euergetes II (Physcon),[26] and he very likely visited Byzantium.[27] But whether, as is so often asserted, he was present, as an old man of seventy, in Scipio's camp at Numantia, remains uncertain. His personal knowledge of New Carthage[28] probably dates to his earlier Spanish journey;[29] and all that is known for certain is that he wrote a memoir on the Numantine War.[30]

However, even without Numantia, his journeys represent a substantial achievement, and one which would have been scarcely possible without the patronage of his aristocratic Roman friends. 'Personal enquiry' he writes[31] 'requires severe labour and great expense' and it is one of his main jibes against the credibility of || Pytheas[32] that 'a private man and a poor man' – ἰδιώτῃ ἀνθρώπῳ καὶ πένητι – 'could scarcely have covered such vast distances on shipboard and on foot'. Pytheas of Marseilles is a shadowy personality, but it is generally thought that, as well as being an outstanding scientist, he was also a merchant; if so, much of Polybius' prejudice against him may spring from the contempt of the Greek landowner for the merchant. It is clear that Polybius did not care for merchants. He admits that it is impossible 'for a single man to have seen with his own eyes every place in the world and all the peculiar features of different places'; hence 'the only thing left for a historian is to enquire from as many people as possible, to believe those worthy of belief, and to be an adequate critic of the reports that reach him'.[33] Thus in choosing the period with which his history is to concern itself he is moved

---

[21] Pliny *HN* v.9 = Polyb. xxxiv.15.7. [On Polybius' voyage see now Walbank, *Comm.* iii, 633–7.]

[22] Cf. Strabo ii.3.4 c.99.   [23] Cf. Honigmann, *RE*, s.v. 'Libye', col.173.

[24] iii.59.7.   [25] xxi.38.7.

[26] Strabo xvii.1.12 c.797 = Polyb, xxxiv.14.6. Physcon reigned from 170 to 163, and again from 145 to 116.

[27] iv.38.11–13.   [28] x.11.4. αὐτόπται γεγονότες.

[29] Cf. De Sanctis (1916) 212.   [30] Cic. *Ad fam.* v.12.2.   [31] xii.27.6.

[32] Strabo ii.4.2 c.104 = Polyb. xxxiv.5.7.   [33] xii.4c.4.

by the reflection that of the events of the years from 220 BC onwards he has
'been present at some and has the testimony of eye-witnesses for others'.[34]
But from such eye-witnesses he is careful to exclude merchants. For instance, in discussing the causes of the constant current flowing from the
Black Sea through the Bosphorus, he contrasts scientific reasoning with
merchants' yarns[35] – ἐμπορικὰ διηγήματα – or, as he elsewhere calls
them 'the falsehoods and sensational tales of merchants' – τῆς τῶν
πλοϊζομένων ψευδολογίας καὶ τερατείας.[36] When Scipio was on his
way back from Spain in 150 BC,[37] he made enquiries from Gallic merchants not only from Marseilles, but also from Narbonne and the trading
city of Corbilo at the mouth of the Loire, concerning Britain, but learnt
nothing from his silent and suspicious informants. Polybius, who was
probably present at the interview and may indeed have instigated it,
vents his anger on || Pytheas, who has nevertheless 'ventured to make
many false statements' about Britain; no doubt, as Müllenhoff shrewdly
observes,[38] anger at the taciturnity of the Gallic merchants had also
something to do with it.

III

The results of Polybius' journeys and enquiries – which no doubt were
generally more fruitful than those Scipio made about Britain – are to
be seen throughout his history. Especially in those parts which concern
Greece his narrative reveals the eye of the native, and frequently he
sketches in a few words the salient features of the locality with which
he is occupied.[39] Books IV and V,[40] with their narrative of the Social
War, are particularly rich in this kind of thing. 'Aegeira is situated in the
Peloponnese on the Gulf of Corinth between Aegium and Sicyon, and is
built on sleep hills difficult of access, looking towards Parnassus and that
part of the opposite coast, its distance from the sea being about seven
stades.'[41] 'Ambracus is a place strongly fortified by outworks and a wall
and lies in a lake with only one narrow approach from the countryside,

---

[34] iv.2.2.   [35] iv.39.11.

[36] iv.42.7. πλοϊζεσθαι means 'commercium maritimum exercere' (Schweighaeuser), not merely
'to sail'; cf. ii.8.1; iv.47.1; v.88.7; 88.9; xxx.8.5. The point is missed by LSJ.

[37] Strabo iv.2.1C.190 = Polyb. xxxiv.10.6–7. This seems the most probable occasion for the incident.

[38] Müllenhoff (1890) 353–4.

[39] We must not, however, suppose, that *every* thumb-nail sketch implies personal acquaintance with
the site in question; there is a traditional element going back to Herodotus and Hecataeus in this
kind of description.

[40] Cf. Cuntz (1902) 5f.   [41] iv.57.5.

and it is so situated as to command effectually both the countryside
and the city (of Ambracia).'[42] 'Triphylia . . . lies on the coast of the
Peloponnese between Elis and Messenia, facing the Libyan Sea and form-
ing the extreme south-west portion of Arcadia: it contains the following
towns . . . [which Polybius then enumerates].'[43] Such concise indications
recur repeatedly in this part of the work, and are reinforced by several
more elaborate, and equally effective descriptions of more important
positions, such as Psophis, on its almost impregnable hillside between
the Erymanthus and a violent torrent which ran into it just below the
city, or the plain around Sparta || and the Menelaion, where a sharp
action took place between the Macedonians and the defenders of the
city.[44] Moreover, the same skill is shown in describing districts farther
afield. A particularly noteworthy example is the detailed account of the
advantages and disadvantages of the site of Byzantium[45] including some
interesting speculation on the current in the Bosphorus and the speed at
which the Black Sea was being silted up and so converted into a fresh-
water lake. We read too of Sinope[46] 'on the southern shore of the Black
Sea on the route to the Phasis and situated on a peninsula running out
to the open sea. The neck of this peninsula connecting it with Asia is not
more than two stades in width, and is absolutely closed by the city lying
upon it; the rest of the peninsula runs out to the open sea and is flat and
affords an easy approach to the town, but on its maritime face it is very
steep, difficult to anchor off, and with very few approaches from the sea.'
There are similar elaborate and vivid descriptions of the topography of
Seleuceia on the Orontes,[47] Agrigentum,[48] and Lissus and Acrolissus in
Illyria.[49]

    The description of Lissus and Acrolissus is however an example of
a difficulty which frequently arises in Polybius' – and indeed in most
ancient historians' – accounts of the lesser-known sites. For in it Polybius
succeeds in giving a perfectly clear picture of the position, the battle, and
the tactics of it: but when we come to place his battle on the map we are
at once in the thick of controversy. The same problem arises again and
again. The battle of Sellasia occupies five long chapters in Book II,[50] and
is on the whole a clear narrative containing many topographical details
and even the names of the two hills on which the Spartan right and left
were stationed. Yet the long controversy between Kromayer, Kahrstedt,
Soteriades and Ferrabino ultimately faded into || silence rather through

[42] iv.61.7.   [43] iv.77.8.   [44] iv.70.3ff.; v.21.3–22.7.
[45] iv.38–45.   [46] iv.56.5–6.   [47] v.59.3–11.   [48] ix.27.
[49] viii.13; on the site of Lissos see now May (1946).   [50] ii.65–9.

the exhaustion of the participants than because they had reached unanimity about the truth. Similarly, when we come further west, we find
the problem of the pass by which Hannibal crossed the Alps occupying a
literature which Professor Kahrstedt (before adding to it) admits that he
has not yet covered for the simple reason that he is not a hundred years
old. Yet Polybius claims to have crossed the Alps himself and to write in
this case as an eye-witness. What then is wrong?

To some extent *we* are: for we habitually ask from ancient historians
what we have no right to ask – namely that their topography shall be
adequate to permit of pin-pointing an action on the contours of a large-
scale Austrian Staff Map. Polybius had not the advantage of such a
map, nor his readers either. For them, a long list of barbarous place
names could have little meaning, and Polybius realistically admits the
fact. 'I am of the opinion' he writes[51] 'that as regards known countries
the mention of names is of no small assistance in recalling them to our
memory, but in the case of unknown lands such citation of names is just
as of much value as if they were unintelligible and inarticulate sounds.'
Anyone who has tried to follow the Russian campaigns of the recent war
without a map will appreciate the truth of these words, and will grant
their reasonableness, though the historian may regret a decision which
deprives him of valuable material.

If then names were useless, what was to take their place? Before coming
to Polybius' own, somewhat naive, answer to this question, let us consider one example of his powers of geographical description, in which
he has produced what is generally agreed to be a minor masterpiece.
Before Polybius wrote, Greek writers had little to say on Italy beyond the
view from the shore.[52] In three chapters of Book II,[53] Polybius makes a
bold use of a system of triangulation to give us the main outlines of the
peninsula, and then to sketch in the smaller triangle which comprises ||
Cisalpine Gaul and the Po Valley. The apex of the larger triangle is Cape
Cocynthus (which is probably the modern Punta di Stilo);[54] the two sides
are the east and west coasts of Italy (neglecting the complications caused
by the 'heel' and 'toe'); and the base of the triangle is formed by the Alps.
The faults of this account are patent: and Strabo has an eloquent chapter
criticising it,[55] and concluding that 'one might call the figure "four-sided"
rather than "three-sided", but in no sense whatever a triangle, except

[51] iii.36.3.　　[52] Ninck (1945) 171ff.　　[53] ii.14–16.
[54] Cf. Nissen (1902) ii.2, 948–9. This seems preferable to Ziegler's identification with Capo S. Maria
di Leuca, at the southern tip of Calabria; cf. *RE*, s.v. Σικελία, col. 2472.
[55] v.1.2 c.210.

by an abuse of the term. It is better, however', he adds 'to confess that
the representation of non-geometrical figures is not easy to describe.'
Indeed it is not. And Polybius' description has at least achieved clarity
through bold simplification, a reduction of physical features to the bare
essentials – seas, mountains and a few rivers – and the use of the fewest
possible proper names; as Ninck observes,[56] it demonstrates a practical
spirit akin to that of the Roman, combined with a power of observation
and a capacity for organising knowledge that is altogether Greek. In
addition, the description of the Po Valley succeeds in giving not merely
the outline of the physical geography, but also the conditions of life, the
fertility of the soil, some significant economic statistics, and what are almost certainly Polybius' own experiences staying *en pension* at a Cisalpine
Gallic inn – all within the space of a chapter.

For brilliant writing of this kind one is not unwilling to pay a price; and
in this case part of the price is our present uncertainty concerning the
pass by which Hannibal crossed the Alps. For the obscurity in Polybius'
account of this famous march springs partly from the principle, already
observed, of giving no proper names in describing barbarous districts,
where they could have no meaning for a Greek reader, but also from the
fact that he has become the victim of his own bold schematisation. As
we || have seen, Polybius pictured the Alps – which, incidentally, he was
the first writer to describe[57] – as a range running from west to east along
the northern frontier of Italy, from Marseilles to the head of the Adriatic[58]
and since it is by these mountains that the Rhone is separated from the
Po Valley,[59] it too is necessarily pictured as flowing from east to west.
Hence when Hannibal leaves the so-called 'Island' to march up the Isère
along the foot of the Alps, Polybius cannot distinguish this river from the
Rhone. This is of course not the whole story of this particular *crux:* but
it plays some considerable part in our – and Polybius' – confusion.

From this it will appear that triangles have their dangers as a solution to geographical problems; and these dangers appear elsewhere in
Polybius. A description of Sicily, for example, could be – indeed must
be – triangulated.[60] Its capes were correctly named, but in giving their
position Polybius sets the island 90 degrees out, so perhaps originat-
ing a vitiated tradition which was later reproduced in both Strabo and
Pliny.[61] In his detailed description of the Sicilian landscape, too, he is

[56] Ninck (1945) 173.   [57] They were *mentioned* by Cato; Servius ad *Aen.* x.13.
[58] ii.14.6.   [59] iii.47.4; cf. 50.1.   [60] i.41.6ff.
[61] Strabo vi.2.1 c.265–6; Pliny, *HN* iii.87. [No: Eratosthenes' view that Rome, Messina and Carthage
lay on the same meridian (Strabo i.93) already implies a 90° error concerning the sides of Sicily.]

inclined to impressionism. Mt Eryx, the modern Mte San Giuliano [Erice since 1924] near Trapani, is admittedly an impressive bulk to anyone approaching from the sea; but it is only 751 m high, and to call it 'much the highest mountain in Sicily after Etna'[62] is manifestly absurd. Similarly in the case of the topography of New Carthage in Spain, where, as Strachan-Davidson, and before him Droysen saw,[63] 'it is hopeless to reconcile Polybius' orientation with the map', his account has given rise to a considerable polemical literature;[64] and it seems clear that on any explanation he has been negligent.

The fault therefore is not wholly in Polybius' readers, but lies || partly in his own failure to devise a satisfactory system of topographical indication. That this is true in his practice we have seen: let us now consider his own theory.

A few pages above I quoted the passage from Book III[65] in which Polybius rejects the use of proper names in referring to outlying countries: it is followed by these words:[66] 'The primary and most important conception, and one common to all mankind, is the division and ordering of the heavens by which all of us, even those of the meanest capacity, distinguish east, west, south and north. The next step is to classify the parts of the earth under each of these divisions, ever mentally referring any statement to one of them until we arrive at a familiar conception of unknown and unseen regions.' In short, instead of mentioning names, one is to give compass points; and as an illustration, Polybius goes on to describe the three continents as lying, Asia between the Nile and the Don and under that part of the heavens which lies between the north-east and the south, Africa between the Nile and the Pillars of Hercules, and under the heavens stretching from the south to the west and south-west, and Europe extending from east to west, from the Don to the Pillars.

As Strabo saw, this passage reveals a remarkable mental confusion. 'No one' he points out[67] 'employs rules and measures that are variable for things that are non-variable, nor reckonings that are made relative to one position or another for things that are absolute and unchanging.' 'The terms East and West, North-East and South-East are not absolute but relative to our individual positions; and if we shift our positions to different points, the positions of sunset and sunrise . . . are different, though the length of the continent remains the same. Therefore, while it is not out of place to make the Don and the Nile limits of continents, it is

[62] i.55.7; cf. Kromayer (1912) 25ff.   [63] Strachan-Davidson (1888) 639; Droysen (1875).
[64] The best recent account is in Scullard (1930) 289ff.   [65] iii.36.3.   [66] iii.36.6ff.
[67] ii.4.7.c.108. The translation follows H. L. Jones (Loeb edition).

something new to use the north-east or the east for this purpose.' In other words, Polybius has tried to define the boundaries of the continents by giving directions, without defining the point from which he takes them. The || cause of this confusion – which does little credit to his intelligence as a geographer – is not far to seek. We know that he believed the course of the Don to be from north-east to south-west,[68] a view which Strabo contests;[69] similarly he asserted that the Straits at the Pillars of Hercules ran due west;[70] and it was common knowledge that the Nile ran from south to north. Apparently then Polybius has confused the direction of the course of these three waterways with the supposed direction of their mouths from the point of view of an ideal spectator – probably situated in the Peloponnese, though this is a point on which he leaves us uninformed.

The naiveté and amateurishness of this chapter makes an even worse impression when one remembers that at the time Polybius was writing Hipparchus of Nicaea was already putting forward his impressive, if still utopian, scheme for a map which should chart the whole world, as far as it was then known, with each important point marked according to its latitude (determined from the altitude of the sun) and its longitude (calculated by observing the times of eclipses). This contrast between Polybius and the professional geographers is indeed fundamental, and can be observed even more clearly in Book XXXIV, which is entirely devoted to geographical problems and the description of the *oecumene*.

IV

The idea of a special geographical book probably came to Polybius from Ephorus, an author for whom he expressed considerable regard,[71] as the only author of a universal history, and who devoted his fourth and fifth books exclusively to questions of geography.[72] Book XXXIV occupies a special place in Polybius' work. It interrupts the historical narrative in the year 152 in order to give a geographical survey of the whole of the *oecumene*, || at a point when, as the historian elsewhere explains,[73] the organised empire which Rome had built up during the previous years was now threatened with trouble and disturbance (ταραχὴ καὶ κίνησις). The remaining five books (XXXV–XXXIX) were to give the details of this incipient chaos, thus balancing Books I–V at the beginning of the work, in the same way that the account of the *oecumene* in Book XXXIV

---

[68] xxxiv.7.10.   [69] ii.4.5 c.107.   [70] xxxiv.7.9.   [71] v.33.3.
[72] Cf. Schwartz, *RE*, s.v. 'Ephoros', cols. 4–5.   [73] iii.4.12

was to balance that of the Roman constitution in Book VI. Between VI
and XXXIV came the twenty-seven books devoted to the rise of Rome
to world empire.

Book XXXIV has therefore its own purpose in the *Histories*, a purpose
which is obscured by those who think, with Professor Schulten, that it
serves merely as a geographical introduction to the Celtiberian War of
153–151 BC.[74] It is rather an attempt to give additional cohesion to the
universal history by describing for us the full geographical framework
of the *oecumene*.[75] Unfortunately it has survived only in a form for which
the expression 'fragmentary' is a gross exaggeration; for most of the
so-called fragments of the book, as assembled for example by Büttner-
Wobst, are mere *testimonia*, or paraphrases taken from the polemics of
later writers such as Strabo, Athenaeus and even Pliny. Moreover two
of the so-called fragments break off quite arbitrarily in the middle of
Polybius' argument, which can only be recovered by consulting the full
text of Strabo.[76] However, from what these later writers tell us, it is
clear that much of the book was taken up, after Polybius' usual fashion,
with attacks on previous geographers, together with discussions of theory
and a considerable number of practical details concerning distances and
topography. Here, as in the famous polemic against Timaeus in Book XII,
Polybius gives full rein to his *penchant* for stating his point of view in
regard to current controversies. A typical example, and one of great
importance for Polybius' philosophical position is his attitude towards
Homeric geography. ||

Homer has been called the Bible of the Greeks: and the Homeric problem overshadowed Alexandrine thought and scholarship as the problem
of the credibility of the Bible overshadowed the nineteenth century. This
was no mere literary dispute, but one affecting every branch of art and
science; for the fundamentalists claimed that the basis of all ordered
knowledge was to be sought in the *Iliad* and the *Odyssey*. The Stoics in
particular believed that Homer held the key to all geographical problems.
As the prototype of the Stoic Wise Man, he must necessarily excel in all
spheres – as an astronomer and geographer, as well as as a poet.[77] Where
this view led to difficulties, these were to be surmounted at all costs, if
necessary by violent means: since for instance the identity of the Erembi
in *Odyssey* iv.84 was uncertain, Zeno had no hesitation in saving Homer's

---

[74] Schulten (1911). [For a reconstruction of the contents of Book XXXIV, which did not include
the whole *oecumene*, see Walbank, *Comm.* III, 565–9.]
[75] Cf. Dubois (1891) 352.   [76] xxxiv.6.14; 7.14.   [77] Cf. Neumann (1886).

reputation by emending καὶ Ἐρέμβους to Ἀραβάς τε.[78] Elsewhere the difficulty was eliminated by assuming that Homer spoke allegorically – a method which has also been known to occur in biblical exegesis. This emphasis on Homer is especially prominent in one of Polybius' contemporaries, Crates of Mallos, the Pergamene critic and philosopher,[79] who believed that Homer already knew that the world was a globe, and attempted to identify the localities touched on by Menelaus and Odysseus in their wanderings after the fall of Troy. Crates, incidentally, was also worried by the Erembi, and therefore emended Homer's Ἐρεμβούς to Ἐρεμνούς, 'the dusky men', and so sent Menelaus voyaging to India.[80] Another Homeric fundamentalist was Asclepiades of Myrlea, who was probably not Crates' pupil, though he was certainly in general sympathy with the attitude of the Pergamene, and wrote a *Periegesis* which accepted the literal truth of Odysseus' wanderings, and found traces of these in the dedications in a Spanish temple in Turdetania.[81] ||

This kind of thing was anathema to Alexandrine scholarship. Eratosthenes, one of the greatest minds of the third century, believed the function of poetry was to entertain, not to instruct.[82] 'Eratosthenes' says Strabo[83] 'asks how it adds to the excellence of the poet for him to be an expert in geography, or in generalship, or in agriculture, or in rhetoric, or in any kind of special knowledge with which some people have wished to invest him.' Poetry, in the opinion of Eratosthenes,[84] was to be judged neither on the reflections it contained nor by the canons of historical truth. As for identifying the wanderings of Odysseus, this he dismissed with the quip that you would find the scene of Odysseus' travels when you discovered the cobbler who sewed the bag of the winds.[85]

On this issue Polybius – as we might expect – appears among the fundamentalists; and in Book XXXIV he dealt at length with Odysseus' wanderings, locating Scylla and Charybdis at the Straits of Messina,[86] and comparing Scylla diving in quest of dolphins, dog-fish and similar creatures to the fishers who harpoon the sword-fish which batten on the shoals of tunny around the Sicilian Straits. Why the controversy about the wanderings of Odysseus should play so prominent a part in a book ostensibly devoted to a description of the inhabited world at the time of the Roman conquest is not immediately clear. A passage in Book XII,

[78] Strabo i.2.34 c.41.   [79] On Crates cf. E. Hansen (1947) 371–80; Mette (1936).
[80] Strabo i.2.31 c.38.   [81] Strabo iii.4.3 c.157.   [82] Strabo i.1.10 c.7.
[83] Strabo i.2.3 c.15–16.   [84] Strabo i.2.17 c.25.   [85] Strabo i.2.15 c.24.
[86] Strabo i.2.15–17 c.23–5 = Polyb. xxxiv.2.4ff.

which is also devoted to polemic, may however offer us a clue.[87] Here
Polybius has been criticising Timaeus as an armchair historian, and has
just quoted Ephorus and Theopompus on the superiority of the man
of action:[88] he goes on: 'Homer has been still more emphatic on this
subject than these writers. Wishing to show us what qualities one should
possess in order to be a man of action he says:[89] ||

> The man for wisdom's arts renowned,
> Long exercised in woes, O Muse, resound,
> Wandering from clime to clime; observant strayed,
> Their manners noted and their states surveyed;
> On stormy seas unnumbered toils he bore
>   (*Od.* i.1–3);

and again

> In scenes of death by tempest and by war
>   (*Od.* viii.183).

It appears to me' continues Polybius, 'that the dignity of history also
demands such a man.'

The implications of this last sentence stand out, immediately we compare a passage already quoted.[90] 'I shall ask those who are curious ... to
give their undivided attention to me in view of the fact that I underwent
the perils of journeys through Africa, Spain and Gaul, and of voyages on
the seas that lie on the farther side of these countries.' Here, disguised
beneath the didacticism of the practical historian, we catch a glimpse of
a romantic, who imagines himself in the rôle of a second Odysseus;[91] it is
a trait we may well remember, in summing up Polybius' character, and
it helps to explain the vigour with which he joins Crates, Poseidonius
and the other Stoics down to Strabo, in resisting the scepticism of
Eratosthenes.

This quarrel with Eratosthenes and Alexandrian science is indeed
something fundamental, which affects more than Polybius' judgement
on Odysseus. It is not that he rejects the use of science outright. Indeed,
in his notes on tactics in Book IX he insists on the importance of some
knowledge of astronomy and geometry for the successful commander;[92]

---

[87] Cf. von Scala (1890) I, 67.   [88] xii.27.10ff.   [89] Pope's translation.   [90] iii.59.7.
[91] If Polybius' affectation was already known in Roman senatorial circles in 150 BC, as indeed it may
   have been, it gives additional point to Cato's quip about Odysseus going back into the Cyclops'
   cave for his cap and belt (Polyb. xxxv.6.4 = Plut. *Cato mai.* 9). Von Scala (1890) I, 67 points out
   that Ptolemy Euergetes also liked to identify himself with Odysseus.
[92] ix.14ff.

but he advocates these sciences for their severely practical use, adding:[93]
'I do not think anyone can fairly maintain that I attach too many quali-
fications to the || art of generalship, by thus urging those who aim at
mastering it to study astronomy and geometry. On the contrary, I strongly
disapprove of all ... superfluous attainments ... and am disinclined to
insist on any studies beyond those that are of actual use.' Naturally this
concept of vocational studies runs entirely contrary to the spirit of free
speculation and the acquisition of knowledge for its own sake which
characterised the new sciences of Alexandria, and not least, the new
developments in geography since the expedition of Alexander.

v

The campaigns of Alexander had given a new stimulus to geographical studies, which had affected almost all the traditional problems. The
new knowledge of India, the Persian Gulf and even Ceylon (Taprobane),
brought fresh material for those who wished to ponder over the dimen-
sions of the earth, the problem of climatic zones, the relations of land and
ocean, and the construction of a map of the world. The results achieved
by Alexander were amplified by his successors. Megasthenes – perhaps
the first Greek to set eyes on the Ganges – and Deïmachus were sent out
by the Seleucids to India, Ariston and Simmias explored the Arabian
Gulf, and the west coast of Arabia, for the Ptolemies. Meanwhile, at
the other extremity of the known world Pytheas of Marseilles had made
his famous sea-voyage in about 325 BC. From Gades he sailed north
along the Celtic coast to the island of Ushant off Brittany, whence he
reached Belerion, the western promontory of Britain, in four days. From
here he probably continued north to circumnavigate Britain in a clock-
wise direction. He obtained information about the Hebrides, Shetlands
and Orkneys, reached a point where the summer night lasted only two
hours, and heard of the midnight sun in Thule. Pytheas' achievements
went beyond mere exploration. It seems evident that he was a scientist
by temperament, and that the driving force behind his voyage was not
primarily gain, but knowledge. It was Pytheas who first equated the latitude of a place with the height of the celestial pole at the same point; and
many of his readings of latitude were subsequently || embodied in the
tables of Hipparchus. Much in the story of Pytheas remains obscure; for
this our sources are largely to blame, for far too often we face a situation

---

[93] ix.20.5–6.

in which we have to consider what Strabo said about what Polybius said about what Eratosthenes said about what Pytheas said somebody had told him. Nevertheless there is little doubt, notwithstanding the jibes of the Stoic-conservative school of Polybius and Strabo, who call him a liar outright, that Pytheas was one of the great explorers of history, of the calibre of Columbus himself.

This extension of geographical experience was followed by new developments in theory. By about 300 BC Dicaearchus of Messana had devised a map of the world based on a central line of latitude running from the Pillars of Hercules along Mt Taurus in Asia Minor, and eastward following the Imaus range in Further Asia, and on a meridian drawn through Lysimacheia on the Hellespont. From the fragments of Strabo which form part of our substitute for the thirty-fourth book of Polybius we know that Dicaearchus also estimated such distances as those from the Peloponnese to the Pillars of Hercules, and to the head of the Adriatic. His map was revised and a new geographical synthesis was undertaken by Eratosthenes of Cyrene, the librarian of Ptolemy III. Eratosthenes in many ways represents the high peak of Greek geography. Beginning with a general survey of his predecessors' work, starting from Homer, but naming Anaximander as the first scientific writer, he went on to a full discussion of all aspects of geography – the shape, size, and position of the earth, the zones, and the problem of the distribution of land and ocean. Perhaps his most notable achievement was the use of the sundial and its shadow, which measured $7\frac{1}{7}$ degrees at Alexandria, and o degrees at Syene on the tropic, at the time of the summer solstice, to calculate the size of the earth's circumference correctly within about 300 km. His map of the world was an adaptation of that of Dicaearchus. His main line of latitude, his *diaphragma*, ran from the Pillars along the Taurus and Imaus ranges, intersecting the main meridian at Rhodes. These two lines were supported by six further meridians drawn at intervals between the eastern and || western boundaries of the *oecumene*, and six further parallels running through Meroe, Syene, Alexandria, Lysimacheia, the mouth of the Borysthenes, and Thule.

The most serious attack on Eratosthenes came from Hipparchus of Nicaea, whose contribution to geography was mainly critical and theoretical. His proposal for a map based on astronomical premises was not yet feasible; consequently, although he criticised Eratosthenes for using unscientific methods – for instance, for arguing from similarities in vegetation to identity of latitude – he produced no map of his own. He was the first man to suggest that longitude might be determined by observing the time of an eclipse at different points; but the lack of accurate chronometers, and the practical difficulties of organising teams of observers, were a serious handicap to the carrying out of such a scheme. In Hipparchus the brilliance of Greek theory seems to have outstripped the possibilities and resources of the time. The tables of latitude and longitude which he compiled were a step towards a new conception of the scientific organisation of knowledge. But for the time being his writings brought geography to an impasse, which perhaps contributed to a reaction towards purely practical, experimental work. Mathematics and astronomy were neglected by the second-century geographer, who limited himself to what was of immediate use.

The whole era of Alexandrian geography had been one of intense activity, keen speculation, and fruitful polemics. When we come to Polybius we have reached the reaction against it, the swing back to Stoic dogmatism and the narrower ideal of geography in the service of some other science – in this case of history.

VI

Usually Polybius' disapproval of the Alexandrians, or lack of interest in their theories, shows itself in silence.[94] On many of the || most important questions, such as the relative proportions of the earth's sphere occupied by land and sea, he feels no urge to speculate or comment. He does not even express any opinion on whether the *oecumene* is an island surrounded by sea – on the whole the accepted view, and the one championed by Eratosthenes – though one passage in Book III[95] has been held to prove that he believed in a junction between Africa and Asia somewhere south of the Indian Ocean, which thus became an inland sea. This fallacy had a long history in antiquity, and was known and combated by Aristotle. Alexander thought at one time that the Hydaspes and Acesines were sources of the Nile. Artaxerxes Ochus had even tried to divert the Nile in India. Even long after Polybius' day, the geographer Ptolemy believed

---

94 Uhden has argued ((1933) (cf. 316, 322)) that Polybius modified Eratosthenes' central meridian (above p.46) by substituting a line Nile–Tanais for the line Nile–Borysthenes; and since the meridian Nile–Tanais appears in the *Tetrabiblos* of Ptolemy, he assumes that Polybius transmitted a map with some kind of mathematical pretensions to the Romans (from whom Ptolemy took it for this work) but not to the Greeks. This theory rests on a misunderstanding of Polyb. iv.39.1 (cf. xxxiv.15.5 = Pliny, *HN* iv.77), which merely says that the Thracian and Cimmerian Bosphori are at diametrically opposite ends of the Pontus – not that they lie on the same meridian. Polyb. iv.39.1 allows no conclusions on Polybius' attitude towards Eratosthenes' map.

95 iii.38.1; cf. Müllenhoff (1890) 350 n.; Honigmann, *RE*, s.v. 'Libye', cols. 167–8; corrected by Gisinger, *RE*, Suppl.-B. IV, s.v. 'Geographia', col. 625.

the Indian Ocean to be an inland sea, and Procopius could still give
the Nile an Indian source. Nevertheless, Polybius has been wrongfully
accused. What he says is this: 'With regard to Asia and Africa, where
they meet in Ethiopia, no one up to the present has been able to say
with certainty whether the southern extension of them is continuous
land or is bounded by a sea.' Now the point where Asia and Africa meet
in Ethiopia is of course the source of the Nile, for that river was taken
by Polybius to mark the division between the continents; so that what
he is leaving undecided is whether the ocean bounding what we today
call Africa comes almost immediately to the south of the source of the
Nile, or whether the continuous land mass of Asia and Africa (no longer
separated by the river) runs for an indefinite distance to the south. In
mentioning this Polybius expresses no opinion on the wider issue.

On one major topic only does he come out with decided views – on the
theory of zones; indeed Geminus tells us in his *Elements* || *of Astronomy*[96]
that Polybius composed a separate work entitled *On the inhabited part of the
globe under the celestial equator.* This may be true, though most scholars assume that Geminus is merely referring, in a slightly confused manner, to a
discussion of the subject in Book XXXIV. In this instance Polybius shows
himself on the side of progress, though unfortunately he has adopted the
right view for the wrong reasons. It had long been accepted doctrine,
based on the existence of the Sahara desert, that the *oecumene* was bounded
in the south by a 'burnt zone' where no one could live. But from the third
century onwards a belief in the habitability of the equatorial zone had
gained ground, and was held by Eratosthenes[97] and probably by Crates[98]
(who placed the Ocean there, dividing our world from the Antipodes);
later Panaetius[99] and Poseidonius both adhered to it.

Polybius, says Geminus, argued from the nature of the sun's motions.
'For at the solstices the sun remains a long time near the tropic circles,
both in approaching them and receding from them, so that we actually
see it in their neighbourhood for about forty days ... So owing to the
length of its stay over the climate lying under the tropic circles, that
region is burnt up and is uninhabitable owing to the excessive heat. But
from the equator the sun recedes rapidly, so that the length of the day
rapidly increases or decreases after the equinoxes. It is reasonable then to
suppose that the climates situated under the equator are more temperate.'
In addition Polybius believed that the equatorial region was 'very high

[96] c. 16 = Polyb. xxxiv.1.7–13.   [97] Strabo ii.3.2 c.97; cf. H. Berger (1880) 83–4.
[98] Gisinger, *RE*, Suppl-B. IV, s.v. 'Geographia', col. 616.   [99] Ibid. col. 624.

[ὑψηλοτάτη – which probably means mountainous] and therefore has a rainfall'.[100]

Nevertheless he divided the earth into six zones,[101] two under the arctic circles, two between these and the tropic circles, and || two between the tropics and the equator: the habitable area around the equator was apparently not distinct from the two tropical zones, but merely formed a division between them. Though superficially straightforward and sensible, this division has its unexpected difficulties. By 'arctic circle' the Greeks meant something different from ourselves. To them the arctic circle was a circle drawn in the heavens, at any latitude, with the celestial pole as its centre, and the distance from the pole to the nearest point on the horizon as its radius, and so containing within it all the stars which at that latitude never set. Thus for the observer at each latitude there was a different arctic circle, and the further north one went, the larger this circle became. What we today call the arctic circle is in fact a line drawn, not in the heavens, but around the earth, along that latitude at which the celestial arctic circle (in the Greek sense) coincides with the sun's daily track through the heavens at the time of the summer solstice – in short it is the most southerly latitude at which it is possible to see the midnight sun on the night of the summer solstice.

Poseidonius, who was acquainted with the fixed arctic circle in our sense,[102] criticised Aristotle[103] for attempting to use a moveable circle to delimit a terrestrial zone; and before him Pytheas, Eratosthenes and Hipparchus were all awake to the difficulty, and knew of the fixed terrestrial circle.[104] But the 'moving circle' was commonly used down to Roman times,[105] and it is not therefore surprising that Polybius falls into the trap, and is justly reproved by Strabo for once more – as in his delimitation of the continents – attempting to define non-variables by points that are themselves variable.[106]

VII

These examples, with could easily be multiplied, show clearly that Polybius could make no serious contribution to the scientific || study of geography. He was however awake to one philosophical problem which

---

[100] Strabo ii.3.2 c.97 = Polyb. xxxiv.1.16. Poseidonius thought it meant 'more bulging' and criticised Polybius, saying that 'there can be no high point on a spherical surface'. Cf. Strabo ii.3.3 c.98.

[101] Strabo ii.3.1 c.96 = Polyb. xxxiv.1.14.   [102] Strabo ii.2.3 c.95.

[103] *Meteor.* ii.5.12; cf. Strabo ii.2.2 c.94.   [104] H. Berger (1880) 82.

[105] Cf. Manil. *Astron.* i.560f.; Macrob. *Somn. Scip.* ii.6.   [106] ii.3.2 c.97.

particularly concerns the geographer, even if the answer he gave was narrowly conditioned both by the tradition established by previous writers and by his own rationalism. What is the relationship between man, his character and his actions on the one hand, and his material environment on the other? This question was first asked in the fifth century in an outstanding work, Hippocrates *On climates, waters and places*.[107] In his refusal to admit the operation of divine causes, Hippocrates insisted that differences of national character and temperament could be deduced from differences of climate: thus a regular climate causes indolence, a varied climate energy and manliness. In addition to the material environment, however, he allows some place for history. For example[108] a free state produces better warriors than one ruled by a despot, and that is why those Asiatic peoples, Greek or barbarian, with a free constitution, surpassed in valour those who were not free.

The same kind of reasoning recurs in many later writers. The author of the pseudo-Aristotelian *Problems*, for instance,[109] asks why the inhabitants of excessively hot or excessively cold regions are beast-like in habits and appearance, and gives the answer that moral energy is correlated with animal warmth, in such a way that excesses of heat and cold cause distortion of both the mind and body. The Ethiopians and Egyptians, whom this writer assumes to be bandy-legged as well as having woolly hair,[110] because their bodies have warped like planks in the heat, had presumably warped and woolly minds as well. Megasthenes[111] on the other hand attributes the intelligence of the Indians to their clear atmosphere and their pure drinking water; and the connection between the damp || air of Boeotia and the stupidity of its inhabitants was a Greek commonplace.[112]

One may note in passing that the theory is not confined to the ancient world. For example, Buckle in England,[113] and Montesquieu in France both said something very similar. To Buckle the fertile curiosity and genius of the Greeks sprang from the fact that in Greece nature is in all things weak and small; while Montesquieu believed that

---

[107] Pöhlmann (1889) 12ff. That there was *some* connection had been assumed by Hecataeus and Herodotus.

[108] Ibid. 35ff.   [109] *Problem.* xiv.1, 909a.   [110] Ibid. xiv.4.   [111] *FHG* ii 402.

[112] Cf. F. Cauer, *RE*, s.v. 'Boiotia', col. 646. We cannot here follow the detailed development of this so-called 'milieu-theory' down to its final notable appearance in Adamantius in the fourth century AD. But one may note the prominent part played in it by Poseidonius, who laid great stress on the fact that the purer and more primitive races such as the Scythians and the Ethiopians, lay on the fringes of the *oecumene*, whereas the more cultured peoples of the Mediterranean area had benefited by racial κρᾶσις. See Trüdinger (1918); Hornyanszky (1929).

[113] Cf. Pöhlmann (1889) 29ff.

virtue and courage grew in proportion to one's distance from the trop-
ics. In the *Laws*[114] he deduced the English free constitution from our national character, and this in turn from our climate. Likewise in Germany
Karl Otfried Müller, the idealiser of Greek aristocracy at the time of
Metternich,[115] derived the history of the state from the *Volksgeist*, and saw
this as organically linked up with the land and climate; 'races' he wrote
'are the children of their soil'.

Of this theory Polybius too is an adherent. But he makes his own
contribution in a curious passage, which owes something to Platonic
doctrine, about his native Arcadia. In that country, he says,[116] music
plays an essential part in the education of youth, and || frequent musical
festivals are held because 'the universal practice of personal manual
labour, and in general the toilsomeness and hardship of men's lives, as
well as the harshness of character resulting from the cold and gloomy
atmospheric conditions usually prevailing in these parts' make it essential
to take steps to counter such adverse circumstances. The wisdom of
this policy was shown by the awful and exemplary fate of the men of
Cynaetha, who refused to take their part in these Arcadian *Eisteddfodau*
and consequently became eventually so brutalised that in no city of
Greece were greater and more constant crimes committed. 'I have said
so much' concludes Polybius[117] '. . . in order to deter any other Arcadians
from beginning to neglect music under the impression that its extensive
practice in Arcadia serves no necessary purpose.'

VIII

How wholly typical of its author! In Polybius' Arcadia, as in Plato's
Republic, music is only allowed entry under a 'utility label'. And in
the long run it is the 'utility label' which stamps the whole of Polybius'
contribution to geography, and marks the place which he occupies in its
development as a science. The permanent work which Polybius did was
in the opening up of the west, in the recording of topographical details,

[114] xiv.13.
[115] Cf. Stier (1945) 22; Meyer (1937) 538, n. 1. The importance of this concept as a forerunner of
the 'Blut und Boden' of the Nazi 'philosophy' is obvious, despite the mysticism of the latter and
the crude rationalism of the former.
[116] iv. 20ff. cf. Wunderer (1901) 14–16. Hirzel (1882) 891–2, tries to show that Polybius' source for
this topic is entirely Stoic; cf. Cicero, *De fato* 7, which attributes the view that climate shapes
character to Chrysippus. But his demonstration breaks down in view of his own admission that
the theory was known to Hippocrates, Plato and Aristotle. Von Scala (1890) I, 204, has further
Stoic references, but fails to show their connection with Polybius.
[117] iv.21.10.

and in the assembling and comparing of distances, rather than in any
contribution to geographical theory. It was his fortune – call it good or
bad – to live on the frontier of two worlds: and though he never ceased
to be a || Greek and to think like a Greek, there is much in him which
was both congenial to Romans and developed by contact with them.
For Greek scientific theory the Romans had neither understanding nor
patience; but they could value the practical contributions of a Polybius.
It is to Rome that Polybius' work as a geographer leads both him and us,
along a route quite different from that of the Alexandrians. The highest
achievement of native Roman geography was the map of Agrippa. Could
there be a || more significant contrast[118] than that between Eratosthenes
measuring the earth's circumference and boldly sketching in his chart
with his eyes on the heavens, and Agrippa solidly building up *his* map
from the evidence of the milestones, which marked off the roads tramped
hard by the legions of Rome?[119]

[118] The comparison was originally made by J. Partsch; cf. Ninck (1945) 72.
[119] This paper was read at the Joint Meeting of the Classical Association, the Hellenic Society, and
the Roman Society in Oxford, on 6 August 1948.

3

*Egypt in Polybius**

Despite a growing number of ostraca and papyri much of the history of
Ptolemaic Egypt still rests largely on the text of Polybius. I hope therefore that my friend and colleague, Herbert Fairman, will accept as a
suitable tribute to his achievements in the field of Ptolemaic language
and culture, and to the generosity with which he invariably makes his
scholarship available to all who approach him, some observations on the
merits of what Polybius has to say about Ptolemaic Egypt and on the rôle
which he assigned to that kingdom in his account of the rise of Rome
to world power. Polybius is especially concerned with the reigns of four
Ptolemies – Philopator, Epiphanes, Philometor and Euergetes II. Since
he was born towards the end of the third century[1] he had to depend for
his account of Philopator mainly on previous writers, whereas to some
extent for Epiphanes and even more for the other two he was a contemporary and could command direct sources of information. Unfortunately
our text of Polybius is incomplete. From the books covering events after
Raphia, 217 BC, we possess only fragments; consequently we are at the
mercy of Polybius' excerptors and can be brought to a halt in mid-stream
whenever their interest flags.[2] Also, a more grievous loss, only six out of
the fifty-three titles of excerpts assembled on the orders of Constantine
Porphyrogenitus have survived.[3] Despite this Polybius remains an indispensable authority and our source for many details that would otherwise
have escaped us – for instance the importance of the Thesmophorion,

---

* [[J. Ruffle, G. A. Gaballa and K. A. Kitchen (eds.), *Glimpses of Ancient Egypt: Studies in Honour
  of H. W. Fairman* (Warminster 1979) 180–9. All references, unless otherwise indicated, are to
  Polybius.]]
[1] The exact date is uncertain, but it is around or shortly before 200 BC; for the evidence see Walbank
  (1972a) 6 n. 26.
[2] E.g. xxxi. 18.16 where the excerptor, weary of Ptolemy VIII's campaign against Cyrene, simply
  concluded with the words καὶ τέλος ἡττήθη.
[3] Cf. Moore (1965) 127–9.

the temple of Demeter and Kore, in Alexandria,[4] the chronology of the
revolt of the natives towards the end of the third century,[5] or Ptolemy
VIII's persecution of the Alexandrians.[6]

I POLYBIUS' SOURCES OF KNOWLEDGE

More than most ancient historians Polybius is given to enlightening his
readers on the methods he uses to collect material. History, he tells
us[7] consists of three parts, 'the first being the study and collation of
written sources,[8] the second the survey of cities, places, rivers, harbours
and in general the peculiar features of land and sea and the distances
between them, and the third political experience'. Written sources, he
goes on to explain, are of course of limited use to anyone whose concern
is contemporary events; for these the reading of books or, as he puts
it, the use of one's ears – for at that time reading was usually thought
of as reading aloud – is less important than the use of one's eyes, by
which he means practical experience, getting around, and developing
one's own criteria based on a public career and the knowledge that this
brings. On the other hand, questioning people (which certainly involves
the ears) is also indispensable to supplement personal experience, since
one cannot always be in the right place at the right time, and no one can
be everywhere at the same time.[9]

How do these principles apply to that part of Polybius' work which
concerns Egypt? For Ptolemy IV, as we can see clearly from his detailed
account of the Fourth Syrian War (219–217), he had access to substantial
written sources; but their identification is virtually impossible.[10] This fact
emerges from an analysis of his account of the rising, defeat and death of
the Spartan king Cleomenes III in Alexandria,[11] events also described in
Plutarch's *Cleomenes*. Comparison of the two versions shows Polybius to be
using at least two sources, one being Phylarchus and the other, probably,

---

[4] See Fraser (1972) I, 199; II, 334 n. 70; as well as in Polyb. xv. 29.8 this temple is referred to briefly
in Satyrus *(P Oxy.* 2465, fr. 2, col. I, line 5).

[5] v. 107.1–3; xiv. 12.4; xxii.16.1–17.7; Fraser (1972) I, 60–1; II, 143 n. 178; for bibliography on the
revolts see Walbank, *Comm.* III, 203 (xxii.16.1–17.7 n.).

[6] xxxiv.14.6; Fraser (1972) I, 60–1.   [7] xii.25c.1–7.

[8] On the meaning of ὑπομνήματα here see Walbank (1972a) 71 n. 20.

[9] xii.4c.3; elsewhere (xii.28a.7) Polybius calls interrogating eyewitnesses the easiest and least important part of history. The inconsistency arises because here, in polemic against Timaeus, Polybius
takes library work and the questioning of witnesses together in contrast to personal experience.
See Walbank (1972a) 72–4.

[10] See Walbank, *Comm.* I, 570 (v.40.4–57.8n.); Huss (1976) 8–20.

[11] v.35–9; the date is winter 220/19.

Ptolemy of Megalopolis,[12] but the blend is such as to offer small hope of identifying Polybius' sources where no second account is available. For the Fourth Syrian War there is no such second narrative; and though in a recent study[13] Huss has attempted to divide Polybius' narrative into passages deriving from a 'Seleucid source near to the court', a 'neutral source', 'other sources' and Polybius' own comments, he admits 'den hypothetischen Charakter dieser Quellenscheidung'.[14] As regards Ptolemy of Megalopolis[15] Huss has shown[16] the weaknesses in the argument which makes him a mere scandal-monger; but it can hardly be doubted that his work retails some scandal and that it is here that Polybius found the details of the courtesans and fluteplayers of Philopator's court.[17]

For the later Ptolemies, who overlapped Polybius' own career, we can only guess at the identity of any written sources and at which parts were derived from these. Despite his criticism of Timaeus for working exclusively in a library,[18] Polybius did not hesitate to use such sources when they were available. One was probably Zeno of Rhodes, whom he criticises for his account of the Fifth Syrian War, including Antiochus' unsuccessful siege of Gaza and his victory at Panium.[19] But we know of no other by name[20] and must presume that for much of his account of Ptolemaic affairs he relied on oral informants. From boyhood onwards his position as the son of Lycortas, a prominent Achaean statesman, gave him special access to information about Egypt. In 187/6, for example, when Demetrius of Athens came to Achaea as Ptolemy V's representative to renew the alliance with the Achaean League, || Philopoemen as General entertained him to dinner,[21] and the conversation around the table turned on the king's hunting prowess, a topic near to Polybius' heart. Ptolemy, Demetrius reported, had once hit a bull with a javelin from horseback. Was Polybius present? It is hard to say, for he will only have been in his teens.[22] But Lycortas, who had been appointed Achaean

---

[12] Cf. Walbank, *Comm.* I, 565–7; Bagnall (1976) 255.
[13] Huss (1976) 8–20; for Antiochus III's battle against the pretender Molon (v.52–4) Bar-Kochva (1976) 117–23, argues that Polybius' use of sources biased against Hermeias and favourable to Epigenes has led him to underestimate the importance of Antiochus' numbers and strategy for his victory.
[14] Huss (1976) 15.   [15] *FGH* II B no. 161; for his career see Bagnall (1976) 255–6.
[16] Huss (1976) 19 n. 77 arguing against the traditional view accepted by Préaux and Fraser.
[17] xiv.11.1–5.   [18] xii.4c.3, 27.
[19] For Zeno as source for Panium and Gaza see xvi.18.1–19.11; Walbank (1972a) 81. On Panium see Bar-Kochva (1976) 146–57.
[20] Against the view that Polybius used Ptolemy VIII's *Memoirs* see Pédech (1964) 233; they were published too late for that.
[21] xxii.3.5–9.   [22] On the date of Polybius' birth see above, n. 1.

envoy for the return visit, will certainly have been there and must have reported this and other details of the conversation to his son. In 181/0 Polybius was himself appointed envoy to Alexandria, though under the official age for such a post, and failed to make the journey only because of the sudden news of Epiphanes' death.[23] He was undoubtedly chosen because he was Lycortas' son; and twelve years later, in 169/8, when a joint embassy from Ptolemy VI and Ptolemy VIII[24] arrived in Achaea to request help against Antiochus IV, they asked for 1,000 infantry and 200 cavalry under the overall command of Lycortas with Polybius as the cavalry commander. This shows that over the years a close family link had been established between Lycortas and the Ptolemaic court. Such a relationship must have placed the young Polybius in a very favourable position for learning about Egypt.

Shortly afterwards Polybius' fortunes suffered a reversal. From 167 until 150 he was detained in Italy along with a thousand other Achaeans suspected of dubious loyalty towards Rome in the Third Macedonian War.[25] But his detention did not interrupt Polybius' channels of communication with Egypt. Allowed, as a special privilege, perhaps through the intervention of Scipio Aemilianus, to remain in Rome when his colleagues were scattered in detention among the towns of southern Etruria, he was favourably placed to meet the constant stream of envoys who came annually to Rome from all over the Greek east, as well as the Greek detainees like himself from many states, with whom he could establish relations. We happen to know of one particular informant for Ptolemaic affairs, Menyllus of Alabanda, whom Ptolemy VI sent to Rome in 163 to counter the manoeuvres of his brother, Ptolemy VIII, with whom he had divided the kingdom.[26] A few months later, in the summer of 162, Polybius enlisted Menyllus' aid in a plot to bring about the escape from Italy of the young prince Demetrius, so that he might seize the Seleucid throne, occupied since 163 by Antiochus V.[27] In that context he describes Menyllus as a man with whom he enjoyed a firm friendship and great trust.[28] When Polybius got to know Menyllus is uncertain; his phraseology does not exclude an acquaintance established in Rome, but it suggests something of longer standing, and it may well be that the two men had met in Achaea before Polybius' detention at Rome.[29] Menyllus could give him useful information on the reigns

[23] xxiv.6.5.   [24] xxix.23.7.   [25] For Polybius' detention in Italy see Walbank (1972a) 7–10.
[26] xxxi.10.5.   [27] xxxi.11.1–15.13.   [28] xxxi.12.8, ἰσχυρὰ συνήθεια καὶ πίστις.
[29] Paton (Loeb edition), 'Polybius had long been intimate with this Menyllus', paraphrases; but a long association is perhaps implied, and Menyllus may have visited Achaea in 180 (xxiv.6.1) or 169/8 (xxix.23.1–8); on neither occasion are the envoys named.

of Ptolemy V and Ptolemy VI, and his influence may have contributed substantially to Polybius' sympathy for the latter in his struggle with his brother.[30] But Menyllus will not have been the only Ptolemaic envoy to visit Rome from whom Polybius could draw information.

Moreover, Demetrius himself must have been a useful informant. Diodorus' account[31] of Ptolemy VI's arrival in Rome in 164, after his expulsion by Ptolemy VIII, follows Polybius and describes how he was met by Demetrius outside Rome;[32] and Polybius will certainly have heard of this incident (and others) from the Syrian prince himself. Indeed, it is highly likely that through Demetrius he got to know Ptolemy VI himself during the latter's stay at Rome – the more so since, as I have shown,[33] Polybius' name was well known in Egypt.

In 150 Polybius was repatriated and it may be assumed – though we have no direct evidence – that from 146/5 onwards[34] he normally resided in Achaea. He still maintained relations with Egypt; and at some unspecified date in the reign of Ptolemy VIII he made the visit to Alexandria of which he had been disappointed in 181/0.[35] This may have been as Scipio Aemilianus' companion on his eastern embassy of 140,[36] but this assumption is really speculation, for there is no positive evidence one way or the other. Whenever it occurred (and it was certainly after 145), it must have brought life and a new dimension to what had hitherto been hearsay; but its importance for the *Histories* can be exaggerated. The view has, for example, been advanced[37] that Polybius' attack on the Sicilian historian Timaeus sprang out of his irritation at discovering in the course of his visit to Alexandria that, despite his own journeys in the Alps and his exploration in the Atlantic, the scholars of that city still regarded Timaeus as the main authority on the west; and further that an elaborate comparison which Polybius draws between history and medicine[38] rests on his knowledge of the medical schools of Herophilus

---

[30] See below, p. 184 [p. 65 in this volume].   [31] Diod. xxxi.18; cf. Fraser (1972) I, 119–20.
[32] It was a different Demetrius with whom he later lodged.   [33] See above, nn. 23–4.
[34] The years 149–146 he spent at Carthage and exploring the coast of Africa; see Walbank (1972a) 10–12.
[35] xxxiv.14.6; this fragment probably belongs to one of the narrative books and may have been included in the context of the revolt of Petosarapis in the early 160s; cf. Pédech (1964) 573 n. 323.
[36] Diod. xxxiii.28 b; cf. Fraser (1972) II, 145 n. 187. Lehmann (1974) 196 n. 1, argues that fg. 76 of Polybius supports the view that he accompanied Scipio on at least part of that mission; this does not seem to me decisive, though he may have met him in Achaea at the outset. See further Walbank, *Comm.* III, note on fg. 76. That the distances recorded in xxxiv.15.2 between Crete, Rhodes, the Chelidonian Islands, Cyprus and Seleuceia Pieria represent stages in Polybius' journey (Pédech (1964) 561), seems to me implausible and ignores the fact that they are prefaced by stages from Gades to the Palus Maeotis and thence to Crete.
[37] Pédech (1961) xxxi–xxxiii.   [38] xii.25d.

and Callimachus acquired in the course of his Egyptian visit. The sneers at Timaeus may indeed have gained something from a stay in the city of the Library, where writers were devoted to the kind of scholarship which Polybius despised. But he did not have to visit Alexandria to learn that Timaeus was held in high regard; and his account of the medical schools seems rather to rest on the categorisation of a medical handbook, supplemented by his own observation of travelling physicians going from town to town.[39]

II THE EGYPTIANS

Polybius' visit to Egypt was undertaken in a very different spirit and in a very different climate of thought from Herodotus'. As a recent study[40] has shown, the concept of Egypt as a land of ancient wisdom, still evident in || Herodotus' description, had given way since 386 to a more realistic picture. Politically Egypt had been opened up to the intrigues of Athens and Sparta; and commercial activity had grown.[41] There were Egyptians now living in Greece, where they sometimes evoked racial hostility.[42] To Polybius Egypt was primarily just one of the larger Hellenistic kingdoms which Achaean interests required to be kept in a reasonable balance.[43] There was a notion, shared by Polybius, that Egypt and the Ptolemaic court radiated a certain pretentiousness, which closer acquaintance would normally dispose of. Aratus of Sicyon, for example, was chaffed by Antigonus Gonatas along those lines: hitherto he had admired the wealth of Egypt, its elephants, fleets and palaces, but after he had been behind the scenes he had discovered that everything in Egypt was play-acting and painted scenery.[44] Likewise, Polybius himself, describing the hostility shown at Alexandria towards Cleomenes III, who was a refugee at Philopator's court, remarks that the king's friends were afraid that Cleomenes would realise the weaknesses of the kingdom, now that he had 'held it up to the light'.[45] To an Achaean Egypt was a state like any other, with which treaties might be made.[46]

---

[39] Cf. xii.25d.6, μετὰ φαντασίας ἐπιπορευόμενοι τὰς πόλεις – which will not be in Egypt.
[40] Froidefond (1971) 232f.   [41] See Milne (1939).
[42] Cf. Hypereides, *Ath.* 3, ἄνθρωπον λογογράφον τε καὶ ἀγοραῖον, τὸ δὲ μέγιστον Αἰγύπτιον; or the ironical attack in Anaxandrides Comicus, fg. 39 Edwards. See Froidefond (1971) 232–3.
[43] On the concept of a balance of power in Hellenistic times see Schmitt (1974) 67–93 (discussion 94–102).
[44] Plut. *Arat.* 15.2, probably going back to Aratus' *Memoirs*.
[45] v.35.10; Plut. *Cleom.* 34.2 (following Polybius) says that Cleomenes had become an eye-witness of the sickness of the realm.
[46] xxii.9.7, οὐσῶν καὶ πλειόνων συμμαχιῶν τοῖς Ἀχαιοῖς πρὸς τὴν Πτολεμαίου βασιλείαν.

The population of Egypt and especially of Alexandria included members of several races; but usually Polybius draws no clear distinction between Greeks and Egyptians. Perhaps not too much should be made of a passage[47] in which, speaking of Aristonicus, who had been sent to box at Olympia by Ptolemy IV, Polybius describes how his opponent Cleitomachus solicited the favour of the crowd, referring to him as an Egyptian – though as an Olympic contestant he was almost certainly a Greek or a Macedonian[48] – since here he is quoting Cleitomachus' words. But elsewhere he himself uses the same terminology, and usually with pejorative overtones. Ptolemy, the governor of Cyprus,[49] was 'not at all like an Egyptian, but gifted with good sense and capacity'; his name certainly sounds Macedonian. After describing the lynching of the clique round Agathocles Polybius remarks[50] that 'people in Egypt are terribly cruel once their anger is aroused'; he is referring to the population of Alexandria which,[51] as we know, included a variety of racial groups.[52] Ptolemy VI, of whom Polybius usually writes favourably, is criticised in an obituary passage[53] for 'allowing his mind to grow relaxed and weakened in times of good fortune and success', so that he suffered from 'a sort of Egyptian profligacy and indolence'. These examples recall Virgil's description of Cleopatra as Antony's *Aegyptia coniunx*.[54]

There was, however, one important passage in the *Histories* in which Polybius distinguished the various groups which made up the population of Alexandria.[55] It is a tantalising reminder of the state of our text of Polybius that what passes for the relevant fragment is nothing more than a piece of Strabo, which gives a résumé of what Polybius said; in addition, at a vital point the passage is vitiated by a textual problem. According to Strabo, Polybius, who visited Alexandria in the reign of Ptolemy VIII Physcon, was disgusted by what he found. The city contained three classes of people – the native Egyptians, the mercenaries, and the Alexandrians proper who, though of mixed stock (μιγάδες), were

---

[47] xxvii.9.1–10.5.
[48] Moretti (1953) 41, shows a Hellenised Phoenician from Sidon contesting at the Nemea; but Aristonicus will hardly be a native Egyptian.
[49] xxvii.13.1; probably Ptolemy Macron, known from a Gortynian inscription *IC* IV 208, possibly from *OGIS* 105, and from 2 Macc. x.12–14, recording his desertion of Antiochus IV and eventual suicide. See Walbank, *Comm.* III, note on xxvii.13.1; Mooren (1975) 187–8 no. 0350; Bagnall (1976) 256–7.
[50] xv.33.10.
[51] Fraser (1972) I, 82, thinks this refers to the native Egyptians; but its reference may be broader, for the mob on this occasion would certainly include Alexandrians as well as the latter.
[52] See below, n. 55.   [53] xxxix.7.7.   [54] Virg. *Aen.* viii.688.
[55] Strabo, xvii.1.12 c.797 = Polyb. xxxiv.14.1–8. See above, n. 35.

nevertheless Greeks by origin and still remembered their Greek ways. This last group had been virtually annihilated by Ptolemy VIII – probably, though this is surmise, as retaliation for his exile from Egypt between 163 and his restoration upon the death of his brother in 145.[56]

Polybius characterises the three groups. The native Egyptians, he says, are ὀξὺ καὶ πολιτικόν. This is an awkward phrase, and the second adjective has been reasonably queried. Jones, in the Loeb edition of Strabo, prints Kramer's emendation, ἀπολιτικόν, and translates 'not inclined to civil life';[57] other suggestions are Müller's ὀχλητικόν, 'moblike', and Tyrwhitt's ⟨οὐ⟩ πολιτικόν. Tyrwhitt's reading is accepted by Fraser in his book on Ptolemaic Alexandria;[58] he points out that a few lines further on Polybius remarks of the Alexandrians that οὐδ' αὐτὸ εὐκρινῶς πολιτικόν, 'they too are not genuinely civilised'. A case can be made for keeping πολιτικόν. As Schweighaeuser remarked, there is some sort of contrast between the native Egyptians, and the mercenaries described as βαρὺ καὶ πολὺ καὶ ἀνάγωγον, 'a numerous, overbearing[59] and uncultivated set' – where βαρὺ . . . ἀνάγωγον seems to balance ὀξὺ καὶ πολιτικόν. Moreover, Strabo elsewhere[60] says of the Egyptians generally that πολιτικῶς καὶ ἡμέρως ἐξ ἀρχῆς ζῶσι, 'they have from the outset lived a civic and cultured life'. Nevertheless, the case is not compelling. In the passage just quoted Strabo is contrasting the Egyptians with the Ethiopians, who live νομαδικῶς . . . καὶ ἀπόρως; hence πολιτικῶς there may mean something like 'living a settled life', which is not relevant in a contrast between the Egyptians of Alexandria and the mercenaries. Further, three adjectives are applied to the latter, βαρὺ καὶ πολὺ καὶ ἀνάγωγον, but to the former only two; and since ὀξύ apparently means 'volatile, headstrong' it does not go well with πολιτικόν. On balance then one must, I think, read οὐ πολιτικόν with Tyrwhitt; the native Egyptians are 'excitable and uncivilised'. It was they,

---

[56] For Ptolemy VIII's onslaught on the population of Alexandria see Diod. xxxiii.6; Justin. xxxviii.8.3–4; and for attacks on the *gymnasia* see Val. Max. ix.2 *ext.* 5. The flight from Egypt enriched other parts of the Greek world as did the flight of Jews from Germany in the 1930s; see Menecles of Barca, *FGH* IIIA 270 F 9, who was perhaps himself a refugee. Another was Aristarchus, who died in Cyprus in 144 (Athen. iv.184 c; *Suda* Ἀρίσταρχος). See further Fraser (1972) I, 86–7; II, 215 n. 232.

[57] Eddy (1961) 260, says: 'Polybios thought those (sc. native Egyptians) in Alexandria quite keen and civilized. But Strabo rejected them as hot-tempered and unpolitical, determined in their hostility to strangers.' He has not observed that 'Strabo' and 'Polybius' are at this point identical texts in which editors have adopted different readings.

[58] Fraser (1972) II, 145 n. 184.

[59] For βαρύ, 'overbearing' rather than 'rough' (so Paton), cf. xxix.27.4 (on Popilius' behaviour towards Antiochus IV).

[60] Strabo xvii.1.3. c.787.

together with the large numbers of insolent and uncouth mercenaries who made up the bulk of the population of Alexandria at the time of Polybius' visit, since Ptolemy VIII had used the mercenaries to destroy most of the native Alexandrians; they, though not truly civilised and a mongrel stock, nevertheless kept some recollection of their Greek origin and were superior to the natives. The generally unattractive character of life in Alexandria as so described Polybius blames on the worthlessness of the kings, which resulted in an absence of disciplined conduct.[61] ||

As a picture of Alexandria in the second half of the second century BC this is clearly inadequate. It is indeed, as Fraser remarks,[62] frankly impressionistic and based simply on what struck Polybius as he walked about the streets. It neglects such elements as the Jews who were both numerous and important,[63] it tells us nothing of the composition of the mercenaries[64] and it exaggerates the extent to which the Greek-based population had been eliminated. Moreover this very period seems to have witnessed a consolidation of the Alexandrian bourgeoisie which was to fill 'the vacuum in the cultural life of Alexandria ... marked by the decline in the number of foreign immigrants, probably of all classes and certainly of the intelligentsia',[65] and of this Polybius says nothing. But Fraser's criticism[66] that Polybius does not do justice to the extent to which the urban Egyptians and lower-class Greeks merged is perhaps unjust in view of his description of the Alexandrians as μιγάδες.

It is however true that one could not discover from Polybius the full extent to which the influence of the native Egyptians had increased within the Ptolemaic kingdom from Philopator's time onwards. He is not of course entirely blind to this movement. In one important passage he draws attention to its beginnings:[67] 'the Egyptians, elated by their victory at Raphia [217 BC], were no longer disposed to obey orders, but were on the look-out for a leader and a figure-head, thinking themselves well able to maintain themselves as an independent power, an attempt in which they finally succeeded not long afterwards'. But this sees the matter solely in military terms and looks forward to the native revolts which persisted until late in the reign of Ptolemy V. It shows no appreciation of other aspects of Egyptianisation as it was reflected, for instance, in burial practices, in religion, and in the supersession of the Greek by

---

[61] xxxiv.14.3, ἐξ ἔθους γὰρ παλαιοῦ ξένους ἔτρεφον τοὺς τὰ ὅπλα ἔχοντας, ἄρχειν μᾶλλον ἢ ἄρχεσθαι δεδιδαγμένους διὰ τὴν τῶν βασιλέων οὐδένειαν. Cf. para. 4, διὰ τὰς αὐτὰς αἰτίας.
[62] Fraser (1972) I, 75–6.
[63] Fraser (1972) I, 83, who dates the influx of Jews largely under Ptolemy VI.
[64] Fraser (1972) I, 81; Cretans and Gauls predominate.
[65] Fraser (1972) I, 78.   [66] Fraser (1972) I, 81.   [67] v. 107.3.

the Egyptian calendar, to mention some of the more obvious of these.[68] In fact, Polybius sees Egypt primarily as the Ptolemaic kingdom, and his interest lies in the personalities and policies of its kings. He makes it clear that it was chiefly in relation to the character of Ptolemy IV (τὴν τοῦ βασιλέως προαίρεσιν) that he described the war against the native insurgents which was raging at the end of his reign.[69] How he deals with the successive Ptolemies who reigned during the period covered by his *Histories* (220–145 without the introduction) must therefore be our next concern.

III THE PTOLEMIES

Polybius' interest in the kings of Egypt is partly the result of his firm belief in the great importance to be attributed to the rôle of individuals in history.[70] But in the case of Egypt it had the further justification that the state was so closely identified with the Pharaoh. Consequently he or his advisers[71] must be held responsible when things went right or wrong. It is noteworthy[72] that in his account of the population of Alexandria, the domination of the mercenaries and the lack of genuine civilisation in the Alexandrians themselves are both attributed to the weakness of the kings. In addition, as we have seen, Polybius enjoyed close personal relations with the Egyptian monarchy at the time of Ptolemy VI and Ptolemy VIII, being a close friend of the former's envoy Menyllus and having probably met the king personally at Rome.[73]

Polybius' account of Ptolemy IV is unreservedly hostile. Partly this reflects the sources available or at any rate those on which he chose to rely.[74] For the Fourth Syrian War, culminating in Raphia, he clearly made substantial use of writers who took the Seleucid side.[75] Whether

---

[68] See Fraser (1972) I, 82; on p. 75 something seems to have gone wrong, since the passage there quoted as Polybius' comment on 'the effect produced on the Egyptian population by their substantial contribution to the victory at Raphia' has only a remote resemblance to what Polybius says in v.65.9 (quoted in Greek in II, 143 n.178). On the 'complete breakthrough of the Egyptian year for dating purposes and . . . (its) triumph over all other systems' in Epiphanes' reign see Mooren (1975) 25ff.

[69] xiv.12.1–5; cf. Peremans (1975) 396.

[70] Polybius repeatedly comes back to the theme of 'what one determined man can do'; cf. i.35.4 (Xanthippus); viii.3.3, 7.7 (Archimedes); ix.22.6 (Hannibal).

[71] Cf. v.12.5; vii.13.1–14.6; ix.23.9 (influence of Aratus and Chrysogonus, Demetrius and Taurion on Philip V); xiii.4.1–5.6 (influence of Heracleides on Philip V); xxviii.21.4–5 (influence of Eulaeus on Ptolemy VI); for the theme of the 'evil counsellor' see Pédech (1964) 234 and n. 141.

[72] See above, n. 61.   [73] See above, nn. 29 and 33.

[74] On the sources available for the history of Ptolemy IV see above, pp. 54–5.

[75] That these included the doctor Apollophanes (v.56.1), as Brown (1961) 187–95, suggests, seems unlikely; he cuts far too poor a figure. Cf. Huss (1976) 10–11, against Pédech (1964) 269.

in addition he used a source sympathetic to Philopator[76] or merely a neutral account[77] is not easily determined. It has been argued[78] that Polybius' picture of the king after Raphia as slothful, dissipated and the tool of his ministers[79] goes back to Alexandrian writers who hated him because they saw in him an enemy of Greek traditions to which they were attached. This would not of course necessarily mean that the picture they drew was inaccurate[80] but it could certainly have helped to generate hostility in Polybius, who was a moralist and did not always dissociate moral and political judgements. It is also likely that Philopator's failure to follow up his victory at Raphia with a more active foreign policy inspired Polybius' contempt.[81] Finally, as Huss remarks,[82] one cannot exclude the possibility that Polybius was influenced by Ptolemy IV's failure to resume Ptolemy III's policy of subsidising Achaea; even if he was not consciously moved by such a consideration, it can have helped to create an attitude towards Ptolemy IV in Achaea which might affect Polybius' judgement.

But this is speculation. Turning to his picture of Ptolemy IV we may note that, exceptionally, Polybius did not let it emerge from a narrative constructed to cover events year by year, which was his usual practice, but instead he treated the last thirteen years of his reign, 217–204, in one long section[83] in which, as I have already mentioned, the main emphasis was laid on the king's προαίρεσις.[84] This procedure can be paralleled in only one other place in the surviving parts of his *History* proper. In a passage in Book XXXII he announces his intention of re-counting the complicated dealings between Athens and Oropus in one piece 'partly reverting to the past and partly anticipating the future, so that the separate details being in themselves insignificant I may not by relating them under different || dates produce a narrative that is both trivial and obscure'.[85] Polybius' reasons for treating most of Philopator's

---

[76] So Schmitt (1964) 175–88.   [77] Cf. Huss (1976) 11ff.   [78] Cf. Préaux (1965).

[79] xiv.12.3. Huss (1976) 242, speculates on the reason why Polybius three times mentions Agathocles before Sosibius, in referring to these two Friends of Ptolemy IV who were powerful at this time, although Sosibius was clearly the more important. Was the recollection of Agathocles more vivid at the time Polybius was writing, he asks. The solution is more simple. Polybius wrote οἱ περὶ Ἀγαθοκλέα καὶ Σωσίβιον because the reverse order would have resulted in hiatus.

[80] It is accepted by Fraser (1972) II, 144 n.180.

[81] So Huss (1976) 269; the suggestion finds confirmation in v.87.3, where Ptolemy IV is crit-icised for not following up his victory at Raphia, ἑλκόμενος ὑπὸ τῆς συνήθους ἐν τῷ βίῳ ῥαθυμίας καὶ κακεξίας; cf. Justin. xxx.1.6f. Ptolemy's policy is defended by Huss (1976) 83.

[82] Huss (1976) 269; but this would have been an unreasonable expectation from a member of Doson's Symmachy.

[83] A manuscript note says that it occupied forty-eight sheets.   [84] Cf. xiv.12.1–5.

[85] xxxii.11.1–6, εὐτελῆ καὶ ἀσαφῆ. On Polybius' reversion here to the Ephorean method of com-posing κατὰ γένος see Walbank (1975) 205–6.

reign in one piece are similar; the war with the native insurgents which occupied much of it[86] was one which, 'apart from the mutual savagery and lawlessness of the combatants contained nothing worthy of note, no pitched battle, no sea-fight, no siege'.[87] In short, by the standards here applied – and they seem to be the common criteria of much Hellenistic history, with its concern for vivid and sensational action[88] – this material was trivial. 'It therefore struck me', Polybius goes on,[89] 'that my narrative would be easier both for me to write and for my readers to follow if I performed this part of my task not by merely alluding every year to small events not worth serious consideration, but by giving once for all a uni-fied picture of this king's character'; as in the case of Oropus and Athens he will thus avoid obscurity. Whether Polybius exploited the advantages offered by this method to assess the significance of the native movement in broader terms we cannot tell, since his narrative is lost; but the refer-ence to τῆς εἰς ἀλλήλους ὠμότητος καὶ παρανομίας suggests that his treatment of it may have resembled his account of the Carthaginian Mercenary War.[90]

In contrast to his father, Ptolemy V is judged rather more favourably, the one exception being the condemnation of his savage suppression of the rebels in the delta,[91] which paralleled his earlier cruelty and breach of faith when he took Lycopolis in 197. As we saw,[92] his prowess as a hunter was discussed over the banquet-table in Achaea; his failure to win military renown is blamed on Polycrates, who was 'unfair' to him;[93] and his plight when Philip V and Antiochus III united in a secret plot to dismember his possessions evokes violent denunciation and much moralising.[94] This plot, however exaggerated in the tradition, occupied a central position in

---

[86] Peremans (1975) 393–402, argues that the war against the native insurgents did not begin effec-tively until about 205/4. See above, n. 5.

[87] xiv.12.4.   [88] See Walbank (1960); (1972a) 34–40.   [89] xiv.12.5.

[90] i.65.3–88.7; Polybius frequently stresses its savagery, e.g. i.65.6–7, 69.9–14, 70.6, 79.8, 80.13, 81.4–11, 88.7.

[91] xxii.17.1–7. The date will be 185; for after executing the rebels Ptolemy went on to meet Aristonicus, apparently just back from a recruiting trip to Greece with mercenaries, and if the date were 186 (as the order of the fragments in Polybius would suggest) this would be hard to reconcile with the fact that the second Philae decree (Sethe (1904) II, 214–30; cf. (1917) 35–49) records that it was Aristonicus who announced the victories of Comanus (?) over Ankhmakis at the synod of priests at Alexandria on 3 Mesore of year 19 of Epiphanes (6 Sept. 186). Further, according to Polybius, xxii. 17.7, Epiphanes was twenty-five years old at the time of the rebels' surrender and execution at Sais, and his twenty-fifth birthday fell on 30 Mesore (2 Oct.) 185. It must therefore be assumed that this is an instance of a dislocation in the order of the Constan-tinian fragments (here the *excerpta de sententiis*). For full discussion see Walbank, *Comm.* III, 11–13 (with addendum), 203–5. [For a revision of this date and the placing of the execution of the rebels in 186 see below, pp. 77–8 n. 34 (extension).]

[92] Above, n. 21.   [93] xxii.17.7.   [94] xv.20.1–8.

the pattern of events which Polybius saw as leading to Roman hegemony
and it will be discussed below. Otherwise references to Ptolemy V (in the
surviving parts) concern his relations with Achaea and his renewal of
the alliance – an affair which produced a *contretemps* in the Achaean
assembly in 185, when Aristaenus performed a smart political operation
to expose Philopoemen, Lycortas and their colleagues, who had renewed
the alliance, as culpably inept since they could not say which of the several
previous alliances they had renewed.[95] On that occasion Ptolemy V sent
the Achaeans 6,000 bronze suits of armour and 200 talents of coined
bronze;[96] and he later followed this up with the promise of a squadron
of pentecontors worth nearly ten talents. It was in connection with this
gift that Polybius was nominated to visit Egypt, a trip which fell through
on Epiphanes's death in 180.[97] These warm and profitable relations may
well have influenced Polybius' attitude to this Ptolemy.

Goodwill towards Alexandria continues to be shown through Polybius'
account of the reign of Ptolemy VI, with whom he clearly sympathised
in his quarrel with his brother, Ptolemy VIII. The death of the former in
145[98] conveniently matched Polybius' revised date, 146/5, for the end-
ing of his extended *Histories*[99] and one of the last surviving fragments
from Book XXXIX[100] is an obituary notice reviewing Philometor's career in favourable terms: he was gentle and good, repeatedly generous
to his younger brother who plotted against him, and open to criticism,
in Polybius' opinion, only in having evinced a kind of profligacy and indolence in times of prosperity.[101] Elsewhere[102] he discusses Ptolemy VI's
character in connection with the bizarre incident in 169 when he was persuaded by the eunuch Eulaeus to abandon Egypt and take refuge from
Antiochus IV in Samothrace. This Polybius regards as the act of a man
whose mind is effeminate and wholly corrupt; but since on subsequent
occasions Ptolemy showed himself to be brave and steadfast in danger,
his cowardice then should be attributed to the influence of Eulaeus. This
judgement arises out of Polybius' view of 'character'.[103] Unlike many ancient authors he did not believe that a man's 'true character' is something
fixed, which circumstances 'reveal'. Character is rather something that

---

[95] xxii.3.5, 7.1, 9.1–12.   [96] xxii.9.3.   [97] Above, n. 23.
[98] Cf. xxxix.7.1–7. Philometor was probably still alive or his death not yet known on 21 Aug. 145; cf. Skeat (1954) 34–5.
[99] On the extension to 146/5 see Walbank (1977).   [100] xxxix.7.1–7.
[101] Polybius calls this characteristic 'Egyptian'; see above, n. 53. Perhaps he associated it with the climate of the Nile valley. For Polybius' adherence to the theory that geographical and climatic conditions contributed greatly to racial character see iv.20.1–21.12; ch. 2 above.
[102] xxviii.21.4–5.   [103] Walbank (1972a) 92–6.

develops, and various factors affect that development; one is his nature, his φύσις, but another is his external circumstances including, especially, the influence of friends. This can be decisive. 'It appears to me', Polybius writes[104] in a discussion of Hannibal's character, 'that not merely in a few cases, but on most occasions, men are compelled to act and speak contrary to their real principles by the complexity of the situation and by the suggestions of their friends'. This is particularly true of kings. Philip II and Alexander owed much to their friends; Philip V was one kind of person when he listened to Aratus or Chrysogonus, another when he followed the evil counsels of Demetrius of Pharos or Taurion.[105] Similarly Ptolemy VI was led to do something 'contrary to his nature' by Eulaeus.

I have already mentioned the close links which had been established with Lycortas and his son Polybius under Ptolemy V.[106] Both states profited from these and they provided the Achaean government with some degree of diplomatic expertise. Another Egyptian expert was the Theodoridas of Sicyon who had accompanied Lycortas to Alexandria in 186/5 to exchange oaths with Epiphanes.[107] Eighteen years later in the winter of 169/8 a message came from Egypt asking that he might raise a mercenary force of 1,000 men.[108] It is unlikely that Theodoridas had had no contacts with Egypt in between. At the same time the Egyptians asked for troops to be sent under the command of Lycortas and Polybius.[109] When the request came up at the Achaean assembly both father and son urged that the help should be sent, countering Callicrates' plea that they should give undivided support to the || Romans in their war against Perseus with the argument that help had been offered the previous year to Q. Marcius Philippus and had been rejected. When on a technicality Callicrates got the matter referred to a special meeting at Sicyon, Polybius there again argued strongly that Alexandria could be assisted without impairing Achaean ability to provide the Romans with any help they might require,[110] and Lycortas supported him by enumerating the favours which Achaea had received from Egypt. Eventually through Roman pressure the Egyptian request had to be refused. But the incident illustrates very clearly how Alexandria had created an Egyptian pressure group in Achaea based on Lycortas and Polybius.

[104] ix.22.10; Walbank, *Comm.* II, 151-3 (notes on ix.22.7-24.8.).
[105] On Philip V see above, n. 71; on Philip II and Alexander see viii.10.5-12.
[106] Above, pp. 55-6.
[107] Cf.xxii.3.6; he was not a professional mercenary captain (cf. Launey (1949) 108. n. 6), but Philopoemen's career shows that the distinction was in many instances a fine one.
[108] xxix.23.6.   [109] Above n. 24.   [110] xxix. 23.8-24.16.

At this time Ptolemy VI and Ptolemy VIII were collaborating. Describing the debate in Achaea Polybius emphasises that the Egyptian request came from both kings.[111] It was only later, after his summons to Rome, that the internal feud developed sufficiently to impinge on Roman policy and Polybius aligned his sympathies with Ptolemy VI.[112] It is unlikely that this was an embarrassment at Rome, since his view was shared by influential men there. Cato, for example, in a speech against L. Minucius Thermus called Ptolemy VI *rex optimus et beneficissimus*,[113] and it is also a fair guess that Scipio Aemilianus and those close to him shared Polybius' view, though it is from a later stage in his career that we learn of the bad impression made on him by Ptolemy VIII.[114] However the Senate as a whole, in a decision based, Polybius says,[115] on self-interest, in 163/2 came out in favour of Ptolemy VIII, assigned Cyprus to him, and a year later cancelled their treaty with Ptolemy VI and expelled his envoy Menyllus from Rome.[116]

Ptolemy VIII figures in Polybius mainly in relation to his brother and their quarrels. It was in his reign that Polybius visited Alexandria[117] and his adverse account of the city and its population can be read as a condemnation of the king whose capital it was and who had destroyed the least noxious element among its people.[118]

Polybius' account of the Ptolemies from Philopator to Euergetes II suffers from several deficiencies. His emphasis on personalities has led him to neglect broader issues which might well have been discussed. For example, given the importance of Coele-Syria, the bone of contention in the Fourth, Fifth and Sixth Syrian Wars, one might have expected a comprehensive discussion of its political and economic importance,[119] and not merely the bare statement in Book V[120] that from their bases in Cyprus and Coele-Syria the Lagids had always been able to menace (ἐπέκειντο) the kings of Syria by land and sea. Since, had Polybius intended to provide such a discussion, the natural place for it would have been in Book V before the Raphia campaign, I think it is reasonable to assume that there was none. Of fundamental importance, too, for the internal development of Egypt was the series of native risings which took place between Raphia and the latter part of Epiphanes' reign, and the growth in Egyptian influence which it both reflected and stimulated. As

---

[111] xxix.23.9.   [112] See especially xxxi.10.7; xxxix.7.5–6.
[113] *ORF* i, M. Porcius Cato, fg. 180; Scullard (1973) 230 n. 4.
[114] Cf. Athen.xii.549c, 350A; Plut. *Mor.* 201A; Diod. xxxiii.28b.
[115] xxxi.10.7; cf. Walbank (1972a) 170.   [116] xxxi.20.3.
[117] Above n. 35.   [118] xxxiv.14.6.   [119] Cf. Pédech (1964) 141.
[120] v.34.6; on the significance of this passage for Ptolemaic foreign policy see Will (1966–7) i, 139ff.

we have seen,[121] Polybius treated the former as of no intrinsic interest or importance; and there is no evidence that he discussed the latter in any detail.[122] Finally, in contrasting the recovery of Egypt with the downfall of the two rival kingdoms, the Antigonid and the Seleucid,[123] he commits himself to a superficial judgement which it is hard to take seriously but which seems to proceed out of a central theme of his work. It is in fact to Polybius' view about the rôle of Fortune, *Tyche*, in the affairs of this period that one must look for the explanation of this sanguine interpretation of the power of second-century Egypt.

IV FORTUNE AND EGYPT

In a striking passage in Book XV[124] Polybius describes the secret compact made by Philip V of Macedonia and Antiochus III of Syria, probably in 203/2, to dismember the possessions of the young Ptolemy V Epiphanes, who had succeeded his father in 204.[125] Whether this compact ever existed is still a subject of debate. Though undoubtedly it has reached our sources in an exaggerated form, complete scepticism seems to me unjustified; but the reality of the pact is not relevant here, since Polybius certainly believed in its existence. An odd feature of his discussion of it is the violence of his feelings and his anger at the behaviour of the two kings, who did not even try to provide a pretext for their shameful, unscrupulous and brutal conduct (τῆς αἰσχύνης... ἀνέδην καὶ θηριωδῶς), in which they resembled fishes which prey on their own kind, the larger eating the smaller. Both were chastised by Fortune, *Tyche*,[126] however, who very soon compelled them to submit to Rome, to pay tribute to her, and to obey her orders, and shortly afterwards re-established the kingdom of Ptolemy, whereas that of Philip was utterly destroyed and that of Antiochus suffered calamities almost as grave.

The downfall of Macedonia and Seleucid Syria are central events in the account of the rise of Rome to world empire; and the dethronement of Perseus and the humiliation of Antiochus IV formed the climax of the *Histories* as originally conceived. This process illustrated the power of *Tyche* (however Polybius really interpreted that word)[127] and if their downfall was to be truly exemplary – a fitting punishment

---

[121] Above, pp. 63–4; see Fraser (1972) I, 82–3.   [122] See above n. 68; Peremans (1975) 402.
[123] xv.20.7–8; cf. xxxix.27.11–12.   [124] xv.20.1–8.
[125] See Walbank, *Comm.* II, 434–7 (xiv.11–12 n.); III, addendum on the same passage (on the chronology of Epiphanes' accession); ibid. II, 471–3 (xv.20 n.); III, addendum on the same passage (on the Syro-Macedonian pact).
[126] See n. 124.   [127] For *Tyche* in Polybius see Walbank, *Comm.* I, 16–26.

(τὴν ἁρμόζουσαν δίκην) and a ‖ warning for the edification of their
successors (τοῖς... ἐπιγενομένοις... κάλλιστον ὑπόδειγμα πρὸς
ἐπανόρθωσιν) – it had to be matched by the corresponding revival of
Ptolemaic Egypt (τὴν... Πτολεμαίου βασιλείαν... ἡ τύχη διώρθωσε).
It is this need to ensure that the victim of the plot emerged on top, as well
as Polybius' personal sympathy for Egypt, that led him to the superficial
judgement that that realm emerged strengthened from the events of
168. This judgement can hardly be upheld. On the one hand, the Sixth
Syrian War, though it undoubtedly ended in a dramatic demonstration
of Roman power which forced Antiochus IV to abandon any aim he
may have had to control Egypt – and provided Polybius with a splendid
incident with which to conclude the last book of the original *Histories* –
left Antiochus in possession of Coele-Syria. But the recovery of that
province had been an object of policy under Ptolemy V[128] and it was
the manoeuvres of Ptolemy VI's guardians in that direction that led
Antiochus IV to launch his attack on Egypt.[129] To that extent the Sixth
Syrian War represented a setback for Ptolemy no less than Antiochus.
Further, those events led to the internal feud between the sixth and
eighth Ptolemies, the fragmenting of the kingdom and, eventually,
the reprisals exacted on the population of Alexandria by the latter,
circumstances which together weakened Egypt and reduced it in reality
to the level of Macedonia and Syria.[130]

Polybius may have recognised this after his visit. Certainly his account
of Alexandria under Ptolemy VIII smacks of disillusion. But if he had
conceived doubts, it was too late to adjust his theme of a Ptolemaic
recovery to balance Antigonid and Seleucid collapse. Altogether then his
treatment of Egypt must be adjudged disappointing. His understanding
of the general effect of Roman policy on Egypt is deficient and the rôle
which he assigned to *Tyche* in the affairs of the three dynasties led him
to credit Egypt with a political revival which is not only unconvincing to
modern readers but had been shown to be false within his own lifetime.

[128] A stele in the Cairo Museum (there is a second copy of the same decree on another, damaged
stele) contains a decree from the 23rd year of Epiphanes which refers (lines 32ff.) to Aristonicus,
the cavalry commander, who seized Aradus (in Seleucid territory) and brought away silver,
produce and other booty. See Daressy (1911); (1916–17); on the dating of the decrees, which
contain only Macedonian months see Mooren (1975) 25 n. 3. Daressy would date the attack
on Aradus shortly after the battle of Magnesia in 189, but it is mentioned towards the end of
Aristonicus' achievements and seems more likely to be an unrecorded incident in the ill-attested
reign of Seleucus IV in the late 180s. But both stelai need re-editing.
[129] Cf. xxxvii.19.2; xxxviii.1.6, 20.5; Diod. xxx.16; Will (1966–7) ii, 265–6; Bunge (1974) 74 n. 83.
[130] See Heinen (1972b) 658–9.

4

The surrender of the Egyptian rebels in the Nile delta
(Polyb. xxii.17.1–7)*

The troubles which afflicted Egypt from the time of Raphia in 217 and culminated in the secession of Upper Egypt under native (or Nubian) kings from 205 to 186 have been the object of much recent discussion.[1] In particular the end of the secession recorded in the second Philae decree, which Sethe published in 1916[2] and commented on in an article in the *Zeitschrift für ägyptische Sprache* in 1917,[3] has received considerable attention. This decree, passed by the synod of priests meeting in the temple of Isis in Alexandria on 6 September 186, recorded the defeat of Chaonnophris by 3*mnws* (who, as Peremans and van't Dack have shown,[4] is probably Comanus,[5] well known from other evidence and perhaps shortly after this date *epistrategos* of the *chora*); at the synod the news of the victory was announced by the eunuch Aristonicus.[6] But this success, though celebrated by the king's declaration of an amnesty and remission of taxes incurred up to his nineteenth year,[7] did not bring an end to the troubles. From a passage in || Book XXII of Polybius[8] we learn of a further incident, when several rebels from the Delta area – he gives their names – were persuaded to surrender to Polycrates at Sais, whereupon Ptolemy incurred some odium by torturing and executing them. The dating of this surrender involves difficulties which have been treated somewhat cursorily; and I hope that Professor Manni,

---

* [[Φιλίας χάριν: *Miscellanea di Studi Classici in Onore di Eugenio Manni*. 6 vols. (Rome 1980) vi, 2187–97]]

[1] See Jouguet (1923); Préaux (1936); Alliot (1951) 435; (1952); Volkmann, *RE* s.v. 'Ptolemaios (23)', cols. 1699ff.; Pestman (1965); Peremans (1975) 393–402; Huss (1976) 83–4 n. 364.

[2] Sethe (1904) 214–30. [3] Sethe (1917). [4] Peremans – van't Dack (1953) 27–8.

[5] On Comanus see Peremans – van't Dack (1950) no. 14611; Mooren (1975) 82–5 no. 042. On the correct name of the rebel leader see Clarysse (1978).

[6] On the eunuch Aristonicus see Peremans–van't Dack (1950) no. 2194 (cf. nos. 1853, 2152); Mooren (1975) 146–9 no. 0191.

[7] But see Müller (1920) 75, who gives a divergent translation, according to which the leader of the revolt was executed.

[8] Polyb. xxii.17.1–7.

who has made so many distinguished contributions to the solution of problems involving chronological *cruces* will accept as a suitable tribute on the occasion of his seventieth birthday a discussion of this problem and of the complications that arise in connection with it for the text of Polybius.

I

It has been clear since Sethe's article of 1917[9] that the events at Sais were quite distinct from the victory recorded in the second Philae decree. Mahaffy,[10] following Revillout, had taken them to be the same, and Bouché-Leclercq[11] felt unable to decide the matter one way or the other. Sethe, however, drew attention to a number of differences between the two events and in particular the discrepancy in the age of Ptolemy who, at the time of the surrender at Sais, was said by Polybius to be twenty-five, ἔχων ἔτη πέντε καὶ εἴκοσιν,[12] which was certainly not true in September 186 at the time of the Alexandrian synod. Unfortunately Sethe was in error concerning the date of Epiphanes' birth. The Rosetta stone[13] records the day and month, 30 Mesore, but not the year, and this Sethe took to be 209. Since, however, we know from the Rosetta stone that Epiphanes was elevated to co-regency with his father on 17 Phaophi – this was the date ἐν ᾗ παρέλαβεν τὴν βασιλείαν παρ<ὰ> τοῦ πατρός[14] – || and since *P. Gurob* 12[15] shows him as already co-regent on 25 Pharmuthi of year 13 of Philopator viz. 5 June 209, his father evidently elevated him on 17 Phaophi (= 30 November) 210, following his birth on 30 Mesore (= 9 October) of the same year. Epiphanes therefore reached the age of twenty-five on 30 Mesore (= 2 October) 185, not 184, as Sethe believed. Hence the events at Sais need not necessarily be more than thirteen months after the synod of 6 September 186 – not the two years required by Sethe nor the three years postulated by Alliot.[16]

---

[9] Sethe (1917) 38ff.   [10] Mahaffy (1899) 159–60.
[11] Bouché-Leclercq (1903) 395.   [12] xxii.17.7.
[13] *OGIS* 90 for the Greek text: for the Greek, demotic and hieroglyphic texts with translations see Wallis Budge (1929) 49–169.
[14] *OGIS* 90 ll. 46–7; the Greek text is here defective but the date is clear in the hieroglyphic version, which has 'the 17th day of the second month of the season Akhet' (the demotic version by a slip refers to 'the season Part'). The reference is to Epiphanes' elevation to co-regency; see Revillout (1883) 1; Walbank (1936) 30.
[15] Smyly (1921) 27–8 no. 12.
[16] Alliot (1952) 23–4, accepted Sethe's date for the birth of Epiphanes and so put the events at Sais three years after the synod of 6 September 186.

Polybius tells us[17] that after executing the rebels at Sais Epiphanes went on to Naucratis. There Aristonicus handed over to him a body of mercenaries which he had raised in Greece, and with these Ptolemy sailed to Alexandria. One has the clear impression that Aristonicus had just returned from his recruiting trip; and Schweighaeuser[18] suggested with some plausibility that these troops were enrolled by virtue of the renewed alliance of 187/6 between Egypt and Achaea[19] – though indeed we have no proof that Aristonicus' mercenaries came from Achaea. Sethe saw[20] that this sequence of events in itself excluded the possibility that the surrender at Sais can have followed immediately on the synod at Alexandria, since Aristonicus could hardly announce the victory in Upper Egypt there and immediately afterwards be at Naucratis, newly returned from Greece. The events at Sais and Naucratis cannot then belong to 186. To which year do they belong?

On this question there has been no unanimity among recent writers. Bevan[21] dated Polycrates' action to 184–3 in view of Polybius' reference to Ptolemy's age. But in an important study of the native movements Claire Préaux[22] attached no date to the surrender at Sais. || Volkmann, in his Pauly-Wissowa article on Epiphanes[23] (published in 1959), mentioned the setting up of the post of *epistrategos* after the victory over Chaonnophris, and after asserting that Hippalus held that office in 184[24] when Epiphanes visited the Thebaid, he continued: 'um diese Zeit brachte Polykrates weitere Führer des Aufstandes . . . sich in Sais . . . zu ergeben'. More recently, Mooren[25] in his book on the aulic titulature of Ptolemaic Egypt dated Aristonicus' recruiting trip to Greece to '*ca.* 185'. But the evidence has never been clearly set out and in particular there has been no discussion of how the excerpts which constitute Polyb. xxii.16–17 are related to the other fragments within the framework of the *Histories*. It is, however, essential that any proposed solution of the problem should take account of the constraints imposed by the interlocking relationship of the relevant Polybian fragments. It is with these therefore that the next section will be concerned.

---

[17] xxii.17.6.   [18] Schweighaeuser (1789–95) VII (1793) 516; cf. Büttner-Wobst (1901) 8.
[19] Polyb. xxii.3.5–6.   [20] Sethe (1917), 38.   [21] Bevan (1927) 274–5.
[22] Préaux (1936).   [23] *RE* s.v. 'Ptolemaios (23)', cols. 1699–1700.
[24] The post of *epistrategos* was probably instituted following the victory of 186 in Upper Egypt; cf. Bengtson (1952) 121–3; Mooren (1975) 85–6 no. 043 (Hippalus). The earliest attested date for Hippalus as *epistrategos* is however 176 (*P. Tebt.* III.895 ll. 62–3).
[25] Mooren (1975) 147.

II

The majority of the fragments which make up the later books of Polybius come from one or other of the sets of excerpts entitled 'On Virtue and Vice', 'On Gnomic Sayings', 'On Embassies to Rome', 'On Embassies from Rome', etc., made on the instructions of Constantine Porphyrogenitus in the tenth century. To reassemble these in the original order of Polybius' text is a complicated procedure depending on various factors, but facilitated (a) by occasional overlaps between passages included under various titles, (b) by the fact that Polybius normally treats events of each olympiad year in a regular and rarely broken sequence of theatres of action in this order: Italy, Sicily, Spain, Africa, Greece and Macedonia, Asia, and Egypt,[26] (c) by the habit of the excerptors of following the order of the original text, and (d) by the possibility of comparing the order of the narrative in Livy or (less often) Diodorus where Polybius is patently their source. By || the use of these and other criteria derived from the general practice of Polybius and his excerptors it is possible in most (but not all) places to establish an order of fragments with some confidence that it is the right one.

Polyb. xxii.17.1–7 derives from the excerpts *De virtutibus et vitiis*, but contains one sentence (17.5) in common with 16.4, which shows these two chapters to be taken from a single original context. Chapter 16 is from the excerpts *De sententiis*, a much damaged Vatican palimpsest (M), and contrasts Epiphanes' treatment of the rebels who surrendered at Sais with Philip II's magnanimity after Chaeronea.[27] It follows that the placing and dating of the combined passage must take account of the neighbouring passages in both sets of excerpts. Now 16.1–4 (exc. 102 in *De sententiis*) is followed in that selection by 18.1–11 (exc. 103), a passage which alleges that Philip V planned the Third Macedonian War fought later by Perseus and was responsible for it. That passage is the basis of Livy xxxix.23.5, which sums up Polybius' argument in one sentence and then goes on to give a list of Philip's grievances which are clearly derived from a passage of Polybius which has not survived; and since Livy puts this passage under A.U.C. 569 = 185 BC, it would appear that Polyb. xxii.18.1–11 forms part of the *res Macedoniae* of Ol. 148.3 = 186/5. But that

---

[26] See Walbank, *Comm.* II, 1.

[27] The commonly used Loeb edition, intimidated by the fragmentary character of the text, omits the first 14 1/3 lines of xxii.16; but its editor had not the same excuse for omitting also 16.4 – presumably because it is identical with 17.5 – thus depriving the reader of the proof that these two chapters must be taken closely together.

assumption carries the unfortunate corollary that Polyb. xxii.16.1–17.7 (which must come from an account of *res Aegypti*) will be from the previous olympiad year (since in any given olympiad year Egyptian affairs come later than Macedonian). That date (187/6) would however be difficult to reconcile with Ptolemy's being twenty-five, since as we have seen he did not celebrate his twenty-fifth birthday until 2 October 185.

We may note in passing that in the excerpts *De virtutibus et vitiis* the passage which precedes xxii.17.1–7 is xxi.34.1–2 (exc. 75) on Moagetes, and belongs to 190/89; and the following passage (exc. 77) is xxii.20.1–8 on Attalus' wife Apollonis, which could be taken from the *res Asiae* of either 186/5 or 185/4.[28] Hence we obtain no help from the excerpts of this collection.

Thus we are confronted with an apparent dilemma. If 18.1–11 belongs || to 186/5, then 16.1–17.7 should belong to 187/6, which is chronologically too early; but if 16.1–17.7 stands in 186/5, then 18.1–11 must be postponed (despite the position of the corresponding Livian passage) to 185/4. But Polybius' account of Macedonian affairs of 185/4 can be reconstructed from Livy xxxix.34–5 and from Polyb. xxii.13.1–14.12, which together give a comprehensive picture of what stood in the *res Macedoniae* for that olympiad year. They show that it would be very difficult indeed to find any place in this context for a discussion of the causes of the Third Macedonian War, for Livy xxxix.33.1–8 (also Polybian) recounts the preliminaries at Rome and 34.1–35.4 gives Philip's actions at Maronea, the interview with Ap. Claudius, Philip's response, and his decision to send Demetrius to Rome, in a form which closely matches Polybius' account in xxii.13.1–14.12. The departure of the Roman envoys to the Peloponnese in Livy xxxix.35.5 follows immediately on a passage corresponding to Polyb. xxii.14.12, and clearly leaves no place here for a discussion of the remote causes of the war. On the contrary Polyb. xxii.14.8 plainly implies the existence of Philip's war-like plans and as something that has already been discussed in an earlier passage.

It therefore looks as if the account in Polyb. xxii.18.1–11 of Philip as the planner of the Third Macedonian War must stand where Livy has it, in 186/5. In that case are there any arguments for neglecting the reference to Ptolemy's age in Polyb. xxii.17.7? It is true that the beginning and end of an excerpt are places especially liable to corruption at the hands of the excerptor, who often trimmed the original to suit the purpose of his selection, introducing proper names at the beginning or rounding off

---

[28] See Walbank, *Comm.* ii, 1; iii, 13.

the end.[29] But this is not invariably so, and in this particular case the presence of the μέν in 17.7 without any corresponding δέ clause[30] suggests an abrupt use of the guillotine rather than any elaborate adjustment. One might also postulate the omission of some qualifying word such as σχεδόν or a failure by either Polybius or the excerptor to distinguish between being twenty-five and being in one's twenty-fifth year. This confusion is common and occurs in fact in Dittenberger's || commentary on *OGIS* 90 (the Rosetta stone) in a discussion of this very passage.[31] But it is unlikely and would not help very much here, since Ptolemy did not enter into his twenty-fifth year until early October 196 when, as we have seen, it would have been impossible for him to meet Aristonicus at Naucratis. None of these evasions even begins to look plausible; and that leaves us with the only possible solution – that the order of the fragments in the *De sententiis* has been disturbed and that xxii.18.1–11 should in fact stand before 16.1–4.[32]

Since the Constantinian excerpts normally follow the order of Polybius' original text scrupulously, this is a solution to be adopted only with reluctance. But there is in fact in the manuscript (M) a possible indication that the text of the excerpts suffered some derangement at this point. The opening sentence of 18.1–11 reads: ὅτι φησὶν ὁ Πολύβιος ἐν τῷ εἰκοστῷ δευτέρῳ. Now it is usual (though not invariable) for an excerptor to indicate that he is beginning to excerpt from a new book by the use of some such phrase or by a note in the margin; examples are xx.4.1, xxvii.12.1, xxxi.6.1. Here however the reference to the new book occurs in the *second* extract from Book XXII; and a possible explanation

---

[29] See Moore (1965) 129, for the tendency of the excerptor 'to take only material relevant to his own subject, omit other parts, and alter the text to provide a continuous narrative': the adjustments at the beginning and end of an excerpt are a part of this procedure (cf. Nissen (1863) 9).

[30] For a parallel case cf. xxxi.19.4.

[31] There is a good example of this equation in connection with Philopoemen's death when, according to Polyb. xxiii.12.1, εἶχε ... ἐβδομηκοστὸν ἔτος (cf. Plut. *Philop.* 18.1, based on Polybius, ἤδη ... γεγονὼς ἔτος ἐβδομηκοστόν, 'already in his seventieth year'). Livy xxxix.49.4, translates 'septuaginta annos iam natus'. So perhaps εἶχε ἐβδομηκοστὸν ἔτος did in fact mean 'he was seventy, and not 'he was sixty-nine'.

[32] As it happens, such a transposition would be implied in De Sanctis' proposal ((1923) 250 n. 1) to bring Polyb. xxii.18.1–11 forward to precede xxii.6.1–6. His reason for this has nothing, however, to do with the passage dealing with the surrender of the rebels at Sais, but depends on the fact that whereas 18.1–11 corresponds (as we have seen) to Livy xxxix.23.5, 6.1–6 is the basis of Livy xxxix.24.6–14. But that transposition is unnecessary, since the change in the order by Livy is due to his having taken the events which Polybius (in 6.1–6) includes in the Italian chapters of Ol. 148.3 = 186/5 and incorporated them for reasons of composition in his narrative of events in Macedonia (see Walbank, *Comm.* III, 184, pointing to the use of pluperfects in the Livian passage). For one transposition in the Constantinian excerpts in a part for which the whole text is available see *De virt. et vit.* 16 (v. 39.6) which precedes 17 (v.34.10–11).

of this anomaly might be that in the original manuscript of the *De sententiis* 18.1–11 was the first extract from Book XXII, but that the copyist of M or some earlier intermediary accidentally omitted it and then, having discovered his error while copying 16.1–4, inserted it one passage late, while retaining the excerptor's introductory words. || This explanation is not wholly compelling, as there is a parallel instance in xxviii.18.1; but that is not entirely comparable since there the book indication consists of a marginal note in the Peirescianus, λογ κη, placed opposite the second excerpt in that collection (*De virtutibus et vitiis*) and not of a phrase incorporated in the text. On the whole, therefore, the words which I have quoted from 18.1 may be held to give some support to a hypothesis which on other grounds imposes itself as the only plausible solution to the chronological problem.

III

If we assume that Polyb. xxii.18.1–11 preceded xxii.16.1–4, it can now stand without difficulty as part of the account of Macedonian affairs of 186/5 (as the parallel passage, Livy xxxix.23.5, would suggest); and Polyb. xxii.16.1–17.7 (for, as we saw, the two chapters must go together) can be part of the account of the Egyptian affairs of the same olympiad year. But need it fall under that year? Ptolemy was not twenty-five until 30 Mesore (= 2 October) 185, and it is only Polybius' practice of extending his account of the events of each olympiad year down to the end of the campaigning season that enables him to include events occurring after Ptolemy became twenty-five under the year 186/5. As we saw, several scholars have dated the surrender of the rebels to Polycrates at Sais to 184; but only an examination of the passages which come next in the *De sententiis* and *De virtutibus et vitiis* can determine whether xxii.16.1–17.7 could in fact belong to any later year than 186/5.

In the excerpts *De virtutibus et vitiis* xxii.17.1–7 (exc. 76) is followed by 20.1–8 on Apollonis, Attalus' wife (exc. 77), 21.1–4 on Ortiagon's ambitions (exc. 78), 22.1–5 on Aristonicus (exc. 79) and xxiii.5.4–14 on Deinocrates of Messene (exc. 80). Of these passages exc. 77 and 78 are from the affairs of Asia, exc. 79 is from the affairs of Egypt, and exc. 80 (which contains an overlap with an extract from another selection) must refer to events at Rome in Ol. 149.1 = 184/3. From this it follows that exc. 77, 78 and 79 must be taken from Polybius' account of the Asian and Egyptian events of Ol. 148.4 = 185/4. Consequently exc. 76 (xxii.17.1–7) must form part of his narrative of the Egyptian events of Ol. 148.3 = 186/5.

In short, the surrender of the rebels at Sais, their execution, and the handing over of the mercenaries to Ptolemy at Naucratis are events of autumn, that is October 185. They cannot have occurred much later for Aristonicus will not have delayed bringing his mercenaries back from Greece much beyond the autumn equinox. ||

The relationship between these events and those celebrated in the second Philae decree is now clear. Following on the synod of September 186 Ptolemy dispatched Aristonicus to Greece to recruit mercenaries, either at once or perhaps in the spring of 185. In the early autumn of that year the rebels still holding out in the Delta, possibly having heard of the imminent arrival of fresh troops, disheartened by the defeat of Chaonnophris, and perhaps encouraged by the amnesty accorded by Ptolemy and referred to in the Alexandrian decree,[33] agreed to turn themselves in at Sais. But they soon learnt to their cost that they had miscalculated.[34]

---

[33] On the assumption that Sethe's interpretation of the Second Philae decree is correct; for a different version see Müller (1920) 75. There may have been further concessions (to commemorate the birth of Ptolemy VI), perhaps on New Year's Day (1 Thoth = 9 October) 196 (cf. Koenen (1962)); see too *P. Kroll = C. Ord. Ptol.* 82–8 no. 34, which some scholars attribute to Epiphanes (cf. Braunert (1960); *SB* no. 9316) – though others, including the original publisher (Koenen (1957) 1–3, 8–39) attribute it to Ptolemy VI. The king and queen were present at Memphis on 22 Thoth = 29 October 185 for the enthronement of the new Apis bull (cf. Brugsch (1884) 125–6, 134; (1886) 27; but the date, of which Brugsch gives contradictory accounts, depends on a reading by J. D. Ray); and Dorothy Crawford [Thompson] has suggested to me that the decree of year 21, raising Cleopatra to the ruler cult and recording the decision to celebrate the birthdays of the Theoi Epiphaneis (Sethe (1904) 198–214 no. 37, the First Philae decree), may emanate from a synod held at Memphis on this occasion. But whether this preceded or followed the surrender of the Delta rebels cannot be determined.

[34] For convenience I list in order the fragments of Polybius, Book XXII, dealing with Ol. 148.3 (186/5) and 148.4 (185/4):

Ol. 148.3	*Res Italiae*	6.1–6
		6.7
	Res Macedoniae	18.1–11
	Res Graeciae	7.1–10.15
	Res Aegypti	16.1–17.7
Ol. 148.4	*Res Italiae*	11.1–12.10
	Res Macedoniae	13.1–14.12
	Res Graeciae	15.1–6
	Res Asiae	20
		21
	Res Aegypti	22

(ch. 19 should stand in Book XXIII) [The chronology proposed in this chapter, putting the execution of the rebels at Sais in 185, has been accepted by McGing (1997) in an important article on the Egyptian resistance to the Ptolemies. I now, however, believe it to be wrong for the following reasons. As explained above, Polyb. xxii.16–17 (consisting of excerpts from *De sententiis* and *De virtutibus et vitiis*) appears to fall in Ol. 148.3 = 186/5, because it makes Ptolemy twenty-five at the time of the execution of the rebels; but xxii.18, which comes later than xxii.16 in the *De sententiis* and so, since it belongs to *res Macedoniae*, should fall in an olympiad year later than the *res Aegypti* of xxii.16–17, can be shown by a comparison with the Polybian passage in Livy xxxix.23.5 to belong, not to Ol. 148.4 = 185/4, but to Ol. 148.3 = 186/5. Faced with the alternatives of ignoring the reference to Ptolemy's age or assuming a rare dislocation in the order of the fragments of the *De sententiis*, so as to put xxii.16–17 before xxii.18, I opted for the latter. This was an act of desperation, which should have been resisted; but I could at the time see no plausible way round the reference to Ptolemy's age.

There is however, a simple and convincing explanation of that reference. Ptolemy's age is mentioned here merely as evidence that he was a fully-grown man and so quite unfairly deprived of his share in the recent fighting by Polycrates (17.7). That he was twenty-five and not twenty-four or twenty-six is not important. In giving his age as twenty-five Polybius is practising age-rounding, as he frequently does elsewhere. This was in fact already implied in my note on xxiii.12.1 (Walbank, *Comm.* iii, 240), where I list the passages (including this one) where Polybius rounds off ages to the nearest five or ten years. The present order of passages in the *De sententiis* need not therefore be disturbed. The events at Sais and Naucratis will fall under Ol. 148.2 = 187/6, probably in early 186 (when Ptolemy was in reality not quite twenty-four). This leaves sufficient time for Aristonicus' recruiting trip to Greece in early 186 before his return to Naucratis (17.6) and subsequent reporting of the defeat of Chaonnophris by Comanus on 27 August 186 to the synod of priests at Alexandria on 6 Sept. 186 (on this see Pestman (1995) 119–20 on the hieroglyphic text *Philae II*; also above, p. 70

I append a revised table of the Polybian fragments covering Ol. 148.2–4

Ol. 148.2 = 187/6	*Res Graeciae*	3.1–9 (*De leg. gent.*exc. 31)	
		4.1–17 (*De leg. gent.*exc.32)	
	Res Asiae	5.1–10 (*De leg. gent.*exc.33)	
	Res Aegypti	16.1–17.7 (*De sent.*exc.102 + *De virt. et vit.*exc.76)	
Ol. 148.3 = 186/5	*Res Italiae*	6.1–6 (*De leg. gent.*exc.34) 6.7 (*Suda*)	
	Res Macedoniae	18.1–11 (*De sent.*exc. 103)	
	Res Graeciae	7.1–10.15 (*De leg. gent.*exc.35)	
Ol. 148.4 = 185/4	*Res Italiae*	11.1–12.10 (*De leg. gent.*exc.36)	
	Res Macedoniae	13.1–14.12 (*De leg. Rom.*exc.19 + *De leg. gent.*exc.37)	
	Res Graeciae	15.1–6 (*De leg. Rom.*exc.20)	
	Res Asiae	20.1–8 (*De virt. et vit.*exc.77)	
		21.1–4 (*De virt. et vit.*exc.78)	
	Res Aegypti	22.1–5 (*De virt et vit.*exc.79)	

5

*Two Hellenistic processions: a matter of self-definition**

Les folies des spectacles était une maladie de leurs très grandes
villes, Rome, Alexandrie ou Antioche.

P. Veyne, *Le Pain et le cirque*, 696

I

A recent trend in Hellenistic studies has been to emphasise the importance of the indigenous peoples within the successor kingdoms to
Alexander at the expense of the Greco-Macedonian element.[1] Within
limits this is to be welcomed, for there can be no doubt that in the past,
for a combination of reasons, native influence on the life and culture of
those states has been underestimated. With the exception of Macedonia
itself, all these Hellenistic kingdoms contained ancient, alien structures,
which the new Macedonian rulers in Persia, Babylonia and Egypt could
not afford to ignore. Relations with their more numerous non-Greek
subjects were always a central problem and one which changed over
the years. In Egypt, for instance, Egyptian influence in the army and
administration, as well as in everyday life, grew steadily from the end of
the third century onwards. How indeed these Macedonian kings – and
their subject populations – saw themselves in this multicultural world
must form a matter of central interest.

Despite this, however, it remains true that the cultural roots of the rulers
and ruling castes, at any rate within the more important of the successor
states, lay in a Hellenised Macedonia and that many of their institutions derived from Macedonia and the Greek *polis*. Ptolemy, Seleucus,
Cassander, Antigonus, Lysimachus were all Macedonians. Their various
kingdoms had been secured or successfully defended in a series of wars;
and when they were not at war, they were actively engaged in numerous

---

* [[*Scripta Classica Israelica* 15 (1996) 119–30]]
[1] See especially Kuhrt and Sherwin-White (1987) and Sherwin-White and Kuhrt (1993).

ways in what may perhaps be called self-validation – through cultural patronage, building programmes both at home and in friendly states, the institution of international festivals and the subsidising of movements abroad, which they hoped might embarrass their rivals.[2] In such ways as these they aimed at projecting favourable images of themselves ‖ throughout the Greek world. In this chapter I propose to look briefly at two famous processions, one in Egypt and the other in Syria, which throw a little light on that activity and also exemplify the way in which these kings reacted to each other – and later to Rome and Rome to them – in a peaceful context.

Processions form the most striking element in most ancient religious festivals and one common to the *polis*, the Macedonian state and Hellenistic kingdoms generally,[3] as well as being important to the indigenous religions existing there. In Macedonia, for example, we hear of the annual *Xanthika*, a spring purification march of the army between the two halves of a severed dog, which is associated with the assimilation of the new year's ephebes into the army;[4] and the assassination of Philip II occurred at Aegeae during a procession bearing statues of the 'twelve gods'.[5] All ancient processions were basically religious. But in the fourth century the popular aspect had tended to grow at the expense of the 'cult' element even within the *polis*.[6] In the classical *polis* the procession, accompanying either the god or goddess, or offerings made to him or her, was a ceremony in which the whole community, as well as the officiating priests or magistrates, was involved. The degree of elaboration varied according to the occasion. Rural ceremonies were simple affairs[7] at all times; but the great *polis* festivals drew in many people and took place, most likely, in all cities. Two examples are the bearing of the *peplos* to Apollo Hyacinthos from Sparta to Amyclae,[8] and the Panathenaea at Athens,[9] the procession of which is probably that depicted on the Parthenon frieze. This procession had, of course, a military aspect, and that is not unusual. But it is an aspect which necessarily grew more marked with Alexander, since while he was in Asia the Macedonian army was – for him – the

---

[2] For examples of this activity see Weber (1995) (with useful bibliography).

[3] For a catalogue of Ptolemaic festivals see Perpillou-Thomas (1993); see also Fraser (1972) I, 189–301.

[4] Polyb. xxiii.10.17; Livy xl.6.1–7; Curt. x.9.12; cf. Hatzopoulos (1994) 89–90 with n. 6 on p. 89 for bibliography.

[5] Cf. Hammond (1994b) 176, 223 with nn. 33 and 34 (with bibliography).

[6] See F. Bömer, *RE* s.v. 'pompa', col. 1894 (attributing the 'turning-point' to the Athenian Panathenaea).

[7] On *komasiai* in Egypt see Perpillou-Thomas (1993) 145.

[8] Bömer *RE* s.v. 'pompa', col. 1920 no. 32.

[9] Ibid. col. 1928 no. 65; cf. L. Ziehen, *RE* s.v. 'Panathenaia', cols. 475–89; Neils (1992).

equivalent of the Macedonian state; and repeatedly, at Ephesus, at Soli, at Tyre, at Memphis,[10] we find him marching in procession with the army.

Where the Hellenistic procession differed from that of the *polis* was in its direction from above and its conscious incorporation of theatrical elements. It || was now less an expression of piety, gaiety and solemnity[11] by the whole community and more of a show put on by those above for general entertainment and instruction.[12] Yet this was not wholly new either. Xenophon[13] sees it as a prime duty of the hipparch to make processions *axiotheatous*, a pleasure to watch, a strictly non-religious aspect. Veyne,[14] who emphasises this 'theatrical world' in its contrast with everyday life, remarks that whereas we distinguish public and private affairs, the Greeks recognised public affairs, private affairs – and festivals.

II

The first procession I propose to discuss is the great *pompe* described in Athenaeus, following Callixeinus,[15] and to be identified with the Ptolemaieia, the penteteric, isolympic festival set up by Ptolemy II Philadelphus in 279/8 in honour of his now-deified father and mother, and perhaps also of his grandfather Lagus and his wife.[16] Two recent

---

[10] Arr. i.18.2 (Ephesus), ii.5.8 (Soli), ii.24.6 (Tyre), iii.5.2 (Memphis).

[11] On this community atmosphere see Veyne (1976) 392; one might compare the English cup final, with its ritual singing of 'Abide with me'.

[12] Like the one put on at Athens by Demetrius of Phalerum (Polyb. xii.13.11), with its large imitation snail, a feature typical of the ingredients of Hellenistic processions.

[13] *Hipparch.* 3.1.

[14] Veyne (1976) 725, quoting Polyb. v.106.2. On the 'theatrical world' of the festival see Raphael (1977); and for a relevant discussion of 'art as public drama' under an autocratic regime see E. Hobsbawm's introduction to the catalogue of the exhibition 'Art as Power: Europe under the Dictators, 1930–1945' (Hayward Gallery, London, 1995).

[15] Ath. v.196D–203B = *FGH* 627 F 2.

[16] The year the procession took place is controversial and its identity with the Ptolemaieia has been challenged; cf. Fraser (1972) I, 230–3; (1954) 57 n. 3; Rice (1983). In a review of the latter book (Walbank) (1984b), I argued that the procession in Athenaeus must form part of the Ptolemaieia, that that festival was inaugurated in 279/8 and that the occasion described is likely to be the original performance of that year. One decisive factor, as Rice has shown, is that Arsinoe II cannot have been queen at the time of the procession, since she is nowhere referred to in the account of it; and she was probably married to Philadelphus by 275/4. My argument is accepted by Ferrary (1988) 502 n. 56. More recently Foertmeyer (1988) has argued that the reference to the Morning and Evening Star at the beginning and the end of the procession (Ath. v.197D) implies that this must have taken place in a year in which the two appearances of Venus could actually have occurred to coincide with a dawn beginning and an evening conclusion of the procession. Since this was held in winter, the only relevant period fitting that requirement was December 275–February 274; hence 275/4 must be the date of Athenaeus' procession. The

studies by Rice and Dunand have greatly illuminated || this procession
and its significance,[17] and I shall be drawing extensively on their work.
As was increasingly true of such occasions in the Hellenistic period,
Ptolemy's procession celebrated several gods;[18] but the selective account
in Athenaeus concentrates on the section devoted to Dionysus, which
was evidently a central feature. Dunand[19] draws attention to two aspects
of the procession, which, she suggests, help to clarify the way in which
the event was conceived. First, the procession was carefully structured
and the groups taking part were clearly defined categories within the
population of Alexandria, based on age and occupation. There were
priests, members of religious organisations, adolescents, children, various female groups, and soldiers. This is true, but its importance should
not be exaggerated, since it is hard to see how the non-military part of a
large procession could have been organised differently. The question is
really one of efficiency. Dunand's second point also needs qualification.
Both the procession and the onlookers, she asserts, were restricted to the
stadium. But this rests on a mistranslation of Ath. v.197c,[20] which, as
Rice has shown,[21] means that the procession 'was led through the city
stadium'. There is in fact clear evidence in Athenaeus' narrative that
it subsequently proceeded through parts of the city, where it will have
been viewed by the very || mixed population of Alexandria – as Ptolemy
must have intended. Accessibility to such festivals was normal in the
city. As we gather from Theocritus,[22] two Syracusan ladies resident in

argument is ingenious; but in fact Athenaeus v.197D merely says that the procession began
(ἀρχην εἶχεν ἡ πομπή) at the time when the Morning Star *appears* (φαίνεται) – not 'appeared'.
He is making a general statement: the section devoted to the Morning Star comes first, because
dawn is the time when that star appears. The section assigned to the Evening Star came at the
end, τῆς ὥρας εἰς τοῦτο συναγούσης τὸν καιρόν, a difficult phrase which perhaps means 'when
the season brought the time to that point'. 'The season' will be winter, perhaps implying an early
nightfall. 'That point' is the moment in the day, twilight, when the Evening Star is wont to appear.
The representation of the morning and evening star(s) can be paralleled by other personifications
of natural opposites such as day and night in the procession at Daphne (Polyb. xxx.25.15). There
is thus no reason to suppose that these representations of the Morning and Evening Star are tied
to any particular date when their appearance might coincide with their place in the procession.
[17] Rice (1983), and Dunand (1981); [see also D. J. Thompson (2000)].
[18] Cf. Rice (1983) 21–7. The absence of Aphrodite, who was closely associated with Arsinoe II,
confirms that the latter was not queen at the time.
[19] Dunand (1981) 150.
[20] The same error occurs in the Loeb translation of C. B. Gulick; cf. too Fraser (1972) i, 230.
[21] Rice (1983) 31, observing (a) that a large crown of gold was in due course hung around the door
of the shrine of Berenice, clearly outside the stadium; this is likely to have been done from the
procession (Ath. v.202D); (b) grape juice from freshly trodden grapes and wine were released to
flow along the street, which implies an area outside the stadium (Ath. v.197E); (c) the marshals
dressed as Sileni would be required in the city streets rather than in the stadium before a sitting
audience (Ath. v.197E).
[22] *Id.* 15. 73–7.

Alexandria have no problems, other than the usual bustling crowds, and encounter no controls in attending the Adonis festival held within the court area. Dunand seems in part to have exaggerated the significance of the structure of the Ptolemaic procession and to have underestimated the breadth of its audience.

At whom, then, was the procession directed? And what reactions was it intended to elicit? Clearly, for an event on such a scale with so many different components this question cannot expect a simple answer. But some elements, both in the presentation and among the spectators, can be identified. To take the latter first, the overwhelmingly Greco-Macedonian flavour of the event – the gods included, the symbolism in the tableaux, the mythology evoked, the emphasis on the Ptolemaic dynastic house and Alexander,[23] and the association of the latter with Dionysus – show that this procession was conceived primarily as a show put on in a Greek *polis*.[24] The *main* audience, those accommodated in the stadium, were certainly Greek and included representatives of the administration and official guests from abroad (these were later feasted separately from the soldiers, *technitai* – artisans or, more probably, Dionysiac artistes – and tourists).[25] But even if they are given no emphasis in our narrative, the procession contained themes to which Egyptians could easily attach their own cultural interpretations.[26] The cornucopia carried by 'Eniautos' (Ath. v.198A), for example, and a second one which appears later in the procession (ibid. 202C) were symbols of fertility connected with Isis, Harpocrates and the Nile, as well as having Greek antecedents. Dionysus is a Greek god; but surely this is not too early in the Ptolemaic period for Egyptians to make a cross-reference to Osiris and/or Sarapis.[27] Egyptians must also have related this procession to those familiar to them from their everyday experience of the processions which formed an integral and important part of native Egyptian festivals, involving the movement of divine images from shrine to shrine, often by river transport on the Nile.[28] But it remains true that on this occasion Ptolemy's interest was focused on his Greco-Macedonian subjects and on visiting Greeks and Macedonians from || abroad; for an important element in this festival was the presence among the privileged spectators of *theoroi*

---

[23] On the Dionysus–Alexander connection see Rice (1983) 83–5.
[24] Rice (1983) 29.   [25] Ath. v.196A.
[26] On the cornucopia cf. Rice (1983) 202–5; on its Greek antecedents see Dunand (1981) 26. For conscious cross-cultural resonances as a basic characteristic of life in Ptolemaic Egypt see Koenen (1993); also (1983).
[27] So Dunand (1981) 33.
[28] Cf. Rice (1983) 180. The triumphalist and often blood-curdling processional scenes on temple walls would be less familiar, since they stood in the area closed to the public.

from other Greek states (some of whom, of course, may have come from cities under Ptolemaic control).[29]

For these, as well as for the local spectators, Ptolemy's greatness is underlined by, *inter alia*, emphasis on imposing, over-life-size figures and objects, and the symbolism incorporated in those elements of the procession. Such symbolism, as Ehrenberg pointed out,[30] had to be broad and simple. Thus 'Corinth' will have stood for the Greek homeland generally.[31] It may also have been intended to suggest a Greek homeland where Ptolemy had a direct interest and might reasonably expect to exercise power, given the current chaos and confusion there, following the murder of Seleucus at Lysimacheia and the death of Ptolemy Ceraunus in Macedonia. But such hints, if they were there, are quite vague and certainly not stressed. For Corinth itself, at this time, was held by Antigonus Gonatas.

The real political emphasis was reserved, in fact, for the mighty military parade rounding off the procession, which was intended to impress both citizens and foreign guests. Dunand speaks of the latter being 'intimidated'. That is perhaps going a little too far, but certainly *theoroi* were expected to report back home on this march-past, which will have lasted several hours,[32] just as in the days of the Soviet Union ambassadors would report on the November parade in the Red Square in Moscow. Supported by some of the symbolism in the preceding sections of the procession – the Alexander theme, the Macedonian 'Mimallones', the Greek cities of Asia formerly subdued by the Persians, the Indian captives and the Ethiopian tribute-bearers, together with large numbers of exotic animals[33] – the procession may well have been designed to celebrate

---

[29] For *theoroi* at the Ptolemaieia see *Syll.* 390 (Nesiotes); *ISE* II, no. 75 (Amphipolis). From classical times the presence of *theoroi* was essential to a festival claiming international recognition and prestige; see Thuc. VI.3; Plato, *Laws* XII, 950 d–e, 951a; Dem. 19.128; 21.115; Arist. *Ath.Pol.* 56.3.

[30] Ehrenberg (1938) 3–4.

[31] Ath. V.201D; it has nothing to do with the 'League of Corinth' set up by Philip II (so Rice (1983) 102–3), for no such name for the league appears in ancient sources and appears to be a modern term. Dunand (1981) believes that Corinth 'certainly' stands for the Greek cities over which Ptolemy sought to exercise control and that there may be a hint at Ptolemy I's expedition of 308, after which he left garrisons in the Peloponnese. Anything so specific, and so long before the date of the procession, seems improbable.

[32] Ath. V.202F–203A. There were around 57,600 infantry and 23,200 cavalry. If, for example, they marched six abreast, at four m.p.h. it would have taken the infantry alone nearly three hours to pass a given point.

[33] See Ath. V.198E (Mimallones), 201A (Indian captives and Ethiopian tribute-bearers), 201D (Alexander), 201D–E (Greek cities of Asia).

victories won or claimed,[34] as well as foreshadowing future conquests going far beyond reality. ||

In addition, the procession contained items designed to entertain, including a mechanical statue of Nysa, and the visual effects of brightly coloured objects and much bronze, silver and gold, underlining the wealth, majesty and generosity of Ptolemy, who also provided gifts, perfumes and wine (for those in the stadium).[35] There were also the carnival 'reversals of normality' common to such processions at all times – children in adult roles, small girls clad as warriors;[36] and finally such symbols as the cornucopia, indicating fruitfulness and fertility.[37] Thus the Ptolemies (like the Pharaohs into whose shoes they had stepped) were presented as conquerors, benefactors and bringers of prosperity.

III

Our second procession was held at Daphne near Antioch by Antiochus IV over a century later, when Rome was already predominant in the eastern Mediterranean. It too is recorded by Athenaeus (who here follows Polybius).[38] Like the Ptolemaic procession, this too has had its date discussed at length. There is, however, little doubt that it took place in summer 166 BC, though whether still in Ol.153.2 (167/6) or in Ol.153.3 (166/5) is uncertain.[39]

---

[34] Both Dunand (1981) 21 and Ferrary (1988) 562 n. 36, believe that the procession celebrated a victory over Syria (but in different wars). See below, n. 47.

[35] Dunand (1981) 27 supposes the wine and grape-juice mentioned as flowing in the street by Ath. v.200B was for the spectators to taste; but if it flowed directly onto the street, this is hard to envisage.

[36] Ath. v.200F. 'Female impersonators' were a regular feature in the annual gala procession in my native Yorkshire town in the early decades of this century. On the 'renversement des moeurs' common to such carnival occasions see Raphael (1977) 115–19.

[37] See above, n. 26.

[38] Ath. v.194C–195D = Polyb. xxx.25.1–26.4; Diod. xxxi.16 (based on Polybius).

[39] Polybius' account forms part of the Asian events of Ol. 153.2 = 167/6. The procession falls in 166, but since Polybius' olympiad year can include events of the following autumn, there is no summer cut-off date for the festival; indeed Bunge (1976) dates it to Sept./Oct. of that year. See further Walbank *Comm.* III, 32–3. (Athenaeus' statement (x.439B) that Polybius described the Daphne festival in Book XXXI has been rightly rejected; it would involve an unparalleled range of contents for that book.) Attempts have been made to date the procession to 165; so Bar-Kochva (1989) 467–73, who dismisses Polybius' linking of the festival with Aemilius Paullus' games at Amphipolis as an interpolation by Athenaeus. He has then to assume a dislocation in the order of the Polybian fragments in order to assign xxx.25.1–26.9 (and xxx.27.1–4, describing Ti. Gracchus' embassy to Syria just after the games) to Ol. 153.3 = 166/5. The arguments in support of this hypothesis are not convincing and this date for the procession (also implied in Broughton, *MRR* I, 438 and adopted without discussion by Sherwin-White and Kuhrt (1993) 220) is to be rejected.

Its purpose, according to Polybius (xxx.25.1), was to outdo the games recently held at Amphipolis by L. Aemilius Paullus to celebrate his victory over Perseus || of Macedonia.[40] The more decidedly military character of Antiochus' procession confirms the truth of this statement, although no military element is recorded for Aemilius' festival.[41] In celebrating his victory in Greece as well as in a Roman triumph, Aemilius was taking the opportunity to publicise Roman policy and Roman success in the Hellenistic mode, as we have already seen it operating in Philadelphus' Ptolemaieia. But he was not the first Roman general with an eye for the fruits of publicity to be gathered in Hellenistic capitals and Greek cities. To take one example, T. Quinctius Flamininus, who had already acted as *agonothetes* at the Nemean games,[42] when about to evacuate Greece, following his much vaunted grant of freedom at the Isthmian Games of 196, marched from the Acrocorinth amid – perhaps orchestrated – cries of 'Saviour and Liberator', a combination of cult titles (Σωτὴρ καὶ Ἐλευθέριος) especially associated with Zeus from the time of the Persian Wars.[43]

From what source Polybius drew his account of Antiochus' procession is unknown,[44] and his description is selective, though adequate to give a general impression of what took place. The procession, like Ptolemy's, was variegated and may well have had more than one aim. It seems probable, though not certain, that, held in summer 166 in the salubrious surroundings of Daphne, it was a special performance of the annual festival held there in honour of Apollo.[45] In attempting to rival Aemilius Paullus, Antiochus was clearly setting up a propagandist challenge to Rome, hoping thereby to repair any damage to his prestige brought about by his acceptance of the humiliating ultimatum presented to him by Popillius Laenas at Eleusis in Egypt.[46] Indeed it is tempting to see

---

[40] On these games, held in 167, see Livy xlv.32.8–33.7; Plut. *Aem.* 28.3–5; Diod. xxxi.8.9; Gruen (1992) 247; Ferrary (1988) 552. Gruen sees these games as expressing a Roman claim to Hellenistic culture, whereas to Ferrary they represent a typical Hellenistic victory-celebration. See also Günther (1995) 83.

[41] Ferrary (1988) 561, thinks that Aemilius Paullus' games must have involved a procession, omitted from our selective account of these events; this is possible.

[42] Cf. Ferrary (1988) 562.   [43] Livy xxxiv.50.9; cf. Jensen, *RE* s.v. 'Eleutherios', cols. 2348–9.

[44] A possibility, but no more, is Protagorides of Cyzicus, who is known to have written *On the festivals of Daphne* (Ath. iv.150CD, 176AB, 183F = *FGH* 853 F 1–2); nothing is known of him.

[45] See Mørkholm (1966) 98; Bar-Kochva (1989) 468, for other examples of this summer festival being used for special celebrations.

[46] Polyb. xxix.27.1–13; Livy xlv.12.3–8; Diod. xxxi.2.

his procession (like Ptolemy's[47]) as a victory celebration, in this case over Egypt, whence Antiochus had brought back much plunder, which helped pay for || the procession.[48] Mørkholm queried this assumption as too much like a sham; but his premature death prevented his witnessing the spectacle of the decisively defeated dictator of a country lying within the boundaries of the former Seleucid kingdom celebrating the 'mother of battles' to considerable internal applause; and reliable information of distant events will have been far more difficult to obtain then than now. The forces taking part in the parade – there were 16,000 mercenaries, more than were fielded at either Raphia or Magnesia – must have been costly to raise and maintain;[49] so perhaps the event was also planned as a send-off, in the Macedonian manner, for Antiochus' eastern campaign, which probably set out in spring 165.[50]

The fact that this procession (unlike that of Ptolemy) *began* with the parade of troops indicates a shift in emphasis towards the military element. The march past of some 45,000 troops of various sorts[51] headed by 5,000 clad in Roman *loricae hamatae* was a significant and challenging gesture, which confirms Diodorus' statement (xxxi.16) that Antiochus, unlike 'the other kings', flaunted his policy of confrontation – a remark perhaps taken from Polybius, who was ill-disposed towards that king. Rank after rank of soldiers could have made a boring start to the celebrations, but this part of the procession was enlivened by the use of coloured shields in various metals – bronze, silver and perhaps gold[52] – gold trappings, purple tunics with gold-embroidered designs, and elephants and chariots. Elsewhere it was distinguished by features similar

[47] See Ferrary (1988) 562, who argues that the procession of Ptolemy II celebrated the Ptolemaic victory in the Syrian War following Seleucus' death (cf. Will (1979) 139–41).

[48] Polyb. xxx.26.9. This passage speaks of robbery (ἐνόσφιτο) and treachery (παρασπονδήσας) toward Philometor, παιδίσκον ὄντα. This is bound to recall the attack planned by Philip V and Antiochus III on another boy-king of Egypt, Epiphanes, an incident which Polybius set at the heart of the structural plan of his *Histories*, interpreting Roman success as the instrument of the punishment inflicted by *Tyche* on the two bandit kings (see ch. 16, below, pp. 245–57).

[49] For the figures see Polyb. xxx.25.4–5; dependent on his source, they are of course subject to the doubts which surround most ancient statistics of troop numbers.

[50] Cf. Habicht (1989) 345 n. 75. Macc. 3.37 puts his departure in *SE* 147, which, on the Macedonian reckoning, is aut. 166-aut. 165. A departure in spring would not (*pace* Bar-Kochva (1989) 468–9) have involved keeping the mercenaries under arms for too long a time after the procession.

[51] For a tabular comparison of the forces at Daphne, Raphia and Magnesia see Bar-Kochva (1989) 34.

[52] Cf. Polyb. xxx.25.5; in my note ad loc. in the *Commentary* I rejected the inclusion of *chrysaspides*. But I was wrong to restrict mention of these to Pollux 1.1175. As a reviewer pointed out, the word also occurs in Plut. *Eum.* 14.5, in Macc. 6.39 and in Onasander 1.20.

to those in the Alexandrian festival, viz. luxury items such as the parading of 800 ivory tusks, and vast quantities of gold and silver plate, with a stress on gold, the great symbol of wealth, throughout. ||

Antiochus also incorporated almost 300 *theoroi* in the procession[53] instead of treating them merely as spectators and guests at the banquet (as Ptolemy had done). In that way he contributed to the picture of a realm lying at the centre of world interest – an impression which it was hoped they might carry back to their cities.[54] Their position in the procession, between the 1,000 sacrificial oxen and the 800 ivory tusks, is not perhaps as odd as it seemed to Schweighaeuser,[55] for it both provided variety and set them between two examples of Antiochus' wealth, prestige and magnificence. The procession also included a vast number of statues of divinities, *daimones* and likenesses (*eidola*) of heroes; the representations of the myths associated with the latter may have been pictures or tableaux (like the Dionysiac myths in the Alexandrian procession). Finally there were symbolic representations of such natural opposites as Night and Day, Earth and Heaven, Dawn and Midday, reminiscent of the Morning and Evening Stars at Alexandria.[56] Here too visual effects were supplemented by the sprinkling of perfume.[57]

The presence of 800 ephebes as a separate and distinctive unit in the later, non-military section of the procession shows that these youths had not yet been taken into the army. But whether, following Macedonian precedent,[58] the Seleucid kingdom preserved the *rites de passage*, which accompanied such incorporation in Macedonia, is not recorded. The organisation of ephebes as a special corps concerned with frontier protection and other 'Home Guard' duties is a development found at Athens and elsewhere well before the Hellenistic period.

Unlike Alexander, neither Ptolemy II nor Antiochus IV took part in the procession in person, evidently preferring to be seen as the power behind it. They were of course rulers of lands (temporarily) at peace,

---

53 Reading θεωρίαι at Polyb. xxx.25.12 for the MS θεωρία; the words βραχὺ λείπουσαι τριακοσίων slightly favour this rather than Casaubon's θεωρίδες, since had individual attendants (of Bacchus or Apollo) been indicated, their number is likely to have been made up to 300. See Walbank *Comm.* iii, ad loc. for discussion.

54 Some no doubt came from Seleucid held cities; cf. Bunge (1976) 68–9.

55 One may assume a slight break in the procession to allow for cleaning operations following the passage of the 1,000 oxen.

56 Polyb. xxx.25.15; and see above n. 16; for the Year and Hours in the Ptolemaic procession see Ath. v.198A–B. Such cosmological personifications are not uncommon in Hellenistic times. The third-century relief showing the 'Apotheosis of Homer', found at Bovillae and now in the British Museum, identifies Ptolemy IV with *Chronos* and Arsinoe, his wife, with *Oikoumene*.

57 Polyb. xxx.25.17.   58 See n. 4.

whereas Alexander was always very consciously leading an army on campaign and so naturally paraded with his troops. Antiochus' rôle is represented, rather absurdly, as that of a steward actually supervising the procession.[59] But Polybius' picture of Antiochus appears somewhat hostile, either because of his admiration for Aemilius Paullus or because his source dealing with that king was hostile – or indeed || because Athenaeus has been selective; the account in Diodorus is slightly more balanced.

IV

The two Hellenistic processions discussed above are exemplary of a highly intensive activity in the field of public relations and propaganda exercises continuously conducted by rulers of the Hellenistic kingdoms both before and after Rome appeared on the scene. The slant and emphasis of this activity necessarily changed with the political climate; though conforming to type, each manifestation was a response to a particular situation in a particular time and place. Both processions, though over a century apart and occurring in different kingdoms, were directed first and foremost towards the world of the Greek states and the Greco-Macedonian populations within the other kingdoms. (What exactly Greco-Macedonian had come to mean by the second century is a separate problem which cannot be considered here.) This does not mean that Ptolemies and Seleucids were blind to the importance of non-Greeks within their kingdoms, of Egyptians, spread all over Egypt, and of Persians, Babylonians and other peoples, living especially in the eastern parts of the Seleucid territories. The rôle of the Ptolemies in connection with native temples as both builders and sharers in their cult is well attested; and there is good evidence for the involvement of the Seleucids in Babylonian religious rituals.[60] The processions are, however, an indication that Greco-Macedonian affairs continued to be at the heart of royal concern. All the major Hellenistic powers were Mediterranean based. Antioch (not Babylon or Seleuceia-on-the-Tigris) was where Antiochus chose to assert his undiminished power, his 'victory' and his forthcoming campaign in the east; and like Ptolemy, he did this in a Greek environment and linked it with the Greco-Macedonian pantheon. His personal image conformed to the Hellenistic concept of the ideal prince. As long as

---

[59] Cf. Polyb. xxx.26.4; Diod. xxxi.16.2; the marginally more favourable traits in Diodorus may go back to Polybius, and may have been omitted by Athenaeus.

[60] See, for Egypt, D. J. Thompson (1988) especially 106–54; and, for the Seleucids, A. Kuhrt in Kuhrt and Sherwin-White (1987) 52.

they survived, these intermarrying dynasties continued to present themselves proudly as Macedonian. A new and significant expression of this
attitude in the third century BC is to be found in a recently discovered
papyrus[61] containing a poem by the Macedonian Poseidippus, in which
Ptolemy II is represented as taking pride in his origins in Eordaea and
his use of the Macedonian tongue.

It was this shared Greco-Macedonian culture that the Romans confronted from the third century onwards and quickly realised that they
must make their own. To win wars was not enough. They had also to
engage successfully in traditional forms of peaceful rivalry, exploiting the
opportunities for self-enhancing cultural patronage and religious celebration exemplified in the processions we have been considering. It was
in this same Greco-Macedonian context that Rome claimed her place
both as the avenger of Troy and as the || successor to Alexander's impe-
rial power; and conquered Greece, in the person of the Greek historian
Polybius, placed her firmly at the centre of the Hellenistic world, when he
interpreted the Roman rise to ecumenical domination as the instrument
employed by *Tyche* to avenge the wrongs inflicted on Egypt by kings of
Macedonia and Seleucid Asia.[62]

[61] Information [reportedly] given in a lecture by G. Bastianini. [But see now Kapetanopoulos
    (1999) 122 for the absence from this papyrus of any reference to the Macedonian tongue.]
[62] See n. 47.

6

*Polybius and Macedonia**

I

For rather more than 150 years Macedonia dominated the history of
the Mediterranean world; and for rather longer – in fact from the reign
of Philip II to that of Perseus – the relations between Macedonia and
the states of Greece proper gave rise to quite bitter and violent political
controversy. The issues debated by Aeschines and Demosthenes during Philip II's rise to power are central in this conflict; but far from
being resolved by Philip's victory, they continued to attract attention
throughout the third century and well into the second, when the historian Polybius is a witness to the importance which the Macedonian
question still held in the new context of the Roman advance to world
domination. Confronted by the fall of Macedonia, Greeks inevitably
pondered upon her rise to power; and commenting upon the final disaster at Pydna in 168, Polybius quotes with wonder the prophetic remarks
uttered by Demetrius of Phalerum after the overthrow of the Persian
empire by Alexander.

'Can you imagine', Demetrius had written in his Περὶ Τύχης,[1] 'that
if some god had warned the Persians or their king, or the Macedonians
or their king, that in fifty years the very name of the Persians, who
once were masters of the world, would have been lost, and that the
Macedonians whose name was before scarcely known, would become
masters of it, they would have believed it? Nevertheless, it is true that
Fortune, whose influence on our life is incalculable, who displays her
power by surprises, is even now, I think, showing all mankind, by her
elevation of the Macedonians into the high prosperity once enjoyed by
the Persians, that she has merely lent them these advantages until she
may otherwise determine concerning them.' Polybius was writing at a

---

* [[*Ancient Macedonia* (1970) 291–307]]
[1] Polyb. xxix.21.4–6 = *FGH* 228 F 39.

time when Rome had already ousted Macedonia as Macedonia had then ousted Persia, and he affects to regard Demetrius' words as 'more divine than those of a mere man – for', he adds, 'nearly a hundred and fifty years ago he uttered the truth about what was to happen afterwards'.[2]

The demoting of Macedonia was the reverse side of the rise of Rome. It || stretched over the years from 220 to 168, which constituted the period covered by Polybius' history in its original form, and it involved problems of allegiance and political decisions affecting both Rome and Macedonia in which the historian was personally involved. That is one reason why he is a valid witness on this theme. A second is his very special position in the controversy. As a Megalopolitan he inherited attitudes towards Macedonia which went back to the fourth century and were very different from those of Demosthenes.

The people of Megalopolis, he tells us,[3] were well disposed towards the royal house of Macedonia ever since the favours received in the time of Philip, son of Amyntas; Megalopolis, we know, had acquired border territories in Sciritis, Belbinatis, and perhaps Aegytis, from Sparta, following on the decisions of the Hellenic League after Chaeronea.[4] It was indeed for this reason that when the Achaeans, threatened by Cleomenes III of Sparta, decided to sound Antigonus Doson of Macedonia on the possibility of an agreement and the sending of military help, the first negotiations were carried out by two men from Megalopolis, Nicophanes and the Cynic writer Cercidas, who might reasonably expect a friendly reception at the court of Pella.[5] Cercidas, we may note, as not without interest, was almost certainly the descendant of the Cercidas who had been attacked by Demosthenes in the *De corona*[6] and by Theopompus in his *Philippica*[7] as a traitor to Greece. Polybius takes up the defence of the elder Cercidas against Demosthenes in the course of a very revealing digression on the nature of treachery. I shall return to this passage below.

II

Polybius' *Histories*, including the introductory books, went back to the beginning of the First Punic War and for Greece they contained a sketch of the rise of the Achaean Confederacy. The revival of Achaea in the

[2] Polyb. xxix.21.9.   [3] Polyb. ii.48.2; cf. ix.28.7, 33.8–12, xviii.14.6–7.

[4] Cf. *Syll.* 665 lines 19–20 (a second-century arbitration settlement between Megalopolis and Sparta referring to this assignment); cf. Livy xxxviii.34.8 (where *Achaeorum* is incorrect). See my comments in Walbank, *Comm.* ii on ix.33.12.

[5] Polyb. ii.48.4.   [6] Dem. 18.295.   [7] Theopompus, *Philippica* xv = *FGH* 115 F 119.

third century and its extension of federal government to cover a large part of the Peloponnese, including Argos, Corinth and Megalopolis, was one of the most significant political achievements of its time and one of which an Achaean historian could be justifiably proud.[8] Looking back from the time at which he was || writing in the first half of the second century, Polybius saw a continuous line of growth from the refounding of the Confederacy in 280/79 down to the inclusion of Sparta under Philopoemen, which he may well have seen as a smaller scale parallel to the rise of Rome to world dominion during approximately the same period.

Unfortunately the relations of Achaea and Macedonia were not wholly free from embarrassment. For Polybius could hardly conceal the fact that whereas the first steps to Achaean unity under Margus and Aratus had been taken in opposition to Antigonus Gonatas, it was this same Aratus who under pressure from Sparta had subsequently brought back the Macedonian phalanx and Macedonian garrisons into the Peloponnese. That the rise of Achaea should involve opposition to Macedonia had been inevitable. Any early attempts at independence had been thwarted by the Spartans or more particularly by Macedonia,[9] whose kings had dissolved the fourth-century confederation,[10] and set up a system of garrisons and tyrants to hold down the peoples of the Peloponnese.[11] From his liberation of Corinth in mid-summer 243[12] it was Aratus' purpose to expel the Macedonians from the Peloponnese;[13] he had no scruple in using any method in opposition to Antigonus Gonatas, and later continued this policy by persuading the tyrants, who were financed by Gonatas' successor, Demetrius II,[14] to lay down their rule. By 228 those of Megalopolis, Argos, Hermione and Phlius had all thrown in their lot with the Achaean Confederation.[15]

For his account of these stirring events Polybius could follow a first-hand, if not wholly impartial, source, the *Memoirs* of Aratus himself.[16] Polybius admits[17] that this work omitted certain details, and these omissions were especially noticeable in the next period, where Aratus came to describe the difficult situation which led to the rapprochement with Antigonus Doson and the return of the Macedonian garrison to the

---

[8] For Polybius' account of the rise of Achaea see ii.37–44.   [9] Polyb. ii.39.12.
[10] Polyb. ii.40.5, 41.9; cf. iv.1.5.   [11] Polyb. ii.41.10; cf. ix.29.6.
[12] Polyb. ii.43.4; Plut. *Arat.* 21.2.   [13] Polyb. ii.43.7.
[14] Polyb. ii.44.3.   [15] Polyb. ii.44.5–6; *Arat.* 34.7,35.5.
[16] Polyb. i.3.2, ii.47.11, 56.2, iv.2.1; Polybius states that he has used Aratus' *Memoirs* for the Cleomenean War (ii.56.2) and he will have done so for the earlier history of the confederation as well.
[17] Polyb. ii.47.11.

Acrocorinth. According || to a passage in Plutarch's *Cleomenes*[18] Aratus later filled his *Memoirs* with abuse of Doson. This assertion creates a problem, for the two men had no contact until Aratus opened negotiations with the king in the autumn of 227 and thereafter relations were cordial down to Doson's death. Why then should Aratus have abused Doson? It has been suggested[19] that Plutarch was referring not to Doson, but to Gonatas; but such careless writing is hard to credit, and it seems on the whole more likely that Plutarch copied this statement from Phylarchus,[20] the pro-Spartan historian who wrote in opposition to Aratus. For elsewhere,[21] in a passage in the *Life of Aratus*, which also appears to echo criticism put out by Phylarchus,[22] Plutarch says that some people judged it wrong that Aratus should have brought back as masters in the cities of the Peloponnese, though in the guise of allies, men whom he constantly defeated in the fields of war and politics and abused in his *Memoirs*. Here the reference is clearly to the pact with Doson, yet the defeating of the Macedonians (and probably the abuse of them) belongs to an earlier period in Aratus' career. It therefore seems likely that in the passage from the *Cleomenes* Phylarchus has tendentiously interpreted this general abuse of the Macedonians as abuse of Doson in person. It is, I suppose, just possible that Plutarch has himself misinterpreted the more general reference which he found in his source; but this seems less likely, since Plutarch was of course familiar with the *Memoirs* of Aratus himself. At any rate, all mention of Doson in Polybius, who will here be following Aratus' *Memoirs*, is favourable. He is a man of energy and sound sense, who claimed also to be a man of honour – though indeed, Polybius adds, it is natural for kings to measure enmity and friendship by the standard of expediency.[23] Faced with the outcry of the Argives, whose territory Cleomenes had ravaged, he remained unmoved 'like a true general and king';[24] and after meeting and defeating Cleomenes || at Sellasia, a battle in which both kings showed themselves to be gifted and equally matched,[25] he went on to treat Sparta with generosity and humanity.[26] In Achaea he was given every honour imaginable

---

[18] Plut. *Cleom.* 16.3.   [19] By Klatt (1877) 6ff.

[20] For Phylarchus see *FGH* 81 and Walbank, *Comm.* i,259 on Polyb. ii.56–63; see also Africa (1961); Gabba (1957).

[21] Cf. Plut. *Arat.* 38.4, μηδὲ οὓς αὐτὸς ἐν ταῖς πράξεσι καταστρατηγῶν καὶ καταπολιτευόμενος, ἐν δὲ τοῖς ὑπομνήμασι λοιδορῶν διετέλει, τούτους ἐπάγεσθω δεσπότας ταῖς πόλεσι συμμάχους ὑποκοριζόμενον.

[22] Cf. Plut. *Arat.* 38.8. where Phylarchus is mentioned as a source for Aratus' early approach to Macedonia.

[23] Polyb. ii.47.5.   [24] Polyb. ii.64.6; for Polybius' attitude towards kings see Welwei (1963).
[25] Polyb. ii.66.4.   [26] Polyb. ii.70.1.

to immortalise his memory,[27] and then returned north to an early death, having aroused high hopes in Greece both by his military skill and even more because of his lofty principles and character.[28]

Doson may indeed have been an excellent man and a trustworthy ally. But one cannot restrain the suspicion that the high praise which he receives in Polybius and (if I am right) received in Aratus' *Memoirs*, cannot be wholly divorced from the political situation which drove Aratus to seek his help against Cleomenes. Whatever the truth of this, for the next quarter of a century Achaea was to be tied to the Macedonian alliance, not always to her advantage. Apart from the substantial power exercised by the Macedonian king through his military occupation of Orchomenus, Heraea, Alipheira, Triphylia, and the Acrocorinth,[29] he seems to have assumed the position of *hegemon* of the Achaean Confederation, and a law was passed requiring the magistrates to summon an assembly whenever he requested.[30] This bond involved Achaea in severe losses during the First Macedonian War against Rome; but Philip V, Doson's successor, gave every help in his power to his Peloponnesian allies, and the alliance was never seriously endangered.

III

The First Macedonian War arose out of Philip V's ill-advised policy of expansion towards the Adriatic and his alliance with Hannibal.[31] The Romans in return, as soon as their position in Italy allowed them to undertake a serious approach to any Greek state, made an alliance with the Aetolian Confederation in autumn 211,[32] the terms of which allowed for the bringing in of Elis, Sparta, perhaps Messene, Attalus of Pergamum, and the Illyrian chieftains Pleuratus and Scerdilaidas. An appeal to Sparta followed quite soon and in the following spring Polybius records speeches delivered at Sparta by Aetolian and Acarnanian envoys, the one urging and the other opposing the proposed Roman alliance.[33] The authenticity of these speeches has || been challenged; and certainly Polybius was to some extent at the mercy of his available sources – in this case perhaps literary, though we do not know what they were. He does, however, insist quite vehemently and on several occasions that the speeches

---

[27] Polyb. ii.70.5; for details see Walbank, *Comm.* ad loc.
[28] Polyb. ii.70.7, τὴν ὅλην αἵρεσιν καὶ καλοκἀγαθίαν.
[29] Polyb. ii.52.3–4, iv.6.4–6; Livy xxxii.5.4–6.   [30] Polyb. iv.85.3, v.1.6; Plut. *Arat.* 38.9; cf. 24.4.
[31] For their treaty see Polyb. vii.9.
[32] Livy xxvi.24.1–14; on the chronology see Walbank, *Comm.* II,11–13, 162–3.
[33] Polyb. ix.28–39; see Walbank, *Comm.* ad loc.

included in a history should record the actual content and not become a vehicle for elegant composition, and we are, I believe, entitled to regard those recorded as having been delivered at Sparta on this occasion as a faithful account of the arguments that were in fact used.[34]

The significant feature of these speeches is that the arguments for and against the Roman alliance were concerned not so much with the immediate situation and the character of the Romans, but with the rôle of Macedonia in Greece – and again not with the person of Philip V, but rather with the record of his predecessors going back to Philip II and Alexander. It is extraordinary how far this discussion in 210 was dominated by the events of fourth-century history and how far the quarrels of Demosthenes and Aeschines were fought out again on the eve of the Roman conquest. For the issue debated at Sparta was briefly: which constitutes the greater danger to Greece, Rome or Macedonia? The arguments were illuminated on both sides with a wide range of *exempla* taken from past history. The two speeches are recorded with great objectivity: and one of the few pointers to Polybius' own sympathies is the fact that the pro-Macedonian speech of Lyciscus, the Acarnanian, is double the length of that of his Aetolian opponent.[35] As a citizen of Megalopolis Polybius could be expected to favour the policy of Philip II, who had humbled Sparta and extended the boundaries of Arcadia; as we saw,[36] he elsewhere attacked Demosthenes and defended the Arcadian patriots such as Cercidas. Naturally, therefore, his sympathies would lie with Lyciscus, who praises Philip II and his successors on the Macedonian throne, rather than with Chlaeneas, the Aetolian, who in urging the Roman alliance denounces Macedonia as the perennial foe of all Greece. Nevertheless, for Polybius the issue could not be a simple one; for he was writing his *Histories* not in Greece at the time of the First Macedonian War, when the Romans were still strangers and, as Lyciscus calls them, barbarians,[37] but in all probability || while still a detainee at Rome after 168, when the victory over Perseus at Pydna had brought Alexander's monarchy to an end and had suggested to Polybius himself the great theme of his *Histories* – 'how and thanks to what sort of constitution the Romans in less than fifty-three years had succeeded in subjecting nearly

---

[34] Cf. Walbank (1965a) 16–17.

[35] The same device appears elsewhere; cf. Polyb. xxxvi.9, where of the four Greek opinions about Roman action against Carthage in the Third Punic War, the last and longest appears to be that of Polybius himself. [on that debate see now, however, pp. 19–20 above.]

[36] Above, p. 92.

[37] ix.37.6; cf. v.104.1, xviii.22.8; Livy xxxi. 29.15 (from Polybius). But Polybius did not himself regard the Romans as barbarians and never so describes them: see my note on ix.37.6.

the whole inhabited world to their sole government – a thing unique in history'.[38]

Since the First Macedonian War, then, the issue had changed. The Macedonian alliance, agreeable though it no doubt appeared to the men of Megalopolis, had turned out to be only a temporary episode in Achaean history. Earlier Aratus had secured Achaean independence at the expense of the Macedonians; and in the Second Macedonian War the Achaeans were to go over to Rome and fight actively against Philip. Throughout Polybius' childhood the Roman alliance had been the dominant factor in Achaean policy; yet it had ended in the *débâcle* of the Third Macedonian War, and had turned sour on its more independent-minded supporters following Pydna, when 1,000 leading Achaeans including Polybius himself were transported to Italy and held there without trial. Looking back to the debate of 210 the issue on which the Spartans were called upon to decide can scarcely have seemed a clear one. Polybius must surely have been asking himself questions such as: Had the Achaeans been correct in their policy? Was the Macedonian alliance right in the first war with Rome and wrong in the second? And if so, what were the true criteria of wise policy – and of political morality? I have elsewhere[39] suggested that it was partly because of the far-reaching nature of these issues that Polybius developed the speeches delivered by Chlaeneas and Lyciscus at such length in his *Histories*.

Briefly their arguments were these. According to Chlaeneas[40] the Macedonians could make no reasonable claim at all on Greek loyalty or support. Philip II had crushed Chalcidice, the cities of Thrace, and Thessaly; his alleged generosity to Athens after Chaeronea was simply a trick to trap others; he had gone on to invade Laconia and had given away Spartan territory to Argos, Tegea and Megalopolis. Alexander had destroyed Thebes. Antipater had sent out his thugs to hunt down refugees. Cassander, Demetrius I and Antigonus Gonatas had held the Greeks in subjection by the aid of tyrannies and garrisons; and Doson had intervened merely to humiliate Sparta and || prevent her from securing hegemony in the Peloponnese. Finally, Philip V himself had committed impious outrages at Thermum and Messene.

To this Lyciscus[41] replies that Philip II was on the contrary the liberator of Thessaly from its tyrants and of Delphi from the Phocians; if he invaded Laconia, it was at the instigation of his allies, and all issues were referred to arbitration. Alexander, his successor, had destroyed the

[38] Polyb. i.1.5; repeated frequently (for references see Walbank, *Comm.* 1, ad loc.).
[39] Walbank (1965a) 17.   [40] Polyb. ix.28–31.   [41] Polyb. ix.32–9.

power of Persia and removed the wealth with which the Great King
had hitherto subsidised either Athens or Thebes against Sparta (an ingenious touch in a speech aiming to win Spartan support!). Next, after
a passage devoted to the misdeeds of the Aetolians, Lyciscus asks the
pertinent question: if we owe thanks to Aetolia for saving Delphi from
the barbarians, what do we owe to Macedonia, which has perpetually
protected the northern frontiers and so acted as a bulwark for Greece?
The catastrophe of Brennus' Galatian inroad was a proof of this, for it
only occurred following the death of Ptolemy Ceraunus. As for Philip V's
alleged impieties, they were merely a reply to Aetolian outrages at Dium
and Dodona; and the Spartans should remember Doson's benevolent
actions, for which they had hailed him benefactor and saviour. Furthermore, the situation had recently changed. Aetolia was now allied with
barbarians. This was no longer a conflict between men of the same
race, ὁμόφυλοι – Achaeans, Aetolians, and Macedonians – but Greece
was threatened by men of foreign race, ἀλλόφυλοι, who once victorious would enslave her. Perhaps at this point a digression is in order, to
draw attention to the fact that to Lyciscus, and probably to Polybius, the
Macedonians were ὁμόφυλοι with the Greeks. There is other evidence
pointing in the same direction. A Macedonian speaker in Livy,[42] who
is here following Polybius, speaks of 'Aetolas, Acarnanas, Macedonas,
eiusdem linguae homines' – though indeed speech and race are not
necessarily identical. The Romans[43] in contrast are *alienigenae*. In this
there is a change since the fourth century when some at least queried
the Macedonian claim to be accounted Greeks. Isocrates, for example,
says of the founder of the Macedonian kingdom – in a work devoted
to laudation of Philip II – 'μόνος γὰρ τῶν Ἑλλήνων οὐχ ὁμοφύλου
γένους ἄρχειν ἀξιώσας' and even Plutarch, perhaps steeped in earlier
traditions (or echoing Aratus' *Memoirs*), describes Aratus' recovery of the
Acrocorinth as an action carried out against an ἐπακτὸν ἀρχὴν ... καὶ
ἀλλόφυλον. But by the third century Macedonia no longer seemed for-
eign in the same way as Romans or Illyrians || – however welcome the
'liberation' by Flamininus. To return to Lyciscus – his final words are on
precisely this theme. Sparta has a great tradition of resisting barbarians,
shown in her refusal of earth and water to Xerxes and the heroic death
of Leonidas; she should not now make common cause with barbarians
against almost the whole of the Greeks (except for Aetolia).

In fact, Sparta joined Aetolia and Rome. The war followed its course
to the separate peace between Philip and Aetolia in 206 and the more

---

[42] Livy xxxi.29.15.   [43] Livy xxxi.29.12, 29.15.

comprehensive Peace of Phoenice in 205. In 200, for reasons which it would be irrelevant to pursue here, the Roman legions were back in Greece, and both the Aetolians and Achaeans had to make the decision whether to join in the war and if so on which side. For Aetolia only questions of expediency were involved: for forty years Aetolia and Macedonia had enjoyed unfriendly neutrality or open hostility. But for Achaea the issues debated at Sparta in 210 had now to be faced in circumstances in which Macedonia could offer little help and the Romans were more completely committed.

IV

The Achaeans postponed a decision for two years: but in October 198 the question was debated at a meeting held at Sicyon, where the Achaean general for 199/8, Aristaenus, a supporter of the Roman side, addressed a confused audience in terms of undisguised self-interest, appealing at once to their sense of self-preservation and to the obvious futility of continuing to support Philip. We have his speech only in Livy,[44] but it represents Polybius' original in substance.[45] The case it made was overwhelming, and Polybius himself has no doubts of its wisdom. 'If Aristaenus', he says,[46] 'had not at this time opportunely caused the Achaeans to leave their alliance with Philip and join that of Rome, clearly the nation would have been utterly ruined.' Nevertheless, so hard was the decision and so strong the ties binding certain cities, in particular Dyme, Megalopolis and Argos, to Macedonia, that despite the high-handed treatment which the Achaeans had at various times received from Philip, the representatives of the first two of these cities and certain of those from Argos rose and left the assembly rather than be a party to the desertion; and recognising their special ties of obligation towards Macedonia, the remainder showed neither surprise nor disapproval.[47] Moreover, || Argos went further. Shortly afterwards[48] she threw off her allegiance to the confederation and called in Philip's general, Philocles. Nor was Argos alone. Already the populace in Corinth had rallied to the Macedonians and resisted an attempt by an Achaean army to liberate the Acrocorinth, perhaps the most famous of the so-called 'fetters of Greece'.[49]

It is clear that despite self-interest Achaea was deeply torn by this decision; and it is significant that Polybius' judgement on it, which I have just

---

[44] Livy xxxii.19–21.   [45] Aymard (1938b) 91–2; cf. Lehmann (1967) 218 n.144.
[46] Polyb. xviii.13.8.   [47] Livy xxxii.22.8–12 (Polybian).
[48] Livy xxxii.25.1–12.   [49] Livy xxxii.23.3–13; Paus. vii.8.2; Zonar. ix.16; App. *Maced.* 7.

quoted, comes in a digression in Book XVIII on the subject of treachery.[50]
This passage has given rise to a great deal of controversy, since the context in which Polybius was led to discuss the subject is not clear from
the extract itself. We know[51] that at the conference held in Locris in
November 198 Philip reproached the Achaeans for their inconsistency
and ingratitude in abandoning him, and Schweighaeuser took the view[52]
that the digression on treachery sprang directly out of Polybius' discussion of the decision at Sicyon. Gabba[53] agreed with this, adding the
further suggestion that the reference to the fourth-century statesmen
accused by Demosthenes of treachery, who were in Polybius' eyes genuine patriots, was a hinted defence of Aratus, whom many Greeks had
accused of treachery to Achaea when he called in Antigonus Doson.[54]
I have pointed out elsewhere[55] that once Polybius has defined a traitor as
a man who calls in a foreign power and admits a foreign garrison,[56] the
conduct of Aratus so obviously falls under this heading that had Polybius
even had it in mind, he must have defended his hero from the charge
by more than tacit hints; it seems then more probable that the case of
Aratus never even crossed his mind. It is, however, clear that the case of
Aristaenus did, for, as we have seen, he refers specifically to Aristaenus'
action,[57] and it seems undeniable that its justification at this momentous
time was one important reason for this digression. On the other hand,
the digression was included in Book XVIII at a point after the conference in Locris, whereas Aristaenus' change of Achaean policy must have
been recorded in the lost Book XVII; || there was no reason why Polybius
should revert to it directly here.[58] There have been other suggested explanations of the digression which I need not consider; for the most likely
theory yet proposed is, I believe, that of Aymard, namely that the act of
treachery to which Polybius is primarily referring is that of the Argive
leaders who had seceded from Achaea and, as I have just mentioned,
had let Macedonian troops into their city. They met with speedy retribution when Philip, unable any longer to defend this now distant outpost,
handed them over to the tender mercies of Nabis of Sparta.

I should like to discuss this digression a little further, because it reveals
very clearly some of the ambiguities and inconsistencies which exist in

[50] Polyb. xviii.13–15; for discussion and bibliography of works dealing with this controversial passage
see Walbank, *Comm.* II, ad loc. [See now Eckstein (1987b), who offers a convincing defence of
Schweighaeuser's view.]
[51] Polyb. xviii.6.7.   [52] Schweighaeuser (1789–95) IV.29, VII.331.   [53] Gabba (1957) 34.
[54] Polyb. xviii.14.   [55] In Walbank, *Comm.* ad loc.   [56] Polyb. xviii.15.2.
[57] Polyb. xviii.13.8–10.   [58] Cf. Aymard (1967) 354–63.

Polybius' attitude and indeed the Achaean attitude towards Macedonia –
inconsistencies brought out vividly in Polybius' remark[59] that Aristaenus
was honoured for his policy ὡς εὐεργέτην καὶ σωτῆρα τῆς χώρας –
words directly recalling the cult-honours widely accorded to Antigonus
Doson after Sellasia! Throughout his discussion at this point Polybius
accepts the principle which can be briefly summed up in the phrase,
'circumstances alter cases'.[60] His criticism of Demosthenes, introduced
at this point, follows the same criterion as his discussion of treachery;
it is based on the principle of success. Because Demosthenes' policy
led to war with Macedonia and defeat for Athens, he is condemned
as responsible for his country's disasters; presumably Polybius was not
aware that the fallacy of *post hoc, propter hoc* implied in this argument had
already been exposed by Aristotle[61] in relation to this precise example of
Demosthenes and Macedonia. This is Polybius' first mistake – to think
that success is necessarily the only criterion of political action. On this
Pickard-Cambridge has some relevant remarks[62] in his book, *Demosthenes
and the Last Days of Greek Freedom*: 'If success is the true and only test of
statesmanship Polybius was undoubtedly right. But if political liberty
had proved itself so precious that without it the whole of life would have
seemed to be lived on a lower plane, success was an altogether unworthy
criterion by which to judge the actions of those who were dominated by
such a sentiment.'

But Polybius was at fault on yet a further point. He judges the issue
of resistance to Philip II not in terms of Greece, but against the narrow
interests || of his native Arcadia and Messenia – and misjudges it at that,
for the notion that after Leuctra Sparta still represented the main danger
to Greece is fallacious. Philip II, he remarks,[63] allowed all the inhabitants
of the Peloponnese 'to breathe freely and entertain the thought of liberty'
ἀναπνεῦσαι καὶ λαβεῖν ἐλευθερίας ἔννοιαν. The words are unfortunate,
for they are precisely the same as he had used three chapters earlier[64]
to describe the proposed liberation from these same Macedonian garrisons after Cynoscephalae; yet the occupation of Corinth and the other
bastions of Macedonian power in central Greece was the direct result of
Philip II's victory.

Polybius then can be charged with miscalculating the real threat to
Greece in 339: what of 198? The switch from Macedonia to Rome,
Aristaenus' policy, can be defended for Achaea if one does not take the

---

[59] Polyb. xviii.13.10; cf. v.9.10, ix.36.5; *IG* v.2.299.
[60] Cf. Polyb. xviii.13.11, κατὰ τὰς τῶν καιρῶν περιστάσεις.   [61] Arist. *Rhet.* ii.24.8, 1401b.
[62] Pickard-Cambridge (1914) 490–1.   [63] Polyb. xviii.14.6.   [64] Polyb. xviii.11.4, 11.6.

view that the Romans were out to dominate Greece. But, as it happens, Polybius believed that they were; and though in fact the Romans were to withdraw from the so-called 'fetters of Greece', the Acrocorinth, Chalcis, and Demetrias, by their services to the Greeks they had established a patron–client relationship which was in the long run to prove an even heavier burden on the land they had liberated than the Macedonian domination.

This discussion of treachery is not, then, one of Polybius' most successful incursions into political and moral theorising; and before leaving it I will simply mention yet one further inconsistency – that the bland assumption that Demosthenes is to be condemned for putting freedom before peace runs directly counter to Polybius' own criticisms, voiced elsewhere, of the Thebans[65] for their neutrality in the Persian War. For there he comments: 'Why do we all vaunt our civic equality and liberty of speech and all that we mean by the word freedom, if nothing is more advantageous than peace?'

v

I have pointed out that the issue of support for Macedonia or Rome was argued largely in terms of historical experience rather than in terms of Philip V's own policy and character. Nevertheless, Philip V occupies a very central position in Polybius' *Histories*. He is presented as the fine young king who suffers a μεταβολή and deteriorates.[66] In his early years he shows magnanimity || and mildness[67] – and a willingness to consult Achaean interests![68] He displays speed of movement,[69] strategical skill and determination,[70] and maturity of judgement.[71] But the bad influence of Demetrius of Pharos which lay behind his sinister intervention at Messene marked the beginning of a downward path,[72] and he soon reveals all the typical traits of the tyrant.[73] Polybius rejects the view common in antiquity that a man's qualities are inborn and that circumstances merely serve to bring them out. In a passage[74] which clearly echoes Stoic

---

[65] Cf. Polyb. iv.31.5.

[66] For Philip's μεταβολή see Polyb. iv.77.4, v.9.1–12.8, vii.11–14, viii.8.1–4, 12.1–8, ix.23.9, x.26.7–10.

[67] Polyb. iv.24.9, 27.9–10, 77.1–4.

[68] Cf. Polyb. iv.72.5–6 (Psophis handed over), 73.2 (Lasion handed over).   [69] Polyb. iv.71.

[70] Polyb. v.2.1–6.   [71] Polyb. iv.82.1, v.29.2.

[72] Polyb. v.9–12, 102.1, vii.11, viii.8.4, ix 22.9, xviii.33.6.   [73] Cf. Polyb. viii.12, x.26.7–8.

[74] Cf. Polyb. ix.22.9; for Stoic parallels see Diog. Laert. vii.89; Galen, *De Hipp. et Plat. plac.* v. p.462 (referring to Chrysippus; see Walbank, *Comm.* ad loc.). Von Fritz (1956) 103–6, would attribute the view to Aristotle; but see Walbank, *Comm.* ii on Polyb. x.26.7–10.

ideas and phraseology he emphasises the complexity of circumstances which sometimes leads men to dissemble and also the fact that men are often influenced by their friends. This was certainly true of Philip V, whose changes in behaviour are frequently linked with the influence of his favourites – Demetrius of Pharos, Aratus, and others.[75] In his case Polybius believes that the deterioration to be observed was due to a defect which Philip acquired in the course of his life through listening to bad advice;[76] to Polybius his inborn characteristics are merely one element among the influences to which in the course of life he was exposed.[77] Together these effect the change that was so apparent.

Polybius then was interested in Philip V because of the development of his character. But even more he was interested in him because he believed that this μεταβολή was an important factor in the process by which Fortune, *Tyche*, brought the whole Mediterranean world under the control of Rome. A central event in that process – an event which Polybius judges by moral criteria – was the pact entered into by Philip and Antiochus III of Syria to plunder the possessions of the child-king of Egypt, Ptolemy V.[78] For it was as the sequel to this nefarious plot that *Tyche* involved both kings in war with Rome and brought about the ruin of their dynasties, while re-establishing || that of Ptolemy. This process was of course an integral part of the operation by which *Tyche* made Rome mistress of the Mediterranean within a period of not quite fifty-three years, and an important aspect of it was the downfall of Philip V at Cynoscephalae and the dethronement of his son Perseus after Pydna in 168.

But the vengeance of *Tyche* on Philip for his treatment of Ptolemy V was not restricted to the destruction of his kingdom; it also involved the ruin of his own house, the murder of his younger son Demetrius and a career of terrorism which made him heartily loathed through-out Macedonia.[79] The Third Macedonian War, which was to effect the downfall of the Macedonian monarchy and so complete the programme organised by *Tyche*, was planned by Philip V (though waged by his successor). By the time Polybius came to write the history of this war he was already committed to a more or less Roman position, and after years spent in the household of Scipio Aemilianus he had come to identify himself with Roman attitudes and prejudices. His treatment of Perseus is free of the ambiguities that had attended his discussion of the switch

---

[75] Cf. Walbank (1940) 261–2.	[76] Cf. Polyb. vii.14.6, ix.22.10.	[77] Cf. Polyb. xvi.28.5–6.
[78] Cf. Polyb. xv.20. with Walbank, *Comm.* ad loc.	[79] Cf. Polyb. xxii.18, xxiii.10.

made by Achaea from Macedonia to Rome under the leadership of Aristaenus. To Polybius Perseus is the instrument of his father's policy. It is a policy which Polybius records with decided hostility; for although it marshalled a good deal of sympathy in Greece, it was a sympathy that Polybius did not share.

When the Boeotians gave their support to Macedonia, the Roman envoys used their influence to secure the arrest and suicide of pro-Macedonian partisans and the breaking up of the confederacy; Polybius, who has decided that political realism means the choice of Rome rather than Macedonia, condemns the Boeotians for 'rashly and inconsiderately espousing the cause of Perseus'.[80] Towards the pro-Macedonian party in Rhodes he is even more uncompromising; he attributes the political affiliations of their leaders Polyaratus and Deinon to their being in debt or else avaricious and unscrupulous,[81] he holds up their policy to abuse and contempt,[82] and he rails against the unfortunate Rhodians who had made the mistake of supporting Perseus for not having shown the courage or self-respect to commit suicide. In this chapter, which to a modern reader must appear as one of the most despicable Polybius ever wrote, he shows that he is first and foremost a political realist with no sympathy at all for the man who proves to have backed the wrong horse. || Just as he regards Demosthenes as responsible for the ills that befell Athens[83] because his policy of resistance to Philip failed, so too with these contemporary Greeks who did not share his own worldly wisdom in supporting Rome. Common to both situations is the fact that Polybius' judgement is delivered *ex eventu*. One must however be clear: Polybius was not a Quisling. His harsh criticism of Callicrates[84] and his careful analysis of the difference between the policies of Philopoemen and Aristaenus[85] show this clearly enough. But he could see no future, but only catastrophe for Greece in the marshalling of support for Perseus of Macedonia. In this he may well have been right; but his percipience is no excuse for the unmitigated contempt which he expresses for those who took a different view.

As Polybius himself tells us, there were many who criticised Rome at this time. Passing judgement on the extinction of the kingdom of Macedonia and the dethroning of Perseus some Greeks, he records,[86] argued that 'far from maintaining the principles by which they had won their supremacy, the Romans were gradually deserting these through a lust for domination like that of Athens and Sparta'; and the treatment

---

[80] Polyb. xxvii.2.10.   [81] Polyb. xxvii.7.12.   [82] Polyb. xxix.10–11, 19.
[83] See above, pp. 92 and 96.   [84] Cf. Polyb. xxiv.8–13.   [85] Ibid.   [86] Polyb. xxxvi.9.7.

of Perseus in 168 represented the prelude to a policy which was to find
its conclusion in the wanton destruction of Carthage twenty years later.
Polybius records these views without expressing his own attitude towards
them; but it seems likely, judging from a passage in Diodorus which
appears to be derived from Polybius,[87] that he approved of terrorism
in punishing rebels as a salutary deterrent. For by now, whether from
proximity to influential circles in Rome or because the theme of his own
history had, as it were, led him to identify himself with the rise of Rome
to world power, Polybius could find neither sympathy nor understanding
for those who differed or failed.

VI

The division of the old kingdom of Macedonia into four republican
states never found favour with its inhabitants;[88] they quarrelled among
themselves because, says Polybius,[89] 'they were unaccustomed to democratic and representative government' ἀήθεις ὄντας δημοκρατικῆς καὶ
συνεδριακῆς πολιτείας. ‖ They preferred of course the more primitive institutions of their own monarchy and the Macedonian people at
arms. Consequently the episode of Andriscus, of the pseudo-Philip fallen
down from heaven, who captured the credulous allegiance of the people throughout Macedonia, defeated the Macedonian armies and was
soon master of the whole country, is simply an incredible story, utterly
improbable and explicable only as a case of heaven-sent infatuation
(δαιμονοβλάβεια), a clear indication of divine wrath. For, he explains,
Macedonia had met with many signal favours from Rome; the country
had been delivered from the arbitrary rule and taxation of autocrats and
now enjoyed freedom in place of servitude, and an end to civil discord
and internecine massacres. Yet its people now gave willing support to
this pretender who exiled, tortured, and murdered them.[90] Polybius, with
his background in Achaean democracy and the orderly processes of the
Roman imperial republic, fails to conceive the enthusiasm which anyone
could inspire, once he had persuaded the simple people of Macedonia
that he was bringing back their ancient monarchy.

As a military man Polybius could not fail to recognise the merits of the
Macedonians as soldiers;[91] and he pays tribute to the great Macedonian

---

[87] Diod. xxxii.2. [Against the Polybian origin of this passage see now Walbank (1974) 18–21]
[88] On this see, however, the contribution of Dr Pierre L. Mackay to the proceedings of this Congress.
(Mackay (1970)).
[89] Polyb. xxxi.2.12.   [90] Polyb. xxxvi.17.13–15.   [91] Cf. Polyb. v.2.1–6, 4.6; cf. iv.69.3–6.

military formation, the phalanx, though he is bound to point out the superior qualities of the Roman legion.[92] But he never shows any sign of *understanding* the things that really mattered to a Macedonian, he judges Macedonian policy invariably in terms of Achaean advantage, and his attitude towards the Macedonian monarchy is ambivalent and contradictory – largely because he cannot shake loose from his Achaean prejudices, and because the switches in Achaean policy towards Macedonia, which are based on self-interest, have to be justified in the more pompous and reputable vocabulary of political morality. The Achaeans are scarcely to be blamed for expelling the Macedonians from their towns when the occasion arose, for recalling them when the threat from Sparta made this move inescapable, and for abandoning their allegiance to the king of Macedonia for Rome when Philip seemed no longer capable of providing Achaea with security. But in the circumstances it would perhaps have been wiser had Polybius not embarked on a digression on the nature of treachery and not become involved in polemic against Demosthenes for leading the coalition that crashed at Chaeronea. The contradictions in which Polybius landed himself in these passages are little to his credit; but they are, in their own context, typical of the general plight of his ‖ countrymen after the time of Philip II. It was the misfortune of the Hellenistic Greeks that they could unite successfully neither under nor against Macedonia, and that the motives which led Greeks to fight as mercenaries in the armies of Darius Codomannus survived to line them up, a century later, on both sides in the Roman–Macedonian wars. The equivocations and self-righteousness of Polybius on the one hand, and on the other his careful account of the detailed shifts in policy which add up to create the overall pattern as Rome succeeds Macedonia as the dominant power, together illustrate both the Greek dilemma and the strengths and weaknesses of the Achaean historian.

[92] Polyb. xviii.29.1–30.4.

7

Sea-power and the Antigonids*

I

An anecdote recorded by Phylarchus[1] relates how Patroclus, who is known from other sources as the admiral of Ptolemy II at the time of the Chremonidean War,[2] once sent a present of large fish and green figs to Antigonus Gonatas 'as a hint at what would happen to him, just as the Scythians did to Darius when he was invading their country. For the Scythians, Herodotus tells us, sent a bird, an arrow || and a frog.'[3] Antigonus was quick to solve the riddle: 'either we must be masters of the sea (θαλασσοκρατεῖν) or else we must eat figs', that is, go short of food.[4] But was the choice a real one? The answer to that question depends on whether Patroclus' point was a general one – that Macedon must be a sea-power or starve – or a particular one, in the sense that at the time of the incident Antigonus had for instance got himself caught in an awkward situation without access to supplies of food. Oddly enough, some sixty years later his grandson Philip V was to find himself in that very plight. Confined within the Gulf of Bargylia in Caria and unable for several months to make an easy getaway through the Rhodian and Pergamene fleets, he was compelled to furnish an illustration of Patroclus' riddle by feeding his troops throughout the winter of 201/200 largely on figs provided by the Seleucid general Zeuxis and by Greek cities like Magnesia which were short of corn.[5] It is not unlikely that it was in some such situation that Patroclus sent his riddling message; and by comparing it to the one the Scythians sent to Darius, Phylarchus may

---

* [[W. L. Adams and E. N. Borza (eds.) *Philip II, Alexander the Great and the Macedonian Heritage* (Washington, DC, 1982) 213–36. This book was dedicated to the memory of Henry J. Dell (1933–1981).]]

[1] Ath. viii.334A; *FGH* 81 F 1; cf. Heinen (1972a) 191–2.
[2] See H. Volkmann s. v. 'Patroklos' (2), *Kl. Pauly* 4 (1975) 558–9.
[3] Hdt. iv.131, where this riddle is elucidated: a mouse was also included in the gift, but omitted by Athenaeus.
[4] So rightly Tarn (1933) 68.   [5] Polyb. xvi.24.5 (= Ath. iii.78e–f).

be implying that Antigonus too was engaged in aggression, in this case against the Ptolemaic empire. Without knowing more of the context of the anecdote – which certainly implied a challenge to a naval battle, and equally implied that when it was fought Antigonus was the victor – one cannot however be sure of this. On the whole, a limited context for the challenge rather than a more general statement about Macedonian sea-power seems the more likely. Nevertheless the story raises in a sharp form the question of how important sea-power was to Antigonid Macedonia, and I offer a brief discussion of this question as a tribute to the memory of a friend and a colleague much of whose own published work was concerned with Macedonia and with naval matters.

The word θαλασσοκρατεῖν is probably not to be taken in a very wide sense. Patroclus was simply challenging Antigonus to meet him at sea: the verb would apply to whichever won. As Tarn observed,[6] thalassocracy has a limited meaning in Hellenistic times; until the Romans came on the scene no one power controlled more than a part of the Mediterranean, and even within a limited area the word || merely implied the ability to meet a challenge (such as Patroclus was making to Antigonus) rather than to exercise a permanent control of the seas and police them. Short of even that restricted kind of thalassocracy there were, of course, many reasons why a state might need to possess ships for certain defined needs, and the question to be asked in connection with Macedonia is to what extent the Antigonids were content to restrict their naval activity to such limited ends – or whether they in fact chose to build up a fleet to expand their power; and if they did, whether that was to the advantage or disadvantage of Macedonia. One must distinguish Macedonia from the dynasty controlling it, because until Antigonus Gonatas made himself master of Macedonia naval power was self-evidently of more vital importance to the Antigonids than it was later.

For Antigonus I, facing a coalition of Ptolemy, Cassander and Lysimachus, a strong fleet was essential to drive a wedge between his opponents, to debar Cassander from access to Greece proper and to secure his own position there. The League of the Islanders, a Macedonian creation (though it was later to be taken over by the Ptolemies),[7] served to reinforce Antigonid power in the Aegean; and Demetrius Poliorcetes affirmed his mastery of eastern Mediterranean waters by his decisive victory over the Ptolemaic fleet off Salamis in Cyprus in 306 BC.[8] Demetrius continued to dominate the eastern Mediterranean even

[6] Tarn (1913) 79–80.   [7] Will (1979) 58.
[8] Diod. xx.47–52; Just. *Epit.* xv.2.6–9; Plut. *Dem.* 15–16; App. *Syr.* 54; Will (1979) 73.

after the defeat and death of his father Antigonus at Ipsus in 301. As king of Macedonia between 294 and 288 he possessed perhaps 300 ships and in 289 he planned to build a further 500 in various shipyards.[9] Even after losing most of these (the ones being built at Pella) to Pyrrhus, he still retained a substantial navy, and it was primarily the desertion of Philocles, the king of Sidon, from his cause that put an end to his naval preponderance.[10]

Until he gained Macedonia Antigonus Gonatas was in a similar position. A fleet was essential to link together his scattered possessions, Corinth, Piraeus and Euboea, and his control of such a fleet is || attested for 283 or 282, when he sailed to meet Seleucus in order to receive his father's ashes.[11] Though he was defeated at sea in 281 by Ptolemy Ceraunus, who had taken over Lysimachus' fleet,[12] his ships, drawn up on shore as a bait to the enemy, played an important part in his victory over the Galatians near Lysimacheia, which led to his final conquest of Macedonia.[13] How big his fleet was at this time is unknown.

II

As king of Macedonia Antigonus was now established with a land base and naval power no longer of such fundamental importance. Macedonia was largely self-supporting and so was not normally concerned with the policing of vital corn-routes which played so large a rôle in Athenian history. Included within the boundaries of Macedonia in Hellenistic times were some of the richest corn-producing lands in Greece, and Macedonia was an exporter of grain.[14] This is attested from Delos, where honours were voted to Demetrius II's σιτώνης, Aristobulus, and to Admetus, both citizens of Salonica and the latter probably a private business-man;[15] and in 227, when following a devastating earthquake at Rhodes, there were many royal gifts to the city, those from the royal house

---

[9] Plut. *Dem.* 43; Tarn (1913) 83.

[10] It was not, as Tarn (1913) 80 supposed, by virtue of his naval preponderance that Demetrius was able to cross over to Asia unchallenged in 287, for it is now known that a peace had already been concluded with Egypt; see Habicht (1979) 62, 63, n. 79.

[11] Plut. *Dem.* 52–3.

[12] Memnon *FGH* 434 F 8 (13); Just. *Epit.* xxiv.1.8: cf. Heinen (1972a) 65–6 (on the date and the site), 190.

[13] *Syll.* 401; Just. *Epit.* xxv.2.6; Trogus *Prol.* 25; Diog. Laert. ii.141; Heinen (1972a) 190.

[14] For Macedonian prosperity in Hellenistic times see Rostovtzeff (1941) i,251–3. According to Jardé (1925) 203, in 1921 41.33 percent of the area of Macedonia was given over to wheat and 23.48 per cent to barley; the yield per hectare of wheat was the highest in Greece except for Arcadia. Similar figures are given in the British Admiralty Geographical Handbook *Greece* ii (1944) 58–60.

[15] *IG* xi 4, 666 (Aristobulus); 664, 665, 1053 (Admetus).

of Macedonia included 100,000 medimni of corn donated by Chryseis, the wife of Antigonus Doson, and probably grown on the royal estates.[16] This does not of course exclude the occasional need of imported corn, especially at times when a full mobilisation might interfere with production. In 168, for example, after three years warfare against the Romans and the loss to them of the rich corn-growing plains of Thessaly, Perseus had to send out a fleet to Tenedos *ut inde sparsas per ‖ Cycladas insulas naues, Macedoniam cum frumento petentes, tutarentur.*[17] But in general the continuing need for a fleet rested mainly on political rather than economic grounds.

It was of course still essential to maintain communications with the military outposts in Greece. But the danger confronting Macedonia from the other major powers was limited and can easily be assessed. Either just before or just after the victory at Lysimacheia Antigonus Gonatas had made a peace with Antiochus I, Seleucus' successor in Asia, which was to last for many decades.[18] In fact, there was never to be any real threat to Macedonia from a Seleucid king again (for though Antiochus III invaded Europe, there is no reason to think that his plans included the invasion of Macedonia).

Later in the third century and still more in the second Pergamum was to become the leading power in western Anatolia and its rulers were persistent enemies of the Antigonids; but as yet the power of Pergamum still lay in the future. The other kingdoms of Asia Minor were small powers and no threat to Antigonus. Indeed for some time his main rival was Ptolemy II Philadelphus. Ptolemy II's foreign policy has aroused considerable controversy. According to Polybius,[19] it was based on the possession of Coele-Syria and Cyprus, on the exercising of strong pressure on the dynasts of Asia Minor and on the control, through the Egyptian fleet, of the islands and the main cities, strongpoints and harbours on the Asia Minor coast from Pamphylia to the Hellespont, together with a number of places like Aenus and Maronea on the European coast which enabled Ptolemy to keep watch over Thrace and Macedonia; but in Polybius' opinion this 'fence of client states' was designed to protect Egypt and was defensively conceived. In short, like his father, Ptolemy II did not aim at attacking Macedonia. In this passage Polybius perhaps over-simplifies the situation. Ptolemy was clearly not above fishing in troubled waters, especially in Greece, where he had a footing at Methone in the Argolid,

---

[16] Polyb. v.89.7.   [17] Livy xliv. 28.1–2.

[18] Just. *Epit.* xxv.1.1; cf. Will (1979) 109. Justinus dates the reconciliation before the battle of Lysimacheia, but that is by no means certain.

[19] Polyb. v.34.2–9.

and where he was always ready to cause embarrassment to the Macedonians. Still, there is a *prima facie* case for thinking that Egypt represented a danger of very limited proportions to Macedonia and that the construction of anything more than the small naval force needed to secure communications and the || safe passage of men and materials between Macedonia and the strongpoints of southern Greece can be taken as evidence of a more forward policy on the part of the Antigonids themselves. In short, with the Seleucids occupied in Asia and the Ptolemies interested primarily in protecting Egypt by means of their outposts in Greece, Anatolia and the Aegean, any breach of the equilibrium was likely to come from Macedonia.

Family traditions were not against that assumption. It was a belief in Greece (attested by Polybius writing in the second century)[20] that the Antigonid house had always cherished ambitions for universal dominion. Certainly Antigonus I had fought tenaciously to maintain the unity (and the control) of Alexander's empire; and Demetrius I had used his powerful fleet to the same end, though with diminishing hope of success. For their descendants any such ambitions are harder to believe in. But the persistence of the tradition indicates that the Antigonids were at any rate not regarded as pursuing a defensive policy.

Evidence for the reign of Antigonus II is still most inadequate. Three events are relevant to the present enquiry: the Chremonidean War and the battles of Cos and Andros. The real causes of the Chremonidean War remain uncertain.[21] It has generally been thought that it was provoked by Ptolemy II, and discussion has concentrated on his motives. But the help which he gave to Athens and Sparta was meagre, and Habicht has recently argued[22] that he was drawn in reluctantly by the Athenians, who took the initiative as the main instigators of the war. It is hard to assess Ptolemy's degree of commitment in Greece so long as we are ignorant of what he had to face elsewhere. His admiral Patroclus was active in Ceos, at Itanus in Crete and at Thera, and he landed some troops at Rhamnus in Attica.[23] Otherwise the Ptolemaic contribution was slight. This can be explained (on Habicht's theory) as due to lack of interest in a war he had not sought. Yet the alliances between Ptolemy and Athens and between Ptolemy and Sparta both preceded the Spartan–Athenian || alliance which led to the war,[24] and it is therefore hard to believe that that alliance was not encouraged, if not sponsored, by Ptolemy; in which

---

[20] Polyb. xv.24.6: cf. v.102.1. [See below, chapter 8.]   [21] See Heinen (1972a) 189–97.
[22] See Habicht (1979) 95–112.   [23] See Heinen (1972a) 142–52; Will (1979) 226.
[24] *SVA* 476; Heinen (1981), reviewing Habicht (1979).

case he was presumably behind the war. Will has argued plausibly that he was provoked into promoting the war by Gonatas' decision to build a fleet and that the Chremonidean War was therefore the Ptolemaic reply to a new phase of Macedonian expansion.[25]

What in fact is known of Macedonian naval activity at this time? On the whole very little. According to Pausanias,[26] Antigonus moved on Athens πεζῷ τε καὶ ναυσίν. Tarn argued[27] that these ships were transports; but elsewhere Pausanias asserts[28] that Antigonus shut off the Athenians from the sea, and despite Tarn's rejection of this statement it could well be true, implying the presence of warships off Attica.[29] The size of Gonatas' fleet is unknown. Heinen quotes[30] Beloch and Will for the view that 'at the beginning of the Chremonidean War the Macedonian fleet was numerically weak'; but Will in fact asserts that only for 272, and his view of what caused the war implies that since then Antigonus had been building new ships. If so, one must suppose that most of these were active elsewhere, not to have left a greater impression on the tradition. They may have been operating somewhere off Asia Minor, as they must have been shortly afterwards when the battle of Cos was fought (see below). Unhappily these are decades for which evidence is still scanty. That some Macedonian ships were active off Attica is suggested by the fact that Athens had serious food problems, as we know from an inscription from Rhamnus,[31] containing a decree honouring the *strategos* Epichares for getting in the grain. This inscription also reveals the fact that Gonatas employed pirates against Athens, but this does not exclude the use of Macedonian ships as || well. The use of pirates was a well-established practice with the Antigonid dynasty as a way of contracting out (for one reason or another) some of one's military obligations. Examples are the Glaucetas who operated under Antigonus I and was captured by the Athenian Thymochares of Sphettus in 315/14,[32] Timocles who fought against Rhodes in the interest of Demetrius I and was captured by the Rhodians in 304,[33] and Ameinias, a Phocian 'archpirate' who had earlier helped Antigonus Gonatas himself to take Cassandreia.[34] Later, in

[25] Will (1979) 219–21.   [26] Paus. iii.6.4.   [27] Tarn (1913) 300.
[28] Paus. i.1.1 ναυσὶν ἅμα ἐκ θαλάσσης κατεῖργεν.
[29] Heinen (1972a) 190 n. 303, who observes that κατεῖργεν could also mean 'he threatened them'.
[30] Heinen (1972a) 190 n. 301, quoting Beloch (1925) 587 and Will (1979).
[31] *SEG* xxiv, 154; cf. Heinen (1972a) 152–9.   [32] *Syll.* 409, lines 10–14.
[33] Diod. xx.97.5. In 302 Demetrius employed a large force of 'light-armed troops' and 'pirates' on land against Cassander (Diod. xx.110.4), but these were perhaps freebooters.
[34] Polyaen. *Strat.* iv.6.18; he was later in Antigonus' regular service and helped save Sparta from Pyrrhus (Plut. *Pyrrh.* 29.6).

205 or 204, Philip V was likewise to employ the Aetolian pirate Dicaearchus to plunder the Aegean islands and cities of the Troad and to help the Cretans against Rhodes.[35] The custom was not of course confined to the Antigonids.[36] There is therefore some, but not a great deal, of evidence for Macedonian naval activity in Greece at this time.[37]

The question cannot, however, be left without some mention of the battles of Cos and Andros. A new treatment of this ancient crux is promised by H. Heinen, who has already discussed Cos in a recent work.[38] Here I need say only that on present evidence the most likely context for the naval battle of Cos, in which an Antigonus (probably Gonatas) won a victory over the Egyptian fleet, which he commemorated with the dedication of his flag-ship to Delian Apollo,[39] is in my view the end of the Chremonidean War. It most likely occurred in the spring of 261, since it must have followed the capitulation of Athens (where Gonatas received congratulations on his victory) but will have preceded the setting up of an inscription at Delos in the archonship of Tharsynon (261) which refers to peace existing in the Aegean.[40] It || was perhaps followed immediately by the Macedonian attack on Miletus known from an inscription from that city.[41] If this dating is correct[42] – and it cannot be regarded as certain – it follows that by this time Macedon possessed a powerful fleet.

When that fleet was built is less certain. Tarn, who dated Cos to the Second Syrian War and (probably) 258,[43] believed that it was not built until well after the Chremonidean War was over. But that war provides the only likely context for a clash with Ptolemy, since there is no evidence at all that Antigonus was involved in the Second Syrian War. (As for Tarn's belief that Gonatas was inspired to build a fleet by the news that 'a great

[35] Polyb. xviii.54.8; Diod. xxviii.1; see below p. 120.

[36] See for example Tarn (1913) 86; Ormerod (1924) 122–4, 126. [See now de Souza (1999) 43–96.]

[37] Tarn (1913) 300 quotes Livy xxxv.26.5 as evidence for Macedonian naval weakness at the time of the Chremonidean War; see against this Heinen (1972a) 192–3.

[38] Heinen (1972a) 193–7. [See now, however, Hammond and Walbank (1988) Appendix 4, 'The battles of Cos and Andros', 587–600, where I date Cos early in 255 and Andros probably early in 245, both being Macedonian victories.]

[39] Plut. *De seipsum laudando* 16; *Apophth. reg.* 183C; Ath. v.209E; the story told here is associated with the battle of Andros in Plut. *Pel.* 2.4.

[40] *IG* xi.2, 114.   [41] A. Rehm in Wiegand (1914) 3 n. 139 = Welles (1934) 71–7, no. 14.

[42] If, as seems likely, Plut. *Quaest. conv.* 676D, with its story of parsley springing spontaneously out of a ship's prow, refers to Antigonus' flagship at Cos, its name was *Isthmia;* according to Moschion (Ath. 5.209E) it was dedicated to Apollo. Plutarch's story need not imply that the battle was fought in a year of the Isthmian games (i.e., one with an even number in the Julian calendar) as argued by Will (1979) 225 and by Tarn (1928) 862. As Tarn had himself suggested earlier (1910), the ship could have been built at Corinth and so named as a compliment to that city.

[43] Tarn (1928) 862–3; earlier ((1913) 461–6) he had made it 246.

landpower, by the adoption of a few simple expedients, had taken to the water with instantaneous and overwhelming success',[44] surely the son of Demetrius Poliorcetes did not need the Roman performance in the First Punic War to teach him lessons in naval warfare.) If Cos was in 261, there had been plenty of time since the outbreak of war in 268 to build a fleet; all the materials were to hand in Macedonia and could easily be transported to Demetrias or Corinth. Indeed, if we accept Will's view concerning the origin of the war, the fleet was already built or being built before 268, since it was this that provoked Ptolemy to war. Nearer than that we cannot get. Nor does it help to bring the obscure battle of Andros into the picture.[45] Its date is uncertain; and indeed the Antigonus involved in it could as well be Doson as Gonatas.

The results of Cos were less important than has often been || supposed.[46] It was the fall of Athens rather than the naval encounter that brought Gonatas his main advantage from the war. Moreover, though Cos was a Macedonian victory, it did not displace Ptolemy from his position as dominant naval power in the Aegean and eastern Mediterranean. The evidence adduced by those who believe it did is indecisive or, in some cases, misinterpreted. Delos, it has been pointed out, was at this time the recipient of Antigonid dedications;[47] but it is now generally agreed that no political conclusions are to be drawn from such dedications, which possess a purely religious and social significance.[48] That Egypt continued to dominate the Aegean is clear from the continued existence of the League of Islanders at least until the Second Syrian War; and this view receives some support from the evidence of the Alexandrian historian Appian, who tells us that at the time of Ptolemy II's death in 246 the royal register recorded a substantial Egyptian war-fleet in commission.[49] The possibility is not to be ruled out that Antigonus acquired control of certain islands. Several inscriptions from Syros, Ios, Amorgos, Cimolos and Cos mention a King Antigonus as influential there; and a similar

---

[44] Tarn (1913) 342.
[45] Trogus, *Prol.* 27; Plut. *Pel.* 2.4. The relevance of *P. Haun.* 1, 6 (cf. Momigliano and Fraser (1950) 107–18) is doubtful. For possible dates of the battle see Will (1979) 237–8. [See also above, n.38.]
[46] See Will (1979) 231–2, 239. For the view that Cos led to a Macedonian control of the Cyclades see Durrbach (1921) 42; Tarn (1928) 713; Huss (1976) 215 n. 288.
[47] Antigonus founded the *Antigoneia* and the *Stratoniceia* (named after Stratonice, the bride of his son Demetrius) in 253; cf. *IG* xi.2, 287 b lines 124–5.
[48] Cf. Fraser (1960) 4–5; Bruneau (1970) 579–80; and more generally Robert (1936) 18 n. 1; Will (1979) 232–3. For an interesting passage showing the strictness with which Delian neutrality was observed see Livy xliv.29.1–2.
[49] App. *praef.* 10. A papyrus (*SB* 9215) refers to the building of new warships by Ptolemy II early in 250; cf. Huss (1976) 216 n. 288.

inscription without a king's name visible comes from Ceos.[50] But until it is clear whether the Antigonus in question is Gonatas or Doson, one may not use these as proof of a Macedonian thalassocracy in the Aegean at this time. New evidence may bring more light to an area and a period of great obscurity. But so far there is nothing to indicate that the victory at Cos brought substantial naval advantages to Antigonus Gonatas. During the next decade his interest was directed rather to central Greece and the Peloponnese, || where his main concerns lay; and it was here in about 249 that he sustained a serious blow when Alexander, who had succeeded his father Craterus, Antigonus' half-brother, as governor of Corinth, declared himself independent, thus depriving his uncle of two vital naval bases and garrison towns, Chalcis and Corinth. Piraeus fortunately continued loyal to Antigonus under an independent command and of course maintained its sea links with Macedonia; but we hear of no large-scale naval operations for the rest of Gonatas' reign.

If Will is right, Antigonus precipitated the Chremonidean War by building a fleet. His purpose in building it can only have been to challenge Egypt, as indeed he did at Cos. If Habicht is right (and for the reasons already indicated this seems less likely) the Chremonidean War was forced on a reluctant Macedonia and a reluctant Egypt by the enthusiasm of Athenian patriots. In that case Gonatas built his fleet in response to the revolt, and his main purpose was to subdue Athens and to restore the *status quo*. In either case, however, the results were unimpressive and brought no positive gain to Macedonia.

III

Gonatas' successor, Demetrius II, succeeded him in 239 and reigned for ten years. There is no evidence of naval activity throughout his reign; and though the alliance which he made with Gortyn and Crete[51] might seem to indicate a widening of political interest beyond Greece proper, it is probably mainly concerned (like the similar treaties made by his successor Antigonus III with Eleutherna and Hierapytna)[52] with raising useful light-armed troops either as allies or as mercenaries. In the main Demetrius was kept busy in central Greece by his war against the

---

[50] *IG* xi.4, 1052 (Syros); xii.5, 1008 (Ios); xii.7, 221–3 (Amorgos); *SGDI* 3611 (Cos); Jacobson and Smith (1968) (Cimolos); *IG* xi.5, 570 (Ceos).

[51] *SVA* 498.

[52] *SVA* 501, 502. That these belong to Doson is conjectural. Huss (1976) 139–42 reverts to the view that the Antigonus of these inscriptions is Gonatas, but his arguments fall short of being decisive.

Achaean and Aetolian Leagues; but obviously he must have maintained his sea connections with Euboea and Chalcis (which Gonatas had recovered along with Corinth in 245)[53] and with Athens. It was a reign in which Macedonia was mostly on the defensive.

His son Philip was a child when Demetrius died; and the || succession went to Antigonus Doson, his cousin. Doson's reign interests our present enquiry on account of an expedition which was long regarded with scepticism, but is now too firmly attested to be dismissed as imaginary. Antigonus' naval expedition against Caria in south-west Asia Minor[54] took place in 227 after he had re-established the Macedonian hold on Thessaly, which had been largely overrun by the Aetolians on the death of Demetrius. It was clearly a reaffirmation of Macedonian naval interests for the first time since the reign of Antigonus II. Trogus asserts that Doson conquered Caria; and a Rhodian arbitration between Samos and Priene, recorded on an inscription from Priene, shows that city accepting Macedonian authority, and mentions both Antigonus and the 'heir to the throne, Phi . . . ' (who must be Philip). Another inscription from a dossier concerning a local Carian dynast, Olympichus, mentions Antigonus' presence in Mylasa. Thus the effects of the expedition were fairly widespread. But it is not clear at whose expense the gains were made. There is no evidence that Ptolemy was the enemy (unless the battle of Andros took place now);[55] more probably Antigonus had seized opportunities presented in Caria following the defeat of Antiochus Hierax by Attalus I of Pergamum – both had been interested in Caria – to reaffirm an Antigonid concern with Asia Minor which went back to Monophthalmus and Poliorcetes. Just how Attalus came into the picture is not clear. Antigonus' gains may have been partly to his detriment or, more probably, given the distance between Pergamum and Caria, made in collusion with him. If that is so, the Carian expedition would be the first break between Macedonia and the Seleucids since the beginning of the reign of Antigonus Gonatas, though Doson could fairly have || claimed that he was setting foot in areas which had already escaped from

53 He had lost Corinth again, to Aratus and the Achaeans, in 243.

54 Trogus, *Prol.* 28; Polyb. xx.5.7–11; Hiller von Gaertringen (1906) no. 37 lines 136–7; Crampa (1969) no. 7, line 12 (presence of Doson in Mylasa). Cf. Walbank, I, 621–2; II, 645; III, 70–1.

55 Above n. 45. W. Otto s. v. 'Hippomedon', *RE* 8 (1913) 1885–7, argued that in the course of Doson's expedition an attack was made on the Ptolemaic island of Samothrace; but the enemy mentioned in *Syll.* 502, like the one in the inscription published by A. Bakalakis and R. L. Scranton in *AJP* 60 (1939) 452–8, is not Antigonus Doson but barbarians from the mainland (either Thracians or Gauls from Tylis) (cf. Rostovtzeff and Welles (1940) 207–8; Rostovtzeff (1941) III, 1645), nor has that inscription anything to do with the Carian expedition. On the expedition see Walbank, *Comm.* III, 70–1. [Walbank in Hammond and Walbank (1988) 343–5.]

legitimate Seleucid control. The size and composition of Antigonus' fleet is not known, nor yet its origin. It can hardly be an inheritance from his predecessor, for there had been, so far as we know, a gap of about thirty years since the last (recorded) major naval activity, the battle of Cos. So probably Doson had built the ships, at Demetrias or Cassandreia, in the winter of 228/7; we know from Polybius[56] that they sailed south through the Euripus (where they temporarily ran aground) before crossing the Aegean. On their financing we have no information. The real scope of Antigonus' ambitions cannot however be assessed, since unexpected developments in the Peloponnese gave him an opportunity to recover Corinth from the Achaeans, and he abandoned his Carian plans, leaving an area under loose Macedonian control for his successor Philip V, who acceded in 221. This control lasted (to our knowledge) until the third year of Philip's reign, but thereafter there is a gap in our records until Philip resumed an Asiatic policy in the final years of the century. The Carian expedition is perhaps to be regarded as a quick response to an opportunity presented by events across the Aegean. It accorded with the traditions of the dynasty; and in addition such a demonstration may have proved very useful to a king who was something of a stop-gap (the obvious heir being still a child) and who had taken over a kingdom which was militarily at a low ebb.

IV

It is unlikely that a substantial Macedonian war-fleet remained in commission after the Carian expedition. During the first few years of his reign Philip V was involved, as a leader of a new Hellenic alliance created by Antigonus Doson, in a war against Aetolia and her allies, and he needed ships mainly for communication with and inside Greece. From the outset he showed himself awake to the importance of the sea for this purpose. A campaign in Ambracia and Acarnania in 219 culminated in the seizure of Oeniadae, an excellent naval base for operations against either Aetolia or the Peloponnese; and in 218 he planned a new programme of naval action, partly under the influence of the Illyrian, Demetrius of Pharos, who had joined him in flight from the Romans the previous summer. But this remained on a rather small scale. Philip mustered his fleet from old vessels already available and amounting in all to no more than twelve decked ships ‖ and forty light craft.[57] They were

[56] Polyb. xx.5.7.
[57] Cf. Holleaux (1921) 158 n. 6, 159 n. 1; Walbank (1940) 51.

to be used for the transportation of troops between various points in the west of Greece, from Lechaeum to Patrae and thence to Cephallenia. In fact, in a war against Elis, Sparta and Aetolia, the only real function for naval craft was to facilitate quick movement and to drive a wedge between these enemy states.

The first signs of a more ambitious naval policy came in the winter of 217, when Philip built a new fleet of 100 *lembi* at Demetrias using Illyrian shipwrights.[58] These *lembi* were light craft, much used by the Illyrians on piratical expeditions;[59] they were quick-moving and could carry each at least fifty men – more, if necessary.[60] 'Philip', says Polybius,[61] 'was about the first king of Macedonia to build such a fleet', evidently in reference to the type of ship rather than the numbers. The war with Aetolia was now over, and Philip's purpose was first to attack Scerdilaidas in Illyria and then perhaps the Roman 'allies' on the Adriatic coast and on the islands off Epirus and Illyria; later, we are told, he proposed to invade Italy.[62] But the sudden approach of a Roman squadron of a mere ten ships from Sicily caused him to beat a hasty retreat to the Aegean; and two years later, in 214, having conveyed a force of 6,000 men to Oricum in 120 *lembi*, he was trapped by the Roman commander Laevinus in the river Aous and forced to burn all his ships and retreat overland to Macedonia.[63] The whole enterprise had collapsed disastrously, the reason evidently being that Philip was banking on his Carthaginian allies organising a diversion against Laevinus, which never in fact took place. ||

These incidents and his treaty with Hannibal (215) had brought Philip into open collision with the Romans. Any plans to invade Italy (if indeed they were ever seriously conceived) now quickly disappeared with the loss of his fleet. It is unnecessary to follow the details of the First Macedonian War. Philip now had to abandon the western waters to Laevinus and very soon found himself under pressure from the combined Roman and Pergamene fleets. In 209 we find him borrowing five Achaean ships in the hope of making contact with Bomilcar, the Punic admiral – who failed to turn up;[64] and the next year, this time using six Achaean ships,

58 Polyb. v.109.3; the ships sailed through the Euripus to round C. Malea the next summer.
59 See Casson (1973) 125–7, for full references and discussion of *lembi* and *pristeis*.
60 Polyb. ii.3.1; Holleaux (1921) 176 n. 1. These figures are based on the likely assumption that Philip's *lembi* resembled the Illyrian. But variations in size and arrangement are found; cf. Livy xxxiv.35.5 for *lembi* with only sixteen rowers. And some of Philip's in 214 were biremes: Livy xxiv.40.2.
61 Polyb. v.109.3, σχεδὸν πρῶτος τῶν ἐν Μακεδονίᾳ βασιλέων; why σχεδὸν?
62 Polyb. v.108.4 (Scerdilaidas); cf. 101.8 (Italy), 101.10 (world dominion). How far Philip believed Demetrius' rhetoric about world dominion is a moot point; but the Illyrian's influence was strong.
63 Livy xxiv.40; Zonaras ix.4.4; Plut. *Arat.* 51.1.
64 Livy xxvii.30.15; cf. Holleaux (1921) 240 n. 2.

he linked up with seven quinqueremes and over twenty *lembi* of his own at Anticyra and, after a plundering expedition in Aetolia, dragged his own ships over the Isthmus and made his way back to Demetrias.[65]

The events of 209 and 208 had demonstrated that there was nothing to be hoped for from the Carthaginians. In addition it looks as if Bomilcar had sustained a decisive defeat at the hands of the Romans.[66] This would help to explain Philip's decision in the winter of 208 to build a new fleet of 100 warships at Cassandreia.[67] The keels were laid down, but when the Romans now virtually withdrew from Aegean waters, Philip evidently shrank from the expense and the ships were left unfinished.[68] Soon afterwards the war ended in the Peace of Phoenice (205). As regards naval activity, the years 217–207 had shown little but misguided effort and even disaster. Once the overambitious plan to invade Italy alongside Hannibal had been abandoned (as it must have been as early as Cannae in 216), the main use for Macedonian ships remained what it had been in the previous war, a means of conveying troops expeditiously from point to point or carrying out small plundering expeditions. The fleet of *lembi* was really a *residuum* from the ambitious plans of 217 and no longer essential. Once it was lost, Philip continued to attack Illyria successfully by land. Indeed his main effort and not inconsiderable achievement in this rashly precipitated war against Rome was on the land. ||

V

Between 205 and 200 Philip turned from Illyria and western Greece to take up the threads which Doson had let fall when he saw the chance to re-establish Macedonian power in Corinth. An expansionist policy in the Aegean, in the approaches to the Straits and in Asia Minor required both ships and money to pay for their construction (and to hire the crews).[69] It was largely because of the methods he adopted to get this money that Philip won himself so evil a reputation during these years. His reversion to a plan for Aegean expansion seems to have been partly a reaction against an Illyrian policy which had brought no lasting results, partly a move away from areas in which Rome had a declared interest, partly a return to aims pursued by his forebears (including most recently

---

[65] Livy xxviii.8.7–13. Whether the quinqueremes were dragged across the *diolkos* or (more probably) left at Lechaeum, we are not told.

[66] See Holleaux (1921) 244 n. 2.   [67] Livy xxviii.8.14, *nauium longarum*.

[68] See Holleaux (1921) 246 n. 2, 285 n. 5.

[69] Cf. Polyb. xvi.7.5 for a distinction between Macedonian troops and non-Macedonian crews.

Antigonus Doson) – and the Antigonids had a strong family feeling – and partly the determination to get in first before Antiochus, who had just got back with some prestige from his eastern *anabasis*; no doubt too he was encouraged by the manifest weakness of the third great power, Egypt, a weakness which was even more patent following the death of Ptolemy IV in the summer of 204 and the accession of a child to the throne.

About the same time (205) war broke out[70] between Rhodes and a group of Cretan cities allied to Philip, and since Rhodes was the Greek state with the strongest interest in policing the seas and putting down piracy, it was in Philip's interest to encourage this war (which he may even have provoked).[71] The most recent studies of this Rhodo-Cretan war[72] suggest that the island was at this time divided into two camps, one led by Gortyn, the other by Cnossus, and that the former group was supported by Philip, while the latter was allied to Rhodes and enjoyed some support from Nabis of Sparta.[73] Despite the involvement of Rhodes, both groups of Cretan cities seem to have practised piracy. In order both to help those Cretans allied to him (since about 217 he had been *prostates* of the Cretan *koinon*) and to || undermine the power of Rhodes Philip employed an Aetolian, Dicaearchus, to sail with twenty ships and indulge in piracy against the rich cities of the Troad and the Cyclades, and also to lend a hand in the Cretan War;[74] and he succeeded in introducing an agent, Heracleides of Tarentum, into Rhodes, where he burnt part of the dockyards.[75] By the early months of 203 Philip could use the proceeds of Dicaearchus' piracy to start the building of a new fleet;[76] and just as earlier he had found it useful to make an alliance with Hannibal to coordinate action against Rome, so now (probably in the winter of 203/202) he made an agreement with Antiochus of Syria to act in consort at the expense of young Ptolemy V.[77]

In 202 the fleet was ready. Its numbers are not recorded but in 201 Philip had forty to fifty decked ships, a few light vessels and 150 *lembi*,[78] so

---

[70] Diod. xxvii.3; *Syll.* 567, 673.

[71] Polyb. xiii.4.2. Brulé (1978) 44, points out that the Rhodian offer to help make peace between the Aetolians and Macedonia in 207 indicates fairly amicable relations: had some special incident occurred since then to cause a rupture?

[72] Errington (1969) 34–48; Brulé (1978) 29–56.   [73] Polyb. xiii.8.2.   [74] Diod. xxviii.1.

[75] Polyb. xiii.5.1–3; Polyaen. *Strat.* v.17 (2).   [76] Cf. Holleaux (1921) 285 n.5.

[77] Polyb. xv.20; see Walbank, *Comm.* ii, 471–4; iii, 785 (discussing Errington (1971), who rejects its authenticity). The compact was probably less precise than the sources suggest. The initiative will have been Antiochus'.

[78] Polyb. xvi.2.9; the fifty-three decked ships which Philip commanded at Chios will include some Egyptian vessels incorporated at Samos.

presumably he had about the same in 202, since he is not known to have
suffered any losses during that year. His campaign led to the seizure of
Lysimacheia, Calchedon (both Aetolian), Perinthus (Byzantine) and Cius
(Aetolian).[79] Cius was sacked and its population enslaved, a profitable operation, and the same treatment was meted out to the free city of Thasos.
Whether he took Lemnos now or possessed it earlier is uncertain.[80] The
object of the campaign seems to have been mixed. In the light of his conviction that the Antigonid house was bent on universal rule,[81] Polybius
interprets it as a first step in that direction. But Philip's real aims were
probably much more modest. On the one hand he was clearly seeking
what he achieved, an extension of Macedonian-controlled territory along
the || Thracian coast towards the Hellespont and the Bosphorus. This
was highly reminiscent of the policy of Philip II, and its similar effect on
Athens, always sensitive to any threat to its corn-supply, can be detected
in the appointment of Cephisodorus as ταμίας τῶν σιτονικῶν.[82] But in
addition the expedition furnished rich plunder, including the proceeds of
enslaving the populations of Cius and Thasos, which would go towards
the cost of manning the fleet.

The next year (201) he sailed out again with a fleet which, after the
seizure of a number of Egyptian vessels stationed at Samos, came to
over 200 ships.[83] Polybius gives a fullish account of the campaigns of
this year, but the order of the main events is controversial owing to the
fragmentary character of his narrative. I have argued elsewhere that
Philip was defeated by Attalus and the Rhodians off Chios, invaded the
territory of Pergamum, gained a victory over the Rhodians at Lade, and
finally sailed south to campaign in the Rhodian Peraea and Caria,[84] in
that order; but the details do not concern us here. That Philip was acting
against Pergamum and Rhodes is clear; but in Caria he was also moving
against Egypt, which he deprived of Samos.[85] The campaign of 201
harks back to earlier Antigonid pretensions, for in seizing the Cyclades

---

79 Polyb. xvi.23.8–9 (Lysimacheia and Calchedon), xviii.2.4, 44.4 (Perinthus), xv.21–3 (Cius), xv.24
    (Thasos). It has been argued that he also took Sestus this year (Polyb. xviii.2.4); but despite the
    absence of any mention of it in Livy xxxi.16.4–6 it seems more likely that Philip seized it in 200
    (cf. Polyb. xvi.29.3: Walbank, *Comm.* ii, 539 ad loc.
80 Walbank, *Comm.* ii, 611 on Polyb. xviii.44.4.   81 Above n. 20.
82 Moretti (1967) no. 33. Three were elected annually, the earliest recorded being in 267/266: *IG*, ii–
    iii², 1272; but Cephisodorus' appointment clearly links with the crisis of this year, as appears from
    his funerary monument, the gist of which is summarised by Pausanias i.36.5–6. The inscription
    says συνδιεξηχὼς τρίτος which Moretti rightly takes to mean that he served along with two
    others ('assieme ad altri due'), not necessarily with superior authority.
83 Polyb. xvi.2.9. For details see above n. 78.   84 See Walbank, *Comm.* ii, 497–500.
85 Above n. 83.

Philip was looking to Antigonus I's creation of the Island League, and by invading Caria he was taking up Doson's interrupted project. The positive character of this programme weighs against Holleaux's view[86] that his main objective was the Straits, but that he was diverted by his defeat at Chios (a view which links with his contention that Philip had no designs on Egyptian possessions).[87] Holleaux || explained the Carian campaign as an improvisation to take revenge on Rhodes for her intervention at Chios. Certainly in 200 Philip again moved in the direction of the Straits; but that could itself have been the result of a general setback in his plans for 201. What Philip's real object was in that year is bound to be somewhat obscure, since his defeat at Chios (like any major defeat) must have caused a modification of plan; and the invasion of Pergamum and perhaps that of the Rhodian Peraea were both motivated at least in part by anger. What is clear is that Philip was prepared to attack free cities like Thasos, Iasus, Bargylia, Euromus and Pidasa, Ptolemaic cities such as Samos, Miletus and Myus and, after the battle of Chios, Rhodian possessions on the mainland;[88] and of course the territory of Pergamum. W. E. Thompson has detected[89] in this campaign a policy of breaking up links between cities and larger units, but his thesis is not proved. On the whole to recover control of the islands and to acquire enough booty to help pay the costs of the operation seem the most likely objects of the campaigns of 202 and 201.

In the later autumn of 201 Philip found himself trapped by the Rhodian and Pergamene fleets in the Bay of Bargylia in Caria, and it was only after spending the winter there that he slipped out by means of a trick the next spring and returned to Macedonia.[90] From there he sent out

---

[86] Holleaux (1952) 334.

[87] See Habicht (1957) 233–41 no. 64 (especially 239 n. 109), an inscription which refers to the Ptolemaic recovery of Samos in the face of Macedonian resistance. It shows that Philip had seized and retained the city by violence and so renders Holleaux's belief in a friendly occupation of the island untenable.

[88] For the political alignment of these cities see Huss (1976) 197 (cities in Caria), 201 (Miletus and Myus), 232–3 (Samos), 235 (Thasos). *Syll.* 572 is a letter from Philip to Nisyros (an island forty miles off Rhodes) together with a Nisyrian decree. It indicates that Philip had seized the island but now granted it the right to use its ancestral laws.

[89] Cf. W. E. Thompson (1971). He argues that Philip detached Nisyros from Rhodes (to which it certainly belonged in the second century) and treats this as typical of a general policy of breaking up larger units, e.g., between Perinthus and Byzantium, between Lysimacheia and the Aetolian League. He also postulates the rupture of a union between Cos and Calymna (Segre (1952) 9–17: the use of the word ἀποκατάστασις implies the restoration of a ὁμοπολιτεία which could only have existed briefly before and been broken by Philip). But there is no evidence that Nisyros was Rhodian before 201, the date of *Syll.* 572. Thompson does not suggest why Philip sought to break up larger political units.

[90] Polyaen. *Strat.* iv.18.2.

some Macedonian ships to carry off four Athenian warships from the Piraeus, but they were soon obliged to surrender these to Attalus, whose fleet along with that of the Rhodians had followed Philip across the Aegean. Philip spent the summer of 200 in a combined land and sea operation in the north-east. He took Maronea, and Aenus was betrayed to him by its Egyptian governor. || These were followed by a series of small towns and forts, Cypsela, Doriseon, Serrheum and then, in the Chersonese, Elaeus, Alopeconnesus, Callipolis, Madytus and others,[91] perhaps including Sestus.[92] Most of these places were Egyptian. Philip then crossed the Hellespont to mount a combined military and naval siege of Abydus. It was here that Roman ambassadors found him and delivered what was in effect a declaration of war. Philip now took the city after most of the men had perished or committed suicide; and returning to Macedonia he learnt *en route* of the landing of a Roman army at Apollonia.

The purpose of this season's campaign is hard to detect. A fragment of Polybius from the *Suda*[93] has been placed by editors at xvi.29.1, just before the siege of Abydus. It states that 'Philip wished to deprive the Romans of the resources and stepping stones in those parts.' But Philip will hardly have attacked Abydus to deprive the Romans of its use. Why he did attack Abydus is stated in the next sentence (xvi.29.2), also from the *Suda*: it was in order to have a bridgehead if he wished to cross over into Asia again. Clearly xvi.29.1 does not belong here and is irrelevant to Philip's intentions. In De Sanctis' opinion[94] these were to establish a land route to Asia by conquering the Thracian Chersonese and the Straits and then with the help of his allies in Asia to crush his enemies on land and 'to prepare the destruction of their fleets as Alexander had prepared the destruction of the Persian fleet'. This ambitious programme seems to forget that Rhodes could not be reached by land (though her Peraea might); and the reluctance Zeuxis showed in providing supplies in 201 suggests that Philip would have been ill advised to look for much help to his 'allies in Asia'. On the other hand, he had acquired a substantial province in Caria (which was to remain Macedonian until after Cynoscephalae) so perhaps his ambitions looked beyond gaining a foothold in north-west Asia, to forestall Antiochus, whose interest in western Anatolia was already apparent.[95] His ultimate aims, however, must remain a matter of speculation, since his campaign

---

[91] Livy xxxi.16.4-6.   [92] Above n. 79.
[93] I hope to discuss this fragment elsewhere [Walbank (1985b)].   [94] De Sanctis (1923) 34.
[95] For his possession of Teos by 204/203 see Herrmann (1965).

was abruptly terminated by the || Roman ultimatum delivered to him at Abydus.[96] For the present enquiry we need only note that the campaign of 200 represents a reduction in the active rôle of the fleet. The defeat off Chios and the embarrassment of a winter spent at Bargylia had cooled Philip's enthusiasm to become a naval power. The advance to the Straits had taken the traditional form of a land campaign (with 2,000 light armed troops and 200 cavalry) relying on the fleet (under Heracleides) for support and provisioning; the assault on Abydus was a joint operation. It was to be almost the last serious naval action carried out by an Antigonid.

VI

Throughout the Second Macedonian War the fleet never ventured out of Demetrias.[97] At the outset Philip had destroyed Sciathos and Peparethos to deprive the enemy of booty and useful bases off the north coast of Euboea.[98] He realised that his fleet of perhaps twenty-five warships and some eighty galleys and light vessels could not face the united fleets of Rome and Rhodes, which together with some Illyrian galleys came to seventy warships and twenty lighter craft.[99] After his defeat at Cynoscephalae, the Romans restricted him to possessing five *skaphe* and a single vessel, a 'sixteen' (*hekkaidekeres*), which he was perhaps allowed to keep as a craft of prestige.[100] Naval power played no part in Philip's subsequent policies. As for Perseus, his successor (in 179), we hear of an attack with *lembi* on Oreus, early in the Third Macedonian War, in which thirty Roman transports were captured;[101] and in 168 he carried out a lively and successful raiding cruise with forty *lembi* and ten *pristeis* commanded by Antenor and Callippus, designed to protect grain convoys proceeding from the Black Sea and Asia Minor to Macedonia and to intercept ships || bringing corn to the Romans.[102] But the Roman victory at Pydna put an end to the war and with it to the kingdom of Macedonia.

[96] His general Nicanor had already conveyed to Philip a warning delivered to him by the Roman embassy at Athens, when Philip sent him to ravage Attica (Polyb. xvi.27.1–5). Whether Philip was aware of the rejection of the war-motion by the centuries when it was first put to them (Livy xxxi.6.3) is uncertain and must depend on the chronology of this year. For one view see Walbank (1940) 313–17, and for other views Will (1982) 116.

[97] Half Livy's statement (xxxi.33.1, referring to 200) that *Philippus impigre terra marique parabat bellum* must be taken with a pinch of salt.

[98] Livy xxxi.28.6.   [99] See Walbank (1940) 147 n. 6.   [100] Polyb. xviii.44.6.

[101] Plut. *Aem.* 9.3.

[102] Livy xliv. 28–9; App. *Mac.* 18.4: ἐς δὲ τὴν Ἰονίαν ἔπεμπε κωλύειν τὴν ἀγορὰν τὴν ἐκεῖθεν αὐτοῖς (sc. the Romans) φερομένην. See Thiel (1946) 402 n. 787.

VII

It is clear that once the Romans had intervened decisively east of the
Adriatic in the Second Macedonian War, one can no longer speak of a
meaningful Macedonian naval policy. Before then naval policy has to be
assessed against a general political background in which the three major
monarchies in practice operated a balance of power which, however,
was never accepted in principle.[103] None of the three had any hope of
reconquering the whole empire of Alexander, yet each was alert to threats
from its rivals and ready in turn to press any advantage to increase its
own security and area of influence; the possible exception was Ptolemaic
Egypt, whose rulers seem to have themselves accepted certain limits on
expansion. In general, the situation is one not unfamiliar in our own time.
Looked at objectively, the Antigonids seem at no moment to have been
in serious danger from the Seleucids and the Ptolemies. The latter, as
we saw, regarded as defensive their ring of possessions in the Aegean, in
Greece (Methana-Arsinoe perhaps from the time of the Chremonidean
War)[104] and towards the Straits,[105] though at the same time they were
ready to subsidise any potential trouble-maker in Greece such as Sparta
or, later, Achaea. The Seleucids were mainly neutralised by the treaty
made between Antigonus II and Antiochus I.[106]

In this context an active Antigonid naval policy indicated a resump-
tion of expansionist aims; and in each case that these were pursued the
results were negative. The first example is in the || Chremonidean War.
As we have seen,[107] there is disagreement as to whether the building of a
Macedonian fleet precipitated the war or (as Habicht implies) occurred
in the course of it. But the war was really decided on land with the surrender of Athens, and the battle of Cos cannot be shown to have changed
substantially the Egyptian dominance in the Aegean. The next attempt
at naval expansion was Doson's Carian expedition. It brought some ac-
quisitions lasting at least until the early years of Philip's reign and perhaps
contacts which persisted in a somewhat dormant form until the Carian
policy was revived by Philip in 201. But it was for his achievements in
Greece, not in the Aegean, that Doson was remembered. Philip twice
took to the sea, in Illyria and then again in the Aegean. Both episodes
were failures and ended in the destruction or curtailment of his navy;

---

[103] See Schmitt (1974); Treves (1970). [See ch. 8, n. 9.]
[104] Cf. Heinen (1972a) 131, 210 n. 465, who points out that Methana was directed towards Ptolemaic
control of the sea, not towards domination of the mainland; Robert (1960) 159 compared it with
Gibraltar.
[105] Above p. 110.   [106] Above p. 110.   [107] Above pp. 111–12.

and the Aegean enterprise could only be maintained by a programme of plunder and terror which made Philip enemies everywhere and eventually provided the Romans with an excuse to resume the struggle against Macedonia, the first round of which had ended indecisively in 205. Further, this led to the collapse of the Hellenic alliance created by Doson and the permanent expulsion of Macedonia from southern Greece. Philip's more substantial achievements were in the north, where he consolidated the frontiers, and in his internal strengthening of the land itself, though the latter was carried out with typical brutality. Perseus, as we saw, could have no naval policy.

That the Antigonids sought world dominion is an exaggeration;[108] but their repeated attempts to create a fleet for objects beyond the minimum needs of communication and security indicated their determination to challenge the Ptolemies and (in the case of Philip's Aegean campaign) perhaps the Seleucids too. In Illyria Philip made the even greater mistake of encroaching on an area pre-empted by Rome. One is tempted to correlate these repeated failures to establish or maintain a naval preponderance with the relative poverty of Macedonia compared with the rival kingdoms. But despite the manifest difficulty which Macedonia experienced in financing a fleet over any considerable period of time, when one looks at the details, it is the human factor that stands out, along with the element of pure chance; the unexpected appeal by the Achaeans to Doson, Philip's poor intelligence at the Aous, his policy of sheer terror in the Aegean || (and the resentment it induced), his being faced with the combined navies of Rhodes and Pergamum at Chios. As regards Antigonus II and the battle of Cos (and Andros?) we know too little to say why his success brought so small a return. But looked at together, one fact emerges clearly from this brief survey, the consistency with which Antigonid naval policy proved a mistake and a disaster.

[108] Above p. iii.

8

Η ΤΩΝ ΟΛΩΝ ΕΛΠΙΣ *and the Antigonids**

I

In 217, Polybius (v.101-2) informs us, Philip V, who had received private information about the Roman disaster at Lake Trasimene, revealed this to Demetrius of Pharos, who thereupon encouraged him to end the war with Aetolia and plan an invasion of Italy as a first step to world conquest, ἀρχὴν τῆς ὑπὲρ τῶν ὅλων ἐπιβολῆς. This suggestion appealed to Philip, who was young, bold and successful and came from a house which had always been inclined more than any other to covet universal dominion, ἐξ οἰκίας ὁρμώμενον τοιαύτης ἣ μάλιστα τῆς τῶν ὅλων ἐλπίδος ἐφίεται.[1] At the subsequent peace conference at Naupactus the Aetolian Agelaus is said (Polyb. v.104.7) to have taken up the same theme and urged Philip to compete at the appropriate moment, σὺν καιρῷ, for world sovereignty, τῆς τῶν ὅλων δυναστείας; and from now on Philip dreamt of nothing else (Polyb. v.108.5).

Are we to believe all this? Was the *oikia* from which Philip sprang so aggressive and ambitious? Or has Polybius got it all wrong? He certainly believed it to be true, for in a later passage, dealing with the year 201 (xv.24.6) and probably referring to Philip's treacherous seizure of Thasos in that year (xv.24.1), he upbraids Philip for his irrational behaviour in cherishing ideas of world dominion (περιλαμβάνοντα ταῖς ἐλπίσι τὴν οἰκουμένην), yet at the very outset of his campaign proclaiming his duplicity and so losing all credibility: for by so doing he sacrificed both honour (τὸ καλόν) and advantage (τὸ συμφέρον).

There are two separate issues here. One is Philip's actual aims and the other the traditional attitude of his *oikia* which these are supposed to

---

* [[*Ancient Macedonia* 3 (1993) 1721–30]]
[1] Polyb. v.102.1. The present tense is used to make a general statement about the Macedonian royal house. At the time Polybius was writing the Macedonian monarchy no longer existed.

reflect. I should like to consider them separately. In a volume devoted to an analysis || of what he takes to be the international conventions regulating the political life of the Hellenistic world, published in 1972,[2] P. Klose argues for the existence of an accepted notion of a balance of power subscribed to by the various main dynastic houses. Polybius' comments on Philip's aims and behaviour Klose rejects as an unacceptable piece of prejudice against that king; in his opinion Philip's ambition to gain universal power is nothing more than a cliché. But this view is not without its difficulties, for Polybius was not the only one of Philip's contemporaries to believe in the latter's unbridled ambitions. In a much discussed epigram[3] the poet Alcaeus of Messene addresses Zeus as follows;

μακύνου τείχη, Ζεῦ, Ὀλύμπια· πάντα Φιλίππῳ
ἀμβατά· χαλκείας κλεῖε πύλας μακάρων.
χθὼν μὲν δὴ καὶ πόντος ὑπὸ σκήπτροισι Φιλίππου
δέδμηται· λοιπὰ δ' ἃ πρὸς Ὄλυμπον ὁδός.

'Make higher the walls of Olympus, Zeus. Philip can scale everything' – an impious claim![4] – 'Close the bronze gates of the blessed ones. Earth and sea lie subdued beneath Philip's sceptre. All that remains is the road to Olympus.' I do not propose to linger over this poem discussing the nuances and whether it represents serious flattery, a reluctant admission of Philip's success by a political opponent, or mere sarcastic jeering. When I discussed it in an article in the *Classical Quarterly for* 1942[5] I followed Arnaldo Momigliano[6] in accepting the first interpretation, namely that it was serious flattery. But in a reply to my article[7] Charles Edson, who, ironically, had himself formerly[8] taken the poem to be serious praise of Philip, now argued – I think convincingly – that it was hostile in tone and bitterly sarcastic. In whichever way one takes it, however, it clearly implies that Philip was an ambitious monarch out to extend his rule as widely as possible – which accords entirely with the picture in Polybius and goes against Klose's interpretation. ||

The practice of what we may call balance of power politics in the Hellenistic period, especially by such medium-sized states as Syracuse or Rhodes, has been cogently analysed in detail in papers by Hatto

---

[2] Klose (1972) 87ff.   [3] *Anth. Pal.* ix.518; cf. Momigliano (1942).
[4] So correctly Edson (1948) 118–19.   [5] Walbank (1942); (1943a); (1944).
[6] Momigliano (1942).   [7] Edson (1948) 118–19.   [8] Edson (1934) 214 n. 4.

Schmitt and Piero Treves.[9] But, as Schmitt makes clear,[10] balance of power policies – which means in effect giving one's support to the weaker power against the stronger in order to curb the power of the latter – were never more than a strategy used by states of middling size. There is no evidence whatever that any great power drew the conclusion even in theory, let alone in practice, that expansion should be limited in order to conform with any such principle of international order. As a Rhodian speaker, as recorded by Polybius (xxi.22.8), observed to the Senate in 189, 'every monarchy by its nature hates equality and strives to make all men, or at least as many as possible, subject and obedient to it'. In a recent article in *Classical Quarterly*[11] Michel Austin has shown how the military character and military origins of Hellenistic monarchy constantly drew rulers into expansionist policies and aggressive warfare, especially those kings who were young and had to prove themselves. So on the first point I would argue that there is nothing at all inherently improbable in Demetrius' having given the advice which Polybius records to Philip nor in his having welcomed it enthusiastically. Whether what he proposed was sensible or even feasible is of course another matter.

II

We may now turn to the second point, that an ambition to achieve world dominion was a tradition of Philip's *oikia*. This claim has generally been rejected as a Polybian exaggeration. When I echoed it in *Philip V of Macedon*, || W. W. Tarn in a review of the book[12] criticised me, but let me off the hook, saying; 'For this Polybius must perhaps take the blame.' The argument against Polybius' claim seemed to be that the later Antigonids from Gonatas onwards had not shown the imperialist traits clearly discernible in Antigonus I and Demetrius Poliorcetes. That is a view that can in some degree be challenged. Circumstances put Antigonus

---

[9] Schmitt (1974); Treves (1970). Treves claims that the Hellenistic kings 'never departed or even dreamt of departing, from an unwritten code of by-laws of war, peace and diplomacy, an etiquette of government, a style of good manners as between brothers (or sisters), which lasted in Europe until Queen Victoria'. This I find unconvincing. In my opinion the main limitation on expansion in the Hellenistic world was the limitation on power rather than respect for a gentleman's code of practice.

[10] Schmitt (1974) 89–90: 'Ein freiwilliger Verzicht auf jede Expansion, als konsequente Folgerung aus dem Gleichgewichtsprinzip, gehört auch in der Neuzeit mehr der Theorie als der Praxis zu. Die Antike kennt, so weit ich sehen kann, diese Folgerung nicht.'

[11] Austin (1986) especially 459 n. 47.   [12] Tarn (1941).

Gonatas largely on the defensive in Greece proper, but, as I have shown elsewhere,[13] Eduard Will may well be right in thinking that one of the main factors which led to the Chremonidean War was Antigonus' decision to build a fleet; and the subsequent naval victories off Cos and Andros both indicate an aggressive policy towards Egypt. Doson's obscure Carian expedition foreshadows Philip V's Aegean campaigns of 201 and certainly represents a policy of expansion, even if his precise aims are hard to discover, owing to the fact that the expedition was soon aborted in favour of a forward policy in the Peloponnese. But I do not wish to dwell too much on the Antigonids, since it is my main purpose to show that, in attributing ambitions of world domination to Philip's *oikia*, Polybius is in fact referring not simply to the Antigonid house, but rather to the Macedonian royal house generally, including the Argeads and possibly – though, as we shall see, this is not entirely clear – to all who sat on the Macedonian throne.

This can be seen from an examination of Polybius' usage. In the first place, he never speaks of 'the Antigonid house', but always of 'the Macedonians' house', ἡ Μακεδόνων οἰκία. *Oikia* is of course the normal Greek word for a royal house. In Polyb. iv.35.11 it is used of one of the two Spartan royal houses. In v.40.4 it refers to the Seleucid house, contrasted with the Ptolemaic, and in v.86.10 to the Ptolemaic house itself. The same vocabulary is to be found in the inscriptions. A decree from Ilium, for Antiochus I, refers to τὴν πᾶσαν βασιλικὴν οἰκίαν;[14] and in a letter to the council and demos of Erythrae Antiochus II speaks of τὴν ἡμετέραν οἰκίαν.[15] The Seleucids in Asia and the Ptolemies in Egypt had of course no Greek-speaking predecessors sitting on their thrones; there was thus a sharp break between their || dynasties and those of the previous native rulers (though this of course did not prevent their cultivating indigenous royal and religious traditions wherever this seemed advantageous). Both houses, Seleucids and Ptolemies, seem in fact to have claimed some kind of connection with the Argeads. But for the Seleucids at least the evidence is scanty. According to Libanius,[16] Seleucus was related to the Heraclids κατὰ τὸν παλαιὸν Τήμενον – which need not of course necessarily involve relationship with the Argeads; but already in the third century BC an inscription from Xanthus asserts the Heraclid ancestry of both Ptolemy IV and Antiochus III of Syria.[17] That Antiochus I of

---

[13] See ch. 7 above, pp. 112–12; cf. Hammond and Walbank (1988) 279.
[14] Frisch (1975) no. 32.   [15] Welles (1934) no. 15 line 7.
[16] Libanius, *Or.* xi.90 ed. Förster; cf. Bikerman (1938) 7 n. 3; Errington (1976) 156–7.
[17] Bousquet (1988) 14–16 line 76 (Seleucids), lines 75, 106, 110 (Ptolemies).

Commagene claimed Alexander as an ancestor by way of his Seleucid wife[18] is Tarn's very hypothetical thesis based on a fragmentary inscription which, when restored, contains a reference (with no clear context) to 'King Alexander, the son of King Philip'. This really tells us nothing about any Seleucid claim to such a relationship. The Ptolemies apparently encouraged two accounts. According to one, Ptolemy Soter was distantly related to the Argeads through his mother Arsinoe,[19] whereas, according to the other, later story,[20] he was Philip II's natural son, though acknowledged as his own by Lagus. Neither Seleucids nor Ptolemies however laid much emphasis on the supposed Argead connection. Indeed the only clear reference to it in court poetry – which is where one would expect to find it – seems to be a mention of Heraclid ancestry and Alexander in Theocritus *Idyll* 17, lines 26–7 – which is perhaps odd, given the original importance of Alexander to Soter and the efforts he had made to ensure that Alexander's body was brought to Egypt. I shall come back shortly to the Antigonid claim to an Argead relationship.

III

First, however, I want to look more closely at Polybius' use of the phrase || οἰκία Μακεδόνων.[21] In many passages this appears to refer to the Antigonids and could be taken as limited to them. Thus in ii.50.9 Polybius speaks of Aratus' offence (ἀδικία) against τὴν Μακεδόνων οἰκίαν in seizing the Acrocorinth, presumably because Achaea and Macedonia were at peace when this took place; the charge is repeated at ii.52.4. When, after his flight from Illyria, Demetrius of Pharos places all his hopes ἐν τῇ Μακεδόνων οἰκία (iii.16.3), he would seem to be thinking of his services to Antigonus Doson and so of the Antigonid house. Similarly, when the Theban Brachylles is appointed boeotarch because he is known to be a friend τῆς Μακεδόνων οἰκίας (xviii.43.3), the reference is to a connection which began only in the reign of Antigonus Doson. It was this Boeotian goodwill πρὸς τὴν Μακεδόνων οἰκίαν (xxvii.2.7) that persuaded the Romans to break up the Boeotian League. It was his kindly treatment at the hands of Philip V that ensured the subsequent friendship of Nicander of Trichonium τῇ Μακεδόνων οἰκία (xx.11.9); and the good relations established πρὸς τὴν Μακεδόνων οἰκίαν by the house of Cephalus

---

[18] *OGIS* 398; cf. Tarn (1929) 139, with the criticisms of Errington (1976) 157 n. 1.
[19] *OGIS* 54 (Adulis inscription) line 5, with Dittenberger's note; Satyrus, *FGH* 631 F 1; Errington (1976) 155.
[20] Curt. ix.8.22; Paus. i.6.2; Errington (1976) 155.   [21] See Mauersberger (1956–) s.v. οἰκία.

in Epirus (xxvii.15.1, cf.15.8) seem to date to Cephalus' lifetime and so can only refer to the Antigonids.

In all these passages the specific reference is to events occurring when the Antigonids were on the throne. But that does not mean that the phrase ἡ Μακεδόνων οἰκία must itself be limited to the Antigonids. In fact there are other passages in Polybius in which it clearly has a wider application. Thus Aratus decided to use representatives of Megalopolis in his negotiations with Antigonus Doson because he knew that Megalopolis was well disposed πρὸς τὴν Μακεδόνων οἰκίαν ever since it had received favours from Philip II. Similarly, at a conference held at Sparta in 210 the Aetolian envoy Chlaeneas recalls the harshness of Antipater who, after the Lamian War, hunted down all those who had given offence to τὴν Μακεδόνων οἰκίαν (ix.29.3), a phrase echoed by his opponent Lyciscus in his reply (ix.33.1). Describing events a generation later at the time of the Third Macedonian War Polybius himself (xxvii.10.3) observes that, had the Greeks who now rashly applauded a victory won by Perseus' Macedonian cavalry called to mind the hardships that Greece had sustained ἐκ τῆς Μακεδόνων οἰκίας, they would surely have refused the king their support. In speaking here of the wrongs done to Greece by the Macedonian house in a passage probably written after 146, Polybius, despite his generally favourable attitude towards Philip II, is probably drawing up a mental balance-sheet of the relations || between Greece and Macedonia during the rule of the Argeads as well as that of the Antigonids and, possibly, all the others who sat on the Macedonian throne between the death of Alexander and the accession of Antigonus Gonatas. Finally, in perhaps the clearest example of them all (v.9.7), in a long discussion of Philip V's sacrilege at Thermum, Polybius compares this, not only with Doson's restrained behaviour at Sparta after Sellasia, but also with Philip II's treatment of Athens after Chaeronea and Alexander's treatment of Thebes in 335, using, as he says, τοῖς ἐξ αὐτῆς τῆς οἰκίας ταύτης παραδείγμασιν, examples taken from this very house. In other words, οἰκία Μακεδόνων embraces for Polybius both the famous dynasties which had ruled at Pella.

IV

This wide interpretation of the phrase probably came more easily to Polybius because by the time he was writing his *Histories* it was generally accepted that the Antigonids were related to the Argeads. I have already referred to the fact that similar pretended relationships existed in the

Seleucid and Ptolemaic royal houses but were never given much prominence there. For the Antigonids, however, the evidence is considerably stronger.[22] In the first place, in the passage dealing with Philip's sacrilege at Thermum, which I have already quoted, Polybius tells us that Philip was at great pains to stress his kinship with Philip II and Alexander, ὡς συγγενὴς Ἀλεξάνδρου καὶ Φιλίππου φαίνηται (v.10.10);[23] and this is confirmed by a passage in Livy, based on Polybius (Livy xxvii.30.9), which describes how the control of the Heraean and Nemean games were placed in the hands of Philip V, because the kings of the Macedonians attributed their origin to that city (Argos), 'quia se Macedonum reges ex ea civitate oriundos referunt'. It was of course the Argeads who made that claim but clearly it is here being extended to Philip V; *Macedonum reges* includes both the Argeads and by implication the Antigonids. The same assumptions arise again in 198, when the Argead connection was a powerful motive at Argos against abandoning the Macedonian alliance for Rome (Livy (= Polyb.) (xxxii.22.11). The relationship with Philip II and Alexander is also mentioned by Plutarch (in his *Life of Aemilius Paullus* 12.5) in reference to Perseus, who claimed a share in their || *arete* through kinship (κατὰ συγγενείαν). In a passage hostile to Philip V Pausanias (vii.7.5) remarks that Philip II was not his ancestor (πρόγονος) but his slave-master (δεσπότης), with the clear implication that Philip had claimed the former connection. That Philip V *imitated* the earlier Philip is not only asserted here by Pausanias, but finds odd confirmation in Photius, who tells us[24] that Philip V made an abridgement in sixteen books of those parts of Theopompus which dealt with Philip II. And Philip's policy during his last decade of shifting populations (Polyb. xxiii.10.4)[25] seems to echo methods used by Philip II. It is also not without significance that at the time of Andriscus' revolt a pretender claiming to be Perseus' son has the name of Alexander (Zonaras ix.28).

As Charles Edson has shown,[26] the Argead link also receives support from the Macedonian coinage, which regularly carries the club of Heracles or Heracles himself – though indeed the appearance of the club on coins of the *Makedones Amphaxioi*, which were not strictly a royal

---

[22] Errington (1976) 153–4, rightly observes that it was the relationship with the Argead dynasty generally and particularly that with Philip II, rather than that with Alexander, that Philip V chose to emphasise.

[23] Alexander is mentioned first only to avoid hiatus.

[24] Photius, *Bibl.* 176 p. 121 a 35, quoting Theopompus, *FGH* 115 T 31.

[25] For similar policies employed by Philip II see Justin. viii.5.7; cf. Momigliano (1934a) 138, 146–7 n. 1. On Philip V's aims see N. G. L. Hammond in Hammond and Walbank (1988) 459.

[26] Edson (1934) 214–16.

coinage, and later on coins of the First Meris and of Roman Macedonia, is perhaps an indication that Heracles has come to be associated with Macedonia generally and not merely with the ruling house.[27] At Pydna, however, Perseus attracted some obloquy and misrepresentation by leaving the battlefield at a crucial time to sacrifice to Heracles (Plut. *Aem. Paul.* 19). I might also mention here the possibility, suggested to me privately by F. Piejko, that a gold stater from Mylasa,[28] showing a laurelled head and a *biga* and inscribed ΦΙΛΙΠΠΟΥ is a coin of Philip V imitating Philip II; but I do not stress this, since others take this coin to be a Seleucid issue.

The use of the Perseus theme, illustrated both by the name of the last king and by a Macedonian tetradrachm figuring Philip V as the new Perseus,[29] also points to the Argead connection since Perseus, like the Argeads, came from Argos. There is some evidence too that the group of statues which adorned a monument set up by Antigonus Gonatas on Delos following his naval || victory at Cos, which was probably in 255,[30] began with an outsized statue representing a god, who will almost certainly be Heracles.[31] The Argead connection is also reflected in literature, especially in epigrams. The *Palatine Anthology* contains three poems by Samus, the son of Chrysogonus, later executed by Philip, celebrating the dedication of a wild boar killed on Mt Orbelus to Heracles.[32] Furthermore, as Edson has shown, the dedicatory epigram for the Colossus of Rhodes[33] stresses the Rhodian descent from Heracles, asserts that lordship by land and sea is the inheritance of Heraclids, and so by implication taunts Demetrius, who had failed in his attempt to capture Rhodes, with not being a true Heraclid. From this, as Edson points out, it follows that the Antigonid claim to Heraclid descent, and so most probably to kinship with the Argeads, was already being made around 283. Edson believes the relationship to have been a real one. It is hard to say, but I think Malcolm Errington is correct in his argument[34] that the fact that Antigonus I never used the claim in his propaganda against Cassander, and especially in his

[27] See Price (1974) nos. 79, 82, 83.
[28] Akarca (1959) Pt. I, no. 1, 13–14; see my additional note on Polyb. v.10.10 in Walbank, *Comm.* III, 771.
[29] See Price (1974) no. 74; a club is featured on the reverse of this coin.
[30] On these statues see Courby (1912) 38–40. On the date of the battle of Cos see F. W. Walbank in Hammond and Walbank (1988) 587–600.
[31] Cf. Edson (1934) 217–19.
[32] *Anth. Pal.* vi.114–16; on Samus see Polyb. v.4.4 with my note in Walbank, *Comm.* III on Polyb. xxiii.10.9 (p. 231) and the additional note on v.9.4 (p. 771).
[33] *Anth. Pal.* vi.171; see Edson (1934) 220f.   [34] Errington (1976) 154 n. 2.

declaration at Tyre in 314 (Diod. xix.61.1–3), is rather against its being true. In any case its truth is not important, since by the time Polybius was writing, it seems to have been generally accepted.

V

If then the Antigonids were widely regarded as an offshoot of the Argeads, Polybius' use of the phrase οἰκία Μακεδόνων is easy to comprehend. In his view, and in it he did not stand alone, the 'house of the Macedonians', that is the single dynasty which included Philip II and Alexander, Antigonus the One-Eyed and Demetrius Poliorcetes, Antigonus Gonatas and Antigonus Doson, Philip V and Perseus, was one traditionally bent on world conquest. Philip II had taken over Thrace, organised the mainland Greeks (or most of them) into an alliance controlled by himself and launched the war against Persia. Alexander's rôle as a world-conqueror needed no elaboration. Antigonus I had fought throughout his life to unite Alexander's empire under || himself; and his son, Demetrius, after waging constant war, had finally perished invading Asia. Antigonus Gonatas had set up tyrannies in Greece to control it on his behalf and had twice challenged Ptolemy at sea and beaten him; and if Demetrius II had spent most of his reign on the defensive, Antigonus Doson had invaded Asia Minor and Philip V had joined Antiochus III in an unprincipled conspiracy to dismantle the Ptolemaic kingdom. Finally orthodox Roman doctrine, with which Polybius was unlikely to quarrel – however unconvincing it may seem to us – made both the last two Antigonid kings, Philip V and Perseus, challengers of Rome for universal dominion. How Cassander and his dynasty and the other weak holders of the Macedonian throne between 297 and 277, including Ptolemy Ceraunus and indeed, a little later, Pyrrhus, fitted into the definition is not clear. No surviving Polybian passage, as far as I know, throws light on this question and I think it is quite likely that Polybius never posed it. From the Macedonian angle it is more than probable that under the Antigonids the historical emphasis was laid on Antigonus Monophthalmus, although he never sat on the Macedonian throne, rather than on Cassander. To Plutarch (*Mor.* 545B) Gonatas is Antigonus ὁ δεύτερος. For Polybius, as various passages make clear,[35] it was the connection and contrast between, on the one hand, Philip II and Alexander, and on the other the Antigonids and especially Philip V and Perseus, that engrossed his

[35] E.g. Polyb. v.9–10, vii.11–14; see Lehmann (1974) 154–7.

attention. In particular he saw the overthrow of the Antigonid dynasty by Rome as the counterpart of Alexander's overthrow of the Persian empire, accomplished in either case in round about fifty years, as Demetrius of Phalerum had so prophetically foreseen.[36] Seen in this context of a single Macedonian dynasty Polybius' remark about the traditions of the οἰκία Μακεδόνων no longer presents any difficulties. Such doubts as we may have felt about his judgement in making it were mainly due to our own failure to understand what this phrase meant in the context of his *Histories.*[37]

---

[36] Polyb. xxix.21.

[37] I was pleased to note, after this paper was already written, that in *Rom und der griechische Osten*, т 30, a course book to accompany lectures given in the University of Munich in the semester of 1988/9, Professor H. H. Schmitt has also explained Polyb. v.102.1 as a reference to Philip's claim to kinship with Philip II and Alexander.

9

Hellenes and Achaeans: 'Greek Nationality' revisited*

I

I have given this chapter, which deals mainly with Hellenes and Achaeans, the sub-title of 'Greek Nationality' revisited. The Greek nationality I am revisiting (though only briefly) is the subject of a paper I wrote long ago in 1951, entitled 'The Problem of Greek Nationality'.[1] I gave it at the general meeting of the Classical Association held that year in Liverpool and in it I discussed and criticised a view prevalent at that time, that Greek history could be usefully interpreted in terms of 'a struggle for Greek unity' and the failure of Greeks to set up a Greek nation. This seemed to me rather an absurd theory for several reasons. One was that to apply the modern idea of a nation to ancient Greece was patently anachronistic. The 'panhellenic' note which can be detected in, for instance, the *Lysistrata*, the Olympian speeches of Gorgias and Lysias or the writings of Isocrates had nothing to do with such a concept. Nor did it seem reasonable to assess people in terms of what they *failed* to accomplish.

Today, indeed, such an approach to Greek history must seem strangely out-of-date. Although it was adopted at that time by such distinguished historians as Gaetano De Sanctis in Italy and Max Cary in England, its real origins lay in the drive to create a united Germany in the nineteenth century and the nationalism of Bismarck's *Reich*. Perhaps that discussion about a Greek nation is mainly important to us today as a reminder of how much our preoccupations as historians may later be seen to have reflected contemporary issues. To take a modern example, have the problems of Northern Ireland and former Yugoslavia nothing at all to do with our current interest in ethnicity?

* [[P. Flensted-Jensen (ed.) *Further Studies in the Ancient Greek Polis* (*Historia* Einzelschrift 138) (Stuttgart 2000) 19–33]]
[1] Walbank (1951).

Certainly 'ethnicity', however we define it, has taken the place of 'nationality' as a historian's tool for interpreting Greek history and trying to understand how Greeks saw themselves. An impressive amount of work has been done in this field in recent decades, especially by Catherine Morgan and Jonathan Hall,[2] to help us to understand what it meant to be an Ionian, an Aeolian, a Dorian or an Achaean. They – and they are not of course alone – have shown convincingly that the identities of these branches of the Hellenic people are often to be seen as something 'essentially changing, flexible and negotiable' and in some cases as comparatively late constructs || rather than clearly fixed and inherited. The relationship betwen the specific political institutions which we encounter at particular dates and their actual (in contrast to their supposed) origins has been illuminated by scholars working in many different fields such as archaeology, linguistics and religion. A special interest has also been generated in the many problems surrounding the early *polis* – how it should be defined, how, when and why it arose, and how it relates to so-called ethnic communities like early Achaea. For example, to take the case of Achaea, was the federal body, which was made up of some dozen *poleis*, and which we know as the Achaean League, a late construct or did it develop out of an earlier, perhaps at one stage a village organisation?

II

In this chapter I have a particular interest. I want to consider first whether and to what extent recent work on ethnicity, which has been more obviously concerned with archaic Greece, can contribute anything to our understanding of the Achaean League in the Hellenistic period. Further, I want to argue that the consciousness of being an Achaean dates from a time well before the political organisation of the Hellenistic Achaean League and that the main deities of the confederation, Zeus Homarios and to a lesser extent Athena Homaria, who play a large part in defining Achaean identity, continued to be important down to the time of the Roman Empire, when they could be invoked in order to express or revive a consciousness of that identity.

The answer to my first problem is not clear cut, for the reconstruction of the Achaean League in 280 took place in a new world of Hellenistic monarchies, which was radically changing the context in which such groups as the Achaeans or the Aetolians operated. It was a world too

---

[2] C. Morgan (1991): Morgan and Hall (1996): Hall (1997): cf. Gschnitzer (1955); Beck (1997).

where in Ptolemaic Egypt, for instance, the very definition of Hellene was to some extent losing its ethnic connotation and even becoming a tax category, occupied by some who might enjoy a dual life-style and bear both a Greek and an Egyptian name.[3] If 'Greek' can mean something quite different, what about 'Achaean'? My question about the relevance of work on ethnicity is, I think, a real one, inasmuch as it remains true that ways of thinking, in which genealogy, myth, location and cult all have an important role, are not restricted to archaic and classical Greece. In the late third century, for instance, the Dorians of Cytinium in Doris, ravaged by Antigonus III of Macedonia, following an earthquake, appeal with apparent confidence for a contribution towards the rebuilding of their shattered walls to Xanthus in Caria on grounds of kinship – though admittedly the contribution they elicited was rather small.[4] But, as we can see from Cohen's new catalogue of Hellenic settlements,[5] the years after Alexander saw a great outburst of new foundations throughout the Near and Middle East, each with its relevant cults and often asserted ethnic links. And divine descent, a basic element in the background of Homeric society and in most myths dealing with ethnic origins, || crops up again in the constructed genealogies of many Hellenistic dynastic families. The Cytinium inscription, for example, refers to Ptolemy Philopator's kinship with the Argeads, descendants of Heracles.

So my object here is to take a look at the Achaean League. The name Achaea has a resonance which goes back to Homer, who uses it of the Greeks at Troy, and subsequently echoes throughout Greek history. Legend brought the Achaeans, expelled by the Dorians from Argos and Sparta, to the shores of the Corinthian Gulf, which they took over from the Ionians.[6] We may not believe this story. But the Greeks believed it and its political repercussions are well illustrated by the story in Herodotus of how the Spartan king Cleomenes pressed his (unsuccessful) claim to sacrifice on the Athenian acropolis with the assertion 'I am not a Dorian, but an Achaean.'[7] Later the Achaeans who inhabited this area figure as an important power in Hellenistic Greece. And their name was still there to describe the province which incorporated most of Greece within the Roman empire. For over a century before the *débâcle* of 146 the Achaean League controlled the whole of the Peloponnese – though not always without encountering resistance. One does not have to believe the nineteenth-century myth about the struggle to win Greek unity to recognise that throughout Greek history the particularism of the Greek

---

[3] D. J. Thompson (1992).   [4] Bousquet (1988); cf. Walbank (1989).   [5] G. M. Cohen (1995).
[6] Paus. viii.1ff.   [7] Hdt. v.72.; cf. Parker (1998), especially Appendix, 27–33.

cities exacted a terrible price. In his chapter in Oswyn Murray's and Simon Price's recent book on *The Greek City* Nicholas Purcell remarks: 'the *polis* in general, one might say, was a cul-de-sac, an unhelpful response to the challenge of Mediterranean reality, if building large and relatively harmonious and inclusive societies is a worth-while goal'.[8] It is from this perspective that the Achaean League seems to have been, on the whole, a rather admirable institution. Its early history and development is, however, somewhat more complicated than I realised when I first started working on it.

III

Before coming to the Hellenistic Achaean League, reorganised in 280, I must digress a little to examine that earlier history; and on this subject we are fortunate to have an excellent study by Catherine Morgan and Jonathan Hall, to which I owe a considerable debt.[9] A basic question is: when did Achaea become organised as a federal league of cities rather than functioning simply as an *ethnos*? Here I have in mind the distinction made in Aristotle's *Politics*,[10] where he contrasts 'an *ethnos* in which people are scattered in villages and one in which they are like the Arcadians' – which must mean one in which they are settled in cities organised to form a federal state, as was the case in Arcadia after the fourth-century synoecism of Megalopolis and the defeat of Sparta at Leuctra in 371. The appearance of cities within an *ethnos* need not of course coincide with or even lead to their union within a federal body. ||

When regular cities first arose in Achaea is highly controversial.[11] Morgan and Hall have argued strongly that it was no earlier than the fifth century. Herodotus, it is true, tells us that Achaea is 'now' – presumably sometime in the second half of the fifth century – divided into twelve parts (μέρεα)[12] – which does not sound exactly like 'twelve *poleis*', except that, like Strabo, who also speaks of Achaean μέρη or μερίδες,[13] he gives them the names of known Achaean cities. Moreover, we know the names and cities – if indeed they were already organised cities – of the Achaean *oikistai* of Sybaris, Croton and Caulonia in southern Italy, which were

[8] Murray and Price (1991) 58.   [9] Morgan and Hall (1996).   [10] Arist. *Pol.* ii.2.1261a27.

[11] See Beck (1997); Funke (1993); Gawantka (1985); Gschnitzer (1955); Koerner (1974); Morgan and Hall (1996); Rizakis (1990); Snodgrass (1991) 1–23.

[12] Hdt. i.145 κατά περ νῦν Ἀχαιῶν τῶν ἐξελασάντων ˮΙωνας δυώδεκά ἐστι μέρεα, 'just as there are now twelve parts of the Achaeans, who drove out the Ionians'. He goes on to list Pellene, Aegeira, Aegae, Bura, Helice, Aegium, Rhypes, Patrae, Pharae, Olenus, Dyme and Tritaea.

[13] Strabo viii.7.4.

founded in the eighth and seventh centuries.[14] They are, respectively,
Ois of Helice, Myskellos of Rhypes and Typhon of Aegium,[15] Aegium
of course continued to be a leading city throughout Achaean history. In
another passage Strabo tells us that Aegium was a synoecism of seven
or eight *demoi* – which are probably villages – Patrae of seven and Dyme
of eight.[16] So perhaps we should think of some sort of protracted process in the transformation of village communities to cities, with a stage
representing what Strabo here calls συστήματα δήμων, village structures. There is evidence from elsewhere that such communities would
not necessarily be without a capacity for political action.[17]

Archaeological work certainly suggests a late development of what
Morgan calls 'high-order sites' in Achaea; and we can, I think, accept the
view of Morgan and Hall that we have no firm archaeological evidence
for fully organised *poleis* before 500. For the fourth century there is, of
course, plenty of evidence both for separate cities and for their combination in a league. From Xenophon we know that the Aetolian city of
Calydon across the Corinthian Gulf was a member of the Achaean
League before 389[18] and Pellene in 370/69;[19] also that the Achaean
cities were allied to Corinth after Leuctra in 371.[20] Both Aristotle and
Dicaearchus wrote *Constitutions* of Pellene;[21] and an inscription records
envoys from Pellene being || entertained at Athens in 344/3.[22] We also
have the text of a treaty between the Achaean League and Κορωνεῖς,
perhaps Coroneia, from the late fourth century.[23] But there is also
evidence for Achaean cities from the fifth century. We know, again
from Xenophon, that the Spartans introduced oligarchies into the
Achaean cities in 417.[24] A fifth-century honorific Athenian inscription
for a ship-owner describes him as Ἀχαιός.[25] But is that evidence, ask
Morgan and Hall, for the existence of an Achaean League at that date?
Not necessarily. And the same doubt attaches to Pausanias' reference to
the victory in the mare race (κάλπη) at Olympia in 496 by Pataikos, an
Ἀχαιός from Dyme.[26]

[14] Foundation of Sybaris: Strabo vi.1.13; Croton: Strabo vi.1.12; Caulonia: Strabo vi.1.10.

[15] Ois (Bérard reads <Συβαρ>ις) of Helice for Sybaris: Strabo vi.1.13; Myskellos of Rhypes for
Croton: Antiochus of Syracuse, *FGH* 555 F 10 = Strabo vi.1.12; Typhon of Aegium for Caulonia:
Paus. vi.3.12.

[16] Strabo viii.3.2; cf. Sakellariou (1989) 317–20.

[17] Cf. *SVA* 110 for a treaty of *c.* 500 between Heraea and Elis before Elis was an organised *polis*;
cf. Sakellariou (1989) 76, 318.

[18] Xen. *Hell.* iv.6.   [19] Xen. *Hell.* vi.5.29.   [20] Xen. *Hell.* vi.4.18.

[21] Cic. *Ad Att.* ii.2 (Dicaearchus); Hypereides in Harpokration 124. 13–16 *s.v.* Μαστῆρες (Aristotle).
The latter passage contains no mention of an Achaean *syllogos* (so Morgan and Hall (1996) 194).
The only reference to such a body is in the title of a play of Sophocles, Rizakis (1995) no. 141.

[22] *IG* ii² 20.   [23] *SVA* 452.   [24] Xen. *Hell.* vii.1.43.   [25] *IG* i² 93.   [26] Paus. v.9.1.

IV

There is, however, one important piece of evidence for the early existence of a federal league of Achaean cities, with its shrine of Zeus Homarios, which I should like to discuss more fully. And may I add now that I am *not* proposing to go into the question, once hotly debated, of how this deity's cult-name should be spelt – Omarios, Homarios, Amarios and Hamarios are all possible – since it is irrelevant to my present topic.[27] The evidence I want to consider is a passage from Polybius,[28] which states that three southern Italian cities, Achaean in origin, namely Croton, Sybaris and Caulonia, combined and agreed first to set up a common sanctuary of Zeus Homarios, in which they held federal assemblies and councils, and secondly to adopt the customs and laws of the Achaeans, ordering their constitution in accordance with these. The value of this statement as historical evidence has been queried by Morgan and Hall on three counts.[29] I want to argue that these are not decisive and that on balance we should accept Polybius' statement.

Their first argument is that Polybius is here writing to glorify his native Achaea. That is perfectly true, but it does not follow that he *invented* this account of a league || of southern Italian cities basing their new constitution on that of mainland Achaea. We should note that not only Polybius, earlier in this same passage, but also Iamblichus, in a passage which probably goes back ultimately to Timaeus, who had no axe to grind on behalf of Achaea, records Achaean intervention in Italy somewhat earlier in the fifth century, following the burning of the Pythagorean club-houses (*synedria*).[30] Nor is it unlikely that the Achaeans should seek to maintain an interest in and influence on their earlier overseas foundations.

The second objection raised by Morgan and Hall concerns Sybaris, one of the three cities mentioned by Polybius. This city had been

---

[27] Nor shall I discuss whether the temple of Zeus Homagyrios (Paus. vii.24.2) is to be identified with that of Zeus Homarios: on this see Rizakis (1995) no. 305.

[28] Polyb. ii.39.5–6; μετά τινας χρόνους (i.e. after the burning of the Pythagorean clubhouses) ὁλοσχερῶς ὥρμησαν (sc. the South Italian Greeks) ἐπὶ τὸ μιμηταὶ γενέσθαι τῆς πολιτείας αὐτῶν (i.e. the Achaeans). παρακαλέσαντες γὰρ σφᾶς καὶ συμφρονήσαντες Κροτωνιᾶται, Συβαρῖται, Καυλωνιᾶται, πρῶτον μὲν ἀπέδειξαν Διὸς Ὁμαρίου κοινὸν ἱερὸν καὶ τόπον, ἐν ᾧ τάς τε συνόδους καὶ τὰ διαβούλια συνετέλουν, δεύτερον τοὺς ἐθισμοὺς καὶ νόμους ἐκλαβόντες τοὺς τῶν Ἀχαιῶν ἐπεβάλοντο χρῆσθαι καὶ διοικεῖν κατὰ τούτους τὴν πολιτείαν. 'Some time afterwards they resolved to model their constitution completely on that of the Achaeans. The Crotonians, Sybarites and Caulonians, having called a conference and come to a unanimous decision, first established a common temple of Zeus Homarios, in which they held their meetings and discussions, and secondly, adopting the customs and laws of the Achaeans, resolved to conduct their government in accordance with these.'

[29] Morgan and Hall (1996) 195.   [30] Polyb. ii.39.1; Iambl. *VP* 263.

destroyed by Croton in 510, restored in 453 and destroyed again in 448. The name Sybaris was then given for a time to the new colony of Thurii, founded in 446 or 445; but the Sybarites soon seceded and founded a new Sybaris on the river Traeis. It is probably to this third city that Polybius here refers.

Against that identification Morgan and Hall object that Strabo tells us that Sybaris-on-the-Traeis was a Rhodian, i.e. a Dorian colony.[31] That, however, is not so. What Strabo says here is that *some people* (τινές) claimed Rhodian origins for both Sybaris-on-the-Traeis and for the city of Siris. In fact we know from Athenaeus that both Aristotle and Timaeus were in agreement that Siris was settled from Colophon (which is of course Ionian in origin);[32] and Strabo himself talks about an earlier city of Siris colonised by Ionians. Since then the τινές were wrong on Siris, it seems not impossible that they were also wrong about Sybaris-on-the-Traeis; for in neither case does Strabo endorse their view. Nor indeed is it very likely that Dorian settlers from Rhodes would want to give their colony the name of the Achaean city Sybaris.

The third objection raised by Morgan and Hall concerns the setting up of a south Italian Homarion in the fifth century. This interests me more, since a common shrine and common deity or deities form one of the most conspicuous defining elements of an *ethnos*. Was there, in fact, they ask, any federal shrine to Zeus Homarios (and Athena Homaria) in Achaea in the fifth century? There is of course abundant evidence that the Homarion, the shrine of Zeus Homarios and Athena Homaria, fulfilled that function within the revived Achaean League from 280 onwards. Morgan and Hall argue, however, that that was not so before the destruction of Helice, the neighbouring city to the south-east of Aegium, by earthquake and tidal wave in 373.[33] It is indeed true that Strabo records the possession by Aegium of the territory of Helice and 'the sacred grove of Zeus, the Homarion, where the Achaeans assembled to || debate matters of common interest'.[34] But that does not have to

---

[31] Strabo vi.1.14; τινὲς δὲ καὶ Ῥοδίων κτίσμα φασὶ καὶ Σειρῖτιν καὶ τὴν ἐπὶ τοῦ Τράεντος Σύβαριν. 'According to some, however, both Siris and Sybaris-on-the-Traeis were founded by the Rhodians.' Τράεντος is the generally accepted emendation of the MSS Τεύθραντος.

[32] Ath. 523c: καὶ οἱ τὴν Σῖριν δὲ κατοικοῦντες, ἣν πρῶτοι κατέσχον οἱ ἀπὸ Τροίας ἐλθόντες, ὕστερον δ᾽ὑπὸ Κολοφωνίων, ὥς φησι Τίμαιος καὶ Ἀριστοτέλης, εἰς τρυφὴν ἐξώκειλαν οὐχ ἧσσον Συβαριτῶν. 'Again, those who settled at Siris, which was occupied first by those coming from Troy and later by Colophonians, as Timaeus and Aristotle tell us, drifted into luxury no less than the Sybarites.'

[33] On the destruction of Helice in 373, see Rizakis (1995) nos. 109, 195, 388, 475, 479, 512 and 513.

[34] Strabo viii.7.5: Αἰγιέων δ᾽ ἐστὶ καὶ ταῦτα καὶ Ἑλίκη καὶ τὸ τοῦ Διὸς ἄλσος τὸ Ἀμάριον, ὅπου συνῆεσαν οἱ Ἀχαιοὶ βουλευσόμενοι περὶ τῶν κοινῶν 'These [i.e. Ceraunia (read Ceryneia) and

mean that the sacred grove of Zeus had formerly been situated on the territory of Helice. Morgan and Hall claim that prior to the disaster the Achaeans had worshipped and held their meetings at a different shrine, in the territory of Helice, which, they think, was in all probability that of Poseidon Heliconios, whose worship was prominent at Helice from Homeric times onwards. They support this view with the argument that the first Achaean coinage, showing on the reverse of the only surviving stater belonging to it a figure of Zeus, was intended to celebrate the adoption of the cult of Zeus Homarios at Aegium in place of the supposed federal cult of Poseidon at Helice.[35] This rather bold argument deserves little credence, however, for this rare issue is one of a series of new coinages which appear in the Peloponnese following the end of Spartan domination at the battle of Leuctra in 371. Head accordingly dated it to that year; and more recently Colin Kraay has linked it with Arcadian and Messenian didrachms which probably date back to the decade 370–360. It is highly improbable that this Achaean issue has anything to do with the adoption of a new federal cult.

v

There is, however, a problem about the Homarion, as is very clear if we examine two passages of Pausanias and one of Livy. In vii.24.4 Pausanias tells us that the Achaeans met at Aegium 'as the Amphictyons did at Thermopylae and at Delphi'. This is a reference to the shrines of Demeter at Anthela and of Apollo at Delphi, and though Pausanias does not specifically say so, his words suggest that the Achaeans likewise met at a shrine, which we have every reason to assume to be that of Zeus Homarios. But was that always true? Livy, who is here closely following the Achaean historian Polybius, tells us that from the beginning of the Achaean League – *a principio Achaici concilii* – meetings of the *gens* were always summoned to Aegium.[36] It could be argued that Livy is here referring only to the revived league of 280; but we know from Polybius

Aegae] belong to Aegium as do Helice and the Amarion, the grove of Zeus, where the Achaeans met to deliberate on affairs of common interest.' Helice was destroyed and its territory annexed in 373.

[35] For Achaean coinage showing Zeus, cf. Head (1911) 410: see Kraay (1976) 101, for a link with Arcadian and Messenian didrachms (370–360).

[36] Liv. xxxviii.30.2 (following Polybius): Aegium a principio Achaici concilii semper conventus gentis indicti sunt, seu dignitati urbis id seu loci opportunitati datum est. 'From the beginning of the Achaean confederacy meetings of the people were always called to Aegium, whether as a recognition of the city's importance or in view of the convenience of the site.'

ii.39.5–6, which we have just been considering, that Polybius believed the Homarion to have been the federal shrine in the fifth century (when the Italians copied it) and knew of no change after the destruction of Helice in 373. So if Livy is referring to the Homarion at Aegium, we may fairly || assume that he (and so by implication Polybius, whom he is following) is speaking of the original confederacy.

At this point, however, we must consider a further passage of Pausanias.[37] Here, with reference to a date all around the time of the Gaulish invasion of 279, Pausanias states that 'the Achaeans decided to meet at Aegium which, following the destruction of Helice, was the leading city in Achaea'. Although he does not actually say so, the implication of this passage would seem to be that the Achaeans had previously met at Helice. Such a conclusion would of course contradict all the other evidence we have just been considering. Accordingly, in 1938, in his important book on the Achaean assemblies. André Aymard proposed an ingenious solution to reconcile the two sets of evidence.[38] To surmount the difficulty which arises if the shrine of Zeus Homarios was the federal shrine at Aegium only after the destruction of Helice in 373 (as Morgan and Hall still argue), he suggested that after Helice was overwhelmed and Aegium took over its neighbour's territory – as Strabo records (viii.7.5) – that territory *included* the Homarion. If that were true, however, we should have to suppose that Pausanias had not appreciated the fact that what occurred after the cataclysm was merely the attribution of the same shrine to a different city and not the adoption of a new shrine in a new locality.

Ingenious though it is, Aymard's theory will not stand up, thanks to evidence that has become available since he wrote. As Robert Parker points out in the important appendix to his recent inaugural lecture as Wykeham Professor at Oxford – it deals with *ethne* cults – several federal inscriptions dating from the fourth century onwards found at a site to the *north-west* of Aegium, towards the coast, and published in 1953 and 1954 by Jean Bingen, render it virtually certain that the Homarion was located in that vicinity, which lies in the opposite direction to Helice and could not therefore have stood on territory annexed from that city after 373.[39]

---

[37] Paus. vii.7.2: ἀθροίζεσθαι δὲ ἐς Αἴγιόν σφισιν ἔδοξεν· αὕτη γὰρ μετὰ Ἑλίκην ἐπικλυσθεῖσαν πόλεων ἐν Ἀχαΐα τῶν ἄλλων δόξῃ προεῖχεν ἐκ παλαιοῦ καὶ ἴσχυεν ἐν τῷ τότε. 'They decided [i.e. in 280] to meet at Aegium. For after Helice had been overwhelmed by the waves Aegium outstripped the other Achaean cities in reputation both from ancient times and then.'

[38] Aymard (1938a) 277–93.

[39] Parker (1998) 31 n. 77; Rizakis (1995) 201 no. 305 n. 2 on the inscriptions recorded by Bingen (*BCH* 77 (1953) 616–28; *BCH* 78 (1954) 402–9) and others from a site to the north-west of Aegium.

VI

So where does that leave us? There are, I suggest, two possibilities. One is that before 373 the Achaeans met at a Homarion in the territory of Helice, but after the disaster transferred the shrine to a new locality to the north-west of Aegium. Recent work on the so-called Helike Project, using 18 m drill-holes and a magnetometer survey, has confirmed that the ancient accounts of the destruction of Helice are substantially correct and that the remains of the original city and its territory were || buried under alluvial deposits ranging between 1.5 m and 12 m in depth.[40] When, after 373, the people of Aegium took over this devastated territory, it is quite feasible that they should have moved the shrine of the now buried Homarion to a new site within their own territory, and as far as possible from the devastated area and the epicentre of the earthquake.

This theory could be reconciled with Pausanias vii.7.2.[41] But it contradicts a strict reading of Livy's statement that it was in Aegium that Achaean assemblies met *a principio*; and, more important, it involves the improbable assumption that down to 373 there existed a shrine of Zeus Homarios, important to the whole of Achaea, *at Helice*, which is nowhere attested in any of our sources. And it is, of course, wholly at variance with Polybius ii.39.5 6.[42]

Alternatively, we can assume that there was no move of the Homarion after 373 and that, despite Pausanias vii.7.2, it does not follow from the decision of the reformed league of 280 to meet at Aegium that the earlier league had not also met there. Between these two hypotheses a decision is not easy, for both present difficulties. But, on balance, it seems to me more probable that the federal sanctuary was *not* moved after 373 and that the decision of the reformed league of 280 to meet at Aegium merely took up a custom that had existed from the earliest days of the Achaean League. Perhaps future archaeological work at Aegium and Helice will throw fresh light on the problem. But, whatever the possible outcome of such work, there is no reason to reject the Polybian account of the setting up of a league of southern Italian cities with its own Homarion in the late fifth century. For there is no ancient evidence to support the view that the Achaeans ever looked to Poseidon Heliconios as their federal deity. Indeed, Strabo (viii.7.3) puts the Achaean adoption of Zeus Homarios back into mythical times, for he thinks the Achaeans took him over from the Ionians when they replaced them on the shores of the Gulf.

[40] On the Helike Project, see *Archaeological Reports* 43 (1976/7) 42; 44 (1977/8) 40.
[41] Quoted above, n. 37.   [42] Quoted above, n. 28. [This is not quite true.]

VII

This has been a long digression: but it seemed necessary to establish that the Achaean League of the fourth and third centuries was in no sense a recent construct, but a direct continuation of the earlier association, with its meeting-place at the Homarion at Aegium, as Polybius ii.39.5–6 implies. The question I now want to examine is this: What did the cult of Zeus Homarios (and Athena Homaria) mean to the ordinary Achaean of the Hellenistic age, not merely when such a person figured in any official capacity, such as occupying a magistracy or attending an assembly, but also as a private individual – and that especially after the expansion of the Achaean League to cover, eventually, the whole Peloponnese? This enlargement began in 251, when Aratus of Sicyon, having liberated his own Dorian city from the local tyrant, took the momentous step of attaching it to the Achaean League. There were in fact several reasons why this act was less surprising than it may at first sight seem. We know || from Pausanias that there was a mythological connection between Sicyon and Achaea.[43] The territory occupied by the latter had at one time been known as Aigialos, a name said by some to have been taken from that of a king of Sicyon (though others, says Pausanias, derived it – and this is perhaps more plausible – from the same word meaning a sea-shore). Furthermore, and perhaps more importantly, such a union had its Achaean precedents, since before 389 Calydon across the Corinthian Gulf had belonged to the Achaean League. And the other great Hellenistic *ethnos*, the Aetolian League, had already set up a significant pattern of expansion by absorbing various peoples of northern Greece during the years prior to the Chremonidean War of 268 – as Aratus will have known. Perhaps the novelty of Aratus' move lay in his *wish* to become Achaean and in the Sicyonian (rather than Achaean) initiative.

Be that as it may, the inclusion of Sicyon in the Achaean League and the vigorous leadership now provided by Aratus himself led to a speedy expansion which I do not propose to trace in detail. The point I want to stress is that for a considerable time the Homarion at Aegium continued to provide both a religious and a secular centre for league activities, although as expansion took in large, long-established cities of the Peloponnese, each with a noteworthy past, such as Corinth, Argos and, after much resistance, even Sparta, Aegium became an increasingly inconvenient meeting place and political centre. Eventually, in 188,

---

[43] Paus. vii.1.1.

after long controversy, and strong opposition from Aegium, Philopoemen of Megalopolis successfully sponsored a proposal to have federal assemblies meet at the various major cities in turn.[44] This took away the *political* importance of Aegium and the Homarion. But there is evidence that, although it must have meant far less to the newer members of the confederacy, which of course already had their own special cults and deities, the *religious* importance of the Homarion, where presumably records of treaties and other public business continued to be kept and honorific decrees of the league to be set up, went on down to and even *after* 146. Clearly it would have been impossible to cart the contents of the whole Achaean record-office around from city to city on the trail of the assemblies.

VIII

In a public sense the shrine and cult of the Homarion thus remained central to the Achaean League, as it had always been. But its *private* significance, at any time, is difficult, perhaps ultimately impossible, to assess. There is, however, one small piece of evidence to show that some individuals looked to Zeus Homarios (and Athena Homaria) as the proper recipients of a personal act of devotion. Around 1900 there was discovered, in the neighbourhood of Damanhour in the Egyptian delta, an inscription on a limestone *stele* which read: Διὸς Ἀμαρίου / καὶ Ἀθῆνας / Ἀμαρίας, 'Zeus Amarios and Athena Amaria'.[45] There has been some controversy over the ‖ years about the date of the lettering of this inscription and the context in which the *stele* was erected. In 1921 P. Perdrizet argued that it was associated with a sanctuary, a view which was widely accepted. But in 1966 Louis Robert showed from a parallel example (*SB* 6664) that it was most probably a dedication associated with a domestic altar. As regards the date, several scholars, including Perdrizet and Marcel Launey, claimed that it was an inscription from imperial times, and envisaged the possibility that it was a later re-engraving of a Hellenistic dedication, a hypothesis which presented several problems. But in 1970 A. Bernard identified it, with great probability, as belonging to the 'haute époque hellénistique'. There is no evidence to support a direct military context for this dedication, but it certainly looks extremely probable that the persons making it had, or had had, some connection

---

[44] Liv. xxxviii.1.5.
[45] Bernard (1970) 1, 523–5 no. 1 = *SB* 1 (1915) no. 357. Earlier discussion in Perdrizet (1921) 281–3; Launey (1950) 953–4; Robert (1966).

with the large body of Achaean mercenaries employed by the early Ptolemies. A group of Achaeans of purely civilian origin and living some 60 km from Alexandria seems altogether less likely. The Achaean connection, however, seems certain, since the Homarios title of Zeus and Athena figures nowhere else in our records. Thus the dedication shows that an Achaean, even when – indeed perhaps especially when – settled in a foreign land, might choose to assert his ethnic and religious identity (and perhaps express a sense of nostalgia) with a dedication to the deities of his native Homarion.

IX

This example of a private dedication to the Zeus and Athena of the Homarion seems to date to a time when the Achaean League was still a leading state in mainland Greece and when association with it could, even in a foreign realm, be a subject of personal pride. But we have also evidence that well after 146 and the Roman takeover,[46] Achaea and the Homarion continued to be of significance as an element in Greek consciousness. As early as 34/33 BC, before the battle of Actium and the establishment of Octavian's principate, an inscription records a dedication to M. Iunius Silanus, pro-quaestor, by a Greek federation composed of Boeotians, Euboeans, Locrians, Phocians and Dorians, that is to say, of ethnic groups situated to the north of the Corinthian Gulf.[47] This group, which apparently bore no overall name, was a forerunner of a series of minor leagues with a fluctuating membership and a succession of different names. Eventually, however, as we learn from an inscription honouring T. Statilius Timocrates,[48] which was shown by Arnaldo

---

[46] The usual view attributes the suppression of the Achaean league to L. Mummius in 146. Kallet-Marx (1995) 77–82, makes a strong case, however, for thinking that it had already disintegrated before Mummius brought the Achaean War to an end.

[47] *Syll.* 767.

[48] *Syll.* 796 A–B; cf. Momigliano (1944) 115–16 [reviewing *CAH*¹ x]. Improved readings in *SEG* document 35304. ἔδοξε τῶι Παναχαϊκῶι συνεδρίωι ἐπαινέσαι τὸν ἄνδρα καὶ ἀναστῆσαι αὐτοῦ χαλκᾶς εἰκόνας ἔν τε τοῖς πανηγυριστηρίοις τῶν ἱερῶν ἀγώνων καὶ τῶι τοῦ Ἀμαρίου Διὸς [τεμ]ένει καὶ ἐν Ἐπιδαύρωι ἐν τῶι τοῦ Ἀσκληπιοῦ ἱερῶι, ἐπιγραφὴν ἐχούσας ν Ἀχαιοὶ καὶ Βοιωτοὶ [καὶ Φω]κεῖς καὶ Εὐβοεῖς καὶ Δοκροὶ καὶ Δωριεῖς Τίτον Στρατείλιον Τειμοκράτη γραμματέα [αὐτῶν] γενόμενον ἀρετῆς ἕνεκα. 'Resolved by the Panachaean Council to praise the man (i.e. T. Statilius Timocrates) and to erect bronze statues of him at the meeting-places of the sacred games and in the precinct of Zeus Amarios and in the shrine of Asklepios, bearing the inscription; the Achaeians and Boeotians and Phocians and Euboeans and Locrians and Dorians to Titus Statilius Timocrates, who acted as their secretary, for his merits.' Nero's speech liberating Greece (*Syll.* 814 = *ILS* 8794) refers only to πάντες οἱ τὴν Ἀχαῖαν καὶ τὴν ἕως νῦν Πελοπόννησον κατοικοῦντες Ἕλληνες ('all the Hellenes dwelling in Achaea and what is up to now

Momigliano to ‖ be concerned with the so-called 'liberation' of the Greece by Nero and hence to be dated to around AD 67, there was by this time a group of *ethne* which, though still predominantly representative of northern Greek peoples, now included the Achaeans, who are mentioned first. The interesting thing about this inscription, which records an event which was believed to be of the greatest significance for Hellas as a whole, is that it reveals that the composite body has now adopted the name of *Panachaioi* and its ambassadors are called ambassadors of the Achaeans. The name of this body, it is true, is not stable. In *IG* VII 2711 the federation is called that of the Panhellenes; but elsewhere in the documents included under this *IG* number it is the 'Achaean *koinon*'. I have no desire to go into the confusing history of these Greek leagues under the early empire prior to Hadrian and their relative chronology. What I do want to emphasise is the fact that, according to the inscription of AD 67, inscribed statues to T. Statilius Timocrates are to be set up not only at the site of the 'Panachaean Games' – which we know from another inscription celebrating the same occasion to be the Olympian, Isthmian and Nemean[49] – and at the Asclepieium at Epidaurus, but also in the shrine of the Homarion. It is certainly noteworthy that this panhellenic body had identified itself so completely with its Achaean forbears and its new Achaean identity as to give the comparatively remote and almost parochial Homarion equal place with these venerable centres of Hellenic religious tradition.

The title adopted by this Panachaean League echoes Homer, *Iliad* ii.404;[50] but the word also exists as an epithet of Demeter[51] and Artemis.[52] A similar form, *Panachais*, is also found as an epithet of Athena;[53] and there is, of course the Panachaean Mountain in Achaea. From this evidence it seems clear that the various ethnic groups, which found themselves within what had now become a province of the Roman empire, eventually agreed on Achaea, or some variant of the Achaean name, as their most appropriate symbol. Their purpose was plainly to assert a Greek identity. It was, in fact, not dissimilar to that which dominated the writers of the so-called Second Sophistic, except that Hellenistic echoes are not common in *their* works. Pausanias tells us[54] that the Romans called the governor of

the Peloponnese'). This clearly refers to both the Peloponnese and the other areas constituting the province of Achaea, i.e. northern Greece up to and including Thessaly and parts of Epirus (Larsen (1938) 438), and so all the *ethne* named in *Syll.* 796 A–B.

[49] *IG* v.2, 517.15 (from Lykosoura).

[50] κίκλησκεν δὲ γέροντας ἀριστῆας Παναχαιῶν, 'He [Agamemnon] called together the most excellent old men of all the Achaeans.'

[51] Paus. vii.24.3.   [52] *BCH* 25 (1901) 350: Delphi.   [53] Paus. vii.20.2.   [54] Paus. vii.16.10.

Greece οὐχ Ἑλλάδος ἀλλὰ || Ἀχαίας, of Achaea, not of Hellas, because they conquered the Greeks δί Ἀχαιῶν, who were at that time the leading people of Greece.[55] So one obvious reason for the decision of the ethnic bodies under Roman rule to adopt the Achaean title will have been to link them to the name of the province and may, as Larsen suggested, have been designed partly to gain their league recognition as a regular provincial assembly.[56] But the decision was not obvious and was not taken at once. In fact, apart from any immediate advantages, this decision was based also upon a long-lasting historical consciousness, in which the name Achaea encapsulated the traditions of the old Achaean League with its revered cult of Zeus Homarios and Athena Homaria and still carried a powerful resonance in the minds of Greeks whose fate it was to live under the Roman empire.

To sum up my argument, I have tried in this chapter to show that the name Achaea carried resonances not only from Homer but from a time before the political organisation of the cities of Achaea, that an Achaean identity was closely associated with the cult of Zeus Homarios and Athena Homaria at Aegium, that Achaeans abroad might express their identity through this cult and that under the Roman empire Greeks living on both sides of the Corinthian Gulf found it appropriate to use the Panachaean name and the cult of Zeus Homarios to express their Greekness in a world dominated by Rome.[57]

Table of relevant dates

720 BC	Foundation of Sybaris
c.708	Foundation of Croton
c.675–650	Foundation of Caulonia
496	Pataikos, an Achaean from Dyme, wins the mare-race at Olympia
c.450	Burning of Pythagorean clubhouses in S. Italian cities, followed by *stasis*
c.430	Achaean intervention in S. Italy
after c.450	Foundation of Sybaris-on-the-Traeis
before 417	Sybaris-on-the-Traeis, Croton and Caulonia form league with Homarion

[55] Mummius' *provincia* had been *bellum Achaicum*. Just. *Epit.* xxxiv. 2.1.
[56] Cf. Larsen (1938) 450–1; on the provincial assemblies, see Deininger (1965).
[57] This paper was read to a seminar in the Institute of Classical Studies, London, on 22 April 1999. I am grateful to several of those present for suggestions and, especially, to Dorothy and John Thompson, whose help and careful scrutiny have improved it in countless ways.

417	Spartans set up oligarchies in Achaean cities
before 399	Calydon a member of the Achaean League
373	Destruction of Helice by earthquake and tidal wave. Aegium annexes territory of Helice
371	Spartan defeat at Leuctra
c.370–360	New Achaean coinage shows Zeus Homarios ||
281/0	Achaean League refounded
279	Gaulish invasion of north Greece
251	Aratus frees Sicyon and attaches it to the Achaean League
3rd cent.(?)	Dedication to Zeus Homarios and Athena Homaria near Damanhour, Egypt
146	Dissolution of Achaean League in course of or after the Achaean War
34/33	Dedication by Greek federation to M. Iunius Silanus (*Syll.* 767)
c.AD 67	Panachaean League honours T.Statilius Timocrates. Statues of him to be erected at the Homarion and other sites

Note: dates before 417 are mostly approximate.

10

*The Achaean assemblies**

I

Since the Achaean meetings recorded in xxix.23–5 are among the most important evidence for the character of the Achaean assemblies in the second century, this is an appropriate place to review recent work on this much-discussed problem. The basic studies are now Aymard (1938a) and Larsen (1955) 165–88. Larsen challenged Aymard's view that the *synodos* was a primary assembly, arguing that, from a date towards the end of the third century, the Achaean assembly ceased to have regular meetings and only came together when, according to carefully defined rules, a special meeting of the primary assembly was called; the four annual *synodoi* were meetings of the council (*boule*) together with the magistrates.[1] Larsen reaffirmed this view in Larsen (1972), replying to A. Giovannini, who had argued[2] || that the *synodoi* continued to be meetings of the primary assembly (along with the Council and magistrates) down to the dissolution of the Confederacy. In a reply to Giovannini[3] I raised some objections and stated that Larsen's theory 'still seems to me the most convincing', though 'no theory yet put forward solves every difficulty to everyone's satisfaction'.[4] Further concern with the problem, encouraged by discussion with G. T. Griffith, has since led me to a different conclusion, and one nearer to Giovannini's, though his account is, in my opinion, partly vitiated by his unwillingness to distinguish adequately between *synodoi* and *syncletoi*.

Larsen's theory accounts for much of the evidence, but leaves some serious difficulties.

(A) Polybius' use of such expressions as ὄχλος, οἱ πολλοί, τὸ πλῆθος of the people attending a *synodos* is anomalous if this was a meeting of

---

* [[Walbank, *Comm.* III (Oxford, 1979) 406–14. All references, unless otherwise indicated, are to Polybius.]]
[1] Cf. Walbank, *Comm.* I, ii.37.10–11n. [2] Giovannini (1969).
[3] Walbank (1970). [4] Walbank (1970) 129.

the Council.[5] This objection can be circumvented by the hypothesis that the new *boule–synodoi* were not substantially smaller than the earlier *ecclesia–synodoi*, with a depleted attendance.[6]

(B) Larsen argued that membership of the Achaean assembly was limited to men of thirty and over (a view resting on a common interpretation of xxix.24.6; see below, p. 156). But this assumption runs up against several passages which imply that the Achaean army, drawn from all adult citizens and in the nature of things containing a preponderance of young men, occasionally acted as the equivalent of an assembly. These are the relevant passages:

(i) iv.7.5 (220): ἐψηφίσαντο . . . συνάγειν τὸν στρατηγὸν τοὺς Ἀχαιοὺς ἐν τοῖς ὅπλοις: ὃ δ' ἂν τοῖς συνελθοῦσι βουλομένοις δόξῃ, τοῦτ' εἶναι κύριον. Following Aymard (1938a) 220f., Larsen (1955) 80 argued that the army was given special authority for this occasion.

(ii) iv.72.5–7 (219/18): Philip calls the Achaean troops together to receive the gift of Psophis: Aymard (1938a) 234f. argues convincingly that the army had some sort of authority to receive this gift.

(iii) x.22.8–9 (before 210): if hipparchs before the year of Philopoemen's office canvassed τοὺς νέους for their support in gaining the generalship, this most naturally suggests that they participated in elections.[7] It is true that οἱ νέοι often simply means 'soldiers';[8] but that does not invalidate Giovannini's argument, since most of these men would in fact be under thirty.

(iv) Livy xxxviii.33.11 (Polybian) (188): the Achaean army exercises judicial functions and executes some Lacedaemonians.

(v) Plut. *Philop.* 21.1 (182): following Philopoemen's death οἱ . . . ἐν ἡλικίᾳ ‖ μετὰ τῶν προβούλων gather at Megalopolis and elect a general. The source is probably Polybius and Casaubon and Schweighaeuser printed the passage as a Polybian fragment. οἱ . . . ἐν ἡλικίᾳ might just possibly mean 'those of age to attend the assembly' (assuming an age limit of thirty), but the more natural sense[9] is 'those of military age'. Larsen argued that the *probouloi* took the real decision;[10] but this really looks more like an army-meeting acting in a crisis as a substitute for an electoral assembly.

Taken separately, each of these passages can be explained away: taken together they suggest that the Achaean primary assembly was open to all men of military age.

---

[5] Cf. Giovannini (1969) 8 nn. 44–8.　　[6] An explanation I accepted in Walbank (1970) 142.

[7] Cf. Giovanni (1969) 9.　　[8] Cf. Walbank (1970) 139.

[9] Cf. Larsen (1955) 178.　　[10] A view I accepted in Walbank (1970) 139 n. 55.

(C) The meeting held at Corinth in 146 (xxxviii.12–13), which, as Aymard argued[11] and Larsen conceded,[12] has every appearance of being a *synodos*, was dominated by working men and a mob spirit, and voted for war with Sparta (xxxviii.13.6), which points to a primary assembly. Larsen suggests[13] that it was a *boule–synodos* and a *syncletos* combined – the assembly having been summoned to meet concurrently with the *boule*. This is not impossible, but no such hypothesis is required if the meeting is a *synodos* of the primary assembly. Furthermore, Polybius says that the war-vote against Sparta was illegal (xxxviii.13.7), ἕτερον ψήφισμα παράνομον giving absolute power to the στρατηγοί, where the word ἕτερον implies that the first illegal decree was the war-vote against Sparta, and this would be so if decisions on war were the prerogative of specially convened *syncletoi*. Whereas on Larsen's hypothesis the vote, having been taken at a *syncletos*, would not have been illegal. However, this point rests on a distinction between the competence of a *synodos* and that of a *syncletos* which will be discussed below (pp. 160–1).

II

The view that the second-century *synodos* was a meeting of the *boule*, and that membership of the primary assembly was restricted to men of thirty and over depends on a number of passages which refer to limitations on the competence of certain bodies or to circumstances limiting the occasions on which they might be summoned.

(A) In 168 a *synodos* at Corinth was prepared to vote for the sending of military aid to Egypt (xxix.23.8–9, 24.5), but Callicrates prevented this, ὡς οὐκ οὔσης ἐξουσίας κατὰ τοὺς νόμους ἐν ἀγορᾷ βουλεύεσθαι περὶ βοηθείας; since his view was accepted, it was clearly felt to have validity – probably because the sending of military aid, in the circumstances, might involve war.[14] || The meaning of ἀγορά here has been disputed. Aymard[15] quoted evidence to show that it frequently means 'primary assembly'; and here it clearly refers to the *synodos* actually taking place.[16] Giovannini[17] argued that it meant 'session', quoting xxviii.7.3, where Attalus' envoys to Achaea arrive εἰς τὴν πρώτην ἀγοράν (which he took to mean 'for the first session', though indeed it could equally well mean 'for the first *synodos*'); but even if this were so, and ἀγορά was

---

[11] Aymard (1938a) 126–33.   [12] Larsen (1955) 187–8.
[13] Larsen (1955) 188.   [14] See below, p. 160; Larsen (1972) 181 nn. 12–13.
[15] Aymard (1938a) 77 n. 3; cf. Walbank (1970) 137.
[16] Cf. Larsen (1955) 183; Giovannini (1969) 5 n. 33.   [17] Giovannini (1969) 6 n. 36.

a technical term for a session of the Achaean *synodos* (which is quite possible), this would merely introduce a nuance, since the reference would still be to a *synodos*.[18] But does this imply that the *synodos* was a primary assembly? Larsen thought that it need not, but that when at some date between 217 and 200 the *synodos* became (as he believed) a meeting of the Council, the word continued in use – a view I accepted in Walbank (1970) 137. Clearly, however, the use of ἀγορά is more natural if the *synodos* was a primary assembly.

Callicrates' points having been taken, the question of military aid for Egypt was deferred. After some time a *syncletos* met at Sicyon ἐν ᾗ συνέβαινε μὴ μόνον συμπορεύεσθαι τὴν βουλὴν ἀλλὰ πάντας τοὺς ἀπὸ τριάκοντ' ἐτῶν (xxix.24.6). This sentence raises many problems – though one can be disposed of immediately. When Polybius says that the *syncletos* happened to have a particular composition, this is merely a stylistic periphrasis, without significance; a study of Polybius' usage shows that συνέβαινε . . . συμπορεύεσθαι is the equivalent of συνεπορεύετο.[19] But why does Polybius mention the Council? And why the age of those taking part? Various answers have been proposed. Aymard[20] argues that Polybius was merely indicating that the *syncletos* was better attended than the *synodos* at Corinth; he does not explain why Polybius refers to the Council and he thinks the thirty years were mentioned because that was the legal minimum age for attending assemblies – though indeed in that case it is not clear why Polybius should have chosen this one occasion to refer to this minimum age. Larsen[21] also believes the passage to imply an age of thirty for membership of the assembly; and from the statement that 'it happened that not only the Council but all over thirty took part' he deduces (*a*) that there could logically have been *syncletoi*, specially convened meetings, of the Council alone (and he quotes an example of one: xxviii.3.10), and (*b*) that the *synodos* held at Corinth was a meeting (though not a specially convened meeting) of the Council. This is clearly more satisfactory than Aymard's view, and I followed it in Walbank (1970) 135–6. Against it, Giovannini[22] supposes Callicrates' argument to have been, not that decisions involving the sending of military ǁ assistance might not be taken in a *synodos*, but that '*deliberation* on such a question was forbidden in a primary assembly, i.e. any primary assembly'; and he claimed that the real issue was the absence of any resolution from the Council at the *synodos* of Corinth. He then went on to argue that

---

[18] Cf. Larsen (1972) 181 n. 11.   [19] Cf. Foucault (1972) 220.   [20] Aymard (1938a) 73ff.
[21] Larsen (1955) 87–8.   [22] Giovannini (1969) 5–6.

the meeting at Sicyon was a *syncletos* with a special composition, a *senatus amplior*, so that decisions could be taken with a proper *probouleuma*.

This view is not tenable. To translate βουλεύεσθαι 'to debate (but not decide)' is very forced, and is not supported by Polybius' usage elsewhere.[23] Further, at one kind of primary assembly – and despite the agreement of Larsen and Giovannini that a *syncletos* need not invariably be a meeting of the primary assembly, the reference to a *syncletos* without qualification in *Syll.* 675 suggests that normally that is what it was – there is no trace of *probouleusis*. True, if a *synodos* was a meeting of a primary assembly, the Council would in the normal Greek way have prepared the business for it; but there is no evidence of *probouleusis* – unless the *probouloi* of Plut. *Philop.* 21.1,[24] who are probably Council members, are so called because of their probouleutic function – and none that the discussion of business without a *probouleuma* was illegal.[25] Nor is it easy to see why the Achaeans should have tied themselves up with a complicated constitutional procedure making *probouleusis* compulsory, which was bound to result in the kind of difficulty postulated here, and then quickly cut the Gordian knot by summoning a special meeting.[26]

Read without presuppositions, xxix.24.6 can carry at least four possible meanings:

(i) 'Not only the *boule* assembled (as on the previous occasion), but all citizens of thirty and over as well.'

(ii) 'Not only the *boule* assembled (as one might have expected), but all the citizens of thirty and over as well.'

(iii) 'Not only the *boule* (which consisted of men of thirty and over) assembled, but *all* citizens of thirty and over as well.'

(iv) 'Not only the *boule* assembled (as would be true if this had been the Roman *syncletos*, i.e. the Senate), but all citizens of thirty and over as well.'

Of these, the last (proposed by Musti)[27] assumes, ingeniously, that the phraseology is for the benefit of Roman readers, who might not appreciate the difference between an Achaean *syncletos* and the Roman Senate (*syncletos*). But such a confusion seems improbable, and Polybius is generally more concerned with explaining Roman institutions to Greek readers than the reverse. Moreover, this implies that Polybius is describing a normal *syncletos*; ‖ but if this was limited to men of thirty and over, it had a smaller potential composition than a *synodos*. This seems unlikely.

[23] See Walbank (1970) 136–7.   [24] See above, p. 154.
[25] Cf. Walbank (1970) 131; Larsen (1972) 181–2.
[26] Cf. Walbank (1970) 133.   [27] Musti (1972) 1156.

Of the first three views, the first is Larsen's and implies that *synodoi* were at this time meetings of the Council. The second is hard to accept, since one would *not* have expected this special meeting to be of the Council. The third implies that the *syncletos* was exceptionally constituted, inasmuch as it consisted not only of the Council (who were men of thirty and over) but of *all* citizens of thirty and over (but *not* of all citizens of military age, as would have been normal in a primary assembly: so Giovannini).[28] On this third view, the *boule* is mentioned because its members were thirty and over. Admittedly, it is slightly odd that Polybius has chosen to emphasise that the *syncletos* was larger than a mere meeting of the Council, if in fact the unusual feature lay in its being smaller than the *synodos* preceding it. But this difficulty may be more apparent than real. For if we assume that when in Achaea someone spoke of 'men of thirty and over' his listeners automatically thought of membership of the Council, then it is not unnatural for Polybius to say 'a special meeting was called for men of thirty and over – not just the *boule*, but everyone of that age'. The idea that a reader might take the mention of the *boule* to be referring back to the previous meeting would of course not cross his mind if the *synodos* was in fact a meeting of a primary assembly.[29]

The unusual composition of the *syncletos* and the reason for this will be considered shortly (p. 160); that it had to be summoned at all was due to the fact that the laws did not allow decisions concerning the sending of aid to be taken at a *synodos* (ἀγορά). The point of such a limitation will have been to prevent snap decisions on delicate issues of vital importance; and this must be considered || in relation to other passages in Polybius which associate such issues with the summoning of a *syncletos*.

(B) In 185/4 Achaean envoys to the Senate defended their magistrates for not having summoned an *ecclesia* at the request of Caecilius (xxii.12.6):

[28] Giovannini (1969) 6–7. The procedure adopted at this *syncletos* corresponds exactly to that described by Livy xxxii.19–23 for the assembly (usually and rightly taken to be a *syncletos*) called to Sicyon in 198 to discuss whether Achaea should abandon Philip for Rome (cf. Walbank (1970) 131). But it does not follow from this that the composition of the meeting of 168 was precisely the same: the procedure may have applied to *syncletoi*, whether of the whole people or (as here) of a more limited section of them (though not, of course, to *synodoi*, which had a different sort of agenda: on this, against Giovannini (1969) 7 n. 40, see Walbank (1970) 135).

[29] An alternative explanation is that the *synodos* was indeed a meeting of the Council by this date, but that this change in the character of the *synodos* and the restriction of membership of *syncletoi* to men of thirty and over was recent. This would get round the difficulties presented by the passages quoted above, in which the army functioned as an assembly, but it would leave the illegality of the decisions of the 146 meeting unexplained; see above, p. 155. Nor is it very likely that such a modification of the democratic machinery of the Confederacy occurred at the peak of Polybius' public career without leaving any trace in our sources.

νόμον γὰρ εἶναι παρὰ τοῖς Ἀχαιοῖς μὴ συγκαλεῖν τοὺς πολλούς, ἐὰν μὴ περὶ συμμαχίας ἢ πολέμου δέῃ γίνεσθαι διαβούλιον ἢ παρὰ <τῆς> συγκλήτου τις ἐνέγκῃ γράμματα (cf. Livy xxxix.33.7). This passage has been taken as evidence that in the second century a primary assembly could only be called for the purposes there mentioned, viz. to consider alliance or war, or to receive a (written) communication from the Senate.[30] This is incorrect. The use of συγκαλεῖν indicates clearly that the reference is not to *any* primary assembly, but specifically to a *syncletos*, in this context clearly identified as a specially convened meeting of the *ecclesia* (τοὺς πολλούς).[31] In describing the original incident when Caecilius' request was refused (xxii.10.10), and in recounting a similar refusal to call a special meeting for Flamininus in 183 (xxiii.5.16, though the circumstances here were not entirely comparable),[32] Polybius uses the more general word συνάγειν; but in neither instance was it essential for Polybius to use the technical expression, since the context showed that a special meeting was being requested, whereas in addressing the Senate the envoys were giving a general explanation which required them to define the kind of assembly to which they were referring. Hence in xxii.12.6, quoted above, he uses the official word συγκαλεῖν (the noun σύγκλητος would have been awkward, in view of the reference to the Senate as σύγκλητος in the next line).[33]

To the argument that συγκαλεῖν τοὺς πολλούς refers only to *syncletoi* the retort could be made that *synodoi* were also summoned. It is true that συνάγειν is used of both kinds of meeting (though always in the passive for *synodoi*).[34] But there is a big difference between a *regular* meeting (for which one merely needed to know the exact date) and a meeting specially convened to discuss one particular issue, and one would expect the summons to have taken a different form for the two kinds of meeting: in the one case something like: 'The first *synodos* will be held at e.g. Aegium as from such and such a date', and in the other 'The Council *or* all adult citizens *or* . . . (some other defined group) are hereby summoned to e.g. Sicyon on such and such a day to debate and vote on the motion . . . ' It is to the second kind of || summons that the technical term συγκαλεῖν (never used of a *synodos*) will apply; and in fact Polybius

---

[30] Cf. Larsen (1955) 89; accepted in Walbank (1970) 133–4.
[31] For the equivalence of συνάγειν σύγκλητον and συγκαλειν τοὺς πολλούς see Musti (1967) 197; (1972) 1153–4; and for the *syncletos* as an extraordinary meeting see Rizzo (1968–9) especially 368–70.
[32] See Walbank, *Comm.* III, 222 ad loc.   [33] Cf. Musti (1972) 1154.
[34] On the distinction see Aymard (1938a) 122.

provides no instance of any specific person summoning a *synodos* (with an active verb).[35]

III

From the passages discussed above it appears that during the second century the conditions under which a *syncletos* could be convened were closely defined; such a meeting was to decide on alliance or war or to receive a communication from the Senate. This limitation will have been designed to prevent the irresponsible and vexatious summoning, perhaps to further political intrigue, of special meetings which must have had a disruptive effect on ordinary life and on the economy. But xxix.24.5 (p. 155) shows that questions of sending armed help might not be decided in a *synodos*. Armed help could lead to war. Hence it seems to follow that the Achaean laws laid down not only that special meetings could only be called to deal with these specific subjects, but that they *must* be called for those purposes, which did not fall within the competence of a *synodos* (but see below, p. 161).

Why the *syncletos* called to Sicyon in 168 (xxix.24.6) had its special composition Polybius does not inform us. We do not know whether this composition was decided on at the previous *synodos* or by the magistrates; but presumably the decision was taken within a formula prescribed by the laws, though this may have been left fairly flexible to suit exceptional circumstances. That there were such circumstances in 168 seems indicated by the fact that Polybius, quite unusually, chooses to say what the composition of the *syncletos* was. In saying that *all* men of thirty and over were present he is of course giving the terms in which the summons was sent out, not indicating that literally all of these (or even necessarily a large proportion of these) actually turned up. We can only guess why on this occasion the younger men were excluded. Despite my hesitation in Walbank (1970) 132, there is much to be said for Habicht's suggestion[36] that it had something to do with keeping the army ready in the uncertain situation just before Pydna; but there may have been some other reason which we do not know.

There remains a final point on the competence of *synodoi* and that of *syncletoi*, competences which Giovannini considers indistinguishable.[37]

---

[35] In 184 (see Walbank, *Comm.* III, 200, note following xxii.14.12n.) Livy xxxix.35.5 (Polybian) reports that 'Lycortas ... concilium indixit' referring to what was probably, but not certainly, a *synodos* (cf. Larsen (1955) 177); but we do not know what Polybian wording this represents.

[36] Quoted in Giovannini (1969) 16 n. 90.   [37] Giovannini (1969) 10–13.

The fact that third-century *synodoi* are found transacting business which is later dealt with at a *syncletos* || confirms the view of Larsen[38] and Aymard[39] that it was only from a date after 217 that the special rôle of *syncletoi* in taking certain kinds of decision was defined. Furthermore, the application of the law may have remained somewhat flexible in the second century. In xxxiii.16.1–8 a *synodos* decides not to send armed help to Rhodes; but perhaps if the vote had looked like going the other way, the matter would have been deferred to a *syncletos*.[40] There must indeed often have been genuine disagreement as to whether certain issues came within the scope of a *synodos* or should be referred to a special meeting;[41] clearly not every formal renewal of a treaty will have required the summoning of a *syncletos*.

To sum up: the Achaeans had a Council and a primary assembly which met at four annual *synodoi* right down to 146. From the time the Romans appeared on the scene, towards the end of the third century, certain delicate issues were removed from the competence of the regular *synodoi* and reserved for discussion and decision at a specially convened *syncletos* with a single item on the agenda; such *syncletoi* would normally consist of the Council and assembly, but (as in 168) exceptionally, following a decision either of the *synodos* or of the magistrates (we are not told which), could have a different composition. Membership of the assembly was open to all men of military age; membership of the Council was probably restricted to men of thirty and over.

[38] Larsen (1955) 92–3.   [39] Aymard (1938a) 228ff., 416.
[40] See Walbank, *Comm.* III, 398–9, xxix.24.5 n   [41] For some examples see Walbank (1970) 140–1.

Polybius as a historian

11

*Timaeus' views on the past**†

I

The question I should like to try to answer in this paper is whether by the Hellenistic period there existed something that we could call a west Greek view of the past. There is no simple answer to this since, until one gets down as far as Diodorus, who was writing at the time of Julius Caesar, all the western Greek historians exist only in fragments; and indeed, after looking at the fragments,[1] I fairly soon reached the conclusion that any discussion of their views about the past would have to centre on Timaeus. For that there is a good reason. Apart from Timaeus, the attested fragments of authors such as Antiochus and Philistus, not to mention lesser figures like Athanis of Syracuse, Timonides of Leucas, Callias and Antander, the brothers of Agathocles, and Alcimus, are so meagre – indeed in some cases we have little more than their names – that they emerge as wholly shadowy personalities. Nor is it simply that the fragments are few in number. In addition there is a strong likelihood that often these writers are being quoted at second hand via Timaeus. Consequently, if the fragments seem to suggest that their authors were interested predominantly in the same kind of things as Timaeus, that may well be because he quoted material from them which happened to fall in with his own interests.

For Timaeus himself the situation is a little better, though by no means wholly satisfactory. Jacoby lists over a hundred and fifty attested fragments of the historian. Many come from Polybius, who consistently sets him in a || bad light, and about a score are from Athenaeus, who had decidedly specialised interests. So at the outset there is the problem of

* [[*Scripta Classica Israelica* 10 (1989/90) 41–54]]

† A paper read at a conference on the Attitudes to the Past in Hellenistic Historiography, held at the Hebrew University of Jerusalem on 14–15 November 1988.

[1] For the fragments of the historians of Sicily (with Magna Graecia) see *FGH* 554–77; Timaeus is no. 566.

recovering Timaeus. About the possibility of doing this there have been two diametrically opposite views. In his monograph on Timaeus,[2] published in 1958, Truesdell Brown took the view that it was dangerous to go beyond the attested fragments; and that was also the judgement of Momigliano in a classic study, originally published in 1959, and reprinted seven years later in his *Terzo contributo*,[3] on the discovery of Rome in the *Histories* of Timaeus. But since then valuable work has been done by Klaus Meister[4] in analysing the chapters of Diodorus dealing with the west and identifying those sections which have drawn on Timaeus. And in 1987 Lionel Pearson published a new study of Timaeus[5] which, I believe, makes it substantially easier to ask the question with which I opened this paper and have a reasonable chance of finding an answer.

Much of Pearson's book is also taken up with analysing Diodorus along with Plutarch and other later writers. A particular problem with which he is concerned is one that I have already touched on, namely whether, when these later writers mention sources other than Timaeus in what we may call 'Timaean' passages, these references reflect their own supplementary reading or are taken over as they stand from Timaeus himself. If, as seems likely, the second alternative is frequently (though not always) true, one can of course be more optimistic about recovering Timaean material from their works. To facilitate this process Pearson has adopted a principle enunciated by the German scholar Geffcken, to the effect that where we have a passage bearing the manifest stamp of Timaeus (as revealed in attested fragments) in at least two authors independently known to use Timaeus, Timaeus may be assumed to be the source; and this law is not, Pearson claims, invalidated by slightly || variant versions in those authors, since slight variations are something one would naturally expect to find. Geffcken's law is obviously *not* equivalent to a proof; but as a rule of thumb it helps things along substantially and extends the amount of material available for establishing Timaeus' views about the past.

Assuming, however, that we can make some sort of shot at reconstructing Timaeus along these lines, can we distinguish between his real views about the past and what one might crudely term the propagandist purpose of his history? To this question I suspect the answer is 'no'. A historian does not simply contemplate the past and apprehend it as something separate from himself. He interacts with it, thrusts his interpretation upon it and in a sense recreates it. Each historian gives us his

---

[2] Brown (1958).   [3] Momigliano (1959).   [4] Meister (1967).
[5] Pearson (1987). [Pearson's use of the 'lex Geffcken' is rejected by Meister (1989/90).]

own version of the past and he may be entirely convinced of the truth of
what he has written although to the critic his version may seem patently
slanted to support a thesis. How Timaeus saw the past is something
to be discovered not simply from what he says about it but also from
how he narrates past events. A good example of this is the account of
the battle of Himera in Diodorus xi.20–6, which draws on Timaeus as
its source.[6] In this passage, as Pearson has shown, Timaeus sets out to
out-trump Herodotus' account of the Persian Wars in mainland Greece.
Thus, instead of Herodotus' synchronism of Himera with the Greek victory at Salamis (vii.166), Timaeus has substituted a synchronism with
the Greek defeat at Thermopylae (xi.24.1); and Himera is portrayed as
so resounding a victory that 'not even a messenger, as the saying goes,
reached Carthage to bring the news' (xi.23.2). The result of the battle was
to encourage the mainland Greeks in *their* coming battle with Xerxes, to
serve as a good omen for their victory and to enable Gelon to offer them
his assistance; and afterwards the Carthaginian prisoners were employed
rebuilding the destroyed temples of Acragas – a boast not open to the
Athenian victors of Salamis in relation to the defeated Persians. These
contrasts are not specifically mentioned by Diodorus or, by implication,
Timaeus: but they are incorporated within the narrative in such a way
that no reader could miss them.

II

For his account of Himera Timaeus seems to have drawn largely on his
patriotic imagination. But for much of his narrative he had of course
sources || to rely on, both earlier writers and – though this is more
controversial – local traditions. I have already mentioned some earlier
west Greek writers, but the only two of real importance were Antiochus
and Philistus.[7] Antiochus had written both *Sicelica* and a shorter work Περὶ
Ἰταλίας. The fact that we have more fragments from the latter work led
von Fritz[8] to attribute many of the Italian fragments to the *Sicelica*; but
that was unnecessary, for the disproportion in the number of surviving
fragments merely reflects the fact that Strabo, the source of many of them,
devoted seventy sections of Books V and VI to Italy and only twelve to
Sicily. Jacoby has made the important point[9] that *Sicelica*, whether written
by Antiochus or his successors, constituted a form of history parallel,

[6] Cf. Meister (1967) 42–3; Pearson (1987) 20–6; *contra*, Brown (1958).
[7] *FGH* 555 (Antiochus), 556 (Philistus).
[8] Von Fritz (1967) I: Text, 507–18; cf. Walbank (1968–9) 479.   [9] *FGH* III B pp. 480–1.

not with Greek *local history*, which usually concerned itself with separate
cities, but with *Hellenica*, that is with mainland Greek history – but filling
a western gap left unfilled by Herodotus. This is both true and important
when we come to Timaeus, who clearly felt himself to be writing history
of that kind.

Written sources could sometimes be supplemented from local traditions – though how extensive or reliable these were is debatable. We have
to distinguish here between two kinds of tradition: first, local legends involving gods and heroes, which might be linked to a particular locality,
but obviously did not correspond to any actual historical events; and
secondly, traditions of early history, including the 'foundation stories' of
the cities of Sicily and Magna Graecia. (Incidentally the latter, legends
and foundation stories concerning Magna Graecia, were often included
in works entitled *Sicelica*, since in early times there existed no geographical concept of Italy comparable to the clear geographical concept of
Sicily.)[10] For both kinds of tradition the evidence is scanty. As Pearson
points out, there is not likely to have been much or any cultural contact
between the Greeks and their Sicel or Sican predecessors;[11] and if there
was any, it is improbable that it elicited any traditions likely to reinforce
Greek legends. In general, however, I suspect that Pearson is too sceptical
about what may have been available elsewhere. A number of terracotta
votive offerings representing Aeneas and Anchises, which were discov-
ered at Veii, may suggest that the legend linking Italy with || the Trojan
War was known in Etruria by an early date.[12] Pearson argues that as a
Greek import the objects can tell us nothing about local traditions. But
imports have to take account of consumer preferences and I think one
must assume that the terracottas meant something to those who dedicated them. The sacred objects which Timaeus records[13] as deposited in
a temple at Lavinium may have been no more genuine Trojan relics than
many sacred objects to be found in our cathedrals – the Turin shroud for
example – are what they purport to be; but what matters is that they are
evidence for the existence of a tradition which regarded them as Trojan.
The strength of that tradition would be enhanced still more if it could be
proved decisively that a building excavated at Lavinium was indeed, as is

---

[10] Cf. Jacoby, ibid.   [11] Pearson (1987) 55.

[12] Cf. Momigliano (1963) 102 n. 37 for earlier bibliography. These terracottas were originally dated
to the fifth century, but Torelli (1984) has recently argued for a date after 390, on the grounds
that the tradition of such terracotta votive offerings in Central Italy does not go back earlier than
the early fourth century.

[13] *FGH* 566 F 59 (Dion.Hal.i.67.4); cf. Pearson (1987) 86 (where 'Lanuvium' is a mistake for
'Lavinium').

argued by several Italian archaeologists, the *heroon* of Aeneas.[14] However, it can, I admit, be argued that the situation in Etruria, Rome and Latium is different from that existing in Sicily and Magna Graecia. But I shall return shortly to the place occupied in Timaeus' *Histories* by Rome.

III

How and what a historian writes and how he views the past are questions that do not depend solely on his sources, his own prejudices and his interaction with the material which the sources provide. He is also deeply influenced by existing literary traditions about different categories of historiography, for example the different scope and expectations proper to history or biography. Timaeus, we must remember, spent fifty years working in libraries in Athens. The subject of his work was western Greece but he would have been surrounded on the shelves by mainstream writers and he must have been thoroughly familiar with their assumptions about different sorts of history and ways of writing it. In a well-known passage from the introduction to || Book IX of his *Histories*[15] Polybius enumerates three different kinds of history-writing which, though he does not say so, had traditionally been associated with a sequence of periods in Greek history.[16] The first of these historical genres he calls 'the genealogical kind'; the second history dealing with 'colonies, foundations of cities and kinship relations (συγγένειαι)'; and the third history concerned with 'ἔθνη, cities and rulers'. Under ἔθνη he includes both tribal states and federal bodies; and in fact it is within this third category that Polybius' own work entirely falls. Polybius does not say, however, that a history had to be restricted to only one of these genres. In fact we know that sections of Ephorus' history dealt with colonies, foundations and the ties of kinship.[17] Since the beginning of the fifth century a branch of history had however arisen which was specifically devoted to bringing the contents of early Greek myth and legend into some kind of order. This 'genealogical kind of history', as Polybius here terms it, was the creation of Hecataeus of Miletus, who sorted out the myths and generations of the epic figures to produce a consistent picture and one that was broadly accepted by his successors. By the early fourth century the 'mythical' and the 'genealogical' were regarded as closely linked together, as they are in the fictional discourse given by Solon to the Egyptians in Plato's

---

[14] See Sommella (1971–2).   [15] Polyb. ix.1.1–5 [see above, ch. 1, p. 6].
[16] On this see Mohm (1977) 27–8.   [17] Cf. Polyb. xxxix.1.3.

Timaeus (22 a). Already Herodotus had accepted the distinction which this implied between legendary and historical times; in iii.122, for instance, he differentiates between Polycrates' thalassocracy and that of Minos. Similarly, Ephorus, by beginning his universal history with the return of the Heracleidae,[18] established that 'event' as an epochal date for the beginning of real history.

Living and working in Athens, Timaeus will have been familiar with these periods and these categories; and Jacoby seems to have established that at the outset of his work he treated the mythical period. His western predecessors had already adopted the habit of beginning their works with the earliest times – unlike the great historians of mainland Greece, Herodotus, Thucydides, Xenophon and, later, Polybius. Unfortunately the 'earliest times' were an age of myth and fantasy rather than of solid historical events. It is rather as if a serious history of Great Britain were to begin with the landing of Brut the Trojan at Totnes or a history of the United States were to open with a first ‖ chapter based on the contents of the Book of Mormon. Polybius' second and third types – or periods – of history fitted the western experience rather well, since foundation legends were an important part of the traditions of those colonial areas. But the first category, ὁ γενεαλογικὸς τρόπος, which appeals to the φιλήκοος, the reader who likes a good yarn, and deals with the mythical period, including all its fabulous elements, presented special problems – but also special opportunities.

IV

One of the merits of Pearson's recent work is his convincing demonstration that Timaeus consciously set out to graft the rich mythology of mainland Greece onto the west. The effect – and perhaps, we may say, the purpose – of this was to stake out a prior Greek claim to large areas of Sicily, South Italy and other parts of the western Mediterranean where, in later centuries, the real Greek colonists would arrive to take up their inheritance. For Timaeus this was not a purely arbitrary procedure. It involved locating places mentioned in the *Odyssey* at specific sites and arguing from survivals of customs and religious rituals, from the supposed origins of still extant buildings and from far-fetched etymologies of place-names, which supposedly 'proved' their Greek character. Alternatively, vaguely situated legends could be firmly attached to some

---

[18] *FGH* 70 T 8 = Diod. iv.1.3.

definite western locality – for example, the rape of Persephone, which was now set in the meadows below Enna, probably by Timaeus.[19] Similarly Demeter's gift of corn to the Sicilians[20] – before she gave it to the Athenians – established Sicily as the birthplace of agriculture and all that that implied for the future of civilisation. The Argonauts were brought to Italy and the island of Elba;[21] Strabo and Diodorus justify this association with strange etymologies which are redolent of Timaeus.[22] Boeotians on the Balearic Islands,[23] the sons of Heracles in Sardinia[24] and Heracles himself at Gades[25] all contribute to the same picture. The list could be || extended. It is interesting to observe that we have a similar phenomenon in the care taken by the historians of Alexander to provide his expedition to India with forerunners in the myths involving Heracles and Dionysus.[26]

As I have already pointed out, it is difficult to discover how far Timaeus actually *believed* all these stories. Many of them contained a miraculous content which a rationalist author like Polybius would have dismissed with contempt. But, as we know, belief in miracles is an odd business. Credulity or incredulity can vary not only from generation to generation, but also from one individual to another. In his *Ecclesiastical History* Bede records miracle after miracle and obviously has no difficulty in believing in them all; and even today many people who refuse to believe that miracles occur in the modern world believe in the miracles recorded in the Old and New Testaments. How far Timaeus was committed to believing all the stories he retails is not easy to decide, since we have not access to his actual words and so are unable to judge the *tone* of his remarks. It may well be that, like Herodotus, he did not necessarily accept as true everything he recorded. But it is useful to be reminded by Pearson that in his account of the sixth-century struggles between the cities of Magna Graecia Timaeus introduced the same kind of marvels and mythical elements that we find in his treatment of earlier centuries – either because he could not find records of a more factual kind or because he preferred a romantic anecdotal treatment.[27] But whatever his innermost beliefs on these matters, I think we must regard his treatment of the 'mythical period' in the west as an integral part of his view of the past.

---

[19] Diod. v.1.3 = *FGH* 566 F 164.   [20] Diod. iv.4.4 = *FGH* 566 F 164.
[21] Diod. iv.56.3–7 = *FGH* 566 F 85.   [22] Cf. Pearson (1987) 63–4.   [23] *FGH* 566 F 66.
[24] Cf. Pearson (1987) 66 n. 54, quoting Geffcken (1892) 55–8.
[25] *Mir.ausc.* 88; Cf. Pearson (1987) 69.
[26] Cf. Pearson (1987) 59 n. 22 for references to Tyre, the oasis of Ammon and Aornus.
[27] Cf. Pearson (1987) 111.

When we come down to the fifth century and later times, the atmosphere changes. There seems no doubt that from then onwards Timaeus saw Sicilian history as a struggle for freedom – externally against the Carthaginians and internally against the rule of tyrants, the latter having frequently gained their position by leading the resistance to the foreign enemy. Timaeus' views on freedom can be deduced from his treatment of the leading figures in Sicilian and Southern Italian history during this period – from his hostility towards the tyrants (with the exception of Gelon, the victor of Himera) and his sympathetic view of Dion and Timoleon and, in the fifth century, Hermocrates, for whom, despite the ambiguities of his career, Timaeus clearly entertained warm feelings. Timaeus' hatred of tyrants partly, of course, reflects his own misfortune in having been expelled from Tauromenium by || Agathocles, just as his sympathy for Timoleon arises out of Timoleon's collaboration with Timaeus' father Andromachus and willingness to leave him in charge at Tauromenium.

v

So far I have said nothing about one aspect of Timaeus' work which is often regarded as highly important both for his historical significance and for his historical understanding: I mean, of course, his treatment of Rome. The trouble about this is that once again our paucity of firm evidence makes it very difficult to find out what Timaeus' considered attitude to Rome was. Writing well over a century before Polybius, he was far less advantageously placed than the Achaean historian for appreciating the rôle that Rome was to fill in the history of the western – and later the eastern – Mediterranean. But, if we could discover what he thought about Rome, it would clearly be relevant to his view of the past, since most historians are apt to interpret the past to some extent in the light of their apprehension of the present.

According to Polybius (i.5.1) Timaeus ended his history in 264, when the Romans first crossed over into Sicily. This is the point at which Polybius himself opened his introductory account of the events down to 220, before embarking upon his main narrative. The year 264, Laqueur remarked, is 'a splendid opening, but no conclusion'.[28] I am not so sure about that. If Timaeus wanted to end his work with a fateful moment and event which set a large question mark against the whole future of the west, 264 would be hard to beat. And why should one assume that every historian will want to end his work at a date which is nicely decisive and

[28] R. Laqueur, *RE* VI A, 1 (1936) col. 1082.

conclusive? The last words of Xenophon's *Hellenica* are surely a clear refutation of that assumption. Closing with the battle of Mantinea he writes: 'After that battle trouble and confusion (ἀκρισία καὶ ταραχή) in Greece were even greater than before.'[29] Certainly by 264 it was clear that Rome was to play an important and probably decisive rôle, at any rate in Sicily – which was Timaeus' main concern. But this may well not have been true at the time when Timaeus was writing his early books – assuming, as I shall, that he wrote those first.

I have already mentioned Momigliano's essay on the discovery of Rome in Timaeus' *Histories*, in which he assigns a major rôle to Timaeus as the man || who first revealed the importance of Rome to the Greek world.[30] In his recent book Pearson is much more sceptical and plays down the rôle of Rome in Timaeus' work and in his vision of the past and present.[31] Rome, he thinks, figured in Timaeus' main work simply as one piece in the early Italian mosaic. Its foundation legends were recorded like those of many other cities: but in no way did it stand out. Let us consider the evidence.

First, there is the problem of the book on Pyrrhus. Discussing the ancient Roman custom of the sacrifice of the 'October horse', Polybius (xii.4 b) refers to Timaeus' views as expressed in Τὰ περὶ Πύρρου, 'The events concerning Pyrrhus', as if this were a separate work, distinct from his main *Histories*. That that is so is confirmed by two later writers. One of these is Cicero who, in a letter to Lucceius (*Ad fam.* v.12.2), asking him to write a monograph on his (Cicero's) consulship, quotes various precedents of historians who have produced such separate works, mainly in fact on individual wars – Callisthenes on the *Phocicum bellum*, Timaeus on the *Pyrrhi (sc. bellum)* and Polybius on the *Numantinum (sc. bellum)*. Cicero clearly implies that his actions against the Catilinarian conspirators constituted another such *bellum*. Pearson[32] claims that we do not know which wars were described in Timaeus' monograph – those which he fought in Italy and Sicily or indeed his whole career. Dionysius (i.6.1), it is true, employs the phrase 'τοὺς . . . πρὸς Πύρρον . . . πολέμους', the wars against Pyrrhus, to describe the separate work (ἰδίαν . . . πραγματείαν). But he does so in order to contrast those wars with τὰ . . . ἀρχαῖα τῶν ἱστοριῶν, the ancient part of the *Histories*, which were recorded ἐν ταῖς κοιναῖς ἱστορίαις, in Timaeus' general history. In both cases it is Rome he is speaking about, Rome's early history and Rome's wars against Pyrrhus (πρὸς Πύρρον).

[29] Xen. *Hell.* vii.5.27.   [30] Momigliano (1959).
[31] Pearson (1987) 84–5.   [32] Pearson (1987) 255–6.

Why then does Dionysius speak of wars in the plural? Clearly the plural does not refer to a variety of wars fought *by* Pyrrhus, including his whole career and his struggles in Greece, Macedonia and Epirus, as Pearson envisages, when he translates 'the wars of Pyrrhus'. For the wars mentioned by Dionysius are fought by the Romans *against* Pyrrhus, not by Pyrrhus against all and sundry enemies. One might, I suppose, assume that the campaign in Sicily was included on the grounds that a war fought against Pyrrhus by Rome's Carthaginian allies was tantamount to a war fought against him by Rome. But that seems on the whole rather far-fetched. And || the use of the plural 'wars' excludes the notion that the Sicilian campaigns were included as forming *part* of the war between Pyrrhus and Rome. On the whole, then, the most likely explanation of Dionysius' plural 'wars' is that he is thinking of the Roman campaigns against Pyrrhus before he left for Sicily and the campaign which took place after his return to Italy as constituting two separate wars. It is more usual to regard them as two episodes in a single war, as Cicero does; but basically we are concerned here merely with a matter of terminology. Τὰ περὶ Πύρρου, on this hypothesis, was a monograph dealing with the war between Rome and Pyrrhus, what looking back at it from the Roman standpoint we usually call the Tarentine or Pyrrhic War. There is no good reason to regard it as a section of the main history. Indeed the combined evidence of Cicero and Dionysius is against that supposition. At this point I should perhaps add that Pyrrhus' war in Sicily will obviously have been treated in Timaeus' *Histories.* But our main surviving sources for that war – Plutarch's *Life of Pyrrhus*, Dionysius and Justin – do not appear to have used him directly and the best Pearson can do here is to pick out passages in those works which seem, if only indirectly, to echo Timaeus' sentiments.[33]

There is also a passage in Aulus Gellius (xi.1.1 = *FGH* 566 т 9 (c)) in which he speaks of 'historiae, quas oratione Graeca de rebus populi Romani (*sc.* Timaeus) composuit'. Jacoby, who by a slip attributes the phrase to Varro (whom Gellius mentions immediately afterwards), assumes that the reference is to Timaeus' work on Pyrrhus; and undoubtedly this monograph can more appropriately be said to be about the affairs of the Roman people than can his main history. We cannot however be sure of this. The context in which Gellius quotes this work and also that of Varro concerns the etymology of the word *Italia*, which Timaeus derived from 'an ancient Greek word "italoi" meaning "oxen" ' – Varro

---

[33] Pearson (1987) 256–9.

probably followed Timaeus in this – and such a context is clearly more appropriate to the early books of the *Histories* than it is to an account of the war against Pyrrhus. Indeed one assumes that Timaeus will have discussed precisely this kind of thing in his early books. Moreover, it would be rather odd to use *historiae* to describe Timaeus' monograph on the war between Rome and Pyrrhus, a word far more suited to the general history, for which he was better known. Nevertheless, I think we have to leave it open as to which of his works was described by Gellius as 'containing *res populi Romani*', while regarding the main history as slightly more probable. ||

The same doubt hangs over an unquestionably significant statement made by Timaeus, namely that Rome was founded in the same year as Carthage, thirty-eight years before the first Olympiad (Dion.Hal. i.74.1 = *FGH* 566 F 60), that is, in 814. Incidentally, this is much earlier than the dates later put forward for the foundation of Rome. But in that it is not unique. Callias, Agathocles' brother, had a version which put it three generations after Aeneas;[34] and Ennius[35] dated it around 700 years before either his own time, which would make it about 900 BC, or (if the relevant passage comes from a speech of Camillus, as Skutsch has indicated)[36] as early as 1100 BC. The coincidence between the foundation of Rome and that of Carthage is very typical of Timaeus, who loved synchronisms. But it can hardly be purely arbitrary and must mean that he saw the two powers as somehow ranged against each other. Unfortunately we do not know *where* in Timaeus' works this synchronism occurred. It is clear from Dionysius[37] that Timaeus dealt with Rome twice – τὰ ἀρχαῖα in his general history, and 'the wars against Pyrrhus' in the separate monograph; and we do not know to which of the two the common foundation date is to be attributed.[38]

It might at first sight seem more likely that a foundation date – like the discussion of the etymology of the word 'Italia' – is more appropriate to the books dealing with the foundation of the Greek and Italian cities. But the monograph could equally well have included material dealing with the earlier history and customs of Carthage and Rome which (in the latter case at least) Timaeus had not thought sufficiently relevant to his main purpose to be included in his *Histories*. It is significant that our only

---

[34] Dion. Hal. i.72.5 = *FGH* 564 F 5.   [35] Fg.501–2 Vahlen = *Ann*.4.5 Skutsch (Skutsch 1985).

[36] On this see Skutsch (1985) 315 n. 1. As he there explains, the suggestion was originally made by Unger in 1880, developed by Holzapfel in 1875, forgotten, and then suggested afresh by Soltau in 1912, and refined by Norden in 1915 and, independently, Klotz in 1942.

[37] Dion. Hal.i.6.1 = *FGH* 566 T 9 b.   [38] Cf. Momigliano (1959) (*Terzo contributo* 44–5).

fragment specifically attributed to the monograph concerns the Roman sacrifice of the 'October horse'[39] 'commemorating their disaster at Troy': one can see how that fitted in to the conflict with Pyrrhus, the descendant of Achilles. And since it was at the time of Pyrrhus that the Romans made their third treaty with Carthage (Polyb. iii.25.1–5), Timaeus may well have drawn attention to a chronological || synchronism which he did not mention when dealing with τὰ ἀρχαῖα. There is a parallel in F 61 (from Pliny), which asserts that 'Servius rex primus signavit aes; antea rudi usos Romae Timaeus tradit'; Momigliano has pointed out[40] that this passage is preceded by a statement that the Romans did not use silver coinage before the time of Pyrrhus and consequently that Timaeus probably dealt with the subject of Roman coinage in his monograph on Pyrrhus rather than in his general history. The same is likely to be true of the synchronism of the two foundation dates.

If that is so, we can, I think, draw the tentative conclusion that Timaeus grew increasingly aware of the importance of Rome and Carthage, despite his seclusion at Athens, cut off from first-hand experience of western developments. The fact that he chose to devote a monograph to the war of the Romans against Pyrrhus and probably included in it the synchronism of the foundation dates of Rome and Carthage indicates that he had some inkling of the coming struggle for power. And that would be confirmed by his decision to end his *Histories* in the year of the great question mark, 264, when the Romans first took their forces overseas into Sicily, the home of Timaeus.

VI

If I may summarise my conclusions about Timaeus' view of the past, the following points seem to emerge. First, Timaeus – and in this he may be following in the footsteps of earlier western historians – looked back to a western past which was comparable to that of mainland Greece and was indeed *equally Greek*. This could be demonstrated from the legends concerning the gods and heroes. Many of these had found their way to Sicily, Magna Graecia and the western Mediterranean generally. As a result the Greek colonists, when they set out to found daughter-cities in the west, came ashore in lands which were *naturaliter Graeca*, lands awaiting the arrival of their destined Hellenic heirs. Western Greece was another Hellas inhabited by men equally devoted to freedom and the struggle

---

[39] Polyb. xii.4 b = *FGH* 566 F 86.   [40] Momigliano (1959) (*Terzo contributo* 45).

against the barbarians, whom they were on the whole more successful in crushing. It is this Greek world that Timaeus in his old age sees as threatened by the imminent struggle between the two barbarian powers, Rome and Carthage. Its forerunner is the Roman war with Pyrrhus, and by treating this in a separate monograph Timaeus may even have been confessing his inability to incorporate the issues which it raised within his main *History*. ||

Jacoby's judgement on Timaeus strikes one as inconsistent. In his commentary on the fragments (*FGH* III b p. 535) he describes him as 'banal, bourgeois and self-contradictory, a writer lacking a philosophy of history or sense of the world around him (*Weltanschauung*)'; yet on the very next page he characterises him as the man who saw the significance of Rome. So phrased, this second claim is not quite as substantially supported as either Jacoby or Momigliano maintains. For it was not simply Rome, but rather whichever of the two great barbarian powers should come out on top in their forthcoming struggle that Timaeus saw as putting the Greek world at risk. If we may believe Polybius, the same point was to be made by Agelaus of Naupactus at the conference of 217, when he made the famous comment about the 'cloud in the west'.[41] For Agelaus it was the Greeks of the mainland who were under threat, for Timaeus those of Sicily and the west. The view that Timaeus saw the significance of Rome has therefore to be qualified. But I hope also to have shown that Jacoby's first claim is dubious and that Timaeus had a clear picture of the past and of a pattern in history which both flattered and legitimised the Greeks of those western lands from which the misfortune of political exile for so many years excluded him.

[41] Polyb. v.104.10.

12

*Polybius and the past**

I

As my thanks-offering for the fifteen years hard labour he has put into producing *LCM* for our common good John Pinsent will expect something Polybian: for he is well aware that old dogs do not easily learn new tricks. I am therefore submitting to his highly critical eye some observations on Polybius' attitude towards the past. By that I do not mean that part of the past which makes up his basic theme – how in just under fifty-three years, from 220 to 168 BC, the Romans made themselves rulers of the whole known world – but rather his attitude towards the whole of the past, Greek and Roman, what in that past he regarded as important and how it linked up with the topic which he chose for his own *Histories*. For how a historian sees the past generally does not merely help to determine how he will approach his own particular topic. It is also relevant to the breadth of his historical understanding and humanity. In Goethe's words:

> Wer nicht von dreitausend Jahren
> sich weiss Rechenschaft zu geben,
> bleib' im Dunkeln unerfahren,
> mag von Tag zu Tage leben.

For Polybius, it is true, three thousand years is more than we have any right to demand. For Greeks and Romans alike the significant past was much briefer than that. But in principle Goethe's words are true for Polybius, as they are for us all.

The historian's relationship to the past is a strange one. Studying history does not mean absorbing the past as if one were drinking coffee. It is a dynamic, dialectical process involving investigation, selection and interpretation. At each stage the historian interacts with his material.

* [[H. D. Jocelyn (ed.) *Tria Lustra: Essays and Notes Presented to John Pinsent* (Liverpool Classical Papers 3) (Liverpool 1993) 15–23]]

The past is in some sense recreated afresh for each person who concerns himself with it. Furthermore, the picture at which the historian finally arrives depends at least in part on his source of information: with poor sources there can be no real depth of historical understanding. Consequently, as Polybius saw, the historian must be prepared to ferret out his version of the past from a variety of sources, not only what previous historians have said, but also oral traditions (such as he used at Locri: xii.5–11) and, for more recent times, eye-witnesses; and there were of course documents available such as inscriptions – vitally important to the modern historian of the ancient world, but already used by Polybius, as they were by Timaeus before him. Sometimes direct evidence is not available, in which case the test of probability may be brought in. Polybius frequently argues from τὸ πιθανόν – what is convincing – and from τὸ εἰκός – likelihood. But he admits that this is always a second-best compared with solid testimony (xii.5.23). Perhaps most important of all, the historian must have a feeling for the ethos of a past age: and this, as we shall see, is an area in which Polybius sometimes falls down.

In both classical and Hellenistic Greece the past was important not simply as the subject-matter of historians, but also as an element in public life and sentiment. Consciousness of the past penetrated political activity to an extent which would seem strange today. References to historical – and pseudo-historical – events, to family links in the distant past and to real or imaginary ties of kinship between mother-city and daughter-colony were repeatedly invoked in serious diplomatic exchanges in order to smooth an approach or gain an end. A recently published example of this from Polybius' time is an appeal by Cytinium in Doris to Xanthus in Lycia for financial help in the rebuilding of its walls, destroyed by the Macedonian king, Antigonus Doson. We possess the appeal and the response (not too generous). In both great emphasis is laid on Xanthus' Dorian origins. Similarly Ilium exploited the Trojan connection to secure privileges from the Romans, the descendants of the Trojans. Past services were remembered or recalled: || obligations thus incurred were not easily ignored. In 198 the representatives of Dyme, Megalopolis and Argos walked out of the Achaean assembly rather than consent to breaking off their old ties of friendship with Macedonia by joining Rome.

The historical perspective in which statesmen made such decisions took in what we should regard as the 'epic' or 'legendary' period. And it is noteworthy that Polybius, like Thucydides, regarded those times as a genuine early stage in Greek history. Thus he mentions Io (iv.43.6), Jason (iv.39.6) and Odysseus as if they were real historical figures. Indeed when he speaks of voyaging on the ocean beyond the Pillars of Heracles, Odysseus is a person every bit as real as Pytheas of Marseilles, who lived in the fourth century. Blatantly mythical elements in Homer's account were easily eliminated. Following Eratosthenes, Polybius interprets Odysseus' voyages along these lines. Aeolus, who gave Odysseus the bag of the winds, was in reality a man who instructed him about sailing around the Straits of Messina; only legend had turned him into a king and 'guardian of the winds'. Similarly Atreus and Danaus were men who, because of their cultural discoveries, had been turned by tradition into seers and kings. Polybius implies, without actually saying so, that the gods were all great inventors and benefactors to mankind who had in consequence been deified. This is, of course, not new. It reflects the teachings of Euhemerus and is very much an aspect of Hellenistic thought. And even among those who did not consciously espouse Euhemerus' theories, it was probably widely assumed that men of past ages were much the same as men of one's own time.

Indeed, somewhat to his detriment as a historian trying to understand the past, Polybius assumes a high degree of uniformity in men's reactions to circumstances, regardless of time and differences in culture. He takes it for granted that people both of his own and of earlier generations must have thought and acted as he would think and act – which means that they would act rationally and from motives of self-interest. Scipio Africanus, for example, a Roman living in the late third and early second centuries, he believes to have been a rationalist shamelessly exploiting the religious sentiments of ordinary Roman soldiers in order to ensure their enthusiasm for his bold plan to capture the Carthaginian stronghold of New Carthage – almost certainly a misinterpretation of Scipio's mentality. But in the same way he assumes that the mythical or semi-mythical Spartan lawgiver Lycurgus pretended to have the backing of the Pythia so as to win acceptance for his famous constitution. And it is in precisely the same spirit that he praises the Romans (vi.56) for cynically using the terrors of Hades to cow the common people into moral behaviour – though, rather oddly, the examples he quotes of strict integrity induced in this fashion are taken from magistrates and ambassadors and not from the lower classes.

If human psychology remained the same, that was manifestly not true of social organisation, which had changed substantially even within historical memory. Life in Homeric society was very different from life in the *polis*; and the many struggles between democrats and oligarchs illustrated the many different social forms under which Greeks (and others) had at various times lived. Historians have frequently been tempted to

try to detect – and in practice this has usually meant being tempted
to superimpose – some sort of pattern on the social and constitutional
changes which constantly occur in history. Early Christian historians imposed one such pattern, which was, to quote Collingwood ((1946) 49),
'universal, providential, apocalyptic and periodized'. Later ages proposed fresh patterns: in the Renaissance, for instance, those of Macchi-
avelli and Campanella and in later times those of Vico, Hegel, Marx,
Spengler and Toynbee. Did Polybius see any such pattern in his interpretation of earlier times?

II

The truth is that our perception of Polybius' view of the past is made no
easier by the fact that he alludes to *several* themes or patterns which he
believes will help the reader to understand the forces of history. Some –
indeed, most – of these themes complement each other; but that is not
true of them all. Let us then examine them, one by one. ||
     The first of these historical patterns is of course his central theme, viz.
that under the direction of a power called Fortune (*Tyche*) Rome rose in a
little under fifty-three years from near defeat at the hands of Hannibal to
become the ruler of the whole known world. The unification of the world
and the interlocking (συμπλοκή) of all its parts during the years from 220
to 168 has also relevance for earlier times, since it implies that hitherto
there had been at least two separate pasts, that of Greece (Polybius is here
thinking primarily of the mainland) and that of the west, meaning in the
first place Rome, but also including her rival Carthage. *Tyche* – Fortune –
is an ambiguous concept for Polybius as it was for most of his contemporaries. The word itself could be used in many ways. At one extreme
it meant no more than saying that 'something happened'. In some contexts it denoted the irrational and incalculable element in human affairs.
And at the other extreme it was the name of a divine power, a goddess
who acted sometimes capriciously to effect a reversal in men's fortunes
and sometimes as a force for retribution, punishing wrong-doing or re-
warding virtue. *Tyche* in all its forms was a popular concept in Hellenistic
times, shaping both the way men saw events occurring and also the language of the *koine* in which they described them. It crops up repeatedly in
historians and in some, like Duris of Samos, it plays an important part.
The problem with *Tyche* is always to separate rhetoric from theology.
     Polybius' own lack of clarity in handling this mercurial word is paral-
leled by other writers, including professional philosophers. All alike are

apt to slide from one meaning of the word to another, sometimes within a single paragraph. But in attributing the rise of Rome to the workings of *Tyche* Polybius seems clearly to be envisaging a conscious and purposeful force more or less equivalent to our Fate or Providence; and in describing her handiwork in detail he is at pains to underline the clues which *Tyche* distributed in the form of synchronisms, by which at certain dates universal movement is signalled by dynastic or other changes occurring simultaneously in several realms. Polybius emphasises these not simply as a *Hilfsmittel* for the reader, but as a sign that *Tyche* is actively effecting a change in human affairs. There are many examples of this kind in the *Histories*. Here are two. First, in ii.71.3–6 the significance of the 140th Olympiad (220–216) is signified by the accession of new rulers in Macedonia, Egypt and Syria, following the deaths of Antigonus Doson, Ptolemy Euergetes and Seleucus III in the previous Olympiad – to which he adds (iv.2.8–9) the accession of Ariarathes IV in Cappadocia and Lycurgus at Sparta. Secondly, the significance of the 124th Olympiad (284–280) is demonstrated by the deaths of Ptolemy I, Lysimachus, Seleucus I and Ptolemy Ceraunus. Yet here too interpretation is clouded by the fact that such synchronisms were already a recognised feature of Hellenistic historiography. Duris, for instance, opened his work with the synchronous deaths of Amyntas of Macedonia, Agesipolis of Sparta and Jason of Pherae. Rhetoric then is an element in this concept too. It does not however impair the reality (to Polybius) of the *Tyche* which directed the rise of Rome. How far the model which incorporates this power is to be extended to the period prior to that with which the *Histories* are concerned is a question to which I shall return later.

First, however, I want to look at two other themes which occur frequently in his work. One of these may seem to detract from the power of *Tyche*, whereas the other arises out of her machinations. The first of these themes is the importance which Polybius attributes to outstanding individuals. Examples are: Xanthippus, the Spartan mercenary captain whose skill brought about the defeat of the Roman general Regulus in the First Punic War (255); Archimedes, whose brilliant devices saved Syracuse for so long from capture by the Romans (viii.3.5, 7.1); Hannibal, since 'for all that happened to both nations, Romans and Carthaginians, the cause was one man and one mind' (ix.22.1); and, to take an example of someone who was a force for evil, the Aetolian Lyciscus, after whose death the Aetolians lived in unison and concord. 'So great, it seems, is the power exercised by men's natures that not only armies and cities, but national groups and in fact all the different peoples which compose the whole world experience the extremities sometimes of misfortune and sometimes of prosperity owing to the good or || bad character of a single man' (xxxii.4.2). This emphasis on what the individual can achieve may seem at variance with the emphasis elsewhere on the power of *Tyche*, but there is really no contradiction, since Polybius allows for many different factors operating in history – for instance the nature of the constitution in the case of Rome. So the importance of the individual can very well coexist within the plan imposed by *Tyche*.

The other theme or subsidiary pattern to which Polybius attributes some importance arises directly out of the growth of Roman power and applies only to his own time. That is the idea of progress. The present, the time at which he is living, is a kind of high point coinciding with the world dominion of Rome. Things now are bigger, better and more highly developed than at any previous time. The world has experienced great material progress. Thus ships are now larger than ever before (i.63.8) – a claim of some importance in its own context, which is a passage seeking to prove that the events of the First Punic War (related in detail in Book I) were on a larger scale than those of any previous war, even those of Alexander's successors. As for the great sea battles of the Persian and Peloponnesian Wars, there could be no comparison between the triremes used then and modern quinqueremes. So here again we find what is apparently a historical statement closely linked with the old historian's *topos*, exemplified in the introduction to Thucydides, that his war is greater than any described by his predecessors.

However, the claim made for progress has a basis in reality and can be supported in other ways. The known world was now greater than ever before (iii.59.1–3), thanks to the achievements of Alexander and the Romans – and, he goes on to imply, in no small measure thanks to himself, Polybius, who has crossed the Alps, visited Africa and explored the outer ocean as a pioneer; for Odysseus' voyages outside the Straits, the ἐξωκεανισμός, as Alexandrian scholars dubbed it, are to be firmly rejected, and the claims of Pytheas treated with the scorn due to a mere merchant, a poor man without the support of a rich Roman patron (xxxiv.5.6). The modern world too has seen the establishment of peace in Greece – he is writing this (iii.59.4) after 146 – and such a growth in the arts and sciences (τὰς ἐμπειρίας καὶ τέχνας) that the student of history is provided with a means of dealing with every emergency that may arise, one could say scientifically (ix.2.5 ὡς ἂν εἰ μεθοδικῶς).

III

So far we have been considering three themes which emerge from Polybius' *Histories*, the first the plan executed by *Tyche* almost within his own lifetime, the second the rôle of the individual and the third the onward march of progress in the wake of Roman domination. Shortly, as I have already indicated, I propose to return to the first of these in order to consider its wider implications. But before doing so I must first examine a passage (ix.1–2) in which Polybius enumerates three different kinds of history-writing which, though he does not say so, had traditionally been associated with a sequence of periods in Greek history. The first of these historical genres he calls 'the genealogical kind', the second history dealing with 'colonies, foundations of cities and kinship relations (συγγένειαι)' and the third history concerned with 'ἔθνη (which includes both tribal and federal bodies), cities and rulers (δυνάσται)'; and he adds the statement that his own work falls entirely within the third category. Elsewhere he describes this work as πραγματικὴ ἱστορία, meaning by that 'political and military history'.

Polybius nowhere states, however, that history has to be restricted to one of these three genres. And in fact we know that Ephorus had sections of his universal history dealing with colonies, foundations and ties of kinship (Polyb. xxxix.1.3), which forms the substance of the second category. Timaeus also included this kind of material in his first books (Polyb. xii.26d.4). Now since the beginning of the fifth century a branch of history had emerged which was specifically devoted to bringing the contents of early Greek myth and legend into some sort of order. This 'genealogical kind of history', as Polybius here terms it, was the creation of Hecataeus of Miletus, who sorted out the myths and generations of the epic figures to produce a consistent picture, one that was || broadly accepted by his successors, though a series of writers, including Acusilaus of Argos and Pherecydes of Athens and going down to Hellanicus of Lesbos, who wrote around 400 BC, made corrections and adjustments and treated the legends of their own cities. By the early fourth century the 'mythical' and the 'genealogical' were regarded as closely linked together, as they are in the fictional discourse given by Solon to the Egyptians in Plato's *Timaeus* (22a). Already Herodotus had accepted the distinction which this implied between legendary and historical times; in iii.122, for instance, he differentiates between Polycrates' thalassocracy and that of Minos. By beginning his own work with the 'return of the Heracleidae' Ephorus established that 'event' as an epochal date for the beginning of

'real history'. Polybius' triple categorisation shows him to be familiar with
this established way of dividing up early Greek history. His first genre,
the genealogical, corresponds to the epic period. Next came the age
of colonisation, which figures largely in Timaeus (who dealt with Sicily
and Magna Graecia) and also in various local historians (xxxiv.2.10).
Where Polybius drew the line between the legendary-mythical period
and what followed is not very clear. He may have accepted Ephorus'
epochal event – the return of the Heracleidae. On the other hand, as
we have seen, his rationalising interpretation of the epic stories led him
to treat the adventures of Odysseus as genuine history; and he was in
fact under no pressure to draw any such line at all, since his own work
fell wholly within the third category, which he defines as the political
and military history of tribes and federations, cities and rulers, the last
being primarily, though not exclusively, the Hellenistic kings. This category (as Mohm showed in his Saarbrücken dissertation of 1977) covered
the whole of Greek history from the period of colonisation and the city
foundations down to Polybius' own time. In fact, however, the main
events mentioned incidentally in his history belong to the period from
the Persian wars onward.

IV

Now this triple division of Greek history into what we may term the
mythical age, the period of colonisation and fully historical times is not
very easily reconciled with a quite different scheme set out in Polybius'
sixth book. As an introduction to his account of the Roman constitution
Polybius there outlines (vi.4–9) a succession of constitutional forms beginning with primitive monarchy which, with the growth of moral concepts,
evolves into true kingship. Under the king's unworthy successors this de-
generates into a tyranny and that, after a revolution, is superseded by
aristocracy. The sons of the aristocrats, like those of the king, then abuse
their position and turn their rule into an oligarchy, until the people rise
up against them, drive them out and set up a democracy. But democracy too is fated to deteriorate – this time into mob-rule, which finds its
outcome in a monarch. At this point the cycle begins all over again. This
succession of political forms, this πολιτειῶν ἀνακύκλωσις (*anacyclosis*),
Polybius tells us, is the 'natural order', the φύσεως οἰκονομία, by way of
which constitutions change, are transformed and return to their original
form. The process is not irrevocably fixed. At Rome, for example, the setting up of the mixed constitution had acted as a brake on the revolving

wheel. Hence this and presumably other factors could thus vary the speed at which the different constitutional and social changes succeeded each other. But in its outline this was a pattern which determined social development from the age of primitive man down to Polybius' own time.

Much has been written about this theory and the difficulties involved in reconciling it both with the mixed constitution (which lies outside it) and also with the natural law of birth, growth, acme, decline and death which Polybius insists that it exemplifies. I do not propose to discuss that problem here. What I do want to consider now, however, is whether in fact this scheme is to be seen as a real tool used by Polybius to analyse the development of societies (and incidentally how far it matches the tripartite division of Greek history at which we have just been looking). Or is it simply an extraneous theory, first borrowed, invented or adapted in order to explain in sociological terms Polybius' central problem, Rome's political and military success, and || then generalised to form a universal model? To answer this we must, I think, consider Greece and Rome separately. Greece, Ἑλλάς, is of course used in different senses; but the western Greeks are clearly included. Let us then briefly consider some passages in Polybius where one might expect to find some reference to the *anacyclosis* if it is really the key to social development that Polybius claims it to be.

In ii.41 there is a brief account of early Achaean history, which at first sight seems to contain some features of the constitutional cycle. The successors of the first king, Tisamenus, ruled the country down to the reign of Ogygus; but when his sons proved despotical and unconstitutional in their rule, the people set up a democracy instead. As we saw, the deterioration of the good king's sons into tyrants is a feature of the *anacyclosis*; but their expulsion should have been followed by the setting up of an aristocracy – not a democracy, as here. Polybius has introduced the democracy because he is committed to the (improbable) view that ever since the original monarchy his native state of Achaea had always been a democracy. Hence Achaea does not fit the cyclical pattern. Nor do Athens and Thebes, as Polybius admits (vi.43.2); for their growth was abnormal and after a sudden blaze of power, the work of chance and circumstance, they suffered a complete reversal of fortune. Both were very much victims of mob-rule, which recalls one feature of the *anacyclosis*; but Polybius does not attempt to apply its other stages, not even in the long passage in xx.4, where he discusses developments in Boeotia after Leuctra. In both these instances *Tyche* seems to be in evidence, but not the constitutional cycle.

Two cities in Italy – Capua (vii.1) and Tarentum (viii.24) – reveal features not dissimilar to those of the cycle. In both, extravagance and luxury, pride and excessive freedom end in their seeking a master, in the one case Hannibal, in the other Pyrrhus. This seems to follow a traditional explanation of the decline of the cities of Magna Graecia as due to extravagance (τρυφή), an explanation exemplified for Tarentum in Strabo (vi.280). Its likeness to the final stage of the *anacyclosis* is striking, but may be coincidental. Finally, there is Sparta, which according to Polybius (iv.81.13) maintained the mixed, Lycurgan, constitution until the battle of Leuctra, after which everything deteriorated, civic discord broke out and land was divided up, until the process culminated in the horrors of Nabis' tyranny. A big step in this decline was the final dissolution of the Lycurgan regime by Cleomenes. Again, at first sight one is reminded of the final stages of the *anacyclosis*. But in fact there is no close correspondence, perhaps because Sparta begins her decline from a position not strictly within the *anacyclosis* at all, for Sparta at her height, like Rome, had a mixed constitution.

In none of the passages just cited is there any systematic attempt to use the *anacyclosis* to illuminate the Greek past. So if this remarkable theory had no application to Greece, how did it stand with regard to Rome? For it was in order to explain Roman success that Polybius brought it in at all. The *anacyclosis* does in fact fit the traditional version of early Roman history rather well. We cannot be quite sure about this, since only a few sentences survive from the chapters of Book VI in which Polybius traced the early history of Rome and it is clearly hazardous to deduce Polybius' views from the account of early Rome in Cicero's *De re publica* ii.1–63. Although it draws on Polybius, Cicero's construction is very much his own and seems designed to explain Rome's mixed constitution rather than how her early history followed the *anacyclosis*. What is clear is that Polybius regarded the year 450 as epochal for the beginnings of the mixed constitution (vi.11.1, with Boissevain's text). Prior to that it seems likely that Romulus may have figured as the primitive monarch, either he or Numa as the good king, with the second Tarquin as the tyrant and the early republic as the aristocracy. The second decemvirate with its oppressive features will then represent the oligarchy, after which Rome slid over into the mixed constitution. The subsequent stages of the cycle lay still in the future. In the absence of Polybius' text we cannot insist on the details. But if this hypothesis is correct, Rome does seem to have been the one and only state for which the *anacyclosis* worked. ||

V

If I may pull together the threads of my argument so far, Polybius evidently conceived the Greek past to be divided in the traditional way into mythological, colonising and strictly 'historical' periods, but although he had rationalising views about the earliest times, his own work and his main interest lay in the history of the period concerned with ἔθνη, cities and rulers. The latest decades of that period had been moulded by the handiwork of *Tyche* and the rise of Rome to world domination; and the early history of Rome had apparently followed a pattern claimed as universal, but conveniently ignored when any state other than Rome was under consideration. I have mentioned one or two passages in which Polybius discusses the earlier development of certain states, πόλεις or ἔθνη. But he also has a series of comments which throw a little light on the quality of his knowledge of the past. This knowledge must have come in the main from reading earlier historians. Obviously then he knew more about the Greek past than his sporadic comments throughout his *Histories* might suggest. He had certainly read Ephorus (iv.73–4 on Elis) and Theopompus (xxviii.6.1); and though he names Thucydides only once (viii.11.3) in the surviving parts of the *Histories*, verbal echoes (iii.6.3, 31.12) show that Polybius was familiar with his work. Whether he had read Herodotus is not clear. On the Roman side he had read Fabius Pictor (who wrote in Greek) and he was acquainted with Roman legends such as that of Horatius (vi.55). About Horatius he is less critical than Livy (ii.10.11), who at one point injects a rather surprising note of scepticism into his account of the legend. How thoroughly Polybius knew these writers is a question less easy to answer. In criticising Timaeus' version of the speech delivered by the Syracusan Hermocrates at the conference of Gela (xii.25k) he makes no mention of Thucydides' version of the same speech, which bears no resemblance to that in Timaeus. Yet, as Gomme pointed out (*Comm. on Thuc.* III, 523), the discrepancy showed either one or the other (or both) to be false. In fact, Polybius' references to fifth-century figures – Nicias and his fatal ignorance of astronomy (ix.19), Aristides and Pericles as 'good leaders', Cleon (and the fourth-century Chares) as 'bad leaders' (ix.23.9) – are superficial; and he mentions Aristides elsewhere (xxxi.22) simply in order to compare his almost legendary integrity with that of Aemilius Paullus. When he lists earlier Greek disasters in order to demonstrate that they were of less moment than that which befell Greece – mainly of course the Achaean League – in 146, all are well-known events: Xerxes' invasion, the defeat of

Sparta by Thebes, the breaking-up of Mantinea, Alexander's destruction of Thebes, the garrisoning of Corinth, Chalcis and other strongholds by the Macedonians. Notably he excludes Sicily and the west from this catalogue. These were events known to every schoolboy. In short, there is no evidence that Polybius' acquaintance with earlier Greek history was at all profound.

From the fourth century onward, however, both his knowledge and his commitment are far greater. Nor is that surprising. For this is the age which saw the rise of Macedonia, a topic which, as we have seen, was to play a prominent rôle in his overall historical picture. Moreover, as it happened, it also saw the foundation of Megalopolis, the historian's native city – thus providing a convenient coincidence of the particular and the general. As an Arcadian, Polybius thus had his own personal reasons for describing the time around the year of the battle of Leuctra as the most brilliant in Greek history (viii.11.3). In his many references to the fourth century he repeatedly draws attention to issues which were to find their echo in his own day. His comments are grouped mainly around some five or six outstanding individuals; for, as we have seen, he regards individuals as a decisive element in historical events.

The most important of these figures is Philip II, the father of Alexander the Great. The rival speeches which he records as having been delivered by Aetolian and Acarnanian representatives at Sparta in the late spring of 210 (ix.28.1–7, 32–8) show that Philip's reputation in Greece varied greatly, depending on which state the person judging him belonged to. Philip was a benefactor to Megalopolis (ii.48.2) and Polybius is strongly partisan. Philip is repeatedly introduced in favourable contexts. His || generous behaviour is contrasted with the cruelty of Ptolemy Epiphanes – his direct descendant, according to the false but officially accepted Ptolemaic genealogy (xxii.16.1–17.7). Polybius also strongly defends Philip's policy in Greece against that of Demosthenes (xviii.13–15) and frequently mentions his leniency towards Athens after Chaeronea (v.10, xviii.14.13–14, xxii.16.2) – sometimes to provide a contrast with his namesake Philip V. He is also lauded as the true author of the war on Persia (xxii.18).

A fourth-century figure almost equally praiseworthy is Epaminondas. Thebes and Boeotia do not normally command Polybius' approval, but Epaminondas, the founder of Megalopolis, is naturally an exception. He is praised as a brilliant soldier, whose march from Mantinea to Sparta and back won universal admiration (ix.8). Along with Pelopidas, he was the man behind the Theban hegemony (vi.43.2–44.9). His counsel to go along with Achaea was wise and the Messenians would do well to heed it (iv.3). Polybius also speaks highly of Dionysius I and Agathocles, rulers of Syracuse (xii.15.1–12, xv.12.35, Agathocles; xii.4a. 3, Dionysius I). But his main commendation is for the Macedonians and for Alexander, who destroyed the Persian empire (ix.34.1–3) and whose destruction of Thebes was unfortunate but excusable (v.10), together with his successors and other Macedonian leaders, whose restrained behaviour was so markedly different from that of Philip V, once his character had deteriorated (viii.10.11). This contrast between the two Philips is an important clue to Polybius' overall view of the past.

VI

Indeed, the most striking characteristic of Polybius' comments on persons and incidents outside the range of his main historical theme is this emphasis on the fourth century. This he clearly regarded as a crucial time for the development of Greek history. In particular it was the events of that period that conditioned the history of the third century down to the time when the Romans embarked on their meteoric rise to world domination. The nature of this link between the two centuries can be detected from the passage in which Polybius describes in terms of awe and wonder the prescience of the statesman and philosopher, Demetrius of Phalerum. To illustrate the mutability (τὸ εὐμετάβολον) of Fortune, Demetrius had pointed to the sudden overthrow of the Persian empire at the hands of the Macedonians, a thing quite unimaginable barely fifty years before it took place, and had then prophesied the superseding of Macedonian rule by some other power – an event which Polybius had himself lived to see and chronicle. The importance which Polybius attached to that 'prophecy' is shown by its position towards the end of the Greek and Macedonian events of Book XXIX, which (apart from the index) will have been the last book of the *Histories* as originally planned. It stands after the battle of Pydna, and the fall of Perseus (xxix.21); and it is followed by an account (xxix.27) of the dramatic encounter at Pelusium in Egypt where Antiochus IV of Syria was humiliated by the Roman envoy, C. Popillius Laenas, who traced a circle round him with his staff and demanded that he accept the contents of the Roman *senatus consultum* requiring his withdrawal from Egypt before stepping outside it. This bringing down at one and the same time of the rulers of Macedonia and Syria not only illustrated the incalculable actions of *Tyche* but also her power as a force of retribution, since, as Polybius earlier explains (xv.20.8), the unconscionable plot of the representatives of the two houses of Macedonia and Syria, Philip V and Antiochus III, against the defenceless boy-king of Egypt, Ptolemy V, was now being avenged on the persons of their respective sons, Perseus and Antiochus IV.

The verbal quotation from Demetrius of Phalerum unites in a single context the rise of Macedonia in the fourth century and the rise of Rome in the late third and early second centuries; and the emphasis on the events of the fourth century in Polybius reveals his deep interest in the earlier period and the theme of Macedonian power which runs through it. But there is also a secondary theme which arises out of the relations of Macedonia to Greece and is for Polybius both more personal and more problematical. As we have seen, Polybius gives us a rose-coloured picture of Philip II and, less plausibly, extends this to Alexander's successors. In particular he contrasts || Philip II with Philip V. But Macedonia's rôle in third-century Greece could not be viewed with entire equanimity by a historian who was both a loyal Megalopolitan and an Achaean states-man. The rise of Achaea under Aratus to become the leading state in the Peloponnese was a process of which Polybius was inordinately proud. But it had been achieved largely by exploiting the weakness of Macedonia and in revolt against her. The expulsion of the Macedonian garrison from the Acrocorinth by a brilliant coup perhaps ranked as Aratus' greatest triumph. The subsequent Achaean absorption of Arcadia and Mega-lopolis had brought the league into conflict with a now aggressive Sparta and when it seemed as if the hostility and successes of the Spartan king Cleomenes would end in the disintegration of the Achaean federation, Aratus with a complete volte-face had brought back the Macedonians into the Peloponnese and had handed over the Acrocorinth once more to a Macedonian garrison. For a little over twenty years – years which saw the birth and early years of Polybius – Achaea at some cost to herself held firmly to the Macedonian alliance and the Hellenic Symmachy set up by Antigonus Doson.

But already *Tyche* was busy switching the location of power in the world and by 198 Achaea had to switch too. To jettison the Macedonian alliance for that of Rome was a painful decision even in retrospect. Polybius defends it, but the defence involves him in some moral and verbal gymnastics about the nature of treason (xviii.13–15), not always very elegantly performed. The immediate outcome of the Roman al-liance was satisfactory for Achaea, but ultimately it was of course to prove disastrous. For Polybius the Third Macedonian War brought exile in Rome followed by a reluctant but eventually a full acceptance of the inevitability and even desirability of Roman predominance. The Roman alliance was made easier to approve by the culpable behaviour of Philip V and later of Perseus, whose faults Polybius also enumerates. The greater the deterioration in the moral character of the Macedonian king, the easier it was to reconcile oneself to the Achaeans' having transferred their support from Macedonia to Rome. Similarly, the excellent character of Antigonus Doson (ii.47.5, 70.7, iv.87.6) – as well as his long-standing links with Megalopolis – had softened any anguish Polybius may have felt at Aratus' decision to call on his help against Sparta. I do not wish to attach too much importance to what might be called the Achaean connection; but it does undoubtedly play some part in colouring Polybius' interests and the way he saw the previous centuries of Greek history. But the main theme is that provided by the sequence of Persia, Macedonia and Rome; and for the fourth century the outstanding rôle of its great king, Philip II.

13

*The idea of decline in Polybius**

I INTRODUCTION

As the historian of Rome's rise to world power Polybius was not particularly interested in the concept of decline. His main concern was to analyse why Rome had got to where she was.[1] But one essential element in his analysis was to assess the merits of the Roman constitution and compare it with other constitutions; and consequently, as a political theorist, Polybius was brought up against decline as a problem. His views on this are interesting for the light they throw on the quality of his political thought and also for the traditions on which he draws. In order to set his views in a proper context, I shall first give a brief sketch of the attested stages in the composition of the *Histories*.

Polybius conceived and began his *Histories* while detained at Rome. After the Third Macedonian War, which ended in the destruction of the Macedonian monarchy in 168, many Greeks, Polybius among them, were summoned to Rome and refused permission to return to their homes until 150.[2] While at Rome Polybius lived on close terms with Scipio Aemilianus, a member of a leading noble family,[3] and having come to appreciate Roman political greatness and to understand its sources (or so he believed) he resolved to write a history, primarily for his fellow-Greeks, which would explain 'how and thanks to what sort of constitution the Romans in less than fifty-three years had succeeded in subjecting nearly the whole inhabited world to their sway'. Polybius had been especially impressed by the downfall of Perseus of Macedonia in the Third Macedonian War. This shattering event, which marked the end of the world-famous Macedonian monarchy, reminded him of a passage

---

* [[S. Koselleck and P. Widmer (eds.) *Niedergang: Studien zu einem geschichtlichen Thema* (Sprache und Geschichte 2) (Stuttgart 1980) 41–58
[1] For Polybius' programme see i.1.5–6, 2.7, 4.1; iii.1.4, 1.9, 2.6, 3.9, 4.2, 118.9; vi.2.3; viii.2.3; xxxix.8.7.
[2] See xxx.13.1–11, 32.1–12; Paus. vii.10.11; Livy xlv.31.9.   [3] Cf. xxxi.23–30.

in the treatise *On Fortune* (Περὶ Τύχης) by the Peripatetic philosopher Demetrius of Phalerum.[4] In that work Demetrius had commented on the destruction of the Persian empire by Alexander the Great – the king of a people which fifty years before was virtually unknown and certainly insignificant – and had remarked that Fortune, the incalculable power which enters into no compact with mortal men, had merely granted the Macedonians the wealth of Persia to enjoy for a time – until she decided to deal differently with them. Polybius saw this as a prophecy, which he had seen fulfilled. Hence the significance of the 'less than fifty-three years' (matching || Demetrius' fifty years) during which Rome rose from her disastrous situation at the beginning of the Hannibalic War to become mistress of the world in 168. There is of course implicit in the reference to Demetrius the concept of a reversal of Fortune – first for Persia and now for Macedonia: Rome too can hardly claim exemption from the law illustrated by the fall of Perseus. This fact emerges from several passages in Book VI. But Polybius never mentions the future fall of Rome in his comments on Demetrius' 'prophecy' and, as I have said, it is an aspect which hardly concerns him as a historian.

II THE SCOPE OF THE *HISTORIES*

Polybius saw the rise of Rome as the work of Fortune (*Tyche*).[5] The notion of *Tyche* was popular in Hellenistic times, but the word was always ambiguous and tended to cover a wide spectrum ranging from 'pure chance' to something like Providence. Polybius himself uses the word '*Tyche*' in a large number of senses,[6] but the *Tyche* which, according to him, raised Rome to world domination strikes his readers as rather different from the *Tyche* of Demetrius of Phalerum. To Demetrius the rise of Macedonia and the downfall of Persia were proof of the mutability, τὸ εὐμετάβολον, of Fortune,[7] who will never allow things to remain stable for very long, whereas to Polybius the swift conquest of power by Rome was more like the manifestation of a providential plan.[8] This does not mean that he regarded history as the handiwork of God. On the contrary, he asserts repeatedly that historical events result from human actions and in one significant passage in Book XXXVI[9] he allows the historian to invoke *Tyche* only as an explanation of those events for which it is difficult or impossible for men to perceive any rational cause – for example, floods,

[4] xxix.21.   [5] i.4.4.   [6] See Walbank (1972a) 60–5; *Comm.* i, 16–26.   [7] xxix.21.2.
[8] *Comm.* i, 25–6.   [9] xxxvi.17: cf. Walbank (1972a) 61.

drought, epidemics and what in English we call 'acts of God'.[10] In his pages '*Tyche*' is frequently little more than a verbal elaboration, a way of speaking or a rhetorical flourish; but in the case of Rome's rise to power he seems, exceptionally, to have invested the process with a teleological character and to have treated the popular Hellenistic goddess as something akin to the Stoic Providence. I have stressed this point because although the rôle of *Tyche* is central to Polybius' main theme, his || constant use of the word with various shades of meaning may indicate that he was not alert to all its ambiguities.

Polybius makes much of the effect which Demetrius' 'prophecy' had upon him. But in setting Rome in the line leading from Persia and Macedonia he was not acting under the inspiration of a sudden flash of enlightenment. We happen to know that these ideas were in the air. Sometime between 189 and 171 a Roman chronologist, Aemilius Sura, had written a book in which he listed the succession of world empires,[11] Assyria, Media, Persia, Macedonia, after which 'when the two kings Philip and Antiochus, who were sprung from the Macedonians, had been defeated shortly after the Carthaginians had been reduced, imperial supremacy passed to the Romans'; and Justinus[12] records that the earthquake which damaged Rhodes and other cities in 198 was interpreted as a sign that 'the rising empire of Rome would devour the ancient empire of the Greeks and Macedonians'. The idea of four successive world empires was well established in the east and no doubt Roman soldiers brought it back to Rome;[13] Polybius may well have become acquainted with it either in Greece or after his arrival at Rome in 167. This eastern tradition may have reinforced – if it did not actually spark off – the impression made on him by Demetrius' 'prophecy'.

His original plan, conceived at Rome, was for a history covering thirty books and the period 220–167 BC. Part of it he wrote while still at Rome,[14] but we do not know how far he had got by 150, when he was allowed to return home. The question is controversial and I cannot go into it here; but he may have reached the end of the Second Punic War (202) by the time he left Rome and he probably completed his work down to

---

[10] For a similar view in Biondo and Bossuet see P. Burke, *Daedalus* (1976) 142 n. 28: 'the function of the concept "fortune" is much like that of "God"; both are invoked when natural explanations seem inadequate'.

[11] Vell. Pat. i.6.6.   [12] Justin xxx.4.4; see also Plut. *De Pyth. or.* ii.399c.

[13] See Swain (1940); Walbank (1963) 8. [But see now ch. 1, p. 8, and the doubts of D. Mendels.]

[14] On the chronology of the composition and publication of the *Histories* see Walbank, *Comm.* 1, 292–7 (on iii, 1–5). In Walbank (1977) I have argued the case that the last ten books were written after Scipio's death in 129. [See now ch.1, p. 20, on the dates of composition and publication.]

167 in Greece. It seems likely that it was quite late in his life, after Scipio Aemilianus' death in 129, that he wrote the extension which took the history down to 146, the year in which Carthage and Corinth were both destroyed after Macedonia had become a Roman province.

The last ten books, which cover these further twenty-two years between 167 and 145, present many problems.[15] Their alleged purpose is to enable readers to judge how Rome exercised her hegemonial power;[16] but this was perhaps not Polybius' main purpose, for he never establishes the criteria by which Rome is to be judged, and although his account of the years 167–151 contains many cynical and critical comments on Roman foreign policy, which seem to reflect the view he formed || about current happenings while he was a detainee at Rome, when he gets down to the wars of 151–146 in Macedonia, Carthage and Achaea, his sympathies are clearly with Rome and against the leaders of the states which opposed her. Andriscus' rising in Macedonia, which was supported by wide sections of the Macedonian people, is explained as 'infatuation' or madness sent by the gods.[17] The disaster that befell Achaea in 146 is described as ἀτυχία, a word with connotations of guilt and shame.[18] The people were bemused and bewitched through following worthless leaders. And although Polybius is so cautious in expressing his own feelings about the responsibility for the Third Punic War that some scholars have argued that he held the Romans to be at fault, that is not the conclusion I would draw from his discussion in xxxvi.9, especially bearing in mind his violent denunciation of the Punic leader Hasdrubal and his own, personal share in the victory, up to the moment when he stood beside Aemilianus at the burning of Carthage.[19]

These events form the climax and the conclusion of the extended version of the *Histories*. They portray the years immediately before 146, in which Aemilianus and to a lesser extent Polybius himself played important rôles, not in any sense as years of Roman decline, but as a time when the central plan of *Tyche*, which had directed the events of 220–167, had given way to what Polybius calls ταρχὴ καὶ κίνησις, confusion and disturbance.[20] But this confusion and disturbance shows itself in the actions of Rome's enemies, not of Rome herself. It is they who are the victims of δαιμονοβλάβεια,[21] divine infatuation: those whom the gods

---

[15] See Walbank (1972a) 173–83.   [16] iii.4.4–13.

[17] xxxvi.17.12–15; for the view that only a minority in fact opposed Rome after 167 see Mackay (1970).

[18] Cf. xxxviii.1.1; Gruen (1976) 46–7.

[19] For discussion see Walbank (1972a) 174–6. [Also ch. 1, pp. 19–20.]

[20] iii.4.12.   [21] xxxvi.17.15.

would destroy, they first drive mad! Rome was led to adopt harsh measures, but she was hardly to blame for that. The *Histories* end with a
personal triumph for Polybius, mediating between the Romans and the
defeated Achaeans, and no suggestion that Rome was in decline.

III SOME PASSAGES IN POLYBIUS RELEVANT TO THE IDEA OF DECLINE

Thus although the general theme of at any rate Polybius' original plan
implied that Rome would eventually decline, this aspect did not seem particularly important. There are however several passages in the *Histories*
which touch on the theme of decline or decay in a non-Roman context
and it may be useful to look at three of these: two fall within the original
scope of the work, i.e. before 168, the third is from the extension. ||

(A) In a passage in Book IV[22] Polybius describes a shocking incident
which befell Cynaetha in his native Arcadia. After a period of political
faction, this city had restored its exiles, but they promptly let in the
Aetolians, who proceeded to a general massacre and eventually burnt the
town. Polybius explains that the rough and mountainous environment
and the cold and gloomy atmospheric conditions prevailing in Arcadia
are such that men by their very nature are forced to adjust to them. It is
only by a determined effort and in particular by the use of music that their
effects can be countered. All other Arcadian cities had therefore instituted
choral singing, dances and festivals to modify the harsher aspects of a
national character shaped by this environment. But the men of Cynaetha
had neglected this and so had become like wild beasts, ἀπεθηριώθησαν,[23]
with fatal results to themselves.

The theory that man's material environment exercises a strong influence on his character is common in antiquity – and in many later writers,
like Montesquieu;[24] it was first propounded by Hippocrates[25] but it also
appears in the pseudo-Aristotelian *Problems*[26] and in Panaetius.[27] Polybius
assumes that an adverse environment corrupts the quality of social life
which, left to itself, will therefore deteriorate (as it did at Cynaetha);
this trend can however be countered by cultural institutions. The word

---

[22] iv.17–18, 20–1.   [23] iv.21.6.
[24] In his *Laws* xiv.13 he attributed the English free constitution to the English national character,
which was the result of the English climate.
[25] See Pöblmann (1889) 12 ff.   [26] Ps.-Arist. *Problem.* 14.1.
[27] Panaetius fg. 76 van Straaten (on the Athenians).

ἀποθηριοῦσθαι, to become like a beast, which Polybius employs here, also occurs in his account of the vicious war fought between the Carthaginians and their mercenary troops in revolt.[28] The mercenaries have adopted the practice of torturing to death any Carthaginian prisoners and returning any allies of Carthage whom they chanced to capture with their hands cut off; and they have just passed a resolution to do this on all occasions. Polybius remarks that just as there are ulcers and tumours in the body, so too the soul has its diseases, a prime cause of which is an evil upbringing and the leadership of violent and unscrupulous men. He uses the word ἀποθηριοῦσθαι both of the mercenaries' behaviour and also in its derived, medical sense 'to become malignant', as applied to tumours.[29] A characteristic of the malignant tumour, θηρίωμα, was that it lacked feeling; this is also true of men who have become ἀποτεθηριωμένοι in their souls.[30] ||

(B) The second passage[31] I want to look at also uses a medical metaphor. It describes how the Boeotians 'somehow or other' let slip the power and fame which they had won after their victory over the Spartans at Leuctra and how they 'changed to the opposite' and after sustaining a defeat at the hands of the Aetolians fell into a state of καχεξία – which is primarily illness, but can refer to moral deterioration or political decay.[32] Instead of following a reputable foreign policy they devoted themselves to rich living and drink, and this sapped their bodies and minds. The picture is one of moral decline; but it also involves political decline, since the Boeotians now joined Aetolia (the hereditary foe of Polybius' native Achaea) and then submitted to Macedonia. Their general deterioration is reflected in the quality of their social life, their suspension of activity in the law-courts and their new habit of squandering money on banquets.

At Cynaetha a failure in the quality of social life leads to political error and destruction, whereas the reverse is true of Boeotia: there political decadence finds expression in luxury and self-indulgence. In Cynaetha the fault lay in an absence of social amenity, whereas in Boeotia the fault lay in its excess. These two examples can scarcely be fitted into a coherent theory of social and political deterioration. They seem rather to show Polybius drawing on traditional themes to suit the occasion; and in the

---

[28] i.81.5–11.   [29] i.81.6.
[30] The metaphor of 'ulcers in the soul' goes back through the Stoics to Plato and ultimately to Solon; see Walbank, *Comm.* i, 145 on i.81.5–11.
[31] xx.4–6.   [32] xx.6.1 cf. 7.4.

case of both Cynaetha and Boeotia his own prejudices and his hatred of the Aetolians also come in to colour the picture.

(C) The third passage to be examined is from Book XXXVI[33] and is one I have already mentioned, in which Polybius in discussing causation defines the area within which one is entitled to attribute events to *Tyche*. As an example of a phenomenon not attributable to Fate or Fortune he quotes the general decline in the population in Greece during his own lifetime and the prevalence of childlessness.[34] This, he says, has led to cities becoming deserted and land remaining untilled, although there have not been continuous wars or epidemics. Such depopulation was due to human shortcomings – to avarice and indolence, refusal to marry or a deliberate limitation of the number of children reared, in order that those surviving might enjoy a higher standard of living. Since the cause is thus entirely 'natural', 'neither prophets nor magic are of any service'[35] in explaining it. What is wrong can be put right only by a change of heart or the passing of laws to compel the rearing of children born, i.e. to make infanticide illegal. ||

Here again the problem arises incidentally and is not related to any general theory of decline, though a passage concerning Rome in Book I may offer a parallel.[36] There Polybius remarks that his readers may wonder why, now that the Romans are masters of the world, they could no longer raise and man such large fleets as those of the First Punic War, and he says that the reason for this will become clear from his account of the constitution in Book VI. However, the passage which was to throw light on this has evidently not survived and we can only guess at what the answer may have been. If the difficulty was that of raising crews rather than building ships, then Italy may have presented some sort of parallel to Greece – with the implication that there had been some degree of falling off since the Romans had become masters of the world (κεκρατηκότες τῶν ὅλων). I shall return to this point below.

These three examples – Cynaetha, Boeotia and Greece generally – are all concerned with aspects of *social* decline – treachery and violence at Cynaetha, degenerate luxury in Boeotia, neglect of civic duty to maintain the population in Greece generally; the causes which Polybius identifies

---

[33] xxxvi.17.

[34] For this as an aspect of economic decline which impressed Montesquieu and David Hume see Burke, *Daedalus* (1976) 141–2 n. 6. It is unlikely that Polybius any more than they had firm statistics on which to base his impression.

[35] xxxvi.17.10. On the exposure of children in Greece see Lacey (1968) 164–7.   [36] i.64.1–2.

are all *internal* to the states concerned, and fall within the sphere of
personal responsibility, as his mention of ulcers in the soul, moral καχεξία
and self-indulgence, or avarice and indolence makes clear. It is true
that in Cynaetha the harsh environment is an *external* factor; but the
success of the other Arcadians in countering this shows that it is the
internal and moral shortcomings of the Cynaethans that bring about
their disaster. In treating social decline as a function of moral defects
capable of being remedied these three examples fit appropriately into
the work of a moralist historian. But for a more elaborate theory of
decline we must turn to consider the special contents of Book VI.

IV POLYBIUS' POLITICAL THEORY

Polybius' *Histories* were designed to explain 'by what means and thanks
to what kind of constitution the Romans in less than fifty-three years had
succeeded in subjecting nearly the whole inhabited world to their sway'.[37]
The Roman constitution is dealt with in Book VI and it is there we find
the fullest and most interesting approach to the problem of decline. In
a manner which would seem natural to any Greek Polybius treats the
possession of the right kind of constitution as a major factor in political
success; and he analyses the Roman constitution against the background
of a theory of political development based on rationalistic assumptions,
for which he claims universal validity. There are, he says,[38] two agencies
which render every kind of state liable to decay (φθείρεσθαι πέφυκε), one
external, the other || internal and self-produced (ἐν αὐτοῖς φυομένου).[39]
For the former no laws can be laid down; but the latter is a regular process.
In fact the distinction between internal and external factors is less clear
than Polybius suggests. The two major illustrations of the power of *Tyche*,
the overthrow of Persia by Macedonia (which impressed Demetrius) and
that of Macedonia by Rome (which impressed Polybius), seem both to be
caused by external factors; but once the gaze moves from Macedonia to
Rome it becomes clear that Rome's ability to overthrow Macedonia was
a function of her own internal development. It is in fact this that Polybius
explains in Book VI. In chapters 3–10 of that book he first sketches and
then develops at greater length a naturalistic sequence of constitutional

---

[37] See n. 1.

[38] vi.57.2; the same distinction occurs in Plato, *Rep.* x.608 e ff. See too Aristotle, *Polit.* vii (v) 10. 36,
1312 b 38 ff. But there is no reason to assume direct borrowing.

[39] See also vi.10.3 for the notion of the 'inborn corruption', which can be compared with rust in
iron, wood-worm in timber, etc.

forms which he claims to be a pattern valid for all states and to which he gives the unique name of the *anacyclosis*.[40]

According to this scheme,[41] social organisation begins when after some general cataclysm due to flood, famine or the like, the survivors, a savage horde without arts and crafts, gather together from weakness and appoint as leader some man who is pre-eminent in strength and physique – as happens among birds and beasts. The next step comes with the birth of children, and the natural expectation that they will be dutiful and a sense of outrage when that expectation is disappointed. From this and similar situations arises a notion of duty and hence of justice; and with the growth of ethical concepts the primitive monarch yields place to, or himself develops into, a king ruling by moral force. However, in due course the king's descendants, who have grown up in luxury and privilege, begin to indulge their appetites in acts of violence against their subjects. Conspiracies arise and at length the best men, supported by the commoners, overthrow the kings, who have become tyrants, and set up an aristocracy. But when in time their children too are corrupted by their privileged position, having never experienced misfortune nor yet knowing the meaning of civil liberty and equality – perhaps, as has been suggested, because this was a concept due to arise only with the next political form[42] – they in turn resort to violent acts, often of a sexual character, until the people rise, expel them and set up a democracy. But once again with the passing of the first and second generation freedom and equality are so common that they cease to be valued; lust for power, corruption of the people and the growth of bribery initiate the rule of violence, massacres, plunder and eventually complete savagery, from which the only saviour will be the monarch, who sets the cycle off once more.

This cycle of constitutions is elaborate and draws on several traditions, including a theory about the origins of culture and another which deals with the causes of || corruption in states.[43] These are best considered separately. According to Polybius primitive, savage men, like other living creatures, gathered together through weakness. This is part of the 'naturalistic' explanation of social development which Plato illustrated in the *Protagoras* with a fable about the creation of man:[44] men were at first preyed on by beasts and came together to found cities – but could only live peaceably in them after Zeus had given them Shame

---

[40] vi.9. 10.   [41] See on this Walbank (1972a) 137.   [42] See Musti (1967) 193.
[43] Detailed discussion and references in Walbank, *Comm.* i, 643 ff.; cf. Ryffel (1949) 189 ff.
[44] Plato, *Protag.* 322 ab.

(Αἰδώς) and Justice (Δίκη). The theory is clearly sophistic in origin and in an impressive discussion Cole has recently sought to derive it from Democritus.[45] His view is plausible but falls short of full proof. More important for the question of decline is the other tradition, the source of which is equally uncertain, though Polybius attributes it to 'Plato and some other philosophers'.[46] The *Republic* certainly envisaged a sequence of constitutions,[47] in which the best form – aristocracy or kingship – is followed by the so-called Cretan or Laconian state, and then by oligarchy, democracy and tyranny. Plato implies that these develop one into another[48] but Aristotle criticised the scheme[49] on the grounds that Plato had not explained how the changes took place and that in any case all kinds of other sequences of constitutions are just as possible as that envisaged by Plato. Neither Plato nor Aristotle, however, nor indeed anyone we know of writing before Polybius, completed the circle by bringing the sequence back to where it started.

Many scholars believe that it was Polybius himself who linked together the two traditions and closed the gap to form the circle.[50] This is possible but not, I think, very likely. In the first place, as I have said, Polybius specifically states that he is merely giving a brief summary of a theory expounded more subtly and at greater length by others.[51] But in addition the vocabulary he uses in his account of the *anacyclosis* differs from his usage elsewhere in such a way as to suggest that he is following a separate source. Briefly, he uses μόναρχος and μοναρχία elsewhere as the equivalent of 'tyranny' (though in a few places μόναρχος has the more neutral meaning of an autocratic ruler, even a legitimate one, like Philip V of || Macedonia); and this usage is found in several parts of Book VI.[52] But in the section dealing with the *anacyclosis* monarchy is the primitive monarchy based on the rule of strength, which with the growth of moral concepts changes into kingship (βασιλεία). When this in turn is corrupted it gives place to tyranny (τυραννίς). At the end of the process, when mob-rule deteriorates into utter chaos, the people turn to δεσπότης καὶ μόναρχος and the cycle recommences. This use of μόναρχος for the primitive ruler and τυραννίς (not μοναρχία) for tyranny points to a source, whose vocabulary Polybius has taken over as it stands, and this suggests that the *anacyclosis* is not his own invention. In what milieu it arose is a question to which I shall revert below.

---

[45] Cole, (1967) summary, 128–30.   [46] vi.5.1.   [47] Plato, *Rep.* viii.544c.
[48] Ibid. v.449 a.   [49] Arist. *Polit.* vii (v) 12, 1316a 1 ff.
[50] Von Fritz (1954) 60–75; Erbse (1957) 275; Pédech (1964) 303 f.; Cole (1964).
[51] vi.5.2.   [52] For details see Walbank (1943b) 76–9; (1972a) 140–1.

The *anacyclosis* explains what changes take place in constitutions; but because these changes follow a zig-zag pattern up and down, and are allegedly valid for all states, the process provides in itself no explanation of either success or failure. The outstanding achievement of Rome in making herself mistress of the inhabited world in under fifty-three years is due, Polybius argues, to something quite different – to her success in clamping a brake on the revolving constitutional cycle by adopting a mixed constitution incorporating the best features of kingship, aristocracy and democracy.[53] The merits of a mixed constitution had already had a long history. We first meet the idea in Thucydides' description[54] of Theramenes' constitution at Athens in 411 as 'a discreet fusion of the few and the many' and from then onwards there are many attempts to define the ideal recipe for such a mixture.

Plato's *Menexenus*[55] contains the first combination of kingship, aristocracy and democracy (bringing in the third element), and this now becomes the standard pattern – though it does not figure in Isocrates until 339.[56] Plato defends the mixed constitution in the *Laws*,[57] where he links it with Sparta. He may have derived it from the sophists and perhaps from the Pythagoreans; evidence for this comes from a spurious work attributed to Archytas of Tarentum, *On Law and Justice*,[58] which treats a mixed state like Sparta as the ideal constitution. By what channel the idea reached Polybius is uncertain. The *Tripoliticus* of Aristotle's pupil Dicaearchus has been canvassed;[59] but by Polybius' time the concept was widespread and accepted by the Stoics, the Peripatetics (who were the source for its later appearance || in Areius Didymus who taught Augustus) and the Elder Cato, who applied it to Carthage. Where Polybius took it from is an unanswerable question.[60]

Both the *anacyclosis* and the mixed constitution seem therefore to have been available independently to Polybius. His personal contribution to political theory consists in having combined them with the object of providing an explanation of Roman imperial success.

His argument is not entirely logical or consistent, and his account both of the *anacyclosis* and of the mixed constitution can be criticised. The former is a cyclical movement; but Polybius depends on an equivocation to close the circle, since the primitive horde which gathers together through natural weakness and finds security in the protection of a strong primitive

---

[53] On the mixed constitution see Walbank, *Comm.* i, 639–40 on vi.3.7; Aalders (1968).
[54] Thuc. viii.97.2.   [55] Plato, *Menex.* 238 cd.   [56] In the *Panathenaicus*; cf. Cloché (1936).
[57] Plato, *Laws* iv.712 de.   [58] See on this Aalders, (1968) 13 ff.
[59] Wehrli (1967) fgg. 70 and 72.   [60] See Walbank (1972a) 136–7 for references.

monarch is really a very different kind of society from the degenerate ochlocracy which, at the end of the cycle, turns to a 'despot and monarch' to bring order into its self-induced chaos.

A further difficulty lies in Polybius' use of the term 'natural' (κατὰ φύσιν). In several places[61] he describes the *anacyclosis* as the natural development of states which, like everything else, have their natural beginnings, growth, perfection, change and end. The concept of a 'biological pattern' running right through nature can be traced back to Anaximander.[62] It very soon became a commonplace, Thucydides remarking that 'it is the nature of all things to grow smaller'.[63] To Polybius this pattern was a law of nature; hence the *anacyclosis*, being also a process κατὰ φύσιν,[64] had to be brought into relationship with it. This was not easy. The biological scheme with its single curve requires an acme, a high point; but it is difficult to find such an acme in the *anacyclosis*. So long as one considers the separate forms and their degeneration, one can detect something like a growth, acme and decline in each (though the scheme suffers some distortion from the fact that both aristocracy and democracy are the product not of gradual change but of revolution).[65] Polybius has this in mind when he remarks that 'he alone who has seen how each form naturally arises and develops (ὡς φύεται) will be able to see when, how and where the || growth, perfection, change and end of each are likely to recur again'.[66] But as if he recognises that this offers no explanation of the 'natural' development of the cycle *as a whole*, he goes on to say[67] that 'it is to the Roman constitution (ἐπὶ τῆς Ῥωμαίων πολιτείας) above all that this method, I think, may be successfully applied, since from the outset its formation and growth have been due to natural causes (κατὰ φύσιν)'. The ambiguity in the use of *politeia* to mean first one of the constitutional forms (and their corruptions) and then the Roman constitution *in toto*, as something continuous throughout the successive phases of the cycle, recurs at vi.9.10–14, where Polybius

---

[61] vi.4.11–13, 9.11–14, 57.1–4. Which states exemplify it is never explained (though vi.3.1 suggests that it is widespread in Greece).

[62] D–K I.12 B 1.   [63] Thuc. ii.64.3.   [64] vi.5.1.

[65] Cole (1964) 449 n.26 argues that this difficulty, and a second due to the fact consequent upon it that the two high points of aristocracy and democracy come at the *beginning* of their respective sections of the cycle, disappear if one thinks of an overlap by which (e.g.) 'the metabole which transfers kingship into tyranny is both the beginning of the decline of one-man rule and the beginning of the rise of the aristocracy'. But he admits that it is unlikely that Polybius explicitly formulated the matter in this way; and it seems a rather forced and unconvincing way of dealing with the difficulty.

[66] vi.4.12.   [67] vi.4.13.

repeats his assertion that the Roman state above all others conforms to the biological scheme of birth, acme and decline.[68]

Nevertheless, despite the difficulty of interpreting the *anacyclosis* in terms of this biological scheme, Polybius clearly regards the two as closely linked. It has been observed[69] that there are other second-century treatises which claim to illustrate the natural law of biological change in various contexts. One example is the work of popular philosophy attributed to Ocellus Lucanus,[70] which sees various levels in the universe, all except the highest being subject to appropriate forms of the 'natural law'. At the second level the four elements move in a flux described as '*antiperistasis*'; at the third level plants move in a cycle of seed, fruit, seed called '*epanakampsis*'; and at the fourth level men and other living creatures pass through a succession of ages. Ryffel,[71] in his study of the changes in constitutions, has suggested that in the same way the *anacyclosis* was the specific form of the law peculiar to constitutions. If that were so, the rare word '*anacyclosis*' would parallel '*antiperistasis*' and '*epanakampsis*' as a piece of pseudophilosophical jargon. There is of course no evidence directly linking the *anacyclosis* with Ocellus Lucanus; but it is not improbable that it was devised in a similar context of popular philosophy. Whether, as Harder suggested, this was closely associated with the Peripatos and to what extent it was affected by Stoicism is a question best left open.

For Polybius the problem of where the acme in the *anacyclosis* lay was to some extent answered in the case of Rome because he had injected the mixed constitution into the cycle and this was by definition superior to any other form. The great merit of the Roman constitution lay in the fact that it had slowed down the cycle by means of the mixed form; and this mixed form gave it, as a whole, an acme lacking in the straightforward *anacyclosis* with its three peaks. True, the correspondence is only partial and leaves many questions unanswered; and this basic difficulty in reconciling || the details of the *anacyclosis* with the biological paradigm which it is supposed to illustrate has led some scholars to suppose that the political theory expounded in Book VI represents two – some would even say three – stages in Polybius' thought. Such hypotheses run up against the objection that the various parts of Polybius' argument are closely interrelated and it is not possible to take them apart without doing violence to sequences which clearly form a single line of thought.

[68] For various possible ways of reconciling the two see Walbank, *Comm.* i, 645–7.
[69] See Ryffel (1949) 203 ff.; von Scala (1890) 237 ff.   [70] Harder (1926).
[71] Ryffel (1949) 203 ff.

The argument certainly contains flaws, but these are basic to the whole elaborate theory of Book VI.

How the mixed constitution came to be grafted onto the *anacyclosis* does not seem to be a matter of great importance to Polybius (despite its relevance to the question of how far the result was 'natural'). At Sparta, Lycurgus foreseeing the course of the *anacyclosis*, based on nature, constructed his mixed constitution by a process of reasoning, whereas the Romans, having followed the early stages of the *anacyclosis* in their formation and growth, had reached the same result, not by ratiocination, but by a long period of struggle and hardship, in which they had taken a series of correct decisions in the light of experience.[72] Polybius expresses no preference for the one method or the other. Insofar as Rome is superior to Sparta, her superiority rests on quite other grounds, namely that Rome is better adapted to warfare and to the acquisition of an empire[73] – a remark which tells us something about Polybius' criteria for a successful state.

V THE IDEA OF DECLINE IN POLYBIUS' POLITICAL THEORY

The mixed constitution is a device for slowing down the movement of the *anacyclosis*, but it cannot hold it up for ever; there are in fact four passages[74] in which Polybius speaks of the mixed constitution in Sparta or Rome as of limited duration, and in a comparison of Rome and Carthage at the time of the Hannibalic War he detects some decline at Carthage. In the First Punic War (264–241) the length of the struggle was due to the fact that 'the two states were at this period still uncorrupted in principle, moderate in fortune and equal in strength',[75] but by the time of the Hannibalic War (218–201) 'the Carthaginian constitution had degenerated and that of Rome was better'.[76] Carthage indeed still possessed a mixed constitution, in which the aristocratic elements hold the balance; but this was already deteriorating since deliberation had ceased to be a prerogative of the Council and was now exercised by the people (perhaps identified with the predominance of the Barca family, which || was believed at Rome to rely for its support upon popular elements). Like that of Carthage, the mixed constitution of Rome must eventually become unbalanced and the *anacyclosis* resume its course; then, as Polybius explains at the end of Book VI (chapter 57), its constitution 'will change

---

[72] vi.10.12–14.   [73] vi.50.3–4.   [74] vi.10.1. 10.11, 10.14, 11.1.
[75] vi.51.3–8.   [76] i.13.12; vi.51.3.

its name to the finest sounding of all, freedom and democracy, but its nature to the worst thing of all, mob-rule'.

This formulation takes up a point made earlier in Book VI where,[77] contrasting Rome with the states of Greece, Polybius asserts that it is an easy matter to describe their past and to pronounce upon their future, whereas the Roman constitution is so complicated that it is hard to explain how it has come to be what it is and equally hard to foretell the future because of Greek ignorance of Roman public and private life. Polybius there raised the question of prognostication; and now, at the end of the book, he reverts to the future development of Rome, and her ultimate decline. In fact he does not mention Rome by name – perhaps out of tact – but since he indicates the general course that a state which has attained supremacy and uncontested sovereignty must eventually follow – clearly it is of Rome that he is speaking.

As I have indicated, some scholars believe that parts of Book VI (as well as the last ten books of the *Histories*) were the product of Polybius' old age[78] and reveal a more pessimistic view of Rome than the one he held when he set out to account for Roman world conquest. There are certainly passages in the *Histories* which suggest that Rome is not the place – or the power – that it used to be. I have mentioned[79] the statement that Rome no longer had the capacity to raise or man fleets of the magnitude of those of the First Punic War. Morally too there had been some relaxation of standards. Since the Romans had undertaken wars across the seas, it was no longer true that all Romans would refuse a bribe.[80] The association of moral deterioration with luxury following the eastern wars – for this and not the First Punic War is what Polybius probably means by overseas wars[81] – later becomes a commonplace, and Livy xxxix.6.7, following an annalistic source, associates the introduction of luxury into Rome with Manlius Vulso's Galatian expedition of 189. This was not simply a later belief imposed on the tradition and adopted by Polybius in his old age, however, since Plutarch records how,[82] after Cato's censorship of 184, a statue was set up in the temple of Salus with an inscription indicating that 'when the Roman state was tottering to its fall, he was made censor and by helpful guidance, wise restraints and sound teachings restored it again'. Later Polybius emphasises the extent to which in the 160s and 150s many Roman || youths gave themselves up to sexual encounters and extravagant living,[83] an accusation perhaps borne out by the accusations made against the young people of Rome by

[77] vi.3.1–4.   [78] Above p. 205.   [79] Above, n. 36.   [80] xviii.35.1–2.
[81] *Contra* Lintott (1972) 629.   [82] Plut. *Cato mai.* 193.   [83] xxxi.25.3.

Polybius' friend and patron P. Scipio Aemilianus in a speech delivered against C. Gracchus in the last year of his life (129).[84]

These passages show Polybius sharing a view prevalent since before his arrival in Rome – that to some extent Rome had deteriorated materially and morally since the time of the Hannibalic War. Primarily, however, they indicate a moralist's interest in reprehending deviations from accepted norms, and are certainly not evidence that either during his stay at Rome or later Polybius was seriously concerned with the problem of Roman decline. Though implicit in his political theory, this was still sufficiently remote not to exercise his concern. He remained the historian of Rome's rise to power.

VI TWO MISCELLANEOUS POINTS

(A) An odd feature of the political theory of the sixth book is how little it is reflected in the history outside that book. Here and there one detects comments which are at any rate consistent with the doctrine of the *anacyclosis*. Thus the people of Capua, unable to sustain their prosperity, summoned Hannibal to be their master and so brought about their own ruin.[85] Tarentum through pride engendered by great prosperity called in Pyrrhus with the same result.[86] In the case of Tarentum Polybius asserts the general proposition that when a democracy has long enjoyed prosperity, it seeks a master, but soon regrets it. This recalls the final stages of the *anacyclosis*; but it does not follow that Polybius or his source has this in mind, for the theme of excessive prosperity leading to softness and luxury (τρυφή) and the calling in of a master was by this time a commonplace, as Hoffmann has shown.[87] In fact, as Momigliano points out,[88] there is virtually no contact between the political theory of Book VI and the history proper, and in the latter Polybius gives no hint at anything like a cyclical view. Indeed Momigliano goes further, for he insists that no historian ever wrote the history of a state (as distinct from such extended historical essays as those of Toynbee or Spengler) in terms of birth and rebirth. This remark is perhaps a salutary warning against reading too much into the theorising of Polybius' sixth book. ||

(B) A word is perhaps in order about the time scale of Polybius' sequence of constitutions. If, as seems fairly certain, he identified the early stages

---

[84] *ORF* 'Scipio Aemilianus' fg. 30 = Macrob. *Sat.* iii.14.6.   [85] vii.1.2.
[86] viii.24.1; see von Ungern-Sternberg (1975) 39–41 on both Capua and Tarentum.
[87] Hofmann (1942) 54 ff.   [88] Momigliano (1969) 27.

of the sequence – primitive monarchy, kingship, tyranny, aristocracy and oligarchy – with the years from 751 to 449, with Romulus as primitive monarch, the elder Tarquin and Tullus Hostilius as kings, the younger Tarquin as tyrant, the liberators as the founders of an aristocratic state, and the second decemvirate as its oligarchic corruption[89] – this gives 300 years of growth, with a subsequent 300 years, from 450 to 150, during which Rome perfected and exploited her mixed constitution to win her empire. On the other hand, this pattern (which was probably expounded in the lost historical chapters of Book VI) implies a period of about 160 years between kingship and tyranny (Numa to the younger Tarquin) but only 60 years from the setting up of aristocracy to its corruption into oligarchy (508–449). Hence, although the *anacyclosis* is 'the course appointed by nature (φύσεως οἰκονομία)[90] and a regular process (τεταγμένη . . . θεωρία)',[91] it does not seem to advance with a *steady* movement; indeed the fact that it is possible to delay it by setting up a mixed constitution shows that Polybius did not picture it evolving at a regular rate. Thus he remarks[92] that 'anyone who understands the *anacyclosis* may in speaking of the future of any state be wrong in his estimate of the time the process will take, but . . . he will seldom be mistaken as to the stage of growth or decline it has reached, and as to the form into which it will change'.

VII LINGUISTIC PROBLEMS IN POLYBIUS' THEORY OF DECLINE

It is clear that Polybius has not been wholly successful in linking the *anacyclosis* with the mixed constitution, or with the biological scheme of birth, growth, acme, decline and end, and it may be worth while considering to what extent ambivalence in the meaning of the concepts with which he was dealing has contributed to this. In particular there appear to be four words which fall into this category.

(A) Τύχη (*Tyche*): This concept carried a whole gamut of overtones drawn from everyday expressions and from Hellenistic popular philosophy and that is reflected in Polybius' usage. His own bias towards a utilitarian view of history debarred him from regarding the *Tyche* which directed the course of Roman imperial power as pure chance, otherwise there would have been no lessons to be learnt. But as Providence *Tyche* still has some of the characteristics of Demetrius' unstable and || fickle goddess,

---

[89] See Walbank (1972a) 147–9.   [90] vi.9.10.   [91] vi.57.2.   [92] vi.9.11.

and the story of the fifty-three years of Rome's rise to world hegemony implies a very ambiguous relationship between Rome and *Tyche*.

(B) Πολιτεία (*Politeia*): There is ambiguity too in the use of this word to describe either a constitution or a constitutional form. By switching from one to the other Polybius is helped to coordinate (up to a point) the *anacyclosis* and the biological model.

(C) Μεταβολή (*Metabole*): should mean 'change', but in the biological scheme of birth, growth, acme, decline and end, it tends to be used to mean 'decline'. Since the second meaning fits the biological model, but the first is appropriate only to the *anacyclosis*, this ambiguity acts as a bridge between the two.

(D) Φύσις (*Phusis*): The notion of 'nature' and in particular the phrase κατὰ φύσιν, 'according to nature', provides a further useful bridge between the *anacyclosis* and the biological model. Polybius seems to believe that as both are 'natural' they must in some way be identical.

VIII SUMMARY

I have suggested that, perhaps because it played so small a part in the pattern of his *Histories*, Polybius nowhere formulates a consistent theory of decline. Although he refers on various occasions to deterioration in communities, he does not distinguish the various fields in which decay can operate – political, economic, social and cultural – nor to what extent they are interdependent. It is true that decline is something inherent in his political theory of the development of states, despite his emphasis on the virtues of the mixed constitution; and this is partly because of the rôle he attributes in his central theme to *Tyche*, whose nature it is to bring about *metabole*, or change. Both words are ambiguous. Polybius' *Tyche* is more purposeful and more providential than that of Demetrius of Phalerum, but she still takes pleasure in unexpected changes and reversals; and *metabole* is used to mean either 'change' or 'deterioration' (or 'decline'). *Metabole* in the second sense fits well into the 'natural' biological sequence of birth, growth, acme, decline and end, a progression which makes decline an inevitable constituent of the political scene, notwithstanding the immobility of the mixed constitution and the repetitive cycle of the *anacyclosis*. Polybius evidently regarded the *anacyclosis* as the particular form of the biological law applicable to states; but he was able to bring the two notions together only by his ambivalent use of *politeia* to mean 'constitution' or 'constitutional form' and by an uncovenanted bonus, that of having introduced the mixed constitution to form an acme in the *anacyclosis*. In the purely historical part of his work, as we saw, Polybius has several acute observations about the factors that make for deterioration or corruption in states; but they do not add up to a || consistent theory of decline. His attempt to prognosticate is invalidated by his caveat over the varying periods of time involved and by the paradoxical suspension of the *anacyclosis* at Rome by means of the mixed constitution.

Finally, Polybius fails to bridge the gap between the political philosopher and the historian. The former is of course bound to concern himself with the schematic and the universal, with the normative and the typical, whereas the historian's interest centres on the particular and the unique. Polybius is not alone in his failure to combine the two trades.

14

*Polybius' perception of the one and the many**

'Leaders and masses' has been chosen as a suitable theme around which to organise a celebration of the author of *Plebs and Princeps*. Zvi Yavetz's work deals primarily with the age of Caesar and the early empire. But what happened then was largely the outcome of developments in Roman public life in the second century, during which Rome achieved predominance in the Mediterranean world. Our guide to that earlier period is Polybius' *Histories* and as my contribution to this volume I propose to examine Polybius' perception of leaders and masses, the one and the many, and the rôle he saw each fulfilling in the Greece where he was brought up and then in the Rome with which he became familiar as an exile and as a historian. It will, I think, emerge that he saw these two opposites as basic elements in the political process which he was concerned to analyse.

I

'The many' is a phrase which at once conjures up the notion of 'democracy'. But the meaning of the word 'democracy', δημοκρατία, in Hellenistic Greece has been the subject of controversy over the last fifty years. In an important article published in 1945,[1] J. A. O. Larsen argued that in the Hellenistic period the words 'democracy' and 'democratic' were used loosely as the virtual equivalent of 'self-governing' and that any contrast implied in their use was not, as formerly, with 'oligarchic', but rather with the idea of domination by an outside ruler. In its || extreme form this went too far. Larsen was careful to speak only of a 'tendency', but the tenor of his argument was to disallow the older and more usual

---

* [[I. Malkin and Z. W. Rubinsohn (eds.) *Leaders and Masses in the Roman World: Studies in Honor of Zvi Yavetz* (Leiden-New York-Cologne, 1995) 201–22]]
[1] Larsen (1945) esp. 88–9; see Walbank, *Comm.* II, 222, note on ii.38.6. Larsen refers to Roussel (1932) 28 n.1; Daux (1936) 283 n.4; Jones (1940) 170; Walbank (1940) 225 n.2, as having contributed in various ways to the formulation of his theory.

sense of the word, and his thesis has been subjected to valid criticism by D. Musti[2] and C. Nicolet.[3] As they show, several of the passages adduced in support of Larsen's view are susceptible of other explanations; and there is no lack of evidence that in political life (and not merely in discussion of constitutional matters, like that in Polybius' sixth book) the word 'democratic' often still carried the full sense of a régime in which all citizens had access to the assembly and organs of government. That, for example, is true of Achaea, which, contrary to Larsen's belief, possessed a primary assembly right down to its dissolution in 146.[4] On the other hand, democratic forms did not necessarily exclude domination from without. In the treaty of ὁμοπολιτεία between Cos and Calymna (late third century)[5] the oath taken by the people of Calymna begins: 'ἐμμενῶ τᾶι καθεστηκυίαι δαμοκρατίαι' (ll. 14–15) – 'I will be true to the established democracy' – and continues later with: 'ὀλιγαρχίαν δὲ οὐδὲ τύραννον οὐδὲ ἄλλο πολίτευμα ἔξω δαμοκρατίας οὐ καταστάσω' (ll. 21–2) – 'I will not set up an oligarchy or tyrant or any other constitution other than democracy.' Yet those swearing also pledged themselves to remain true to the 'friendship and alliance' of Ptolemy and both states clearly fell within the Ptolemaic sphere of control sufficiently to require a mention of Ptolemy to be included in the agreement. Moreover, as Nicolet points out, there are many inscriptions in which δημοκρατία appears to be used in Larsen's sense of 'autonomous republic' or 'free ancestral government',[6] especially from cities dominated by the Seleucids. Here again, royal domination does not exclude || δημοκρατία. It is of course undeniable that many cities with constitutions democratic in form contained timocratic elements and in practice assigned power, influence and honour to their richer citizens.

So 'democracy' is a flexible concept in the Hellenistic age. What were Polybius' views about it and about the 'many' on whose power it rested? Polybius grew up in Achaea, and this, as we have just seen, was a democratic federal state.[7] From his *Histories* and in particular from Book VI it is clear that he was acquainted with various theoretical works dealing

---

[2] Musti (1967).
[3] Nicolet (1983a), esp. 15–35, 'Polybe et la "constitution" de Rome: aristocratie et démocratie' (= Nicolet 1983b).
[4] See ch. 10, above.   [5] *SVA* 545.
[6] Nicolet (1983b) 23, where he adduces inscriptions (quoted already by Holleaux (1942) 153 n. 1) from Smyrna, Iasus and Lampsacus. Musti (1966), esp. 138–45, discusses these and other inscriptions and attributes a fuller content to δημοκρατία, justified, he argues, by the special circumstances of each inscription. But it is hard to resist the implication that δημοκρατία is being given its weaker sense, if one takes these inscriptions together.
[7] On the federal aspect see ii.37.7–11; see also Walbank (1976/7).

with political development and different types of constitution. But his notion of 'the many' is based primarily on observation and on his reactions as a member of an upper-class Achaean political family. His view of the masses can be reconstructed from scattered observations, some his own and some incorporated in speeches attributed to orators of different states and with varying political views; but the picture that emerges is consistent, something on which all are agreed. The people – οἱ πολλοί, ὁ ὄχλος or ὁ δῆμος – do not normally assume the initiative. They are there to be played on, easily swayed, liable to lawless passions, irrational rage and violent anger.[8] An unidentified speaker (the relevant passage is an unassigned fragment) explains that because the mob is irrational, any alliance with a democracy needs the support of considerable goodwill.[9] The masses are like the sea, whose appearance is governed entirely by the winds playing over it – a simile attributed first to Scipio Africanus[10] and then, later, to an Aetolian, Leon the son of Cichesias.[11] On the second occasion Polybius remarks, rather oddly, that the simile was 'apt to the present situation', viz. Leon's defence of his fellow-countrymen for having called in Antiochus: whereas to Livy, drawing on and adapting this very passage of Polybius,[12] Leon || was employing a commonplace (*vulgata similitudine . . . usus*). In fact the same figure is to be found in Solon (fg. 12 Bergk), in Artabanus' speech to Xerxes in Herodotus (vii.16α) and in Demosthenes (xix.136), and later in Curtius (x.7.11). The mob is also seen as quick to jealousy[13] or to love or hate.[14] Polybius singles out the mob at Athens (a city he dislikes) as particularly prone to be whipped up by demagogues, whom it in turn encourages.[15] But, according to a Polybian passage in Livy,[16] the populace of Syracuse is no better: 'ea natura multitudini est: aut servit humiliter aut superbe dominatur.' There is, however, one consolation: the cosmopolitan Alexandrian mob is worse than that of any of the older Greek cities.[17]

Given these views on the masses, it may seem a little anomalous that Polybius is so enthusiastic a supporter of democracy and of the qualities which he attributes to it. Achaea, he says, is an incomparable example of a

---

[8] vi.56.11, πᾶν πλῆθός ἐστιν ἐλαφρὸν καὶ πλῆρες ἐπιθυμιῶν παρανόμων, ὀργῆς ἀλόγου, θυμοῦ βιαίου. That is why οἱ παλαιοί wisely devised stories of gods and the terrors of Hades, to keep them under control. (All subsequent references without an author's name are to Polybius.)

[9] x.25.6: the context is obscure.

[10] xi.29.9.   [11] xxi.31.9.   [12] Livy xxxviii.10.5.

[13] xxiii.12.8; hence it was remarkable that, though he spoke out, Philopoemen avoided incurring ill-will.

[14] xxxiii.20, an unplaced fragment.   [15] vi.44; cf. Livy xxxi.44.3 (drawing on Polybius).

[16] Livy xxiv.25.8.   [17] xv.25ff.; cf. Musti (1967) 205.

political system based on equality, freedom of speech and democracy. The combination of equality (ἰσηγορία) and freedom of speech (παρρησία) is peculiarly characteristic of democracy.[18] Thus Perseus' envoys flatter the Rhodians by referring to them as champions of equality and free speech;[19] and Polybius several times employs the phrase in reference to Achaea.[20] In one place,[21] it is true, he uses the word ἰσηγορία to describe the traditional freedom with which Macedonians addressed their king. But this is a specific situation, an unusual phenomenon, not normally present in a monarchy. It does not indicate equality generally, nor do we have the typical combination || of ἰσηγορία and παρρησία which is associated with the quality of life in a democracy.

In fact, there is no real contradiction between Polybius' admiration for Achaea and his contempt for the masses; for Achaea was not the kind of democracy where the πλῆθος habitually had full rein. On the one occasion[22] when it uses its παρρησία in a manner of which he disapproves, Polybius utterly condemns the proceedings of an assembly 'full of factory-workers and common men', which was so unwise as to insult Roman envoys. That meeting took place in spring 146 at Corinth, a centre of trade and manufacture and probably most of the πλῆθος came from that city. Normally, as J. L. O'Neil has recently shown,[23] the real power lay elsewhere. Achaea was 'a democracy, but one dominated by a rather narrow élite drawn from the well-to-do families which had provided the leadership of the original Achaian League, of Sicyon and of Megalopolis'. Achaea, Polybius also points out, though a democracy, was πολυειδής, multiform,[24] and much in its workings depended on the relations between the magistrates, the council and those generally attending the assembly.[25] The events at Corinth were exceptional and a symptom of the widespread disarray in Achaea at the time of the Achaean War, when, in Polybius' opinion, the wrong sort of people led

[18] ii.38.6, ἰσηγορίας καὶ παρρησίας καὶ καθόλου δημοκρατίας ἀληθινῆς σύστημα καὶ προαίρεσιν εἰλικρινεστέραν οὐκ ἂν εὕροι τις τῆς παρὰ τοῖς Ἀχαίοις ὑπαρχούσης.

[19] xxvii.4.7.

[20] In addition to ii.38.6 (above, n.18) cf. ii.42.3, iv.31.4 (probably referring to Achaea). For Achaean democracy cf. ii.44.6, iv.1.5 (adopted immediately after the reign of Ogygus), xxii.8.6, and *Syll.* 665 l.17, δα[μ]οκρατούμενοι καὶ τὰ ποθ᾽ αὑτοὺς ὁμονοοῦντες.

[21] v.27.6. On Macedonia ἰσηγορία see Adams (1986) 43–52. For Nicolet's contention that ἰσηγορία and παρρησία were characteristic of other 'good' constitutions see below, p. 222, with n.65.

[22] xxxviii.12.4–5, πλῆθος ἐργαστηριακῶν καὶ βαναύσων ἀνθρώπων ὅσον οὐδέποτε.

[23] O'Neil (1984–6) esp. 42; cf. xxviii. 7.7.

[24] xxiii.12.8: Philopoemen was active ἐν δημοκρατικῷ καὶ πολυειδεῖ πολιτεύματι. πολυείδης has been variously interpreted: I take it to mean 'composed of various elements'. See my note ad loc. (Walbank, *Comm.* III, 242); also Musti (1967) 164.

[25] See further, O'Neil (1980).

the mob to take disastrous decisions.[26] In better times, before Polybius'
exile, Achaean statesmen had been of a different ilk.

II

Polybius' Greek experience down to 168 had also brought him into contact with 'the one' and had shaped his opinions on this element in the
political scene. His judgement on 'the one' appears || in two quite distinct
contexts. In the first place he is impressed by what an individual who has
the right qualities and applies them can achieve in the face of all kinds of
difficulties. Such men usually call for admiration, but occasionally their
qualities can be ruinous. Thus, commenting on Lyciscus of Stratus in
Aetolia,[27] 'a turbulent and noisy man', after whose death the Aetolians
were able to live in peace, he remarks that 'the power inherent in men's
natures is so great that not only armies and cities, but also national groupings and in fact all the different peoples which compose the whole world
experience sometimes the greatest misfortune and sometimes the greatest prosperity because of the good or bad character of a single man'. But
most of his examples are of men whose achievements merit wonder and
admiration: Xanthippus, for instance, the Spartan mercenary captain[28]
who destroyed the Roman army of Regulus and restored Carthaginian
fortunes in the first Punic War, Archimedes,[29] whose engines and military
ingenuity saved Syracuse from capture for eight months, or Hannibal
himself[30] – for 'of all that befell both the Romans and the Carthaginians
the cause was one man and one mind – I mean Hannibal'.

But Polybius was also interested in 'the one' as an element dialectically
engaged in various political constellations with 'the many'. 'The one'
could take various forms. In the political life of Greece he could be a
general, a statesman (or demagogue, according to one's point of view), a
tyrant or a king. The two latter are the most important; as we have seen,
the word 'democracy' *could* be used to mean simply 'not subject to a king'.
Both kings and tyrants were well in evidence in the Hellenistic world, and
sometimes the same individual could appear in both rôles. The Spartan
Cleomenes, for instance, began as an excellent king but became a most
cruel tyrant;[31] and the same was true of Philip V of Macedonia.[32] Nabis,
though a Eurypontid || and an accepted king of Sparta, is invariably

---

[26] See esp. xxxviii.15.1–18.12.   [27] xxxii.4.1–2.   [28] i.35.4–6.
[29] viii.3.3, 7.7.   [30] ix.22.1, 22.6.
[31] ix.23.3, cf. ii.47.3, iv.81.14. On Polybius' view of Cleomenes see Walbank (1966).
[32] iv. 77.4; cf. v.11.6, vii.13.7.

referred to by Polybius as a tyrant.[33] On the other hand, Dionysius I and Agathocles began as tyrants at Syracuse and 'were afterwards recognised as kings of the whole of Sicily';[34] and Hiero II, though he also seized power by force, is described as a king.[35] Obviously the distinction was to some extent fluid. A successful ruler might be whatever he chose to call himself. At the same time, Polybius seems to have been influenced by value-judgements as well as legal forms in his choice of the terms he used.

With his Peloponnesian background, Polybius had a long-standing experience of both kings and tyrants. Several cities had had tyrants imposed on them by Antigonus Gonatas, 'who planted more tyrannies in Greece than any other king';[36] and Aratus, the hero of the early third century Achaean Confederation, had spent many years expelling these. Polybius followed the orthodox line in loathing tyranny; in this, tradition matched his own personal experience. To a Greek, tyranny was the greatest of crimes. 'Great is the honour bestowed not on him who kills a thief,' says Aristotle,[37] 'but on him who kills a tyrant.' Polybius agrees: 'the slayer of a tyrant', he remarks,[38] 'everywhere meets with honour and the assignment of special seating at the theatre'. This is all fairly schematic and foreseeable. But on kings Polybius' views reveal greater nuances.[39]

There was a traditional criterion which distinguished the king ruling according to law over willing subjects from the tyrant ruling as he wished over unwilling subjects. Xenophon attributes it to Socrates, but it also crops up in Plato and Aristotle and || indeed something like it had already been adumbrated by earlier writers.[40] Polybius concurs in this definition (though, as we have just seen, his practice is less consistent). It is ultimately a moral distinction. His own formulation is one which draws on the

[33] iv. 81.13, xiii.6–8, xxi. 11.10. Nabis' kingship is well attested; see Walbank, *Comm.* ii, 420 on xiii.6–8.
[34] xv.35.3–4. In fact Dionysius never took nor was given the title of king.
[35] vii.8.2; cf. i.8.3.
[36] ii.41.10; cf. ix.29.5 (a speech by Chlaeneas the Aetolian, which however closely echoes the former passage in grouping together the garrisons imposed by Cassander and Demetrius and the tyrannies of Gonatas).
[37] *Politics* ii.7.13, 1267 a 12ff. It is a view later taken over by Cicero, *Off.*iii.32; cf. *De re pub.* ii.48 (no doubt having acquired new urgency since the Ides of March 44).
[38] ii.56.15,τιμῶν καὶ προεδρίας τυγχάνει παρὰ πᾶσιν; cf. 59.6 (in reference to Aristomachus, the tyrant of Argos).
[39] Cf. Welwei (1963) 185: 'Er hat die Herrscher nicht schematisch charakterisiert.'
[40] Xen. *Mem.* iv.6.12; similar distinctions are drawn in Plato, *Plt.* 291e and Aristotle, *Politics* iii. 14, 1285 a 24–9. As Welwei (1963) 123–4 n.1, points out, the concept of ἑκόντων ἄρχειν as the mark of the king is in Eur. *Hel.* 395f., *Or.* 1167f., Thuc. i.96.1, iii.72.2 and Gorgias fg. 11a, 14. In Herodotus, iii.82.2 the king rules on the basis of γνώμη ('judgement').

vocabulary for the ideal king, as it is revealed in various Hellenistic sources. 'It is the tyrant's rôle,' Polybius declares,[41] 'to do evil so as to make himself master of men by fear against their will, but that of a king to do good to all and so to rule and preside over a willing people, earning their love by his beneficence and humanity (διὰ τὴν εὐεργεσίαν καὶ φιλανθρωπίαν ἀγαπώμενον).' Beneficence (εὐεργεσία) was of course a characteristic of the good king so outstanding that 'Benefactor' (*Euergetes*) was taken as a title by both Ptolemaic and Seleucid rulers, and humanity (φιλανθρωπία) and love (ἀγάπησις) figure as the supreme royal virtues in Aristeas' *Letter to Philocrates*.[42]

Welwei[43] has assembled a list of other passages in Polybius which mirror the 'ideal king'. A generous spirit (μεγαλοψυχία) is above all the kingly virtue, especially when combined with gentleness and moderation (εὐγνωμοσύνη and μετριότης). These are qualities found in Philip II[44] and also, on one recorded occasion, in Antiochus III.[45] Hiero II showed his true character in youth by acting with gentleness and generosity (πρᾴως καὶ μεγαλοψύχως); later he never killed, exiled or injured anyone.[46] Antigonus Doson treated the conquered Spartans with generosity and humanity;[47] and even Philip V, when in adversity, showed a generous and kingly spirit and firmness of purpose.[48] But it does not follow from this that Polybius approved of kingship as an institution. || Rather it was something one had to live with (or preferably without). Hellenistic kings presented a constant threat to Greek cities and the whole history of the Achaean League from its reformation in 281/280 had been bound up, often disastrously, with the struggle against Macedonia and its Antigonid rulers. Consequently, for Achaea the word democracy (δημοκρατία) carried its full significance both as the antithesis of autocratic or oligarchic government and as the assertion of independence from outside domination. In one passage (xviii.41.5) Polybius appears to come close to approving kingship as an institution. We should admire Attalus' μεγαλοψυχία in devoting all his resources exclusively to the attainment of kingship (πρὸς βασιλείας κατάκτησιν), 'than which nothing greater or more splendid can be named'. But it is not kingship

---

[41] v.11.6; for a short account of the idealised picture of the Hellenistic king see Walbank (1984a) 81-4.

[42] Aristeas, *Letter* 265.   [43] Welwei (1963) 123.

[44] v.12.1, μεγαλοψύχως καὶ βασιλικῶς, 10.2, εὐγνωμοσύνη καὶ μετριότης.

[45] viii.23.5, μεγαλοψύχως καὶ βασιλικῶς.   [46] i.8.4; cf. vii.8.2.

[47] ii.70.1, μεγαλοψύχως καὶ φιλανθρώπως.

[48] xvi.28.3, τὸ ... βασιλικὸν καὶ μεγαλόψυχον καὶ τὸ τῆς προθέσεως ἐπίμονον. After Cynoscephalae he did not neglect his duty, but very properly burnt all the state papers (xviii.33.2).

per se, but the single-minded concentration on acquiring it that arouses Polybius' admiration,[49] for he thinks this reveals a generous spirit (μεγαλοψυχία). In this he appears not to be conscious of the inconsistency which we might detect in admiring the disposition to acquire something while regarding with dislike and suspicion the thing acquired.

That Polybius regards kingship with suspicion is quite clear. Kings may be good or bad (mainly the latter), but the institution itself is flawed. It is the nature of kings to judge everything in terms of self-interest.[50] Moreover, when behaving rationally, kings begin by talking about freedom and calling their adherents friends and allies, but later they treat them despotically.[51] There are also two passages in which Polybius attributes similar views on monarchy to others in speeches. The Rhodians, in a speech before the Senate directed against Pergamene ambitions, allege that 'every monarchy hates equality (τὸ ἴσον) and strives to increase the number of its subjects';[52] and Apollonidas of Sicyon, opposing the acceptance of a proposed gift of money from Eumenes, tells the Achaeans that the interests of kings and democracies are by nature opposed (ἐναντίαν φύσιν ἐχόντων).[53] ||

As has been pointed out, behind his general disapproval of kingship as an institution Polybius distinguished between good kings and bad. And there is one noteworthy example of a king who consistently earns his praise, namely Philip II of Macedonia. In Book VIII he offers a long defence of that king against Theopompus who, despite his admission that Philip was the greatest man Europe had ever produced, and his claim that he was 'richly endowed by nature with every quality that makes for virtue' employs the vilest language to abuse him and his 'collaborators and friends' (many of them being the future Diadochi, who were to dispute Alexander's empire after his death).[54] Elsewhere, in several places,

---

[49] Polybius writes οὗ (not ἧς) μεῖζον κτλ: the antecedent is the whole action, not βασιλείας or even κατάκτησιν.

[50] ii.47.5, in relation to Aratus' approach to Antigonus Doson.

[51] xv.24.4: Philip in his pact with Antiochus III was too irrational even to conceal his true motives for the time being.

[52] xxi.22.8: summing up this speech (23.13) Polybius says that the Rhodians 'seemed to all to have expressed themselves modestly and well about the situation'. Evidently he concurs in their statement about monarchy.

[53] xxii.8.6; it is noteworthy that in a passage based on Polybius, Livy (xliv.24.2) makes Perseus' envoys to Antiochus IV and Eumenes put forward the same argument in order to try to win their support against Rome. But there the regime opposed to monarchy is not democracy, but a 'free state': 'natura inimica inter se esse liberam civitatem et regem'. Was the Polybian original another example of the approximation in meaning of 'democracy' and 'a free state'?

[54] viii.9.1–11.2.

Polybius praises Philip II for his generosity to Athens after Chaeronea;[55] and in a speech attributed to the Acarnanian Lyciscus at a meeting at Sparta in late spring 210 – it is a reply to that of the Aetolian Chlaeneas – Philip is praised as a benefactor of both Greece and Sparta. This is clearly also Polybius' own view, for his home city of Megalopolis had long-established ties with the Macedonian royal house ever since Philip gave the city territory taken from Sparta.[56] Consequently there were special political reasons why Polybius should favour Philip II. There were also quite other reasons connected with the overall structure of his *Histories*. I have discussed these elsewhere,[57] and since they are not relevant to the present subject I shall not go into them here.

III

In 168 Polybius was in his early thirties,[58] an experienced statesman and cavalry commander and probably already the author || of a memoir on Philopoemen and perhaps a book on *Tactics*. As we have seen, he had clear views about the nature of the masses and those who led them, whether statesmen, tyrants or kings. And, as regards monarchy, it is likely that his family, in particular his father Lycortas and himself (like the family of Aratus of Sicyon), had special links with the Ptolemaic royal house.[59] To that extent at least Polybius' theoretical and instinctive views about kingship will have been tempered by pragmatical considerations. In 167, however, following the Roman victory over Perseus of Macedonia at Pydna, Polybius was shipped off to Rome as part of a general *épuration* of the Achaean League. How on his arrival in Italy he was able to exploit the friendship of Scipio Aemilianus to be allowed to remain in Rome and how he there conceived the idea of his *Histories* and set about writing them is a story, often told, which need not be repeated here. The point I would emphasise is that as a critical viewer of the Roman scene and the author of a history which was to deal with the rise of Rome to world power, Polybius now needed to set his ideas about the one and the many in a new, Roman context.

---

[55] v.10.1–5; cf. xviii. 14.6–8, 14.14, for his μεγαλοψυχία and φιλοδοξία; xxii. 16.2, contrasting him with Ptolemy V.

[56] ii.48.2; the territory in question was the Sciritis, Aegytis and Belbinatis and the award is referred to in *Syll.* 665 ll.19–20.

[57] Chapter 16, below.

[58] His date of birth is unknown, but it was probably towards the end of the third century; see Walbank, *Comm.* I, 1 n.1.

[59] Cf. xxii.3.5, xxiv.6.3–7, xxx.23.3–5. I have discussed this question in chapter 16, below, pp. 252–3.

The *Histories* themselves provide the evidence for how he did this. They also show that he was now consciously attempting to relate his ideas about the distribution of power within a state to his new purpose – the explanation of why Rome came to be mistress of the inhabited world, the *oecumene*. That is why the formulation of his views about 'the one' and 'the many' during his active years in Achaea is reflected in odd remarks throughout his work, whereas his views about those elements at Rome are mainly concentrated in one place, Book VI. This book contains, among other things, an analysis of the Roman constitution in which the two contrasted concepts (and the fleshing out of these in the realities of Roman public life) play an essential part.

As the background to this discussion Polybius describes an elaborate model of political development, the so-called *anacyclosis*, involving a kind of circular succession of constitutions, by way of primitive monarchy, kingship, tyranny, aristocracy, oligarchy, democracy, mob-rule (ochlocracy) and so back to monarchy, ‖ where the process began.[60] A brief survey of this sequence will show that the relationship between 'the one' and 'the many' is basic to it at almost every stage. At the outset we are presented with a primitive horde, the survivors of some natural cataclysm, who come together for mutual protection, herded like animals and led by the strongest individual among them – as is the case, Polybius adds, with bulls, boars, cocks and the like. This strong man is the monarch (μόναρχος), and his strength is the measure of his rule.[61] The rôle of 'the many' at this stage is passive: they are like a herd of animals except in one respect – their possession of reason (νοῦς καὶ λόγισμος). In time and thanks to this quality of reason, the primitive group becomes infused with moral ideas. Polybius is at pains to show that that occurs as part of a 'natural' process. Natural instincts lead to sexual intercourse and the birth of children; the behaviour of children towards their parents is observed by others and if they show ingratitude this is remarked on with indignation. Likewise ingratitude in someone who has been helped in time of danger is ill regarded, whereas acts of bravery are noted and honoured. There thus grows up a notion of duty (τὸ καθῆκον). When the monarch identifies himself with this new moral code, he becomes a king (βασιλεύς), whose rule is based on reason (λογισμός) and is willingly accepted by 'the many'.[62] Basic to this stage of the cycle is the existence of reason in 'the many' and 'the one'; but whereas the growth of moral ideas in 'the many' is seen as a 'natural' development, the ruler's identification

---

[60] vi.4.6–10 (outline); 5.4–9.9 (full exposition).   [61] vi.5.4–9.   [62] vi.5.10–7.5.

with this moral order depends on a conscious choice on his part. Thus
it is with him that the initiative lies, and through him that monarchy
advances to become kingship.

The next stage arises when the king's offspring, who inherit the throne,
are corrupted by their privileged position and resort to outrageous behaviour, which precipitates conspiracies led by the best people, i.e. the
noblest, the most generous and the most courageous. The kingship has
now become a tyranny and this is overthrown and replaced by an aristocracy in a process in which the people (πλῆθος) combines with the noble
element to || oust the tyrant. Once again 'the many' fail to take the
initiative but merely follow the lead given them by the nobles; and after
the victory they entrust these with power, believing them to merit that
trust.[63] But the process of deterioration is about to be repeated, with the
sons of the aristocrats emulating the sons of the king in their behaviour;
and that for two reasons. First, they have had no experience of 'evils' (i.e.
tyranny) as had their fathers; and secondly 'they have had no experience
whatsoever of political equality and freedom of speech'.[64] This second
reason creates a problem of interpretation. It is Nicolet's contention[65]
that 'political equality and freedom of speech' are to be found in all 'good'
constitutions, i.e. in kingship, aristocracy and democracy, but are absent
from their corrupt forms. It is because aristocracy has been perverted
into oligarchy in the second generation that the new rulers have had
no experience of equality and free speech. This can hardly be right. If
equality and free speech existed under the *first* generation, Polybius could
not reasonably say that the second generation had had no experience of
them whatsoever, since they had been brought up by their fathers, under
whom *ex hypothesi* these values existed. It seems far more likely that the
reason the oligarchs had had no experience of equality and free speech
is that these were a characteristic of 'good' democracy and so had not yet
put in an appearance.[66] We have already seen that the combination of
these two institutions was peculiarly democratic. Polybius never speaks of
them in reference to aristocracy nor indeed monarchy (for, as we noted,
Macedonian ἰσηγορία is something different).[67]

The oligarchs soon go the way of the tyrants. And here again the initiative comes, not from 'the many', but from one individual who speaks out
against the rulers and is supported by the people. But this time the people
do not hand over control to their leader, having learnt from experience
of the dangers inherent in that course. Instead they set up a democracy.[68]

[63] vi.7.6–8.1.   [64] vi.8.2–4, ἄπειροι ... καθόλου πολιτικῆς ἰσότητος καὶ παρρησίας.
[65] Nicolet (1983b) 27.   [66] Cf. Musti (1967) 193.   [67] See above, n. 21.   [68] vi.8.4–9.3.

This collapses when the grandchildren of the first generation begin to ||
aim at getting more than 'the many' and reject equality and free speech.
These men are described as rich (for ἰσηγορία is of course political, not
economic equality)[69] and it is through them that the state begins to lapse
into mob-rule. How that process works out in relation to 'the one' and
'the many' I shall consider shortly. But at this point it would be as well
to ask how this schematic evolution of constitutions applied to Rome.
For Polybius, after completing his account of the *anacyclosis*, asserts that
'especially in the case of the Roman state this method of examination
will give us the clearest insight into the process whereby it was formed,
grew and reached the zenith of its achievement as well as the changes
for the worse which will follow these'.[70]

Polybius will have shown how the *anacyclosis* applies to Rome in the
lost section of Book VI, of which only the fragments assembled as vi.11a
survive. The likelihood is that monarchy, kingship and tyranny were illustrated by the reigns from Romulus to the younger Tarquin, aristocracy
by the early republic and oligarchy by the decemvirate.[71] But from that
point[72] Rome succeeded in applying a brake to the cycle by acquiring a
balanced or mixed constitution (Polybius never actually calls it a 'mixed
constitution' though that is what it is) and this constitution avoided the
corruption to which all the simple forms were liable. Polybius analyses the
powers exercised by the monarchic (i.e. the consular), the aristocratic (i.e.
the senatorial) and the democratic elements in the state and the checks
each applied to the other two,[73] and in due course sets up a comparison
between Rome's 'mixed' constitution and the constitutions of a select
number of other states. Of these, it appears, both Carthage and Sparta
were also exceptional in having or having had mixed constitutions.[74] One
cannot help wondering, therefore, how far the *anacyclosis*, || the 'course
appointed by nature for constitutional change',[75] could really be thought
of as being of universal application and how far it could provide the sure
guide to future constitutional developments that Polybius claims for it.

---

[69] Cf. vi.8.4.   [70] vi.9.12–14.

[71] See Walbank *Comm.* I, 663–4, note on vi. 11a; the general line of Polybius' argument can be
cautiously recovered from Cicero's *De re publica*, which drew in part on Polybius. [See below,
pp. 285–8.]

[72] vi.11.1: for the reading see R. Weil in the Budé edition (1977) 85 and 146. Weil has shown that
there is no lacuna and the date for the beginning of the onset of the perfected Roman constitution
is therefore firmly established as 450 (i.e. the decemvirate).

[73] vi.11.11–18.8.   [74] Cf. vi.10.1–14, 48.1–50.6 (Lycurgan Sparta); vi.51.1–8 (Carthage).

[75] vi.9.10, αὕτη φύσεως οἰκονομία, καθ᾽ ἣν μεταβάλλει καὶ μεθίσταται καὶ πάλιν εἰς αὑτὰ καταντᾷ
τὰ κατὰ τὰς πολιτείας.

In the mixed constitution 'the one' and 'the many' no longer play the dynamic and diachronic rôle that they play in the *anacyclosis*. Here Polybius' analysis is schematic, since he is describing a constitution with the brakes on. He is concerned with elements (μέρη) in the state and the monarchic or kingly element is represented by the consuls.[76] In this Polybius followed a Roman tradition stressing the continuity of the consulate with the royal power which preceded it.[77] A good example of the strength of that tradition is to be found in a passage of Livy, based on an annalistic source, which describes an attempt by M. Aburius in 187 to intercede against the proposal that a triumph be awarded to M. Fulvius. When Aburius suggested postponing a decision until the return of the consul M. Aemilius to Rome, Ti. Gracchus interjected that the tribunate was intended, not *pro consulari regno*, but *pro auxilio ac libertate privatorum*.[78] As regards the 'democratic element' it has long been noted as an oddity that the restraint exercised on this by the 'aristocratic element' is illustrated by the extent to which the *publicani* find it necessary to rely on the Senate to secure their contracts.[79] Here 'the many' is being interpreted in a very restricted sense. But Polybius speaks of the people in a broader context when he underlines its power to confer honours (at elections) and inflict punishments (through the courts), especially on capital charges. The people also legislates and decides on war and peace (after deliberation) and ratifies alliances, terms of peace and treaties.[80] Its powers are thus substantial.

But what of the aristocratic element, which appears to fall outside the categories of 'the one' and 'the many'? At Rome || this is represented by the Senate and Nicolet has argued[81] that Polybius really saw Rome as an aristocracy. This would seem to distort Polybius' perception of the Roman state. In one place,[82] it is true, he speaks of P. Scipio 'pursuing fame in an aristocratic state'. But this passage occurs in the course of a comparison with Philopoemen who, on Polybius' reckoning, had died the same year and had 'pursued fame in a democratic state'.[83] In this rhetorical *syncrisis* Polybius seems to be far away from the ideas of the *anacyclosis* and the mixed constitution. The remark about Scipio is certainly

---

[76] Cf. vi.11.12, ὅτε μὲν γὰρ εἰς τὴν τῶν ὑπάτων ἀτενίσαιμεν ἐξουσίαν τελείως μοναρχικὸν ἐφαίνετ' εἶναι καὶ βασιλικόν.
[77] Cf. Dion. Hal. vi.63; Cicero, *De re publica* ii.56, 'potestatem . . . genere ipso ac iure regiam'.
[78] Livy xxxix.4.1–5.   [79] vi.17.
[80] vi.14.   [81] (1983b) 21–2, 31. [On this see below, pp. 281–3.]
[82] xxiii.14.1, φιλοδοξήσας ἐν ἀριστοκρατικῷ πολιτεύματι.
[83] xxiii.12.8, φιλοδοξήσας ἐν δημοκρατικῷ καὶ πολυειδεῖ πολιτεύματι (on πολυειδεῖ see above, n.24).

inconsistent with the detailed analysis and conclusions of Book VI and raises the question which of the two is more likely to represent Polybius' considered view of the Roman constitution. It seems to me that the very detailed and carefully argued account in Book VI must take precedence over an isolated comment apparently inserted in order to create a rhetorical antithesis. And if, as is not impossible, the third figure in the *syncrisis*, Hannibal,[84] was represented as examplifying a love of glory (φιλοδοξία) of a monarchic type, that would reinforce the view that this passage completely ignores the constitutional discussion of Book VI. That Hannibal was so represented is of course hypothetical. But of the part of the discussion relating to him only one fragment has survived; and some comment about the type of state he operated in seems to be required, to match the comments on Scipio and Philopoemen.

Against the assumption that Polybius regarded the Roman constitution as an aristocracy is the whole tenor of the argument in Book VI, which represents Rome as having a balanced constitution of the Lycurgan type;[85] and though, as Nicolet points out,[86] the Senate, identified as οἱ ἄριστοι, is in charge of deliberation at Rome, that is not an argument for identifying the Roman government at that time as an aristocracy. On the contrary, the retention of the right to deliberate by the Senate was || an indication that Rome had not yet begun to abandon its *mikte* as Carthage had done; for there deliberation was already in the hands of οἱ πολλοί .[87] Indeed, if the Roman constitution is to be characterised as 'aristocratic' ('même si elle est composite'), it is hard to see why Polybius should have gone to such pains to elaborate the theory of the mixed constitution and the way in which it avoided the 'congenital vice', the σύμφυτον κακόν, inherent in each simple constitutional form.

IV

For states which remained within the circle of the *anacyclosis* the stage following democracy was mob-rule; and Polybius has a succinct account of how that came about.[88] But Rome too, although thanks to the mixed constitution she had been able to put a brake on the wheel, could not evade the onset of change for ever; for 'all existing things are subject to decay, a proposition which scarcely requires proof, since the inexorable

---

[84] xxiii.13. Hannibal's command in Italy, often represented as independent of effective Carthaginian control (though wrongly), may well have seemed to possess some monarchic features (cf. n.30).

[85] vi.10.14, ἦλθον ἐπὶ ταὐτὸ μὲν Λυκούργῳ τέλος.   [86] Nicolet (1983b) 21–2, 31.

[87] For this point see Pöschl (1936) 61.   [88] vi.9.6–9.

course of nature is sufficient to impose it on us.'[89] In one of the last chapters of Book VI Polybius therefore outlines the process of decline as he saw it coming at Rome.[90] The book thus contains two accounts of ultimate constitutional decay, one within the *anacyclosis* of democracy into mob-rule and final monarchy, the other specifically of the Roman mixed constitution, as it dissolves and sets Rome back on the wheel of change. As one might expect, the two contain some similar features; but they are not identical, and for a proper understanding of what Polybius was saying, it seems desirable to distinguish between them.[91]

In the first passage (vi.9.6–9), dealing with the end of the *anacyclosis*, the rich leaders, grandsons of the founding fathers of || the democracy, become contemptuous of equality and free speech (ἰσηγορία and ἐλευθερία) and bankrupt themselves by bribing the people (τὰ πλήθη) to give them the power they cannot secure on their merits. This creates among the people an appetite for such hand-outs; and since their original corruptors no longer have the wealth necessary to continue these, the people fall for the blandishments of a leader (προστάτης) who is bold and ambitious, but poor. They therefore take to violence, and institute massacres, exiling, plunder and the division of land (γῆς ἀναδασμός) and so, having resorted, to complete savagery, end up with a master and monarch (δεσπότην καὶ μόναρχον). Polybius does not say, though he perhaps implies, that this monarch, who in order to close the cycle has to correspond to the original leader of the primitive horde, is the bold and ambitious poor man who has initiated the reign of violence. This picture contains elements familiar from earlier Greek writers. 'Is it not always particularly characteristic of the people,' asks Plato,[92] 'to set some individual over themselves and to nourish him and raise him up to greatness?' Such a man is of course a tyrant and, as Nicolet correctly points out, the whole setting of this passage in Polybius is Greek. The leader excluded from public honours through poverty would be an absurdity in a Roman context, and in this part of the *anacyclosis* Polybius is simply drawing on his experience of Greek political life in the third and second centuries.[93]

---

[89] vi.57.1.   [90] vi.57.1–9.

[91] The distinction is not made in two important recent discussions of this matter. Claude Nicolet ((1983b) 33) takes both passages to be describing 'la détérioration éventuelle d'un équilibre "aristocratique"': par deux fois au livre *vi* il précise sa pensée'; and Millar (1986) 5 n.12 quotes with approval a suggestion of John North that vi.9.6–9 'can be read as an implicit prediction of the course of events in the last century of the Republic'. [See further below, pp. 289–91.]

[92] Plato, *Rep.* viii.565c οὐκοῦν ἕνα τινὰ ἀεὶ δῆμος εἴωθεν διαφερόντως προΐστασθαι ἑαυτοῦ, καὶ τοῦτον τρέφειν τε καὶ αὔξειν μέγαν;

[93] Nicolet (1983b) 33; cf. also von Fritz (1954) 309.

In fact Polybius does not claim this passage as a forecast of future developments at Rome. That is reserved for the later chapter (vi.57.5–9) with which he rounds off his description of the Roman state, a striking passage, which inspired Schweighaeuser to an uncharacteristic digression on the state of affairs in his contemporary France.[94] At the very outset, however, this chapter || presents a problem. States can decay, says Polybius,[95] as a result either of external or internal causes; and the latter operate in a regular process. That process is, of course, the *anacyclosis*, and those who have followed his exposition of it from beginning to end will be able to foretell the future unaided (προειπεῖν ὑπὲρ τοῦ μέλλοντος); and what that will be, he adds, is clear. But logically the *anacyclosis* should only enable one to foretell the future for a state developing inside it. Thanks to her having acquired a mixed constitution, Rome's decline is bound to diverge in some degree at least from that of a state whose progress has followed the 'normal' path. Polybius, perhaps from a certain sense of embarrassment, does not specifically say that the development in chapter 57 is that of Rome. He speaks only of 'a state' (πολιτεία), unnamed;[96] but at the end of the chapter he claims to have described its origin and growth, its prime and present condition and the differences for better or worse between it and others, so that there is no doubt that Rome is the state in question.

Decline begins at Rome when after many perils she achieves supremacy and uncontested sovereignty (ὑπεροχὴν καὶ δυναστείαν ἀδήριτον). This reference to Roman imperial domination is a new feature, not found in the account of the *anacyclosis* and not applicable to any of the other states enjoying a mixed constitution either; its realisation is the central theme of the *Histories*.[97] What that supremacy implies in practice, as Peter Derow has explained, is that everyone is now subject

---

94 When in the preface to Vol. I of my *Commentary on Polybius*, vii, I wrote that Schweighaeuser's work was 'virtually untouched by the stirring events going on at the time', I did him an injustice; for I had overlooked the remarkable note on vi.57.7, which deserves to be transcribed: 'Eum dicit statum [sc. Polybius], qualem nostris his diebus esse novam Franciae constitutionem calumniose clamant hi, qui, fractas suas immodicas opes et repressam insolentiam dolentes, ignosrere philosophiae non possunt, quod adflictum miserata statum quo nimis diu populus Francorum depressus iacuerat, descendere tandem de coelo, sedemque inter nos figere, et ordinare moderarique res nostras dignata est' (Tomus VI (Lipsiae, 1792) 399). The reference to the new French constitution is probably to that adopted by the Constituent Assembly in 1791. The early years of the revolution were of course rich in symbolism, theatrical personification and pageantry. Even so, it was an imaginative gesture to picture the revolution in the guise of the goddess Philosophia, making her epiphany to live in France and there regulate and control men's lives.

95 vi.57.2.   96 vi.57.5.

97 Cf. i.1.5–6; see Walbank, *Comm.* I, 40 for a note on this passage and other references to this theme throughout the *Histories*.

to Rome and, in Polybius' own words, that 'henceforth all must submit
to the Romans and obey their orders'.[98] The result of this supremacy is
a high degree of prosperity, which leads to an extravagant life-style and
greater fierceness in rivalry for office and the like and this will be the
beginning of the decline.[99] ||

The situation described in this passage coincides in detail with that
which Polybius later claims to have existed after 168. In Book XXXI,
in a character-sketch of Scipio Aemilianus, he asserts that it was precisely from that date that vicious and extravagant behaviour became
widespread because 'since the fall of the Macedonian kingdom it appeared that Rome enjoyed undisputed universal dominion, and because
after the riches of Macedonia had been brought to Rome there was a
great display of wealth, both public and private'.[100] Moreover, Scipio was
exceptional in spending his time hunting when the other young men were
busy in the forum occupied with legal cases and levees (χαιρετισμούς,
Latin *salutationes*) in the attempt to court the favour of the people.[101]
Clearly the prognostication in vi.57 is developed from the situation at
Rome, as it appeared to Polybius after 168, and not on Greek parallels
like vi.9.6–9.

There are other ways in which this chapter differs from the earlier
passage. In the first place those responsible are not the grandsons of
the democratic founding fathers, for the simple reason that the state in
decline here is not a democracy, but a mixed constitution. Furthermore,
it is not contempt for equality and freedom in a spoilt generation, but an
extravagant life-style due to exploiting the fruits of supremacy abroad
that has led to excessive political ambition. Obviously the two passages
are not to be read as two versions of the same analysis.

Polybius now proceeds to assess responsibility in a manner absent from
his account of the *anacyclosis*. The 'credit for the change', he says, will
go to the people (ὁ δῆμος), who will clearly have grievance (ἀδικεῖσθαι
δόξῃ)[102] against greedy politicians and will become conceited at the
hands of those flattering them 'in the hope of office'. It is the tone of this
passage which deserves to be noted. The phrase 'λήψεται τὴν ἐπιγραφὴν
τῆς μεταβολῆς', the people 'will get the credit for the change', has an
ironical ring which creates quite a different impression from the more
dispassionate account of the decline in the *anacyclosis* (9.8–9), though the

---

[98] Derow (1979) 4; cf. iii.4.3.   [99] vi.57.5–6.   [100] xxxi.25.6–7.
[101] xxxi.29.8–9, διὰ τούτων συνιστάνειν ἑαυτοὺς ἐπειρῶντο τοῖς πολλοῖς; cf. Astin (1967) 30–1.
[102] This is probably the meaning rather than 'the people think they have a grievance'; see Mauersberger, *Polybios-Lexikon* s.v. δοκέω II (a) (β).

context is not dissimilar. For the populace, swayed by passion and anger, is no longer willing to obey or || even be the equals of those in control (τοῖς προεστῶσιν) but demands the largest share, indeed the whole. In short, they upset the balance on which the mixed constitution depends: the result is democracy only in name, mob-rule in reality. Two further points distinguish this account from the earlier one. First, it does not incorporate the *communis locus* of *largitiones* leading to tyranny, which is to be found in vi.9.8, συνειθισμένον γὰρ τὸ πλῆθος ἐσθίειν τὰ ἀλλότρια καὶ τὰς ἐλπίδας ἔχειν τοῦ ζῆν ἐπὶ τοῖς τῶν πέλας ('the people have become accustomed to feed at the expense of others and their prospect of winning a livelihood depends upon the property of their neighbours'). Here, on the contrary, the excesses of the people take a political form. They seek the lion's share in government, not material advantage. Secondly, the account in chapter 57 does not include the two stages of democracy and mob-rule. Instead, these are two names for the same kind of state, the second indicating the reality (perhaps another example of Polybius' irony and an indication of an emotional involvement not present in the account of decay in the *anacyclosis*).

V

It is clear, then, that Polybius presents only chapter 57 as a prognostication of the further development of Rome. What still requires explanation, however, is the dislike of the populace evinced in his account of the approaching decline. That explanation is, I believe, to be found in the similarity, to which I have already alluded, between the conditions outlined in chapter 57 and those amidst which the youthful Scipio, encouraged by Polybius, set out to establish his moral superiority over his peers. The object of the canvassing, on which the latter spent their efforts and to which Scipio took such objection, was to secure the favour of the masses. Scipio's reluctance to take part in this canvassing is an indication of his contempt for the people and their rôle in Roman political life. The importance of the popular or 'democratic' element at Rome at this time has recently been underlined by Fergus Millar in two articles,[103] in which he successfully defends Polybius against the charge of seeing popular power || where there was none. As Scipio's friend and mentor, Polybius understood the importance of self-presentation in the Roman political scene. The chapters in Book XXXI dealing with Scipio's early

[103] Millar (1984), (1986). [On Millar's views see above, p. 16.]

life[104] read like the successful completion of a well-designed programme to draw Scipio's abstemiousness, his generosity and his courage to the attention of the Roman populace and so to provide a valid substitute for the usual canvassing. In all this, Polybius implies, Scipio was a contrast to the majority of his contemporaries. It is in this context, I would suggest, that we should interpret Polybius' expressed dislike of the populace. The part assigned to the people in Polybius' prognostication of Roman decline, in fact, reflects the milieu in which as a friend of Aemilianus he now lived.

Developing his thesis that Polybius was wiser than many of his critics in assigning so important a rôle to the people, the 'democratic element', in second- (and by implication in first-) century Rome, Fergus Millar has drawn attention to the vital relationship between 'the one' and 'the many' which that rôle implied. If the people possessed real power, they were also, as Polybius repeatedly insists, like the sea when strong winds blow over it. In fact, the Roman system with its law-courts and popular assemblies preceded by *contiones*, gave great scope for the demagogue. Criticising the traditional view of senatorial supremacy – of which Nicolet's theory of a mixed constitution which is really an aristocracy is a newer version – Millar observes[105] that 'the unconscious fiction of the collective parliamentary rule of the Senate has obscured the centrality of this much more important relationship, that is, of the one to the many, of the individual orator and/or office-holder and the crowd': and he adds, pertinently, a reference to 'the analyses of the relation of the individual and the people in Z. Yavetz, *Plebs and Princeps*'.

In this paper, which will, I hope, commend itself to Zvi Yavetz, I have tried to show that Polybius was well aware of this dynamic relationship in its various forms and that it forms a central feature of his account of political development in general and of the Roman constitution in particular.

[104] xxxi.23.1–30.4.   [105] Millar (1986) 4.

15

*Profit or amusement: some thoughts on the motives of Hellenistic historians**

I

There are two main obstacles when one tries to analyse the aims of Greek historians of the fourth to the second centuries BC: one is the failure of most of them to survive other than in fragments, the other is the fact that among those fragments it is only the rare passage that touches on purpose and method. The outstanding exception on both counts is of course Polybius: but, as I hope to show, he is not entirely representative. One of the themes that arise repeatedly in his work is the contrast between history for instruction and history for pleasure.[1] In the brief space here available I want to take a look at this theme and ask what it can reveal about the general aims and practices of Polybius and his predecessors and contemporaries.

At the outset we should note that the antithesis use/pleasure is not one peculiar to history-writing. Many years ago Pohlenz demonstrated the existence of a theory of art, probably going back to the sophist Gorgias, which saw enjoyment, ψυχαγωγία, as a means of improving the reader, the listener or the onlooker, both morally and intellectually.[2] All arts shared this function, but especially poetry and tragedy. The general acceptance of this theory had been partially obscured by the fact that two of the most outstanding critics – Plato and Aristotle – either attacked the claim or ignored it. For Plato the content of poetry was untrue and could not therefore provide useful lessons. The Gorgianic || claim to improve through deceit, ἀπάτη, was a paradox;[3] and even when ἀπάτη

---

* [[H. Verdin, G. Schepens and E. De Keyser (eds.) *Purposes of History: Studies in Greek Historiography from the 4th to the 2nd Centuries B.C.* (Studia Hellenistica 30) (Leuven 1990) 253–66]]
[1] E.g. Polyb. i.4.11; ii.56.11; v.75.6; vi.2.8; vii.7.8; xi.19a.1–3; xv.36.3; xxxi.30.1.
[2] Cf. Pohlenz (1920); see also K. Ziegler, 'Tragoedia' *RE* VI A 2 (1937), cols. 1899–2075, for a summary.
[3] Cf. Ephorus, *FGH* 70 F 7 (= Polyb. iv.20.5): μουσικὴν . . . ἐπ' ἀπάτῃ καὶ γοητείᾳ παρεισῆχθαι τοῖς ἀνθρώποις. For the evidence that this theory of ἀπάτη goes back to Gorgias see Pohlenz (1920) 162. In ii.56.12 Polybius uses ἀπάτη of tragedy.

was redefined by Plato[4] as μίμησις, representation, poetry remained a dubious activity and one to be excluded from the ideal state. Aristotle,[5] who in the *Poetics* in turn exploited and developed the concept of μίμησις, stressed, not the improving aspects of poetry, but the pleasure, ἡδονή, that arose out of the purging of the emotions, κάθαρσις. The immense influence of these two writers of genius has tended to conceal the fact that later writers, including both Stoics and Epicureans, continued to suscribe to the Gorgianic view of poetry as contributing to our improvement by way of pleasure.[6] The classic formulation came in Horace's *Ars poetica*, which expounds what throughout antiquity remained the popular view of the matter.[7]

II

Where then does history slot into this general theory? Thucydides clearly intended his history to be useful; not, it is true, in providing a series of formulae or blue-prints for future generals and statesmen, but certainly in giving his readers an extension of that generalised experience which, as von Fritz puts it,[8] enables || a ship's captain – or, one might say, the driver of a car – to know the right thing to do in a particular emergency. For Thucydides this experience was primarily political and military. In the fourth century, especially through the influence of Isocrates, the impact of rhetorical training became more marked. In his speeches Isocrates set out to be a teacher of morals,[9] and this aim was echoed by his pupil, the historian Ephorus,[10] and by Theopompus, who was probably also his

---

[4] Cf. *Rep.* iii.393ff. for criticism of μίμησις and its exclusion from the πολιτεία. It seems likely that Plato took over the definition of μίμησις from a predecessor; cf. Ziegler, 'Tragoedia', *RE* vi A 2 (1937) cols. 2018–19.

[5] See Arist. *Poet.* 6, 1449 b 28, for κάθαρσις through pity and fear; for this as pleasure, ἡδονή, ibid. 14.1453 b 12–13.

[6] For a convenient collection of relevant passages see Ziegler 'Tragoedia', *RE* vi A 2 (1937), cols. 2053–63.

[7] Cf. Hor. *Ars P.* 333–5:

> 'aut prodesse uolunt aut delectare poetae
> aut simul et iucunda et idonea dicere uitae';

see the commentary on this and the following sections in Brink (1971) 352f.

[8] See especially de Romilly (1958). Against Fornara (1983) 106, who rejects the view that Thucydides had any lessons for the statesman as a 'nineteenth-century prejudice', see the judicious comments of von Fritz (1967) ii.274ff.

[9] Cf. Avenarius (1956) 24.

[10] Cf. Ephorus, *FGH* 70 F 42 (Strabo vii.3.9 c 302). Fornara (1983) 110f. would deny the existence of this purpose in Ephorus, but his argument rests on a mistranslation of the fragment in question; see my comments in Walbank (1985c) 211.

pupil (though this has been queried).[11] But already in Xenophon[12] the didactic element in history is primarily directed towards moral improvement, and later this emphasis is reinforced by the Stoa: it is the task of history to furnish examples of conduct to emulate or avoid, παραδείγματα.[13]

When we come to Polybius, however, the picture is more complicated. Aristotle, in the famous chapter of the *Poetics*[14] in which he contrasts tragedy and history, had come down in favour of tragedy as being 'more philosophical'. Against this Polybius, who provides far and away the greatest number of references to the rôle of use and pleasure in history, asserted a different priority. But the general thrust of his argument was directed, not against Aristotle (whose κάθαρσις theory he completely ignored), but || rather against the popular view, derived from Gorgias, which (despite Plato's disapproval) continued to assign both profit and enjoyment to various art-forms which were basically a mere representation (μίμησις) of the truth and so, to Polybius' way of thinking, false.[15] Taking up the theme of 'use' and 'pleasure', Polybius insists on the superiority of history to poetry because its subject-matter is true; but he also has to work out his own conception of how the two aspects of use and pleasure were related in history-writing. Both – τὸ χρήσιμον and τὸ τερπνόν – needed redefining within the context of political history.

III

In considering his exposition it will be best if we look first at τὸ τερπνόν, enjoyment. There are clearly various ways in which any narrative, historical, poetical, rhetorical, can give pleasure to a reader or listener. Judging by what critics had to say on the matter,[16] style was always judged important – though Dionysius later accused Hellenistic historians

---

[11] Cf. Dion. Hal. *Ad Pomp.* 6.6–8; Avenarius (1956) 24. For a full discussion of Theopompus' relationship to Isocrates see R. Laqueur, 'Theopompos aus Chios', *RE* vᴀ 2 (1934), cols. 2176–2223, who defends the tradition making Theopompus Isocrates' pupil against the scepticism of Schwartz, Wilamowitz and Jacoby.

[12] For moral lessons in Xen. *Hell.* v.1.4 and 3.7, see Fornara (1983) 107.

[13] Cf. Avenarius (1956) 25, and 27 n. 37. Specific references to historical παραδείγματα appear in later historians, e.g. Diod. i.1.4; xvi.70.2; Dion. Hal. v.56.1; 75.1; xi.1.5; Joseph. *AJ* xvii. 60; Plut. *Aem. Paull.* 1.5 (quoted by Avenarius).

[14] *Poet.* 9.2–4, 1451 b 1–11.

[15] Cf. Polyb. i.14.6; xii.12.3; 'history stripped of truth is an idle tale' (ἀνωφελὲς . . . διήγημα); xxxiv. 4.2 (Strabo, probably deriving from Polybius). For the contrast between true history and the ἀπάτη of tragedy cf. ii.56.11.

[16] See for instance Dio i.1.2; Joseph. *AJ* xiv.2–3 (quoted by Avenarius (1956) 26–7).

generally of neglecting style.[17] The proper organisation of subject-matter was also a means of making the narrative attractive. Both organisation and style were the concern of rhetoric, and rhetoric of course played a great part in Greek education from the fifth century onwards. Thucydides was thinking of such rhetorical elements when he spoke of the 'show-piece for the moment', the ἀγώνισμα ἐς τὸ παραχρῆμα, which he did not wish his history to be.[18] Polybius recognised the importance of style – though he did not rate it very highly.[19] In his opinion one could get by without much || concern with style, as Timaeus had rightly observed.[20] The organisation of subject-matter was rather more important. Indeed Polybius paid great attention to this with his effective framework of Olympiad years, within which events were treated in sequence according to theatres of action.[21] He points out that by constantly shifting from place to place his narrative creates a variety of content, which prevents his readers becoming bored by getting too much of the same thing.[22] In this way a sophisticated arrangement of the material contributed to the reader's pleasure and was not to be despised.

Style and organisation of subject-matter are of course elements essential in all forms of composition and by no means the prerogative of the historian. But was there any recognised form of pleasure peculiar to history which was not shared with other genres? In a study of Greek and Roman historiography published in 1983 C. W. Fornara has argued that there was such a peculiar pleasure and that it was exemplified in the work of Duris of Samos. His argument rests on a much discussed passage,[23] in which Duris criticises Ephorus and Theopompus for their lack of μίμησις, and of the pleasure that such μίμησις affords. Fornara, who takes μίμησις here to be 'an imitation of the emotions aroused by history', argues[24] that Duris must have gone further than that: as an Aristotelian he must have asked

---

[17] Dion. Hal. *De comp. verb.* 4, p. 30: Hellenistic historians neglected τὸ κάλλος τῶν λόγων.

[18] Thuc. i.22.4; Polyb. iii.31.12–13 echoes this passage (cf. Walbank (1965a) 250).

[19] Polyb. xvi.17.10: the proper reporting of events μεγάλα συμβάλλεται ... πρὸς τὴν ἱστορίαν; but it is not to be regarded as ἡγεμονικώτατόν γε καὶ πρῶτον ... παρὰ τοῖς μετρίοις ἀνδράσι. In xii. 28.10 Polybius praises Ephorus for his phraseology (φράσιν), treatment (χειρισμόν) and the working out of his argument (ἐπίνοιαν τῶν λημμάτων); but he is deeply critical (xvi.17.9) of Zeno of Rhodes, not only for the factual errors which marred his work, but more particularly because his main concern was with elegance of style, on which (like several other distinguished historians) he especially prided himself.

[20] Cf. Polyb. xii.12.2: the ultimate criterion was not whether there was deficiency in style, treatment or any other particular, but whether a history was true.

[21] For an analysis of this structural system see Walbank (1975).

[22] For a defence of this see Polyb. xxxviii. 5–6.

[23] *FGH* 76 F 1 (= Phot. *Bibl.* 176 p.121 a 41); on Duris see Kebric (1977).

[24] Fornara (1983) 122–6.

the question: What is the pleasurable emotion peculiar to history?'[25] – and || come up with the answer: 'Surprise – and, in particular, surprise at the workings of Fortune, *Tyche*, in human affairs.' I can only say that this hypothesis seems to me to outstrip such evidence as we possess.[26] Indeed, it is perhaps a positive argument against it that in his criticism of the third-century historian Phylarchus[27] Polybius has nothing at all to say about *Tyche*. For if Fornara is right to interpret μίμησις as 'an imitation of emotion', Duris' methods and technique will have closely resembled those attributed to Phylarchus – as indeed Fornara claims to be the case.[28]

The matter is, however, to some extent complicated by a long-standing uncertainty about the meaning of μίμησις in this passage of Duris. Several scholars, including myself,[29] have taken μίμησις to mean 'vivid representation', which went along with a concentration of sensational events – a view not very far from that of Fornara. But in a recent and, in my opinion, convincing re-examination of the problem V. Gray[30] has shown that the word is most likely being used by Duris in a sense found in the later writers Demetrius, Dionysius and Longinus – if indeed Demetrius was not Duris' contemporary. For them historical μίμησις, she argues, implies that both in his narrative and in reported speeches the historian is using vocabulary, arrangement of words, sentence construction and all the other available stylistic devices in a manner *appropriate* to each character and each situation, so as to produce a work that is 'true to nature';[31] the || content of such a work would not of course be limited to sensational material. Now whether in fact we interpret μίμησις in this way, as I am now inclined to do, or continue to associate the word with subject-matter having a high emotional effect, it undoubtedly implies pleasurable reactions, as Duris specifically says. But, on either interpretation, μίμησις and the pleasure that goes with it are not something restricted to history; and I know of no evidence that Greek literary theory

---

[25] Aristotle believed that there were various pleasures peculiar to various art-forms; cf. *Poet.* 14.2, 1453b.10–11: οὐ γὰρ πᾶσαν δεῖ ζητεῖν ἡδονὴν ἀπὸ τραγῳδίας ἀλλὰ τὴν οἰκείαν.

[26] Fornara (1983) 126 admits that 'the evidence is slight'. It appears to rest largely on the argument that *Tyche* in history is the equivalent of the *deus ex machina* which Plato (*Cra.* 425d) and Aristotle (*Poet.* 15, 1454b.2–6 regarded as epitomising poor tragic technique, and subsequent writers (cf. Cic. *De nat. deor.* i.54.4 on *tragici poetae*) seized on as characteristic of tragedy generally. Accordingly Fornara regards *Tyche* as providing links between tragedy and the kind of history Phylarchus wrote.

[27] Polyb. ii.56–63.

[28] Fornara (1983) 126: 'it seems reasonable to associate the two men'.

[29] Walbank (1960) 227; see also Sacks (1981) 147–70.   [30] Gray (1987).

[31] Meister (1975) 109–26 also takes μίμησις to be 'an imitation of reality', but he does not lay the same emphasis as Gray on the *method* of achieving that 'imitation'. Meister has a useful survey of the different ways in which scholars have interpreted the fragment of Duris.

laid down any specific form of pleasure as being peculiar and exclusive to historiography.

The work of Duris and Phylarchus does, however, illustrate another way, besides attention to style and the organisation of material, in which the historian could make his narrative attractive to the reader, viz. by his choice of what elements to include and to emphasise. He could, for example, introduce false and fabulous details of the sort later reprehended by Tacitus as 'remote from the seriousness of his work';[32] or trivial, gossipy stories to titillate the imagination, such as seem to have been common in Duris – wonder-tales, travellers' yarns, prodigious births, scandalous customs, love-intrigues, elaborate costumes, like those sometimes worn by Demetrius Poliorcetes, disguises or almost human animals, such as the dolphin that fell in love with a boy.[33] Phylarchus, on the other hand, chose to emphasise the sensational and pitiful aspects of his narrative. In a famous passage[34] Polybius attacks him for his account of the sack of Mantinea with its stress on the dragging away of hosts of captives, or on the torturing to death of the ex-tyrant Aristomachus of Argos. Such scenes were calculated to arouse pity and anger,[35] emotions which can give rise to pleasure of a kind. That Phylarchus, in describing events in this way, never explained the causes behind them,[36] is an additional criticism levelled against him by || Polybius; for it ensured that the pity and anger aroused in the reader could have no rational basis. But this is a secondary objection.

IV

Polybius' criticism of Phylarchus does not of course mean that he himself rejected pleasure as an appropriate aim of a historical narrative – but only pleasure of an illegitimate kind. What kind of pleasure, then, did he regard as legitimate? This question receives special attention in a

---

[32] Tac. *Hist.* ii.50.

[33] See the fragments in *FGH* 76; in a well-balanced survey Kebric (1977) 21ff., argues that behind this sensationalism there lay a moral purpose.

[34] See n.27; Walbank (1938) 57–8.

[35] Not the Aristotelian 'pity and *fear*' (which Fornara (1983) 125, would attribute to Duris).

[36] Polybius argues (ii.56) that (a) Phylarchus is constantly aiming at arousing pity and emotion in a way peculiar to tragedy, but not to history; (b) history has a different purpose, to be useful (χρήσιμον) by instructing and convincing serious students through an unvarnished account of the facts. He then adds, as a fresh point (56.13, χωρίς τε τούτων), independent of what has gone before, that Phylarchus recounts most catastrophes (περιπέτειαι) without saying why things are done and to what end. Hence, even on his own premises concerning the nature of history, he makes it impossible to feel legitimate pity or proper anger. This is of course a criticism of Phylarchus' exposition and has nothing to do with the rôle of Fortune in the events he is narrating.

Saarbrücken dissertation of 1977 by S. Mohm,[37] who points out – what has not always been appreciated – that Polybius distinguished clearly between two sorts of pleasure, only one of which was acceptable.

As evidence for this Mohm quotes a passage in Book VII,[38] where Polybius criticises – without naming[39] – 'many historians', who have written filled-out accounts of the brief reign of the young king Hieronymus of Syracuse, whereas they would have done far better to direct their readers' attention to the lives of Hiero and Gelo. Such an alternative account, says Polybius,[40] would have been both more pleasurable (ἡδίων) to casual readers (τοῖς φιληκόοις) and more useful (χρησιμώτερος) to serious students (τοῖς φιλομαθοῦσι) than a discussion of Hieronymus' reign. On both these counts such a narrative would apparently have had Polybius' approval. Mohm argues further[41] that the use of the || comparative implies that in Polybius' opinion there is *some sort* of pleasure to be derived from a sensational narrative. That that was Polybius' belief is indeed true, as we shall see in a moment. But I hesitate to press the passage on Hieronymus as evidence for that belief, for if the comparative ἡδίων (more pleasurable) is to be given its full force, the same must also be true of the comparative χρησιμώτερος (more useful) – which would mean that Polybius thought that a sensational account could be of *some* use to the serious student. And that is hard to believe.

There are, however, other passages which show that Polybius conceded that pleasure, though of a short-lived kind, could be gained from a sensational narrative. One such passage is in Book XV, where he discusses the downfall of the Alexandrian politician, Agathocles.[42] The events surrounding Agathocles' fall are there said to be 'unnatural' (παρὰ φύσιν) and 'contrary to normal human experience', yet to have been worked over by many historians,[43] who have either over-emphasised the rôle of Fortune (*Tychē*) in them or tried to rationalise the whole story. There is indeed, says Polybius, some pleasure in reading of such events just once, simply in order to convince oneself that what seems impossible is actually possible.[44] But that is not a lasting pleasure nor one appropriate to history; for an over-generous measure of what is sensational (ὁ πλεονασμὸς ὑπὲρ τῶν ἐκπληκτικῶν συμπτωμάτων) contributes neither to pleasure

---

37 Cf. Mohm (1977) 121–33.   38 Polyb. vii.7.

39 He calls them λογογράφοι, perhaps pejoratively; the reference is probably to Baton of Sinope and historians writing on Hannibal, such as Eumachus; see Walbank, *Comm.* ii, ad loc.

40 Polyb. vii.7.8.   41 Mohm (1977) 122.   42 Polyb. xv.36.

43 One of these is probably Ptolemy of Megalopolis, but whether he over-emphasised Fortune or rationalised the narrative we cannot tell; see Walbank, *Comm.* ii, ad loc.

44 Polyb. xv.36.5: χάριν τοῦ γνῶναι τὸ μὴ δοκοῦν δυνατὸν εἶναι διότι δυνατόν ἐστιν.

nor to profit. Polybius' insistence that only a brief pleasure can be derived from the description of such incidents as Agathocles' fall is interesting as an indication of one more way in which such narratives might be compared to tragedy, which likewise thrills and charms the audience only for the moment (κατὰ τὸ παρόν).[45] But where || Polybius accepts pleasure as a proper aim of the historian, it is the lasting kind of pleasure to which he is referring.[46]

There is, however, one difficulty in Mohm's account of this. His argument assumes that the brief and the lasting kinds of pleasure are also distinguished from each other by their relationship to truth. What is sensational and unnatural, he assumes, takes no account of the truth,[47] whereas the more lasting kind of pleasure springs from a narrative which is based on the truth and consequently creates an effect going beyond the immediate reaction of the reader. But this is an over-simplification, since it is quite clear that the account of Agathocles' end, though sensational, is in fact true; for Polybius explains[48] that the pleasure – the wrong sort of pleasure – which it conveys comes from our perception that what seemed impossible was in fact possible. What showed it to be possible was of course the fact that it had actually happened. Truth and falsehood are not then inseparable criteria of the two sorts of pleasure. Moreover, when we examine the 'right sort of pleasure' more closely, the result is somewhat surprising. In a fragment of Book VI[49] Polybius asserts that 'what at one and the same time delights and benefits serious students' (τὸ ψυχαγωγοῦν ἅμα καὶ τὴν ὠφέλειαν ἐπιφέρον τοῖς φιλομαθοῦσι) is the study of causes, which leads to skill in making correct choices. Here, paradoxically, the pleasure – the right sort of pleasure – which history can offer is virtually identified with what is most useful; thus the traditional antithesis between τέρψις and ὠφέλεια is in effect dissolved by the identification of the two.

Here, however, I should perhaps point out that this theoretical (and, it might appear, restrictive) identification of use and pleasure does not in practice prevent Polybius from making his account of historical events attractive to the reader by using a lively and what one might even regard

---

[45] Polyb. ii.56.11.

[46] See i.4.11: vi.2.8; vii.7.8 (see above nn.40 and 41); xv.36.3; xxxi.30.1. In ix.2.6 and xi.19a.1–3 pleasure seems to be excluded.

[47] Mohm (1977) 123, 'Die eine – die er ablehnt – nimmt keine Rücksicht auf die Wahrheit und ist nut für den Augenblick gegeben.'

[48] See above, n.44.

[49] Polyb. vi.2.8; cf. i.4.11, where a study of all the particulars of universal history and their interconnection provides both benefit and pleasure.

as a sensational presentation of his material || – the only proviso being
that what he was describing was, in his opinion, true.[50]

That Polybius relegates what is neither useful nor, in his opinion,
capable of yielding lasting pleasure to tragedy[51] is an idiosyncracy which
puts him in direct opposition to the orthodox view of tragedy, going
back to Gorgias, as an art-form which both instructs and entertains. This
heresy has unfortunately encouraged many scholars in what I consider
to be the misguided belief that Polybius is here attacking a specific school
of so-called 'tragic historians', among whom the object of his polemic,
Phylarchus, is held to be an outstanding example.[52] But that is something
I have dealt with elsewhere and it need not concern us here.

v

The blurring of what is pleasurable with what is useful in the passage of
Book VI dealing with the study of causes[53] suggests that we should perhaps now take a closer look at the utilitarian claims made for the study
of history. There were clearly various ways in which one could envisage
history being useful to the reader and none of these is inherently inconsistent with producing the right sort of pleasure. Indeed, in a passage
which emphasises those simple lessons of history which, if taken to heart,
will save us from being duped in military situations, Polybius points out[54]
as a further advantage that we can gain this useful experience 'while enjoying well-justified repose and relaxation'. The benefit here is military;
for Polybius, like Thucydides, was writing a political and military history.
But with the exception of Polybius – as far as the fragmentary nature
of the Hellenistic historians allows us to judge – it was not the practi-
cal, but the moral || lessons furnished by history that historians chose
to underline. The evidence for this, it is true, comes largely from later
writers[55] who follow the Hellenistic tradition and are almost unanimous
in making moral ὠφέλεια the great prize which history has to offer.

For Polybius too history provides moral and psychological, as well as
practical lessons; and these are of several kinds. History, for instance,

[50] On this aspect see D'Huys (1987) 224–31 and his contribution to this colloquium (1990); for
Polybius' treatment of the last years of Philip V see my discussion (1938).

[51] Polyb. xv.36.7.

[52] So most recently Fornara (1983) 133, who attributes it to Duris of Samos; for a different view see
Walbank (1960).

[53] See above, n.49.   [54] Polyb. v.75.6.

[55] See, for instance, Diod. i.1.4–5; Dion. Hal. i.6.4; Joseph. *AJ* vi.343; Dio Chrys. *Or.* 18.9 (quoted
by Avenarius (1956) 25). Two exceptions (Dion. Hal. v.56.1; xi.1.1–4) offer statesmen ὠφέλεια of
the sort found in Polybius.

can assist readers to endure the vicissitudes of Fortune by describing the calamities of others,[56] or alternatively provide examples of virtues to emulate or vices to avoid. It is with some such object in view that Polybius is wont to interrupt his narrative with an assessment of the careers and characteristics of selected outstanding individuals, from which his readers are evidently intended to derive benefit. Examples are Regulus, who met with catastrophe in the First Punic War, Philip V of Macedonia, whose deterioration is traced at several points in his life, Achaeus and his tragic end at Sardes, and, as someone to emulate, Scipio Africanus.[57] There are also many other passages[58] where Polybius specifically draws attention to the value of such assessments in providing his readers with patterns to imitate or avoid. Many of these assessments, that of Philip V, for instance, involve moral judgements. But since their background is usually military or political, they are moral judgements delivered in the context of public behaviour, so that it is often hard to distinguish them confidently from political judgements.[59] Consequently, although || in offering moral teaching Polybius stands close to the Isocratean tradition, his repeated insistence that men of affairs and statesmen (πολιτικοί and πραγματικοί) form a substantial element among his readers[60] indicates the primary importance which he attached to political, rather than moral, lessons. The study of speeches and the analysis of lines of causation[61] are both seen as a help to effective political action; while two books (IX and X) are especially concerned with citing examples of military matters designed to instruct the general or the soldier in the stratagems and devices necessary to his craft;[62] for Polybius thought of himself as living in an age of high military technical achievement.[63] This refusal by Polybius to draw a clear line

[56] Cf. Polyb. i.1.2: μετ' εὐσχήμονος ἀναπαύσεως ἅμα καὶ διαγωγῆς.

[57] Cf. Sacks (1981) 132; the references are i.35 (Regulus); iv.77.4; v.10.11; vii.11–14; x.26.7–10; xviii 33.6 (Philip V); viii.21 (Achaeus); x.40.1–9 (Scipio Africanus). It is clear from x.26.9–10 that similar 'moral examples' had been provided by earlier historians (but mainly in their prefaces, not scattered throughout the work); cf. Meissner (1986) 348.

[58] See e.g. x.21 (Philopoemen); xxx.6 (various Rhodian statesmen); xxxi.23–30 (Scipio Aemilianus); cf. Sacks (1981) 133; Mohm (1977) 218–19.

[59] Polybius' judgement on Roman policy abroad (cf. Walbank (1974); (1977) 156–9) involves more ruthless criteria in which the moral background is more obscure.

[60] See, for instance, Polyb. ii.61.11; iii.7.5, 21.9–10, 35.5–10, 118.12; vii.11.2; ix.1.4.

[61] On speeches in Polybius see Walbank (1960); on the importance of causes see i.1.5; vi.2.9–10; viii.2.3; xxxix.8.7 (forms of government); xii.25b.1–4, 25i.1–9 (speeches); xi.19a (causes of success in military contexts). See further Sacks (1981) 124.

[62] On the rôle of Books IX–X as a single unit especially concerned with military matters see Sacks (1981) 124.

[63] Cf. Polyb. ix.2.5: τὰς ἐμπειρίας καὶ τέχνας ἐπὶ τοσοῦτον προκοπὴν εἰληφέναι καθ' ἡμᾶς ὥστε πᾶν τὸ παραπῖπτον ἐκ τῶν καιρῶν ὡς ἂν εἰ πεθοδικῶς δύνασθαι χειρίζειν τοὺς φιλομαθοῦντας; cf. also x.47.12.

between moral and political lessons has its parallel – as we have already seen – in his unwillingness to make a rigid distinction between profiting and pleasing the reader. An example of this is the long account of the very consciously and deliberately virtuous youth of Scipio Aemilianus which is likely, Polybius tells us, to be agreeable (ἡδεῖαν) to the old and salutary (ὠφέλιμον) to the young;[64] presumably the old are beyond the need of *exempla*. It is largely through this combination of practical with moral and psychological lessons that Polybius broadens the concept of usefulness in history well beyond the purely moral criteria of the rhetorical tradition.

VI

Polybius' work thus provides an expanded concept of the ways in which the study of history can be useful. But it was an || expanded concept which was not to catch on. For most historians of the Hellenistic age the lessons of history remained moral lessons. That was what the public mainly wanted; and it is perhaps a reflection of a certain unease in Polybius' stance that he feels it necessary to argue so determinedly for the view that his lessons of practical utility – directed towards statesmen and soldiers – would also prove a source of pleasure to the ordinary reader.[65] For one must, I think, admit that it is highly unlikely that the reader who looked to history for moral guidance, still less the reader who enjoyed the highly coloured and sensational anecdotes in Duris or the emotional incidents and pitiful accounts of horrors in Phylarchus would – as Polybius claims – find equal (or greater) delight in the exposition of causes,[66] or in a didactic description of, for example, a new system of fire-signalling,[67] or in Polybius' cautionary remarks about making sure that one had ladders of the right length before setting out to take a city by surprise.[68] Polybius left a legacy. In one of his most entertaining lectures[69] A. Momigliano traced the later reputation of Polybius' *Histories* as a handbook of military expertise from the renaissance onwards. But for the writers of his own generation and those who followed him, the lessons to which he was most attached fell largely on deaf ears. For the historians of the Hellenistic world – and equally for those writing later under Rome[70] – it was above all a moralising Clio who officiated as *magistra vitae*.[71]

[64] Polyb. xxxi.30.1.   [65] E.g. in vii.7.8 (above n.40).   [66] See n.49.
[67] Polyb. x.43–7.   [68] Polyb. v.98; ix.18.5–9.
[69] Cf. Momigliano (1974a) especially 10–15; see also his lecture (1974b).
[70] See e.g. Livy *praef.* 10–11; Tac. *Hist.* i.3; Justin. *praef.*, cited by Avenarius (1956) 25 n.37.
[71] Cic. *De orat.* ii.36.

Polybius on Rome

16

Supernatural paraphernalia in Polybius' Histories*

Polybius is, of course, our main guide to the seventy or so years during which Rome achieved domination over the eastern Mediterranean – a domination that consisted in every people henceforth being obliged to do what the Romans told them to do.[1] Like Thucydides before him, Polybius was active as a statesman and general and was personally involved in many of the events of the early second century. His own career had many ups and downs – first as a politician in Achaea, then as a detainee at Rome, and finally as a protégé of the influential Scipionic family, playing an active rôle in decisive wars and their aftermath. It would indeed be odd if his own career and changes of personal fortune had had no impact upon his work; and one of the objects of the present chapter will be to try to analyse the nature of that impact.

Polybius frequently emphasises the importance of truth and impartiality in writing history.[2] But in fact his work contains || several examples of plain bias, arising out of his own particular background. The hated rival Aetolian League was of course a *bête noire* to the Achaean historian;[3] and he is not very fond of Athens either,[4] for she had consistently refused to join the Achaean Confederation. Achaea itself and especially his home town of Megalopolis usually get favoured treatment. But there are other states and individuals about whom he is less than impartial. One particular example of this is Philip II of Macedonia, whom he admires inordinately and defends against criticism contained in the account given by

---

* [[I. Worthington (ed.) *Ventures into Greek History* (Oxford 1994) 28–42. This volume is dedicated to N. G. L. Hammond.]]
[1] Cf. Derow (1979) esp. 4–6.
[2] Cf. i.14.6, xii.12.3, xxxiv.4.2 (if his remark and not Strabo's); Walbank (1972a) 43–4; Vercruysse (1990).
[3] Frequently noted since Brandstaeter (1844).
[4] Examples in Walbank (1972a) 169 n.81; add Livy (following Polybius) xxxi.44.2–4.

the fourth-century historian Theopompus of the king himself and of his companions and emphasising what they had achieved both under and after Alexander (viii.9–11). It may seem a little strange that in a history nominally concerned with Rome's rise to power between 220 and 167 Polybius should pay such attention to this fourth-century king. But Polybius is extremely interested in the fourth century, and that for more than one reason. In the first place the fourth century had brought about the unification of Arcadia and the founding of Polybius' native city, Megalopolis. But it had also seen the rise of Philip II who, Theopompus had claimed (and Polybius does not question it), was 'the greatest man Europe had yet produced' (viii.9.1). And Philip had of course been a benefactor to many Peloponnesian cities – to Megalopolis, Messenia, Tegea, and Argos – which he had rewarded at Sparta's expense (xviii.13.6–7). There were thus good reasons why Polybius should have chosen to dwell on his great reputation. But Philip II was also important to Polybius for quite another reason and one more directly related to his own theme, the rise of Rome to world power.

II

The relevance of Philip II to Polybius' main subject becomes clearer when one examines a more general characteristic of the *Histories*, namely that, although Polybius is commonly regarded as a rational or 'factual' historian, his work reveals an obsession with what I may call historical patterns. It is an observed fact || that many historians have a strong inclination to create some sort of overall structure or pattern for the events with which they are dealing. They usually see themselves as eliciting such a pattern, though to their critics they frequently seem to be imposing it, not always without violence. I have in mind the kind of pattern to be found in early Christian historians, or in Machiavelli at the time of the renaissance and later the patterns in Vico, Hegel, Marx, Spengler, or Toynbee. Other examples will no doubt spring readily to mind. Despite the 'factual' nature of much of his work, Polybius falls very clearly into this category. Indeed, when one begins to examine the *Histories* from this aspect one is struck by his introduction of such patterns at two vital points of his work. At the very outset (i.1.5) he outlines his purpose as being to explain 'by what means and under what form of constitution the Romans succeeded in less than fifty-three years in bringing under their rule almost the whole of the inhabited world'. It has often been noted that of these two aspects – 'by what means and under what form of constitution' – the first is answered by the narrative of Books III to XXIX (i.e. down to the battle of Pydna) and the second in Book VI with his account of the Roman constitution. What has not perhaps been equally noted is that in dealing with both these two elements in his *Histories* Polybius has superimposed an extraneous 'pattern'; and that these two patterns are different in kind.

The second – which he claims as 'natural' – φύσεως οἰκονομία (vi.9.10) – is of course the elaborate system expounded in Book VI to explain the rise and fall of states, the so-called *anacyclosis*, which involves a kind of circular constitutional development by way of primitive monarchy, kingship, tyranny, aristocracy, oligarchy, democracy, mob-rule (ochlocracy), and so back to monarchy where it began (vi.4.6–13, 5.4–9.14). This scheme provides the background for the 'form of constitution' under which Rome conquered the world, although, rather oddly, that 'form' does not itself figure in the cycle. It was, of course, the famous mixed constitution, which the Romans, by a process of trial and error and at a particular point in their history – around 450 – had succeeded in evolving and had thereby attained (for a time at least) a stability not available to most other peoples, who still remained trapped on the tread-mill of the *anacyclosis* (vi.10.12–14; || described in detail in vi.11.1–18.8). Rome's passage through the early phases of that process seems to have been traced by Polybius in the now lost *archaeologia* of Book VI. But, as far as we can see, it is a scheme which fits the development of no other state, nor does Polybius try to apply it elsewhere. I shall therefore not spend further time on it now, beyond noting that it indicates a general disposition in Polybius to cast events into a pattern.

To some extent any pattern introduces some degree of determinism into one's historical perception. But an aspect of Polybius' thought which seems implicitly to contradict any determinist pattern is the outstanding importance which he attributes to the rôle of great men – for example, Xanthippus, the Spartan mercenary captain employed to such effect by the Carthaginians in the First Punic War (i.35.4–5), Archimedes with his wonderful devices at the siege of Syracuse (viii.3.3, 7.7), and Hannibal himself, since, as he says, 'for all that happened to both nations, Romans or Carthaginians, the cause was one man and one mind' (ix.22.1, 22.6). The individual could do great harm as well as great good, Polybius explains (xxxii.4.2), referring to the Aetolian Lysciscus. But the 'great man' view of history does not figure as an overall explanatory scheme in his work. It merely crops up from time to time, and where it does it can without difficulty be accommodated to other more all-embracing explanations of events.

III

I turn now from the question of the Roman constitution to the other element in Polybius' programme – 'how in less than fifty-three years the Romans became masters of the inhabited world'. Here the surprising thing about this rational and factual historian is the extent to which he subjects the pattern of those fifty-three years to supernatural guidance. For it was *Tyche*, Fortune, he claims, that raised Rome during those years from near defeat at Hannibal's hands to the position of mistress of the inhabited world (i.4.5), following her victory over King Perseus at Pydna. *Tyche* occupied a special place in the religion, art, and rhetoric of the Hellenistic age. Polybius makes frequent and ambiguous use of the word, employing it with a wide range of || meanings. I have discussed this elsewhere,[5] and need only observe here that whereas in some passages *Tyche* is no more than a verbal equivalent of saying that something happened, in other passages it can refer to the irrational and incalculable factor which so often comes in to upset human plans. In one place Polybius attributes to *Tyche* such natural disasters as plague or drought, for which mortal man cannot perceive the cause – what we term 'acts of god' (xxxvi.17.2); but *Tyche* also serves to explain human events – like the Macedonian revolt under Andriscus – for which Polybius at any rate can see no rational explanation (xxxvi.17.13–16). In the context of Roman imperial growth, however, *Tyche* figures as a divine power, the Hellenistic goddess who acts either capriciously to put down the mighty from their seats or retributively to punish wrong-doing and reward virtue. In many passages featuring *Tyche* it is hard to tell just what sense Polybius is giving to the word. Indeed, one often suspects that he has not thought it out clearly and slides without much trouble from rhetoric to theology. As regards the rise of Rome, however, the picture seems clearer. There *Tyche* is portrayed as a conscious and purposeful power directing world events towards a closely defined end. But if events are being manipulated from above in this way, where does that leave the rational historian – Polybius – who proposes to set out lessons for his readers? There is certainly an *aporia* here – and probably some residual confusion. But perhaps a partial answer is that while the supernatural control operates in a general way, the ordinary laws governing political and military action and its likely results still hold good. It may be *Tyche* who ensures the ultimate success of Rome, but whether Philip V captures Melitaea or not can still depend

---

5 Walbank, *Comm.* I, 16–26; cf. (1972a) 60–5; for *Tyche* in Hellenistic art see Pollitt (1986) 2–4. There is an interesting discussion of *Tyche* in Green (1990) 800ff.

on the length of his ladders (v.97.5–98.11, ix.18.5–9). The contradiction is perhaps not too serious. As we all know, Oliver Cromwell trusted to God but also believed in keeping his powder dry. Moreover, Polybius does not see the favour of *Tyche* and the merits of Rome as in any way exclusive of each other: on the contrary, divine favour was a recognition of Roman worth (cf. Walbank, *Comm.* 1, 129–30). ||

Tyche then brought about the rise of Rome to supremacy. But how did she engineer this in detail? Clearly through Roman victories in a series of wars. But what *led* to the wars? What was Rome's rôle in starting or even causing them? In order to attempt answers to these questions, one must turn to Polybius' discussion of causality and the scheme by which he seeks to explain the events leading up to some of the more important of these wars. I say 'the more important', since he does not apply his scheme to minor clashes nor indeed to every major war, let alone other situations – to which indeed it is ill adapted. Polybius mentions three words, between which he draws a slightly pedantic distinction. They are αἰτία πρόφασις, and ἀρχή, being the cause, the pretext, and the beginning of a war respectively (iii.6.1–7). In some Polybian contexts αἰτία can mean 'guilt' or 'responsibility', but that is not its meaning here. In his elaborate scheme of causation αἰτία is defined as anything that contributes to the taking of the decision to go to war (iii.6.7). *Who* takes that decision appears, rather curiously, to be a secondary consideration. The word αἰτία can embrace political or military acts, unjust clauses in a treaty and the resentment they create, psychological hang-ups and states of mind – briefly anything which leads someone to decide on war.

Now there are five major wars in the period 220 to 168, the Hannibalic War, the First and Second Macedonian Wars against Philip V, the War against Antiochus of Syria, and the Third Macedonian War against Perseus. Polybius only expounds his scheme of causation fully in rela-tion to the Hannibalic War (iii.9.6–10.6), but he applies it sketchily to the Roman wars against Antiochus (iii.7.1–3) and Perseus (xxii.18.1–10) and, in addition, to a war quite outside the period under consideration, namely the war in which Alexander the Great overthrew the Persian empire (iii.6.10–14). Polybius also indicates that none of the events usu-ally adduced as causes of the war with Perseus can in fact be causes, for the simple reason that the decision to fight that war had already been taken by Perseus' father Philip V (xxii.18.9–10). We are not of course concerned with whether that is a plausible proposition or not. It is, how-ever, Polybius' view and, moreover, it brings out a very strange aspect of the way in which he applies his scheme – which is, that for three of

the wars in question – Alexander's war against Persia and the wars of ||
Hannibal and Perseus against Rome – in each case he alleges that the
decision to make war was taken by someone other than the person who
actually waged it. It was Philip II who decided to make war on Persia
(iii.6.13, xxii.18.9) and Hamilcar Barca (iii.9.6) and Philip V (xxii.18.10)
who decided to make war on Rome; but the three wars were fought by
Alexander, Hannibal, and Perseus.

This curious feature of Polybius' causal scheme, or rather of the way
in which he applies it, calls for an explanation. There can of course have
been more than one reason for it. In the first place it serves to confirm
a general proposition about wars which Polybius makes explicitly in
Book III (xxxii.6–7). 'By far the most essential part of history-writing,'
he says, 'lies in the consideration of the consequences of events, their
accompanying circumstances, and above all their causes (αἰτίαι). Thus I
regard the war with Antiochus as having originated from that with Philip,
the war with Philip from that with Hannibal, and the Hannibalic War
from the one fought for the possession of Sicily, while the intermediate
events, however many and diverse they may be, all converge upon the
same issue.' Now if a decision to fight a war had already been taken by
a predecessor, clearly the interconnection between one war and another
is thereby reinforced. There is also (as so often with Polybius) a *personal*
reason, namely that this interconnection makes the only person equipped
to deal properly with the causes of a war the universal historian (i.e.
Polybius himself), rather than the writers of monographs, against whom
he so often inveighs: for example, iii.32.3–5, vii.7.6, viii.2.1–11, ix.44.2,
xii.23.7, xvi.14.1. Here then are two possible explanations of the oddity
of Polybius' procedure in identifying the causes of war. However, there
is also a third. But before coming to that, I need to examine a little
more closely the motivation of *Tyche* in raising Rome to her position of
dominion in the world.

IV

Polybius traces and comments on the procedure of *Tyche* as follows:
(i) Rome's rise to world dominion is the greatest achievement of Fortune
and one most profitable to contemplate (i.4.4). This achievement had
already been foreseen prophetically || by the Peripatetic philosopher
Demetrius of Phalerum, who in his work Περὶ Τύχης had observed that
no one fifty years before the time when he was writing could have foreseen
the overthrow of the Persian empire and the appearance of a Macedonian

empire in its place (xxix.21.4). (Demetrius was writing at Alexandria under Ptolemy I and so sometime between 307 and 285. Fifty years take us back to a date between 357 and 335 – and probably nearer to the latter than the former.) At the same time Demetrius had foretold that in due course *Tyche* would likewise contrive the overthrow of Macedonia (xxix.21.5–6). (ii) The fulfilment of this 'prophecy', which was, he says, 'more divine than the words of a mere man', had been witnessed by Polybius himself in the overthrow of Perseus at Pydna in 168 (xxix.21.8). And corresponding to the fifty years mentioned by Demetrius is the period of almost fifty-three years which had brought Rome from her low ebb in the early Hannibalic War to dominion over the whole *oecumene* (i.1.5).

But Polybius is not satisfied simply to identify Roman success as a turn of the 'wheel of Fortune'. In addition he introduces a further element into his picture. As I mentioned above, *Tyche* could be seen either as a force intervening arbitrarily in human affairs (as she was by Demetrius) or as a power exacting retribution. It is in the latter guise that she is here represented by Polybius. But retribution for what? An answer to that lies in Book XV (20.1–4), where Polybius describes the monstrous crime committed by Philip V of Macedonia and Antiochus III of Syria, who in 203/2 made a common pact to plunder and dismember the kingdom of the infant Ptolemy V of Egypt. The historicity of this pact has been much debated.[6] My own view is that an agreement of some kind was actually made; but some question this, and in any case its reality is irrelevant, since here, as over the war against Perseus, our concern is only with what Polybius himself believed. After giving his account of the contents of the pact Polybius goes on to explain that 'Fortune brought the Romans upon them [sc. Philip and Antiochus] and justly and fittingly visited them with the very wrongs which they had wickedly tried to practise against others. For both kings were very soon conquered in battle, and were not only prevented from coveting || the possessions of others but were forced to pay tribute and submit to the commands of Rome. Finally, within a short space of time Fortune raised up again the kingdom of Ptolemy, while as for the rival dynasties she dealt them in the one case total destruction and in the other a series of misfortunes almost as crushing' (xv.20.5–8).

The climax of this process of retribution occurs in Book XXIX, which was originally designed to be the last book of the *Histories* going down to 168/7, if one makes the reasonable assumption that Book XXX (like Book XL in the extended plan) was to have been an index volume.

[6] For recent discussion and bibliography see Gruen (1984) II, 387–8. [See now, for new evidence supporting the reality of the pact, Wiemer (2001) 74–85.]

Book XXIX recounts the battle of Pydna, which spells the end of the Macedonian monarchy, and soon afterwards the humiliating incident at Eleusis in Egypt, where Antiochus IV was compelled to yield to the insolent ultimatum of the Roman envoy Popillius Laenas (xxix.27.1–13). Already before then Philip V had compounded his crimes by allegedly murdering his younger son Demetrius (xxiii.10.12–14; Livy xl.23–4, based on Polybius). The account of the events leading up to this disaster was worked up by Polybius in an unusually dramatic form (carried further by Livy). Antiochus III too (according to Livy xxxv.15.4–5, who is here following Polybius) was suspected of having murdered *his* son, another Antiochus, thus reinforcing the parallel between the two villainous monarchs.

The Syro-Macedonian pact and its sequel are thus shown to be essential elements in the process which led a retributive *Tyche* to take vengeance on Philip and at the same time fulfil Demetrius' prophecy. This retributive aspect of the historical pattern brought Syria as well as Macedonia into the picture – but in a subordinate way. For the prophecy was concerned first and foremost with *Macedonia*, the imperial realm of Philip II and Alexander. It was Macedonia that had overthrown Persia and was in turn to be overthrown by Rome. And so, appropriately, it is Macedonia that is destroyed, whereas Syria is merely humbled! But why, one may fairly ask, does Polybius feel so strongly about the wrongs done to Egypt – so strongly that the Syro-Macedonian pact becomes the key incident, upon which the whole oecumenical reversal engineered by Fortune rests? He may indeed have been moved by righteous anger and generous indignation at an unjust plot against a child – a plot which, we || should, however, note, was never fully carried out. But I should like to venture another, perhaps more likely, explanation.

In 187/6 Polybius' father Lycortas was sent as an envoy to Alexandria to renew the treaty between Ptolemy V and the Achaean League (xxii.3.6, 9.2); and in spring 180 Lycortas, Polybius himself, and Aratus, the grandson of the great statesman, were appointed as members of a similar embassy to thank Ptolemy for various substantial gifts, including ten pentekonters (xxiv.6.1–7). The presence of Lycortas on the first of these embassies is given by Polybius as a reason for the choice of his father and himself for the second – which in fact never came off, owing to the king's sudden death. Aratus was chosen because of his family's connection with the Ptolemaic royal house, a connection which went back as far as Aratus' great-grandfather, Cleinias (Plut. *Aratus* 4.2). Later, in 169/8, Lycortas and Polybius both supported sending Achaean aid to

Ptolemy VI and his brother Ptolemy VIII, who were temporarily reconciled and united against Antiochus IV (xxix.23.3). This aid was to have
consisted of a force of 1,000 foot and 200 horse and, at the request of the
Ptolemies, it was to have been officered by Lycortas and Polybius; but
the proposal was rejected and later Polybius, probably out of caution –
though he says 'out of consideration (διά) for the Roman consul, Marcius
Philippus' – withdrew from the debate about it (xxix.25.5).

What I would tentatively suggest is that these events indicate a connection, perhaps of ξενία,[7] between Lycortas' family and the Ptolemaic
royal house, such as clearly existed between that house and the family
of Aratus. Such a link would account for Polybius' exaggerated reaction
to the Syro-Macedonian pact. Against this suggestion it might be urged
that Polybius mentions the family connection for Aratus and not for the
other two. But that is very understandable, for Aratus' connection was
an ancient one and was moreover the only justification for appointing
that apparently insignificant person; whereas in the case of Lycortas
and Polybius there was already a record of diplomatic activity in relation to Alexandria. If such a bond of ξενία did exist it did not prevent
Polybius from criticising Ptolemy V for cruelty to the conquered rebels
in 186/5 [187/6: see above, pp. 77–8], comparing him unfavourably ||
with Philip II (xxii.16). But a ξενία relationship might help in part to explain why Polybius chose to relate a feat of marksmanship performed by
Ptolemy V while hunting on horseback as something 'of minor importance perhaps, but worth mentioning' (xxii.3.8–9). I would not indeed
press this, for Polybius' love of hunting is probably reason enough for
the anecdote. In any case a link of ξενία with Lycortas' family can only
be hypothetical, though it would indeed explain satisfactorily Polybius'
extreme indignation over the pact.

A final point before I leave the subject of *Tyche*'s vengeance. If the
offence of Philip and Antiochus was a compact made in 203/2, why
had *Tyche* already started on the retributive process of raising Rome to
world power and planning the destruction of Macedonia as early as the
first Olympiad of Philip's reign (220–216)? Perhaps one should not insist too strongly on such an apparent illogicality. But in fact there is no
real inconsistency in Polybius' position. For already by 217 Philip was
plotting against Rome and shortly afterwards his political and military
interference in Messene is dramatically denounced by Polybius as indicating 'the revolution in Philip's character and his notable change for

[7] On ξενία see Herman (1987).

the worse' (vii.11.10). The instigator both of this change and of his anti-Roman policy was of course the Illyrian, Demetrius of Pharos (vii.13.4–14.6), who provides a good illustration of Polybius' theory about the importance of certain individuals in history for good or evil. Seen in this context the Syro-Macedonian pact is simply one vital and revealing stage along the road to Philip's destruction of his kingdom, which had begun over a decade earlier.

V

This supernatural pattern which interprets the ruin of Macedonia and the rise of Rome as the work of a divine power exacting retribution for moral delinquency is, however, the clue to a further and quite central reason for Polybius' emphasis on the historical rôle of Philip II of Macedonia. We have seen how he interpreted the downfall of the kingdom of Macedonia as retribution for the crimes of Philip V, with special emphasis on the pact with Antiochus to dismember Egypt. We have also seen how the final stage in that downfall, the war between Rome and ‖ King Perseus, was portrayed by Polybius as due, not to Perseus himself, but to Philip V, his father, inasmuch as it was he who took the decision to wage it. But if it was Philip V who brought about the destruction of Macedonia, it was Philip II who raised the kingdom to mastery over the whole of the Middle East.[8] Philip, not Alexander, since, as Polybius makes clear, the war against Persia was planned by Philip; and it is significant that in the passage in Book VIII, where Polybius praises Philip and his Companions as having been largely responsible for the victory over Persia, Alexander himself is played down: 'we may perhaps (ἴσως) allow him some credit' is all that Polybius will admit (viii.10.8). In the same passage, moreover, Polybius is drawn into a digression in which he discusses Theopompus' treatment of Philip II (viii.9.1–11.1). This appears to have arisen out of the contrast between that king and Philip V, who at that point in the *Histories* has just shown his true colours by his breach of faith at Messene. Nor is this the only passage where Polybius contrasts the two Philips to the disadvantage of the later one. Another occurs in Book V, where Philip V's vengeful sacrilege at Thermum, the Aetolian religious centre, is contrasted with the alleged gentleness and moderation of Philip II (v.10.1–8). No doubt Polybius was partly influenced by the coincidence in name between the two very different kings.

---

[8] In xxii.18.10 Polybius specifically links together the two Philips as the authors of the two decisive wars.

For similarly in xv.34–6 discussion of Agathocles of Alexandria leads him to comment on Agathocles of Syracuse; and likewise in xii.4a.3, a reference to the younger Dionysius of Syracuse is an excuse to speak about the elder tyrant of the same name. But in addition, Philip V himself went out of his way to stress the connection with his predecessor and claimed him as his kinsman (v.10.10) – a claim accepted by Polybius, who uses the expression 'the Macedonian royal house' (οἰκία Μακεδόνων) to include both the Argeads and the Antigonids.[9] But the contrast between the two Philips also, and perhaps more importantly, reflects the fact that in planning the Persian War Philip II was primarily responsible for engineering that reversal in the fortunes of world powers that had so impressed Demetrius of Phalerum and led him to pronounce his || famous 'prophecy'. Philip II, like Philip V, thus served as a major instrument in the working of *Tyche*, as Polybius saw it.

Polybius undoubtedly idealised Philip II in some degree. He was aware of the hostile case against him, for one can read it in the speech he gives to the Aetolian Chlaeneas at Sparta in 210 (ix.28–31); and he cannot approve of Theopompus' subordination of the history of Greece (*Hellenika*) to the history of Philip (*Philippika*): viii.11.3–5. But by and large he regards Philip II as an admirable ruler who conforms to the Hellenistic concept of a 'true king' and illustrates the importance of great men in history for good or evil – in his case and as far as Greece was concerned for good.

VI

A final question remains. How far does Polybius' addiction to patterning and his use of this supernatural paraphernalia affect his value as a source? For the 'nuts and bolts' of his history – his account of particular events and campaigns, battles, embassies, and the like – hardly at all. For these his reliability is generally acknowledged and is not affected by the matters I have been discussing. There is, indeed, room here for some slight qualification on other grounds. As the Belgian scholar, V. D'Huys, has recently shown,[10] Polybius' battle accounts sometimes exploit rhetorical commonplaces repeated from earlier writers; and the status of the speeches, a traditional element in Greek historical writing, also presents some residual problems, despite Polybius' vigorous claim to be recording what was actually said.[11]

---

[9] For references see ch. 8, above.   [10] D'Huys (1990).
[11] On Polybius' speeches see Walbank (1965a); Sacks (1981) 79–95.

The effect of his patterning is, however, more apparent in two other areas. His identification of the period which saw the Roman rise to world power with the fifty-three years from 220 to 167 is in some ways arbitrary and seems to be in part at least influenced by his recollection of the fifty years mentioned in Demetrius' 'prophecy'. The correspondence between these two || figures is of course not an exact one. In speaking of the downfall of Persia, Demetrius was giving a round figure calculated from the time he was writing his Περὶ Τύχης; whereas Polybius' 'nearly fifty-three years' is a precise figure covering the period between two specific events. Moreover, the rise of Rome to supremacy was a more drawn-out process than the fall of Persia – though indeed that also occupies several decades, if it is assimilated to Philip II's reign and judged against the background of Polybius' αἰτίαι, which include the march of the Ten Thousand and Agesilaus' campaigns in Asia (iii.6.10–11), and not simply as something accomplished between Alexander's crossing of the Hellespont and the battle of Gaugamela. Of Polybius' two dates, 220 and 167, the second was chosen partly for personal reasons: it was the year when, thanks to the Roman victory at Pydna, Polybius himself was reduced from the rôle of an active statesman and general to the level of a detainee – and historian. And the year 220, following an established historiographical tradition, was chosen partly to fit the synchronism provided by the accession of the three Hellenistic kings of Egypt, Macedonia, and Syria in the preceding Olympiad (ii.70.6–8, 71.3–4), but also because Aratus' *Memoirs* happened to finish at that point (i.3.2, iv.2.1). One can think of other possible dates relevant to Roman expansion – 275, the end of the war with Pyrrhus; 264, the opening of the First Punic War (Polybius himself uses this date in his introductory books); 146, the terminal date of the revised edition of Polybius' *Histories*; 133 (or 129) with the acquisition of Asia – and so on. Good historical reasons can be adduced for stressing any one or more of these as marking important stages in a continuous process; and probably no great harm has been done by Polybius' patterning – unless it leads us to attribute greater and more exclusive significance to his parameters than they in fact possess. It is however noteworthy that we are still using Polybius' divisions. For example, the central chapter in Peter Green's new study of the Hellenistic age, *Alexander to Actium* (pp. 267–432), covers the years between 221 and 168.

Polybius' patterning also influenced his notions about causes. As Peter Derow has shown ((1979) 9–13), his scheme of causation with its distinction between the αἰτίαι, πρόφασις, and ἀρχή of a war is concerned more to describe || steps in a process than to assign responsibility at each stage; and this may well be because he saw the general direction of events as being already laid down by *Tyche*. He is interested not so much in apportioning blame, as in what led to the taking of vital decisions, what reasons were alleged, and at what point hostilities actually broke out – in short the process of events. Finally and most importantly, Polybius' portrayal of some of his main characters appears to have been affected by the overall scheme into which he has fitted them. In particular, Philip II and Philip V are assessed very largely in the light of the rôles they have been chosen to fill – as the creator and the destroyer of the Macedonian empire which was the predecessor of that of the Romans.

In this paper I have tried to show how, out of a wide range of historical material available to him, Polybius constructed a narrative in which certain incidents were selected for special emphasis. That selection was made in the light of an Aristotelian philosopher's *obiter dictum* on the rise of Macedonia (a topic close to the heart of the Achaean historian), a generally accepted Hellenistic belief in *Tyche*, and, probably, his family involvement with Ptolemaic Egypt. The result is an account of the rise of Rome to world power which, in certain crucial respects, reflects those arbitrary and idiosyncratic features.

17

'Treason' and Roman domination: two case-studies, Polybius and Josephus*

I

The sweep of overwhelming Roman military power eastwards confronted members of the ruling class in the states threatened (and eventually absorbed) with desperate problems. How they should (and did) respond depended on several factors, among them the nature and imminence of the threat, current relations with Rome and the degree of 'national' consciousness[1] – or self-definition – in any particular state. Few, if any, states, moreover, were monolithic, most containing class and factional divisions, so that one man's compromise with Rome was another man's treason. In judging such compromises the modern historian is liable to be swayed by hindsight and the temptation to make immediate success or failure the overriding criterion. On closer investigation, however, the background of most political decisions is more complicated than at first sight appears; nor is it always possible to establish the circumstances in which they were made. In the present paper I propose to examine two cases, those of Polybius and Josephus, not as a pair of Plutarchean parallel lives, but as two examples of very different figures who had to face, each in his own time and manner, the dilemmas inherent in confronting Rome.[2]

As historians, both illustrate from the evidence in their works as well as from their own lives the impact of Rome upon the states in which they lived. Polybius, especially, enables us to trace in some detail the developing response of the Achaean Confederacy to the growing pressure from republican Rome during his own lifetime and years of political activity.

* [[C. Schubert and K. Brodersen (eds.), *Rom und der griechische Osten: Festschrift für Hatto H. Schmitt zum 65. Geburtstag* (Stuttgart 1995) 273–85]]
[1] On nationality in the Greek and Roman world see Walbank (1951); (1972b); Finley (1975).
[2] Eckstein (1990) discusses the two historians, but mainly to establish the considerable extent to which Josephus borrows themes from his predecessor.

In 198 BC, in the course of the Second Macedonian War, the Achaeans by an almost unanimous vote abandoned their alliance with Macedonia in favour of a new one with Rome;[3] but in the subsequent years there was disagreement between Aristaenus and Philopoemen on the policy to be adopted towards the Romans.[4] Aristaenus was for accepting and even anticipating each Roman demand, whereas Philopoemen took up his stand, as long as he could, on Achaean law and the terms of the Roman alliance.[5] Lycortas, the father of Polybius, followed Philopoemen's line and strongly opposed Callicrates, who urged the Romans to tighten the screw on || Achaea.[6] In the Third Macedonian War, in 171/70 BC, Polybius, on the eve of his election to the important post of cavalry commander, broke with his father, who favoured neutrality, to join Archon, who was about to be elected general of the confederacy for 170/69 BC, in collaborating with Rome. Archon despatched Polybius to make contact with the Roman consul in southern Macedonia, where, with an eye to Achaean interests, he postponed meeting the consul and only made the offer of Achaean troops when he thought they were unlikely to be accepted.[7] The outcome was not very happy for Achaea, for peace was followed by a general purge, in which all leading citizens throughout Greece other than the most rabid pro-Romans were sent to Italy and detained there. Polybius, who was one of these, did not return to Achaea until 150 BC; and soon afterwards he was again absent for several years, indeed until after the fall of Corinth at the close of the disastrous Achaean War. By this time Achaea was firmly within the Roman sphere of control and Polybius himself had established close links with some eminent members of the Roman aristocracy. His account of the Achaean War is extremely hostile to those directing Achaean affairs at this time; he

---

[3] Opposition came from Dyme, Megalopolis and Argos, cities bound by old ties to Macedonia; cf. Polyb. ii.48.2; Livy xxvii.30.9; xxxii.22.10-11.

[4] Polyb. xxiv.11-13; see Walbank (1972a) 166-7. Polybius (xxiv.13.8) describes Philopoemen's policy as καλή and that of Aristaenus as εὐσχήμων. Ferrary (1988) 297 n.102, has shown convincingly that εὐσχήμων means 'honourable', not 'plausible': the word 'indique un degré inférieur, mais non pas un simple apparence, un faux-semblant, de l'honneur'. [Baronowski (1995) 17 n.3 translates εὐσχήμων as 'presentable' and καλή as 'honourable'.]

[5] Polyb. xxiv. 11.4-6; 13.6-7, suggests that Philopoemen knew what was coming, but sought to postpone it; on the latter passage see Lehmann (1967) 246 n.208, arguing against the view that Polybius exaggerated Philopoemen's pessimism in order to defend him from the charge of being anti-Roman.

[6] For modern assessments of Callicrates' policy see the works quoted in Walbank, *Comm.* III, 263 on Polyb. xxiv.10.8.

[7] Polyb. xxviii.6-7 (on the different policies), 12-13 (on the embassy to the Roman consul), with Walbank, *Comm.* III, 344-5 on 12.2; cf. Eckstein (1985) 277-81, discussing Polybius' policy towards Rome. See also Lehmann (1967) 203 on Polybius' delay in making contact with the Roman consul.

regards them as responsible for the disasters and the dissolution of the confederacy.

Two hundred years later Josephus, in his *Jewish War* and *Jewish Antiquities* gives us a detailed account of the events leading up to the destruction of the Jewish state; and Martin Goodman has recently thrown fresh light on the historic reasons which rendered the Judaean ruling class singularly inept at controlling a disaffected populace, along with several other factors peculiar to Judaea, which are directly relevant to our assessment of the decisions taken by the Jewish leaders, and, incidentally, of the writings and career of Josephus himself.[8]

We are well informed on Achaea, less so on Judaea. But the issues faced in both states and the sort of political decisions taken were, *mutatis mutandis*, common to other peoples confronted by Rome until (and even after) she reached her final frontiers.

II

A comparison between Polybius and Josephus was suggested to me by a question, which has been put to me more than once after a lecture on Polybius. 'Was he', I have frequently been asked, 'a traitor – like Josephus?' The question is perhaps simplistic, indeed doubly so, with its unquestioning assumption of Josephus' guilt. But similar views on Polybius have been advanced by highly regarded historians. Throughout his life Gaetano De Sanctis displayed a growing dislike of Polybius both for 'accepting' the Roman advance eastward (which diverted Rome from her 'true mission' in north-west Europe) and even more for his failure to come out against Rome in the Third Macedonian War – a 'velato tradimento', in which De Sanctis saw Polybius as no better than his many fellow-countrymen who had consented to take the fascist oath to Mussolini.[9] No one in antiquity levelled such a charge of treachery against Polybius; but De Sanctis is not alone in doing so in modern times, when the comparison with Josephus has frequently been made.[10] It is not, however, altogether clear what 'treachery' or 'treason' might mean in the Greek or Roman context.

Polybius claims to have devoted much thought to the problem of treason and he discusses it in a digression probably inspired by the events surrounding the switch in Achaean policy in || 198 BC.[11] In this passage

[8] Goodman (1987).   [9] See ch. 20, below, 310-21.
[10] See, for example, S. J. D. Cohen (1980) especially 366-7; Mendels (1992) 358.
[11] Polyb. xviii.13-15. Eckstein (1987b) argues persuasively that the occasion for this digression was, as Schweighaeuser thought, Aristaenus' move to persuade the Achaeans to abandon Macedonia

Polybius not only defends Aristaenus, who effected the change, but also the politicians from many Greek states who, in the fourth century, threw in their lot with Philip II rather than Demosthenes. He defines as traitors those who, for personal or factional reasons and to further their own ends, subject their countries to the control of a superior power. His definition includes both those in office who operate through state decisions and the more obvious sort of traitor who secretly opens the city gate to the enemy.[12] He appears not to be conscious of the possible application of this definition to the Achaean statesman Aratus, who had handed over Acrocorinth to Antigonus III of Macedonia; but perhaps he would have regarded Aratus (like Aristaenus) as acting in the manifest interest of Achaea. The phrase 'to further his own ends' is yet another qualification which would let Aratus off the hook. It is, however, ironical that Polybius sees the fourth-century politicians bring 'hope and freedom' to their states by embracing the cause of Philip II of Macedonia, whereas Aristaenus achieves the same end by abandoning that of Philip V.[13] Polybius' discussion is not wholly happy; in the first place he never attempts to deal with the case of the statesman or general who sees his country embarking on a policy which he regards as suicidal or simply wrong and so feels constrained to take action against it. And, equally important, he never appears to feel the need to ask to whom or to what political entity loyalty is owed. Yet in the Greek world this was not self-evident.

III

The fourth-century supporters of Philip II are specifically described as not being προδότας ... τῆς Ἑλλάδος.[14] So treason (προδοσία) was a crime that could be committed against Hellas as well as against one's own particular city;[15] presumably too against a confederation, such as Achaea, though no specific example of such a charge is recorded.[16] Polybius'

---

for Rome, and not (as I had argued in Comm. II, 564–5, following A. Aymard) Philip's surrender of Argos to Nabis, the traitors on that view being the Argives, who had let the Macedonians into their city. See also. Musti (1978) 72–4.

[12] Polyb. xviii.15.1–7; see especially 15.3.

[13] Polyb. xviii.14.6 (the fourth-century Peloponnesians and Philip II) and 11, 4–6 (the second-century Greeks and Philip V): in both passages Polybius uses the same phrase ἔννοιαν λαβεῖν ἐλευθερίας. Different circumstances demand different solutions. On Polybius' conscious contrast of the two Philips see ch. 16 above, especially 254–5.

[14] Polyb. xviii.14.2.

[15] See E. Berneker, RE xxiii 1 (1957), s.v. προδοσία, col.90, quoting Gorgias (D–K) ii no.82, 11a 3 (on Palamedes).

[16] Cf. Berneker, loc.cit.

discussion takes place against the background of the city, with its strong feeling of identity.[17] As one moves over into Asia and the lands which formed part of the Achaemenid empire before Alexander, issues become more cloudy. Loyalty now meant primarily loyalty towards a king. The Hellenistic kingdoms – especially Seleucid Asia – with their royal courts recruited from various cities and their partially mercenary armies, found it difficult to inspire a sense of loyalty. Nor was it easy for cities within the kingdoms to evoke loyal feelings. Alexandria 'ad Aegyptum' was, typically, a magnet drawing in Greeks of all sorts and persuasions, poets, scholars, politicians and army officers and men, but it hardly exercised the patriotic pull of an Athens or a Rhodes. Similarly, the various native peoples who lived under such monarchies, though usually clearly distinguishable to the outside gaze, did not necessarily have a strong sense of self-definition || and patriotism;[18] but the truth is that such feelings are now difficult for us to locate and identify. It is hard to discover just what it meant to be a Nabatean.

There is however one striking exception. On the Jews we are relatively well informed. For them, as for the other subject peoples, the Roman conquest was, in many respects, a continuation of the Hellenistic situation. They perhaps counted for less within a multiracial Palestine; and, more important, as Goodman has shown, the reign of Herod the Idumaean had led to the deliberate imposition of a succession of ineffective high priests. Judaea lacked the kind of landowning élite, locked into the social structure, on which the Romans tended to rely in governing other areas of the near east.[19] The Jews saw the Romans, like the Ptolemies and Seleucids before them, not only as the ruling power, but also as representing a cultural opposition, which continued to be Greek rather than Latin;[20] for increasingly Greek was the language associated with the dominant power in the areas surrounding Judaea. Whereas for Polybius, in Achaea in the second century BC, Rome was an alien non-Greek threat (comparable, in the famous metaphor of the cloud in the west, with Punic Carthage),[21] in the Palestine of Josephus Roman power was identified

---

[17] This sense of city identity was less strong in earlier times, when bonds of ξενία between members of the aristocracies of different cities were often closer than those binding fellow-citizens, cf. Herman, (1987).

[18] On this point see Millar (1993) 220–2, 225–35.

[19] See Mendels (1992) 193–4 on the reduced importance of the Jews; Goodman (1987) 29–50 and *passim* on the weakness or absence of a ruling class after AD 6.

[20] See Mendels (1992) 193–4; Momigliano (1981) 337–8 (Hellenisation as an upper-class attitude in Judaea).

[21] Polyb. v.104; Walbank (1972a) 69 n.11.

with the preponderance of a Greek (or at least a hellenised) upper class: a good example, from the diaspora, is the Jew Ti. Julius Alexander, procurator of Judaea (AD 46–8) and prefect of Egypt (AD 66).[22] It is this Greek upper class, springing from and mainly resident in the Greek cities within the eastern provinces, which produced the Greek literature of the late republic and early empire and, not least, such historians as Poseidonius from Apamea, Dionysius from Halicarnassus, Arrian from Bithynia and Appian from Alexandria, all drawn in various ways to Rome. Where Josephus differs from these is in his strong and persistent identification with his native Jewish origins and with the Jewish state, to which Rome represented a cultural as well as a political threat. He was never a member of a hellenised élite; his earliest writings, even after his arrival in Rome, were in Aramaic and his Greek had to be learnt.

IV

It is interesting to examine in parallel the careers of Polybius and Josephus. Although, like Polybius, Josephus found his life and work shaped and dominated by his relationship to Rome, the background and consciousness of the two men were very different. Polybius came from an upper-class landowning family of Megalopolis in Arcadia, now an integral and influential part of the Achaean Confederation. His prime loyalty was clearly to Megalopolis and Achaea.[23] As we have seen, from his youth onwards the politics of Achaea were dominated by the problem of its relationship to Rome. Polybius praises the policy of Philopoemen, who favoured loyally maintaining the Roman alliance, but doing nothing that might hasten Achaean subjection. But, as Eckstein has shown, his own policy, from the time he became involved in political life, was one of full accommodation towards Rome.[24] His seventeen years away from Achaea were rendered considerably easier by the friendship (or patronage) of Scipio Aemilianus, thanks to which he was able to visit Spain, Africa and Gaul. Later, after his release, he || watched the destruction of Carthage from the victor's camp and explored some of the African shores of the Atlantic in a specially provided ship, before returning to

---

[22] See Vidal-Naquet (1977) 24–6; Burr (1955); A. Stein, *RE* x 1 (1917), 153–7, s.v. Julius no. 59.

[23] The 'Greek nation', which De Sanctis believed him to have betrayed (see ch. 20, below) was a tenuous and dubious entity; see Walbank (1951).

[24] On Philopoemen's policy see above, n.4; and for Polybius' policy of accommodation to Rome see Eckstein (1985) 265–6, who points out that the kings of whom Polybius approves (Hiero, Attalus I, Eumenes II, Masinissa) are those who collaborated with Rome, whereas her enemies (Hieronymus, Philip V, Perseus, Andriscus) are broadly condemned.

Greece when the Achaean War was already over, but in time to help mitigate Roman anger against his country.[25]

Josephus also came from an upper-class landowning family, Sadducees in their social and religious affiliations.[26] But Judaea was a temple-state and Josephus' family had priestly connections, which coloured the whole of his career and work. Judaea furnished the central focus for his loyalty. The whole body of Jewish sacred writings, as well as Josephus' own works, reveals the intense national and religious consciousness of the Jewish people. In this respect Judaea stands apart in our perception from the other peoples of the Near East, who by the first century AD were also directly under Rome.[27]

Judaea was governed by a Roman prefect (later a procurator) with troops at Caesarea.[28] Though violent when they occurred, clashes between the Jews and the Roman authorities were not frequent, for it was a long-standing tradition of the Jewish upper class to avoid confrontation and to seek a peaceful accommodation with whatever great power controlled Palestine.[29] When things went wrong, their usual practice was to blame the local governor – such as Gessius Florus (AD 64–6) – rather than the emperor at Rome;[30] and generally they succeeded in carrying the more intransigent lower classes of the towns and the country people along with them. There existed, however, a radical opposition in Judaea, which took various forms and was spread over several sects, each with its own political and religious convictions.

These were all alike in being hated by Josephus, who in his narrative rarely differentiates clearly between them,[31] regarding them all as cruel and violent, sinful and seeking to tyrannise the masses. That is partly because these groupings were fluid in character and liable to merge, but also because Josephus usually refers to them in generalised terms, as οἱ νεωτερίζοντες (*BJ* ii.407, 652), οἱ νεωτερίζειν βουλόμενοι (*BJ* ii.274), οἱ στασιασταί (*BJ* ii.330. 406), τὸ στασιάζον (*BJ* ii.422), or – of

---

[25] Cf. Walbank (1972a) 8–13. It is not clear whether, when he embarked on his Atlantic voyage, Polybius already knew that there was trouble in Achaea; but it certainly suited him to be away.

[26] See Applebaum (1971) 157, for Josephus as a Sadducee; for his land cf. Josephus, *Vita* 422.

[27] See above n.18.

[28] Until Claudius' reign Palestine was under a praefectus, not a procurator (a point missed by Rajak (1983) 67–8 and by Goodman (1987) 7). The evidence is in the Pilate inscription (*AE* 1963 no.104); cf. Sherwin-White (1964); Reynolds (1966) 119–20.

[29] Cf. Josephus, *BJ* v.390 (Josephus' speech from the walls of Jerusalem, adducing occasions when non-resistance had brought victory).

[30] Cf. Rajak (1983) 76, who notes that Josephus approves the sentiments in Agrippa's speech, that the emperor should not be blamed for the faults of procurators, who come and go.

[31] Cf. Rajak (1983) 83, 85.

Menahem, a hated popular leader – τύραννος (*BJ* ii.442).[32] The upper class, which also had its groupings, was in the main successful in restraining these radical sects, but the Jewish War of AD 66 developed because the ruling class was weak and Roman provocation made such restraint no longer possible.[33] In this situation Josephus, though by upbringing and disposition favourable to Rome, took up a post as commander of the Jewish forces in Galilee.[34] His motivation is unclear. It is Rajak's belief that he was trying to 'buy his way' into favour with the popular forces;[35] but Mendels and Cohen assume that the youthful Josephus perhaps entertained radical views which, in the light of experience, he later || discarded.[36] Whatever the truth of this, he undoubtedly grew increasingly disillusioned with the way the war was going and its likely outcome, until eventually, in AD 67, when taken prisoner at Jotapata he successfully defected to the Romans.[37]

Josephus' defection is the turning-point in his life. He insists that it came about as a result of dreams,[38] which revealed to him the fate of the Jews and the destinies of Roman sovereigns and made clear that God had gone over to the side of Rome and was resolved, as a punishment for the sins of the Jews, to destroy the Temple in Jerusalem.[39] This religious perception of Josephus has usually been interpreted as a gradual process,[40] but, in a striking article, already mentioned, Cohen makes Josephus' realisation of it much more instantaneous,[41] and that is the impression given by his text. Be that as it may, in fighting Rome and defecting to Titus while actually holding a Jewish command, Josephus was certainly in a far less favourable position for meeting criticism, both at the time

[32] Similarly John of Gischala was a brigand (ληστής) Josephus, *BJ* ii.587; see Rajak (1983) 84 on this word, elsewhere used in its literal sense. On the various groups see Applebaum (1971) 163f.; Goodman (1987) 198–227.

[33] On this see Goodman (1987) 152–75, who demonstrates that faction struggles within the ruling class were a decisive factor in both the outbreak and the disastrous conclusion of the war.

[34] Rajak (1983) 130 argues that Josephus and others of his class (*BJ* ii.562–8) were accepted as generals because of their political experience (and wealth) and their willingness to go along with the opposition; according to *BJ* ii.562 they were won over by a mixture of violence and persuasion. The version of Josephus' appointment given in *Vita* 29 – that he was to reduce and disarm 'anti-Roman brigands' – is clearly a self-serving distortion of what happened; cf. Eckstein (1990) 192 n. 50.

[35] Rajak (1983) 75.   [36] Mendels (1992) 263; S. J. D. Cohen (1979) 97–100.   [37] *BJ* iii.340–92.

[38] *BJ* iii.351; for God's desertion of the Jews see *BJ* ii.360; 373 (Agrippa's speech stressing divine support for Rome; v.367 (τύχη and ὁ θεός); 368 (ὁ θεός); 412 (τὸ θεῖον).

[39] Rajak (1983) 95–6 with n.95, compares the prophets of the First Temple period.

[40] Cf. Mendels (1992), who notes that Philostratus attributed the sentiment to Titus; he argues that it was a view common to many Jews at that time.

[41] S. J. D. Cohen (1980).

and in the later judgement of his countrymen and posterity, than was Polybius.

The later life of both men is shrouded in some obscurity. It is generally assumed, probably rightly, that after his final return to Achaea in 146 BC Polybius stayed there, apart from occasional visits to Rome, to Alexandria and, probably, to Numantia in 133 BC.[42] His service to his country in 146/5 BC clearly brought him (officially at least) renown and gratitude in Achaea. He could (and no doubt did) regard himself as an elder statesman; and there is a substantial record of some of the honours accorded to him.[43] We know nothing directly of his personal life – unlike Josephus, who records his three marriages[44] – but he evidently had a wife and family, for there is epigraphic evidence for a descendant, T. Flavius Polybius, living (probably) at Messene, in the third century of our era.[45] Whether Polybius ever resumed an active career we do not know. It has been suggested that his sketch of Achaean history in Book II was designed to further such a return to political life.[46] But the plausibility of that assumption depends on the date when he composed and published the various books of his *Histories*; and even if that was his intention, it need not follow that he ever actually carried it out. When Polybius died is also uncertain, but if (as I have argued)[47] it was around 118 BC, he had a further twenty to twenty-five active years before him following his return to Achaea in 146 BC.[48] The Roman connection seems to have been maintained at least during the lifetime of his friend Scipio Aemilianus, who died in 129 BC. ||

Josephus, on the other hand, never returned to Judaea: his reputation there would scarcely have encouraged it. Yet his sense of Jewishness was

[42] For Polybius' visit to Rome cf. Polyb. xxxix.8.1; to Alexandria cf. Strabo xvii.797 = Polyb. xxxiv.14.6; to Numantia cf. Cic. *Ad fam.* v.12.2 and for Scipio's ἴλη φίλων, which probably included Polybius, App. *Hisp.* 84, cf. 89.

[43] For honours paid to Polybius see Polyb. xxxix.5.4–6 (many cities); Paus. viii.30.8 (Megalopolis); Walbank, Comm. I, pp. ix–x (for Messene); *IG* v 2.304 (Mantinea).

[44] Cf. *BJ* v.419; *Vita* 414; 415.

[45] See *IG* v 2,370 = Hiller von Gaertringen, *Hist. gr. Epig.* no.112 for a dedication by this man at Olympia. Since Polybius could have married and had children before 167 BC this is not proof that he retired to Greece to stay; it does however strengthen that assumption.

[46] Ferrary (1988) 279–81 argues that Polybius published Books I–II in 150/49 BC and III–IV in 145/4 BC. For my own view see Walbank, *Comm.* I, 292–7 (iii.1–5 n.) and III, 739–40 (xxxix.8.1–8 n.), with the criticism of Derow (1984) 235. In reverting to Gelzer's view that 37–70 were a later insertion in Book II I may have pressed the wording of the final summary (xxxix.8) too hard. When Polybius composed the Achaean chapters and when they became an integral part of Book II is, I think, still an open question.

[47] See Walbank, *Comm.* I, 1 n.1; cf. III, 768, addendum on Polyb.iii.39.8.

[48] If he died from a fall from his horse at 82 (Ps.-Lucian, *Macrob.* 23), clearly he remained vigorous to an advanced age.

never diminished and his work contains many passages which demonstrate his concern for his country and offer his defence against the charge of treason. His *Against Apion* is a well-argued critique of the arguments raised by those hostile to the Jews.[49]

v

If Polybius and Josephus differed greatly in their lives and circumstances, that was less true of their writings, which were for both a direct response to the events through which their authors had lived. Polybius seeks to inform the world of the Greek *poleis* (whether independent or a constituent part of one or other of the new Hellenistic kingdoms) – and also, to a lesser degree, the Romans – about the significance to other peoples of Roman oecumenical domination.[50] Josephus, whose *Jewish War* was written first in Aramaic for readers in eastern provinces of the empire and beyond, and only later in Greek, sets out to describe the end of the Jewish state and the destruction of the Temple.[51] But in recording the fulfilment of God's purpose, he too is at the same time urging the acceptance of Roman rule. The fact that both men are writing within the conventions of Hellenistic historiography (though Josephus consciously modelled himself on Thucydides) and using the same language results in some similarities; and these are all the more striking because, as Eckstein has impressively demonstrated, Josephus deliberately takes up many themes – and not least the interpretation of Roman success exclusively in terms of power – directly from Polybius.[52] In addition the works of both writers contain a personal element (Josephus' more than Polybius'); for both too their histories are in a sense a substitute for a public life from which their authors are now debarred.

Nevertheless, the style and atmosphere of Josephus' work is very different from that of Polybius. How far Polybius' speeches contain a genuine historical content is a subject of controversy.[53] But those of Josephus, following a common Greek convention, are clearly a confection.[54] He is also

---

[49] For his strong Jewish commitment cf. *BJ* vi.107; *AJ* xx.263; for his concern for the land of Israel see Mendels (1992) 264.

[50] For Polybius' purpose in writing his *Histories* cf. i.3.7–10; 63.9 (with Walbank, *Comm.* I, 129–30 ad loc.); III.4 (with Walbank (1972a) 27–31). See also Walbank (1977).

[51] *BJ* 1.6; cf. Rajak (1983) 175.

[52] Cf. Goodman (1987) 5, 9, 199, 211; Josephus only twice mentions Thucydides (*Contra Apionem* i.18; i.66) but implicitly recalls him at several points (e.g. *BJ* i.1 on the magnitude of the war). See also Eckstein (1990) 178 with n.7.

[53] On Polybius' speeches see Walbank (1965a); (1972a) 43–5, 69 n.11 (on Agelaus' speech).

[54] See Rajak (1983) 60.

addicted to the sensational kind of writing not uncommon in the Hellenistic period and attacked by Polybius in his onslaught against the historian Phylarchus.[55] Like Phylarchus Josephus piles on the horrors of war and its aftermath, and revels in the macabre penalties of sin such as cannibalism and death from outlandish diseases, often unknown to the modern medical profession.[56] Eusebius comments on the τραγικὴ δραματουργία of his account of the strange retribution that befell Herod's family as divine vengeance for the (apocryphal) massacre of the innocents.[57] Josephus includes lamentations in the Jewish || tradition;[58] and unlike the rational Polybius[59] – though he had forerunners in Herodotus and Xenophon – he believes firmly in omens and dreams.[60]

Both wrote at Rome and whether they wrote wholly of their own volition has been queried. Polybius was probably already a writer at the time of his detention[61] and needed something (besides teaching the young Aemilianus and hunting)[62] to occupy his time; there is no evidence that he required a spur from the Scipios to set him off – though his last ten (added) books do indeed contain an *aristeia* of Scipio Aemilianus.[63] For Josephus the answer is less certain. He was in receipt of a pension from the Flavians and had lodgings in Vespasian's former house;[64] his narrative is strongly slanted towards Vespasian and Titus and the merits of Rome.[65] But if one accepts the religious motivation so strongly emphasised by Josephus himself, that gave him sufficient impetus to embark on his history without Flavian intervention; and indeed it is perhaps a little unlikely that the new emperor would want to sponsor a work to be written originally in

[55] Polyb. ii.56.1–16.

[56] E.g. *Vita* 173; *BJ* iii.522–3 (slaughter on Lake Gennesaret), vi.280 (in Jerusalem). The whole account of the fall of Jerusalem is presented in dramatic and sensational terms. On Herod's horrible death (*BJ* i.656; *AJ* xvii.169) see Africa (1982) especially 9–11. see also Rajak (1983) 98.

[57] *Hist.eccles.* i.8.4 referring to Josephus' account of Herod's death.

[58] E.g. for the Temple (*BJ* v.19–20).   [59] Cf. Walbank (1972a) 59–60.

[60] For Josephus' dreams see *BJ* ii.112–16; iii.352–3; cf. *Vita* 208–9.

[61] It is likely – though it cannot be conclusively proved – that Polybius' *Life of Philopoemen* and his *Tactics* were early works, written before his banishment to Rome; see Walbank (1972a) 14–15.

[62] For hunting see Polyb. xxxi.29.8; for Polybius' rôle as teacher of Aemilianus ibid. 23.6–25.1.

[63] Polyb. xxxi.25.2–29.12, with Walbank, Comm. III, 499; also Walbank (1977) 143–5.

[64] Josephus, *Vita* 422.

[65] Josephus, *BJ* iii.236 (Vespasian); vi.623, Titus' τὸ φιλάνθρωπον φύσει despite his celebration of Domitian's birthday with the execution of 2,500 Jewish prisoners by beasts, gladiatorial combat or fire, or (*BJ* vi.284) the massacre of 6,000 women and children by his 'angry' troops, or his ghastly progress through the cities of Syria (*BJ* vii.96). Contrast too Josephus' account of Roman massacres without comment (*BJ* iv. 445–6) with his condemnation of Simon Ben Giora (*BJ* iv.540–1). On the merits of Rome see his account of the Roman army, ἀρετῆς κτῆμα (*BJ* iii.71). Momigliano (1934b) 884 assumes the *BJ* to have been written at the behest of Vespasian, but see Rajak (1983) 185, 196.

Aramaic.[66] Both bodies of work, those of Polybius and Josephus, were however plainly very acceptable to the Romans, some of whom no doubt read them.

Both Achaea and Judaea were small countries, marginal to the greater developments of Roman history and even to Roman expansion. But whereas Josephus wrote a monograph, the *Jewish War*,[67] which placed his own people at the centre of the stage, Polybius' universal history had to concern itself with a larger canvas and the particular question of how Rome took over the rôle of world power from Macedonia. In that context Achaea had a minor part to play though in his narrative Polybius makes as much of it as he can.[68] By contrast, when he is discussing constitutions and the superiority of that of Rome in Book VI, Achaea is remarkable for its absence – perhaps as a federal body and perhaps to avoid an embarrassing comparison.[69] Here one is struck by the difference in emphasis in the themes of the two historians.

VI

In several other respects, however, the histories of Polybius and Josephus show a striking similarity. The first of these is the degree to which their writing is coloured by class prejudice. Both in their public careers and as historians they were patently members of the rich landowning class. Various scholars, and especially Goodman, have remarked on the difficulty in reaching a clear definition of the ruling element in Judaea,[70] owing to complications springing both from the predominance of religion in the Jewish community, with the Temple at the centre || of Jewish life, and, down to AD 6, from the presence of the monarchy or tetrarchy, a second centre of power. The priestly connection is of vital importance to Josephus, whereas the conditions of second-century Achaea assigned little political significance to religion; what mattered there was the holding not of priesthoods, but of magistracies and places on embassies.

---

[66] Thackeray (note on *BJ* iii.108 in the Loeb edition of Josephus) and Momigliano (1934b) both however argue that the work was intended as a warning to peoples further east, including some under Parthia, of the danger of resisting Rome, and was officially inspired.

[67] The title of the work might suggest a Roman slant (cf. Vidal-Naquet (1977) 13); but it is a natural way to describe a war fought within the Roman empire, regardless of the author's sympathies.

[68] For Polybius' emphasis on Achaean and Peloponnesian affairs see Walbank (1972a) 5–6 (Achaean based synchronisms), 27 (growth of Achaea), 49 (Megalopolitan standpoint), 85–6 (favourable view of Philip II).

[69] On the absence of the Achaean constitution from Book VI see Walbank (1972a) 150–1.

[70] See especially Goodman (1987) *passim*; Rajak (1983) 108–9; Millar (1993) 360.

Despite these differences in their constitution, however, both ruling classes had to face the common problem of reaching and maintaining a comfortable relationship with the power of Rome, while at the same time keeping an eye on the lower classes and their demands. P. A. Brunt has made a collection of passages from Josephus illustrating this basic factor in the *Jewish War*.[71] Social conflict also played a part in the life of second-century Greece. In Achaea, however, contrary to what was long the orthodox belief,[72] the war of 146 BC was not primarily a social rising; it sprang out of political divisions within the confederacy and a recrudescence of the perennial dispute between the confederacy and Sparta, always a reluctant member.[73] Polybius' (unfortunately fragmentary) account of the war exaggerates the rôle of the lower classes in the rising, and employs derogatory class expressions to designate its supporters.[74] He seeks to give the impression that the rising was provoked and controlled throughout by popular demagogues; and it is indeed true that in the earlier stages support for it came predominantly from the lower class, the ἐργαστηριακοὶ καὶ βάναυσοι (handworkers) of whom there were many in Corinth, where the war-decision was taken.[75] His detailed account of the course of the war, however, shows that eventually it came to command almost complete support from all classes and, what is more, that it spread to embrace many other states outside Achaea. In short, the pattern was not dissimilar to that in Judaea in AD 66, where opposition to Rome was first evident among the lower classes, but developed from that base to embrace eventually the pro-Roman upper classes and end as a national rising.

One reason why events followed this course in Achaea was the Roman Senate's insistence on obedience to any orders it might impose and its determination to allow several member-states to secede from the Achaean Confederacy.[76] Polybius asserts that the Romans merely intended to curb

---

[71] Brunt (1977) (quoting Kreissig (1970) and Applebaum (1971)). See also Goodman (1987) 64–6, making the interesting point that the Jewish concept of charity, which looked to the giver rather than the recipient, contributed to the growth of a class of subsidised poor, with no social ties to any individual rich man or woman and dependent for subsistence on public or royal works in a society lacking the usual Hellenistic examples of private euergetism. For the connection between the class conflict and opposition to Hellenism Goodman quotes Kreissig (1969).

[72] See Fuks (1970) 78 for this 'orthodox' view in Kahrstedt, Oertel, Rostovtzeff and others.

[73] See Harris (1979) 240–4; Gruen, (1984) II, 520–3; Derow (1989) 319–23.

[74] E.g. τὸ πλῆθος (opposed to τὸ σωφρονοῦν μέρος: Polyb. xxxviii.10.6–7), οἱ χείριστοι (Polyb. xxxviii.10.8), οἱ ὄχλοι (Polyb. xxxviii.13.6).

[75] Polyb. xxxviii.12.5.

[76] Corinth, Argos, Arcadian Orchomenus and Heraclea in Trachis were to be allowed (encouraged?) to secede (Paus. vii.14.1; Justin. xxiv.1.6; Livy, *epit.* 51; *Ox. epit.* 51; Dio xxi.72).

Achaean arrogance and by no means wished to go to war;[77] but this is true only in the sense that they hoped to impose their will without fighting. His statement is to be regarded as a reflection of his pro-Roman attitude throughout his description of this war, which took place when he was absent with Scipio at Carthage.[78] Ferrary has argued that for Polybius the Achaean leaders at the time of the Achaean War resemble the demagogues and 'tyrants' to be found in many other Greek states – Callicrates in Achaea itself (till his death in 150/49 BC), Charops in Epirus, Lyciscus in Aetolia, Mnesippus in Boeotia and Chremas in Acarnania[79] – || who had been given a free hand after the thorough purge of moderates by the Romans after Pydna. For example, Ferrary points out, Polybius uses the same uncommon word δελεάζειν 'lead astray', of both Charops and Critolaus.[80] But the parallel is not to be pressed, for apart from the fact that there was no reign of terror in the Peloponnese, Diaeus and Critolaus (unlike Callicrates) led the Achaeans in revolt against Rome, whereas the demagogues in north-west Greece and Boeotia relied on Roman support or acquiescence for their domination.

It is, of course, one aspect of their membership of the ruling class in Achaea or Judaea that Polybius and Josephus were both military men, who had commanded troops; and this was reflected in their works. Both are fascinated by the sheer power and skill of the Roman army; indeed it seems overwhelmingly likely that Josephus' account of the imperial army in *BJ* iii.70–109 was inspired by the famous description of the republican army and camp in Polyb. vi.19–42:[81] Josephus says he included it to console his defeated countrymen and to deter others from futile revolt! Both Polybius and Josephus were active men, who favoured autopsy in preference to armchair work as the basis for their writings.[82] And both could offer the Romans something of value, Josephus as an interpreter

---

[77] Polyb.xxxviii.9.8; this is accepted by Gruen (1984) II, 520 n.193, Ferrary (1988) 34 and Bernhardt (1984) 16–28; contra Harris (1979) 240–4. See now Derow (1989).

[78] Orosius v.3 = Polyb. xxxviii.14.3.

[79] Ferrary (1988) 344–6. On Charops see Polyb. xxxvii.15.3; for Callicrates Polyb. xxiv.8.1–10.15; and for the rest Polyb. xxx.3.3–4 (with Walbank, *Comm.* III ad loc.).

[80] Polyb. xxxvi.6.2 (Charops), xxxviii.11.11 (Critolaus); it means 'demagogic action leading to ochlocracy' (cf. Polyb. vi.9.6).

[81] See Eckstein (1990) 204, who shows that Josephus borrowed directly from Polybius in many places and not least in the expression of admiration by both for Roman skill and power (rather than for civilising influence, which later became a commonplace of imperial rhetoric). See also S. J. D. Cohen (1980) 368 for several (not always convincing) parallels between the two historians.

[82] For Josephus see Rajak (1983) 75; for Polybius see Polyb. iv.4.1–2 and Walbank (1972a) 24, 42 and 119–20; also Eckstein (1990) 180–1 on this aspect, common to both historians.

and go-between, addressing the Jews in revolt (though not indeed very effectively), Polybius as a skilled military engineer.[83]

Among the many similarities between the works of Polybius and Josephus there is one feature which has been noted, but not perhaps sufficiently appreciated. The main difference between the Jewish revolt of AD 66 and the Achaean struggle of 146 BC lay in the religious element evident in the former.[84] Josephus' account is primarily concerned with the destruction of the Temple and the question of why God allowed this to happen. As we saw, this is a question to which he offers a religious answer: God has withdrawn his support from the Jews, and *Tyche* has gone over to Rome.[85] Rajak has remarked that this implies the introduction of a theological component into a Greek-style political history.[86] The different ethos of the two types of history is undoubtedly important; but its rôle here should not be exaggerated. Despite Momigliano's comments on the absence of religious motifs from Greek histories,[87] supernatural forces do play a rôle in Herodotus.[88] As for Polybius, it is true that he attributes Roman success primarily to Roman military supremacy and the virtues of the mixed constitution;[89] as Momigliano remarked, 'no one has yet made out a reasonable case for Polybius or Tacitus as religious interpreters of history'.[90] Nevertheless, at another level of interpretation, Polybius attributes quite a basic rôle in the destruction of Macedonia (and the humbling of the Seleucid monarchy) in 168 BC to *Tyche*, Fortune, who in this way brings about the rise of Rome to world hegemony in just under fifty-three years. This *Tyche*, moreover, is not just blind || chance;[91] she is a consciously retributive force, who employs the war planned by Philip V and fought by Perseus to put an end to the Macedonian hegemony acquired in the war planned by Philip II and fought by Alexander

---

[83] For Polybius at Carthage see Walbank, *Comm.* III, on Polyb. xxxviii.19.1; Paus. viii.30.9 (where ὁ Ῥωμαῖος is probably Scipio rather than 'the Romans' generally).

[84] Momigliano (1971) 4–5 observes that the introduction of religious emotions and the reporting of divine intervention are alien to Greek historiography; he does not mention Josephus, presumably because he regards him as lying outside the Greco-Roman area he is considering.

[85] See above, n.38.   [86] Rajak (1983) 78.   [87] Momigliano (1971) 4–5.

[88] On the supernatural element in Herodotus see Fornara (1983) 77–9; Walbank (1972a) 58–9.

[89] Cf. Polyb. i.1.5, where Polybius links together the course of military events (πῶς) and the Roman constitution (τίνι γένει πολιτείας) as the two aspects of his work; Eckstein (1990) 204.

[90] Momigliano (1971) 75.

[91] Like the *Tyche* of Demetrius of Phalerum, whose remarks made so great an impression on Polybius (Polyb. xxix.21). In choosing the fifty-three years from 220 to 168 BC as the period during which *Tyche* raised Rome to world domination, Polybius was to some extent influenced by his recollection of the fifty years which encompassed the rise of Macedonia in Demetrius' 'prophetic' passage (Polyb. xxix.21.4; see ch. 16, above).

against the Persians. In so doing *Tyche* is punishing Macedonia for the sins of Philip V and above all for the shocking compact with Antiochus III to rob the boy-king of Egypt, Ptolemy V, of his possessions[92] – just as, for Josephus, God has destroyed the Temple in Jerusalem to punish the sins of the Jewish people.

How Polybius' *Tyche* relates to the gods is never made clear.[93] As for the *Tyche* in Josephus that passed over to Rome, there is considerable disagreement on how it should be interpreted. The orthodox view is that it represents the will of God; but Eckstein has recently argued that Josephus has taken it lock, stock and barrel from Polybius, as a convenient way to present his ideas to a Greek public.[94] That is by no means impossible. *Tyche* does not go well with Hebrew conceptions of God, but is a common notion easily recognisable throughout the Hellenistic world. But even if this is accepted to be a Polybian borrowing, there is still a substantial difference in the tone of the two works; for whereas Josephus is passionately involved in the fate of his country, which has been revealed to him in a series of dreams,[95] Polybius is not personally locked into the central issue of Macedonia and Rome, which he describes objectively and, apart from the occasional cynical comment, dispassionately.

It is of interest, however, that Josephus and Polybius, with their very different outlooks, should both have come to the conclusion that in the last resort Roman success was the result of the action of a supernatural power. This is a conclusion not perhaps strange in Josephus, but certainly rather odd in Polybius. By adopting it and at the same time showing as historians how *Tyche* operated through events occurring at the sublunary level, they may have found it easier to justify their own eventual appearance in the Roman camp; for in so doing they were following the path of history. Confrontation with Rome and the right response to Roman threats and eventual domination were part of the common experience of everyone living in the areas Rome subjugated. But as historians writing about contemporary events in which they were personally

---

[92] For a fuller exposition see ch. 16, above.

[93] For Polybius' views on religion see Walbank (1972a) 59–60 and works there quoted; add van Hooff, (1977).

[94] For Josephus' references to *Tyche* and God see *BJ* iii.394; v.54–66, 88 (God and *Tyche* and Titus), v.412 (τὸ θεῖον), vi.267 (εἱμαρμένη), vi.399 (God and the Roman *Tyche*). This all reflects Hellenistic Greek terminology; and in *BJ* vi.411 Titus attributes Roman success to God (θεός) – which god? In agreement with Stählin (1974), Eckstein (1990) 200–2, argues (against S. J. D. Cohen (1979) 369–73 and Rajak (1983) 101) that for Josephus *Tyche* is an independent force separate from God's will, which he has in fact taken over from Polybius.

[95] For Josephus' dreams see above n.60.

involved – in 170 BC and AD 66–70 – Polybius and Josephus could not discuss the fortunes of Rome without reference to their own personal careers. In short, because they were historians, they were obliged to confront, and find a solution to a problem which faced others equally, but which non-historians who ended up conforming could quietly forget.

VII

Finally, to return to the point from which we set out, both Polybius and Josephus have at various times been designated traitors. In the light of the above discussion, how far is that a just assessment? Josephus was well aware of the accusation,[96] but, naturally, he never accepted its validity. In a series of passages he asserts his innocence and his patriotism. 'Although || he might look for pardon from the Romans', he writes, referring to his arrival in Tiberias, 'he would have preferred to suffer a thousand deaths rather than betray his country and disgracefully abandon the command which had been entrusted to him, in order to seek his fortune among those whom he had been commissioned to fight.'[97] Surely he could not have written these words, had he genuinely believed (as many clearly believed) that that was precisely what he later did. In fact, from the outset of the rising the practical arguments for surrendering to Rome were very strong; resistance might be heroic but it was hopeless, and Josephus sets out those arguments clearly in the speech attributed to Agrippa.[98] But more important to him were the religious arguments, which seem to have come to him later: first the conviction that God had gone over to the Romans[99] and secondly his belief, reinforced by dreams, that he had been personally selected by Heaven to convey that information as a messenger and as God's minister.[100] This belief sounds genuine – though admittedly his sincerity can only be decided on the basis of a subjective judgement. But if it is genuine, the practical and the religious arguments together must have presented a powerful incentive for his defection. It was a defection which, it is true, turned out very much to his advantage, though it must have required both courage and ingenuity to carry it through to success. Josephus admits managing it

---

[96] BJ iii.137, 354, 359, 361, 381, 439; *Vita* 416, 424, 429; cf. Rajak (1983) 104.
[97] *BJ* iii.137; cf. *BJ* ii.345–401; vi.107 (in his speech, uttered with tears!).
[98] *BJ* ii.345–401.   [99] See above n.38.
[100] *BJ* iii.353–4, μαρτύρομαι δὲ ὡς οὐ προδότης, ἀλλὰ σὸς ἄπειμι διάκονος (in a prayer) 'I call you to witness that I go, not as a traitor, but as your minister.'

'Treason' and Roman domination

adroitly;[101] but to have played his cards other than to the best of his ability would have been folly. Judged from without, on the basis of his actions, he was beyond doubt a quisling.[102] But, I would suggest, if one takes into account both the objective circumstances of the revolt and Josephus' religious convictions, the charge of treason against him does not result in a straightforward verdict.

Polybius was fortunate in not having to face a similar decision. His policy of accommodation was one widely accepted;[103] and the emphasis throughout his work on rationality in decision-taking clearly pointed towards accommodation with Rome and at all costs not provoking her anger. However, in 198 BC, when Achaea abandoned the Macedonian alliance for Rome, he was a child; and later, during the war with Perseus, as cavalry commander he did the best that circumstances allowed; his detention at Rome was an unavoidable fate he shared with a thousand other Achaeans. Finally, during the Achaean rising, thanks to his friendship with Scipio Aemilianus he did not reach Corinth until the short war was over and was thus spared difficult decisions. It could all so very easily have turned out otherwise, had he remained at home after his original return to Achaea along with the other surviving detainees in 150 BC. How he would have reacted in these circumstances is anyone's guess. As we saw, his discussion on traitors never dealt with the dilemma of the man who is persuaded of the suicidal policies of his own government. My own personal view is that, had he been faced with the decision of what to do at the time of the Achaean War, Polybius would not have come out against Rome. But who can tell?

VIII

Our comparison of Polybius and Josephus has produced no novel conclusions. But it has, I hope, thrown some light on two individuals whom, because they happen to be historians describing events through which they lived, we are able to question in some detail. Both members of the upper class in a subject, or soon to be subjected, people, they faced a common dilemma, which must have taken different forms in different places, but is nowhere likely to have been wholly evaded. The solutions

---

[101] *BJ* iii.387, ὁ δ᾽ ἐν ταῖς ἀμηχανίαις οὐκ ἠπόρησεν ἐπινοίας ('In his dire straits his resource did not forsake him'); and indeed to have managed the lots so skilfully that he survived until the last pair was a remarkable feat.

[102] Vidal-Naquet (1977) 30 rightly points to his vanity, his class bias and his cynicism; but these are not decisive one way or the other.

[103] See Eckstein (1985).

which they reached were unheroic; but they were rational, advantageous to themselves, in no way harmful to their own people – in the case of || Polybius positively advantageous – and indirectly responsible for two major histories. Would any alternative have ended with a better balance-sheet? A question difficult to answer; so perhaps in these and similar cases the modern historian would be well advised to follow the old maxim and abstain from moral judgements.

18

*A Greek looks at Rome: Polybius VI revisited**†

I

In 217 BC a conference was held at Naupactus on the Corinthian Gulf to try to bring to an end the war between the Macedonian Confederacy, led by Philip V, and the Aetolian League. It became famous for a remarkable speech by Agelaus of Naupactus, who, if we can believe Polybius' account, urged all Greeks to bury their differences and to turn their eyes to the 'cloud in the west', that is to the struggle between Carthage and Rome, since the winner in that conflict was likely to go on to destroy Greek freedom.[1] Almost exactly fifty years later, in 168, at the battle of Pydna, that prophecy was fulfilled: for in that year the Macedonian monarchy under Perseus was abolished and the Seleucid king Antiochus IV was humiliated by a Roman envoy at Eleusis in Egypt.[2] Henceforth Rome was the undisputed superpower. The Roman victory was followed by a purge throughout Greece, as a result of which most men of influence found themselves detained in Italy. Among them was the Achaean statesman and future historian, Polybius, who was to spend the next sixteen years in Italy, where he planned and began his great history of Rome. In this he set out to show 'how and thanks to what kind of constitution' (πῶς καὶ τίνι γένει πολιτείας) Rome had become mistress of the inhabited world, the *oecumene*, in not quite fifty-three years.[3]

In its original form this history was designed to cover the years 220 to 167 in thirty books. These were later extended to forty to provide a closing date in 146/5, when both Corinth and Carthage had been destroyed and Polybius' native Achaean Confederacy disbanded. But this extension will not concern us here, since what I am concerned with now is Book VI,

---

* [[*Scripta Classica Israelica* 17 (1998) 45–59]]
† This paper was originally read on 25 May 1997, at the 26th Conference of the Israel Society for the Promotion of Classical Studies held at the Hebrew University of Jerusalem.
[1] Polyb. v.104. Henceforth references are to Polybius unless otherwise indicated.
[2] xxix.27.   [3] i.1.5.

which was unquestionably part || of the original plan;[4] for if the *Histories* as a whole described *how* Rome rose to her dominant position, the other half of the enquiry – 'thanks to what kind of constitution' – was to find its answer in Book VI. An Italian scholar has recently argued[5] that the purpose of Book VI was to contrast the orderly world of Rome with the confusion rife in the Hellenistic kingdoms, as could be seen in the wars of Macedonia and Syria described in Books IV and V. A good historian, it is true, often has more than one reason for including particular items in his work: but the contrast Lucio Troiani wishes to draw is one of minor importance and not such that, alone, it would justify devoting a whole book to a description of the Roman *politeia*. Like most scholars who have interested themselves in this topic, I translate *politeia* here as 'constitution'; indeed that is the basic meaning of the word. But *politeia* often includes more than simply the political arrangements within a state. It can, and frequently does – for example in Plato's *Politeia* – embrace social customs and a general way of life, ἔθη καὶ νόμιμα, to use Polybius' phrase. In Book VI the account of the *politeia* is extended to include such topics as Roman religion and the organisation of the army with which Rome conquered the world.

II

Book VI of Polybius' *Histories* is an extraordinary and complicated piece of writing. Polybius places it at the point in Roman history when Hannibal's victory at Cannae had brought Rome to her knees. From then on the way was to be all uphill. I have been interested in this book for over fifty years[6] – as long as it took the Romans to rise to world dominion! – and my reason for returning to it now is that some distinguished scholars have recently shown themselves to be not entirely clear about what exactly Polybius is trying to say. As I have just observed, the book is complicated. That is because it represents a mixture of theorising on the basis of doctrines set out by earlier Greek political writers, including Plato, members of the Peripatetic school and perhaps others, together with Polybius' own observation of Roman political institutions and customs during sixteen years spent as a rather privileged detainee at Rome.

---

[4] Cf. especially iii.2.6 and vi.2.3. There is nothing in Book VI which cannot have been written by 150; see Walbank (1972a) 134.

[5] Troiani (1979).

[6] See, for example, Walbank (1943b) superseded by Walbank (1954); Walbank, *Comm.* I, 635–746; Walbank (1972a) 130–56.

What he is trying to do in Book VI is to interpret what he saw there in terms of certain || traditional Greek views about the nature of states and human society. In the process he sometimes forces his material into an over-schematic form and, moreover, simplifies and abbreviates, to make the evidence fit the pattern he imposes. Nevertheless, though open to justifiable criticism in places, his attempt to apply Greek political theory to Rome is a striking innovation, which deserves our full attention. As far as we know, this had never been attempted before.

Unhappily, Book VI is incomplete; but we can reconstitute its original shape with some confidence from the fragments contained in the Codex Urbinas and in the so-called Constantinian excerpts, together with passages in later writers who quote Polybius, not least Athenaeus, who had the useful habit of quoting the number of the book from which he took his passages. There are also one or two helpful indications elsewhere in the *Histories*. So let me now briefly sketch its contents. After a short introduction Polybius explains that there are various kinds of constitution, but that whereas those found in Greek states are simple and therefore easy to understand, that of Rome is quite the opposite, because it is complicated; and its future is hard to foretell, through ignorance about its past.[7] Simple constitutions are of three kinds, kingship, aristocracy and democracy. And each of these has a perverted form, tyranny, oligarchy and ochlocracy (or mob-rule). Historically the simple constitutions follow each other in a natural succession of primitive monarchy, true kingship, tyranny, aristocracy, oligarchy and, following that, democracy, which declines into mob-rule and eventually ends in monarchy once more. At this point the cycle begins again. To these simple forms, however, another must be added, namely a mixed constitution, such as Lycurgus set up at Sparta. This was a mixture of the three simple, uncorrupted varieties. Polybius then traces in detail the way in which the successive constitutions succeed each other; this process he calls the *anacyclosis*, a word otherwise unrecorded in this sense.[8] For convenience I shall call it simply the constitutional cycle.

Rome, like Sparta, was fortunate in having acquired a mixed constitution. But, whereas that at Sparta had been set up by one individual, the famous lawgiver Lycurgus, that at Rome had been reached 'by the discipline of many struggles and troubles, and always choosing the best in the light of experience gained in disaster'.[9] At this point in the book there is, unfortunately, a long lacuna. We know, however, that Polybius here

---

[7] vi.3.1–4.   [8] vi.3.5–9.14.   [9] vi.10.14.

had a substantial section describing in some detail the early development
of Rome down to the year 450, the date of the Decemvirate; but, apart
from a few trivial details and a handful of dates, this section has been
entirely lost.[10] It was followed by a passage that has survived || complete,
in which the powers of the consuls, the Senate and the people – which
represent the royal, aristocratic and popular elements in the state – and
the checks which were exercised on each of these by the other two, are
described at length.[11]

Next comes an account of the Roman army and military system,
nominally as it existed at the time of Cannae.[12] This is important, since
it was through the army that Rome rose to world power during the
fifty-three years from 220 to 167. The army is also the element in which
Rome is superior to Sparta, for Sparta, we are told, was unsuccessful
when it came to foreign conquest; and foreign conquest is something
that Polybius rates highly.[13] In the next section the Roman constitution
is compared with those of other noteworthy states, in particular those of
Sparta and Carthage, especially Carthage;[14] and finally Polybius sketches
the probable future development of Rome and rounds off the book with
an anecdote illustrating the high Roman morale which existed after
the defeat at Cannae, thus bringing us back to the point at which he
interrupted his narrative.[15]

III

As one can clearly see, the book contains a bewildering variety of loosely,
but logically connected themes, and I shall now discuss one or two of
these in greater detail. To begin with, there is an obvious problem, which
Polybius has not wholly surmounted, concerning the cycle of constitutions. This cycle, Polybius emphasises,[16] was a natural development;
and by 'natural', κατὰ φύσιν, Polybius means that it follows the biological pattern, to which he repeatedly refers and which requires all
things to have their birth, growth, prime, decay and end. But it is not
at all easy to reconcile such a scheme with that of the constitutional
cycle, which has no clear prime but, once started, is subject to perpetual
change in a circular form, with a series of high points in kingship, aristocracy and democracy, each of them followed by a corresponding low
point in their successive perversions. Various attempts have been made to

---

[10] vi.11a.1–10; cf. xxi.13.11 = vi.1.9, on the Salian priests.   [11] vi.11.1–18.8.   [12] vi.19.1–42.6.
[13] vi.48.6–8.   [14] vi.43.1–56.15.   [15] vi.57.1–58.13.   [16] vi.4.12–13.

reconcile this cycle with the biological sequence, but never, I believe, with success.[17]

Another difficulty concerns the nature of the revolutionary changes within the cycle, thanks to which the perverted forms of tyranny and oligarchy are || superseded by the next 'good' forms, namely aristocracy and democracy. As Wilfried Nippel has recently pointed out,[18] these transformations do not, as one might expect, reflect changes in power within society. In each case it is the *people* who overthrow the corrupt rulers and then hand over power, first to the noble leaders, aristocrats, and later, when aristocracy declines into oligarchy, no longer either to kings or to a select few, but to themselves. Thus the changes here contemplated do not correspond to changes in the power relations of various groups in society, as they do in Aristotle. The social base is always 'the people' and the circumstances leading to the violent change are of a moral nature, namely corruption in the rulers, which arises 'naturally', just as rust arises in iron or woodworm in timber. This is a profoundly pessimistic view of the effects of power and of the limited life and effectiveness of all political forms. Polybius nowhere suggests that this 'inbuilt evil' (σύμφυτον κακόν) within the successive simple constitutional forms can be corrected by exercising moral pressure on the offending elements. The only long-lasting solution is to be found in a constitution which embodies various elements rather than in any single form.

IV

What Polybius actually says is that there are three kinds of constitution (τρία γένη πολιτειῶν), namely kingship, aristocracy and democracy, but that the best constitution is a combination 'of all the afore-mentioned forms' (πάντων τῶν προειρημένων ἰδιωμάτων).[19] This certainly appears to be a reference to the 'mixed constitution', which was by this time a well-known concept, going back at least as far as Thucydides, who praised that set up at Athens by Theramenes as a moderate mixture (ξύγκρασις) as regards the few and the many.[20] And indeed Aristotle[21] even regarded Solon's constitution in sixth-century Athens as a mixture. That this is what Polybius is here talking about has been generally agreed. Recently, however, the eminent French scholar Claude Nicolet has argued that this 'ideal' Roman constitution was not a mixed constitution

---

[17] See Walbank, *Comm.* I, 645–7 on the *anacyclosis* and the biological theory.
[18] Nippel (1980) 142–56.   [19] vi.3.5–7.
[20] Thuc.viii.97.2.   [21] Arist. *Pol.*ii.12, 1273 b 35ff.

at all, but an aristocracy.[22] We should, I think, glance at the arguments he puts forward for this paradoxical view.

First, he alleges that Polybius is not describing a constitution composed of three different forms, but one which contains 'characteristics' of those forms. He bases this somewhat arcane argument on the meaning of the word ἰδίωμα in the || passage I have just quoted, which refers to 'all the afore-mentioned ἰδιώματα'. Now ἰδίωμα does commonly mean a 'specific quality', a 'characteristic' of something, as in Polyb. ii.38.10, where it is used of the characteristics of the Achaean political principles (προαίρεσις) and constitution. But Polybius uses it in relation to the three single constitutional forms for quite another reason. Having just mentioned 'three constitutional forms (πολιτεῖαι)', he now wants to say that the best πολιτεία is one consisting of all three. But that would involve a rather clumsy repetition of the word πολιτεία and so, for euphony, instead of saying 'of the three πολιτεῖαι' he substitutes the phrase 'of the three ἰδιώματα'.[23] In his *Polybios-Lexikon* Mauersberger renders ἰδίωμα in this passage as '*Staatsform*', 'constitutional form'. This must be right, for Polybius cannot here mean 'afore-mentioned characteristics', as Nicolet alleges, since he has not mentioned 'characteristics' before, but only constitutional forms, i.e. kingship, aristocracy and democracy. So Nicolet's first reason for thinking that Polybius is not describing a 'mixed constitution' vanishes.

His second reason lies in a passage in Book XXIII[24] where, in an obituary on Scipio Africanus, Polybius describes him as 'pursuing fame in an aristocratic state'. That is indeed inconsistent with the argument in Book VI that during the third and second centuries Rome had a mixed constitution. But Polybius has a very good reason for this remark about Scipio. He specifically wants to contrast him with the Achaean leader Philopoemen, who died in the same year and who 'pursued fame in a democratic state' viz. The Achaean Confederation.[25] If then one asks, as one must, which is Polybius' more considered view, the fully argued exposition in Book VI or this isolated comment in Book XXIII, introduced to create a rhetorical contrast, then I think there can be no doubt that one must opt for the former. The whole tenor of the argument in Book VI, including the comparison with Sparta, where Lycurgus

---

[22] Nicolet (1983b).
[23] In a discussion following the reading of this paper in Jerusalem, Professor A. Laks suggested that an additional reason for Polybius' choice of the word ἰδίωμα might be its suitability to describe a *specific* constitutional form, as opposed to the *mikte*.
[24] xxiii.14.1.   [25] xxiii.12.5.

had introduced a mixed constitution, is against the view that Polybius seriously regarded third-and second-century Rome as an aristocracy. It is true that he tells us that at Rome, in contrast to Carthage, at the time of the Hannibalic War deliberation was still in the hands of the 'best people', the aristocracy;[26] but, as Viktor Pöschl pointed out long ago,[27] that is where deliberation *should* be in a mixed constitution and Polybius' mention of it here shows that the Roman constitution had not yet begun the downward || decline evident at Carthage, where deliberation was already in the hands of the people (οἱ πολλοί). That is why, to the outsider, who cannot get the whole picture,[28] the Roman constitution, falsely, appears to be aristocratic (τελείως ἀριστοκρατικὴ φαίνεθ' ἡ πολιτεία).[29] It is, moreover, difficult to see why Polybius should have gone to such pains to describe the mixed constitution as a means of avoiding a built-in tendency to corruption in the separate constitutional forms, if it was not relevant at Rome, where there was an aristocracy containing only certain 'characteristics' of the three best separate forms.

If then we agree that Rome enjoyed a 'mixed constitution', how exactly is this to be envisaged? The similar Lycurgan constitution at Sparta is 'mixed' in the sense that it is in a state of equilibrium, like a balance (ἰσορροποῦν καὶ ζυγοστατούμενον).[30] This was not a new idea. The Pythagorean Archytas of Tarentum had described Sparta in much the same terms in the fourth century.[31] The Roman constitution was mixed in a very similar way. It was not, that is to say, like a cake made out of well-mixed ingredients. On the contrary, its three main elements remained separate, but exercised a series of checks or restraints over each other, in such a way as to create a balance and ensure political stability. For Polybius does not define those elements as constitutional forms such as kingship, aristocracy and democracy, but rather as concrete, political entities operating in a political continuum – the consuls, the senate and the people, which embody, respectively, the royal, the aristocratic and the democratic elements in the state. As we saw, he devotes a long section of Book VI to listing the powers exercised by each of these entities and to showing how any two can limit and constrain the power of the third.[32]

v

Having described the mixed constitution and how it functioned, Polybius was faced with a serious problem. He had to show how it could have

---

[26] vi.51.5–8.   [27] Pöschl (1936) 61; see Walbank, *Comm.* I, 736.   [28] vi.12.3.
[29] vi.13.8.   [30] vi.10.7.   [31] See Walbank, *Comm.* I, 640–1.   [32] vi.11.11–18.8.

arisen 'naturally' out of a constitutional cycle which, in its natural form, had no place for it. As we saw, it had arisen, not like the one at Sparta, at the hands of a single lawgiver, nor by any process of reasoning, but 'by the discipline of many struggles and troubles and always choosing the best in the light of experience gained in disaster'.[33] We know that Polybius' account of the operation of the || constitution was followed by a section describing the early history of Rome and it is a reasonable assumption that this account was designed to explain how Rome moved over from the revolving wheel of the cycle to the relative stability of the mixed constitution. Since Johannes Schweighaeuser's outstanding edition of Polybius at the end of the eighteenth century, it has been usual to call this section the *archaeologia* – a term not, as so many scholars assert, without any ancient authority, but one taken from a passage in the *Roman History* of Dionysius of Halicarnassus,[34] where Polybius is listed among those historians who have written on early Rome – though in fact the word *archaeologia* is there used specifically in reference to Hieronymus of Cardia. Unfortunately, of this section there survive only a few dates and some isolated and rather trivial, if sometimes illuminating, comments, such as the information that it was customary for Roman men to kiss their female relatives on meeting them, in order to ascertain whether they had been illicitly drinking wine.[35] Otherwise the whole of the *archaeologia* is lost. As one can imagine, scholars over the years have devoted a great deal of effort to trying to recover what it said. On this Professor Nicolet judges it wiser to remain silent: 'plus sage de garder le silence'.[36] He may be right. But if we are to understand Polybius' argument in Book VI, I think we have to take a chance and see how far we can get with this question. In tackling it, we are not entirely helpless.

As I have already indicated, we know that Polybius' account went down to 450 and the Decemvirate.[37] So it is a reasonable assumption that it was from that date that the mixed constitution came into existence. We also know that Polybius thought that it was at its best at the time of the Hannibalic War[38] – which perhaps implies that it was no longer at its best in the mid-second century, when he was writing. If, however, the mixed constitution came into existence in 450, then between 751, the year Polybius gave for the foundation of the city, and 450 Rome presumably followed, somehow or other, the constitutional cycle as he describes it.

[33] See above, n.9.　　[34] Dion. Hal. *Ant. Rom.* i.6.　　[35] vi.11a.4.　　[36] Nicolet (1974) 211n.

[37] Cf. vi.11.1 with the note in Walbank, *Comm.* I, 674 and that of Weil (1977) 85, with the complementary note of Nicolet, ibid. p. 146.

[38] vi.51.5.

In fact, the events of early Rome can, with a little help, be fitted into that cycle, if we assume that Romulus was the original primitive monarch, Numa, who introduced many religious institutions at Rome, and perhaps the elder Tarquin or Servius Tullius were the good kings, Tarquinius Superbus the tyrant, the early republic the aristocracy and the second Decemvirate the oligarchy – after which the mixed constitution took over. ||

This seems a plausible scheme, in outline, but it leaves a good many problems and difficulties. For example, the conditions in which Romulus set up his monarchy are quite different from those which followed some natural cataclysm, as described in the cycle. What is more important, did the Roman constitution pass directly from oligarchy to a mixed form, avoiding democracy, in the year 450? This seems very unlikely, for it would run directly counter to Polybius' insistence that Rome acquired her mixed constitution by choosing the best course in a series of crises over a period of time. So should we perhaps think of Rome as taking on board, from the outset, first the aristocratic and later the democratic elements that eventually enabled it to enjoy a mixed constitution? That was the view of Fritz Taeger, who wrote a striking but harshly criticised book about Polybius' *archaeologia* in 1922.[39] In particular, he was attacked, a decade later, by Viktor Pöschl,[40] who rightly pointed out that he had loaded his case with some very unconvincing hypotheses on the extent to which we can recover Polybius' original argument from Diodorus, Dionysius and Cicero, all of whom he assumed to have drawn on Polybius. On the other hand, Pöschl misunderstands Taeger's argument at some points and, I would now argue, is wrong to reject it outright. For Taeger was certainly justified in trying to relate the development of Rome to the constitutional cycle: otherwise why should Polybius have included both a detailed account of that cycle and a sketch of early Roman history in Book VI? But before I take this argument any further, I must turn to an essential piece of evidence which is directly relevant to our problem.

VI

In 1821 Angelo Mai discovered the lacunose text of Cicero's *De re publica* on a palimpsest in the Vatican Library and it became immediately clear that for the earlier books of this work Cicero had drawn on Polybius; for he describes him there (speaking in the person of Scipio Aemilianus) as

---

[39] Taeger (1922).   [40] Pöschl (1936).

'our friend Polybius, who is unsurpassed in chronological accuracy'.[41]
This reference to Polybius suggested that Cicero had taken at least his
dates for the reigns of the kings from his work; but had he utilised this
for more than that? There is good reason to think that he had. As we
saw, Polybius interpreted a mixed constitution as one in which various
elements were balanced to create stability. Now Cicero says, in *De re
publica* ii.42, a passage in which he compares the Roman state at the time
of the kings to those of Sparta and Carthage, that the three elements of
kingship, aristocracy and democracy 'were mixed, but in such a way that
there was no proportion whatsoever' (*ita mixta . . . ut temperata nullo fuerint
modo*). In his scheme, apparently, the various elements were there from the
start, but they were properly || combined only with the acquisition of a
fully mixed constitution. May we then assume that Polybius had sketched
a similar development in Book VI? That is a question not easy to answer.
As Pöschl has shown, Cicero used other sources besides Polybius; and,
although Cicero's mixed constitution is 'properly combined' (*temperata*),
that combination is not achieved by the various elements in the state
exercising a check on each other, but by something far more reminiscent
of the *concordia ordinum*, Cicero's own ideal, in which those elements were
integrated under the guidance of the *optimates*. Furthermore, in Cicero's
dialogue C. Laelius is made to say[42] that the ideal state which Scipio is
describing is 'a new style of discussion (*ratio ad disputandum nova*), nowhere
employed in the writings of the Greeks', which certainly sounds like a
claim to originality. Laelius goes on to explain, however, that by this
he means that Scipio is not inventing an ideal state wholly in the air, *suo
arbitratu*, like Plato, nor yet discussing various types of state in the abstract,
like Plato's successors (i.e. Aristotle and Theophrastus). On the contary,
he is dealing with a real state, Rome, and assigning a rationale to its
development. But this is surely what Polybius was doing in the *archaeologia*.
So perhaps we should not take Cicero's claim to originality too seriously.
After all, we know that Cicero's normal practice in his philosophical
works was to draw extensively on Greek sources; and to claim originality
was a regular *topos*. I think we can therefore make cautious use of Cicero,
as indeed Pöschl admits, in our attempt to recover Polybius' *archaeologia*.
    In so doing we must, however, be clear about certain limitations im-
posed by an obvious divergence between Cicero's account and what we
know must have stood in Polybius. Cicero, for example, has nothing
corresponding to the passage at the beginning of the cycle, in which

[41] Cic. *De re pub*. ii.27.   [42] Ibid. ii.21.

Polybius discusses the earliest stages of human society after some great natural cataclysm, when a primitive horde, in fear, seeks the protection of a monarch, whose main characteristic is physical strength.[43] Indeed Cicero specifically refuses to go into the question of the origins of human society here,[44] though elsewhere[45] he makes clear that (unlike Polybius) he regards the earliest association of human beings in society as springing not from fear and a feeling of weakness, but rather, like Aristotle,[46] 'from a certain social spirit, which nature has implanted in man' (*non tam imbecillitas, quam naturalis quaedam hominum quasi congregatio*). Furthermore, he begins his account of his constitutional cycle, what he calls 'the orbit, whose natural motion and circuitous course you are to recognise' (*ille . . . orbis, || cuius naturalem motum atque circuitum a primo discite agnoscere*), only from the reign of Tarquinius Superbus, the tyrant.[47]

We must not, therefore, expect to find anything like a close reflection of Polybius in Cicero's *De re publica*. We can, however, as Pöschl argued, assume that, like Cicero, Polybius described a natural growth and blossoming of the state, which gradually, by way of the cycle, developed from the sequence of single constitutions to a more stable mixed constitution, and he will have traced that path through the history of early Rome, probably emphasising the critical occasions when Rome chose the right solution.

There are, however, still some unresolved difficulties. Are we, for instance, to assume that all three elements – the royal, the aristocratic and the popular – were present, in some form, at Rome from the outset, but not in due proportion? That is certainly the case in the scheme put forward in Cicero's *De re publica*. Or did society begin with a monarch and then move on first to aristocracy, while retaining a monarchic element, and then to the acquisition of the democratic element essential to the mixed constitution? The second alternative might seem to gain some support from a passage in Book VI,[48] where Polybius, describing the perversion of the aristocratic regime at the hands of the children of the original aristocrats, says that they had no experience of political equality and freedom of speech (πολιτικῆς ἰσότητος καὶ παρρησίας) Why not? Nicolet has argued that it is because political equality and freedom of speech are characteristics of all the three 'good' regimes, but *not* of their corrupt forms.[49] This, however, is an unsatisfactory explanation, since the second generation of aristocrats had been reared by their parents, under whom *ex hypothesi* these qualities did exist. I think we must rather assume that the second-generation aristocrats' ignorance of these two

---

[43] vi.5.4–9.　　[44] Cicero, *De re pub.* i.38.　　[45] Ibid. i.39.　　[46] Arist. *Pol.* i.2, 1253 a 1ff.
[47] Cicero, *De re pub.* ii.94.　　[48] vi.8.4.　　[49] Nicolet (1983b) 27.

virtues sprang from the fact that they only appear at that point within the constitutional cycle at which one achieves democracy or, in the case of Rome, the mixed constitution, which took its place.

This need not mean, of course, that *all* elements belonging to aristocracy and democracy only entered the cycle at the point at which those forms of government became dominant. That is clear when one bears in mind that Polybius prefers talking about specific state institutions – the consuls, the Senate and the people – rather than about political abstractions. These institutions were all there from the beginning of the republic (and in some form from the foundation of the city), though (as Cicero said) their powers were not proportionately mixed. What changes in the various stages of the cycle is the amount of influence each of them exercises. And it is on that that our characterisation of the state as a monarchy, an aristocracy or a democracy depends. ||

Indeed, as Nippel has shown (and as we have already seen),[50] the people plays a vital rôle from the beginning of the cycle, overthrowing each corrupt regime and replacing it by its 'good' successor. So what we should perhaps envisage Polybius as having described in the *archaeologia* is a developing society in which the various organs – magistrates (representing kingly power), leading citizens and the people in general – gradually, or in a series of political acts, some of them violent, assume new relations towards each other, which can be described as kingship, aristocracy and then, elsewhere, democracy but at Rome the mixed constitution.

VII

This hypothetical reconstitution of the *archaeologia* is to some extent confirmed by what happened after Rome acquired her mixed constitution. For clearly Polybius regarded this, not as a permanent solution to the problems inherent in the constitutional cycle, but merely as a kind of brake on movement. When, towards the end of Book VI, he draws a comparison between the two states locked in a conflict which was to decide the fate of the Mediterranean world, he points out that Carthage also had a mixed constitution[51] – as indeed Cato had recorded[52] – but that at the time of the Hannibalic War Carthage was worse (χείρων) and Rome better (ἀμείνων); and the reason for that was that at Carthage the populace (δῆμος) had acquired the chief voice in deliberation, whereas at Rome this was still under the control of the Senate. As we have already

---

[50] Nippel (1980).   [51] vi.51.1–8.   [52] *HRR* Cato, fg. 86.

seen, that was not, as Nicolet believes, because Rome was really an aristocracy, but because in a mixed constitution at its prime deliberation is
one of the prerogatives of the aristocratic element within the state, viz., at
Rome, the Senate. This tells us something about where Polybius wanted
to locate true power within a mixed constitution. It also opens up the
question of what would succeed that constitution. If the balance had
already slipped a little at Carthage, would this also happen at Rome?
And if it did, what would that mean?

Polybius answers that question in chapter 57, almost at the end of
Book VI; but he does not emphasise it, for his purpose in writing that
book was not to prophecy doom, but to explain Roman success. There
are, however, two passages in Book VI describing how states eventually
decline; for though it is true that his constitutional cycle logically has
no overall decline, but continues from good to bad and then, after a
revolution, to good again, in a circular movement, Polybius at the same
time tries to combine this with the 'natural', biological pattern of political
birth, growth, prime, decline and destruction. As he says,[53] || 'all existing
things are subject to decay, a proposition which scarcely requires proof,
since the inexorable course of nature (ἡ τῆς φύσεως ἀνάγκη) is sufficient
to force it upon us'. Seen in that perspective decline into ochlocracy
seems to bring the cycle to its end.

The first of these two passages dealing with decline is to be found at
vi.9.6–9, where Polybius sketches the last stage of the cycle, in which
democracy is corrupted and becomes mob-rule, declining eventually
into complete savagery from which the only escape is a new master. The
second is in vi.57, which describes the decline of a particular state, clearly
Rome, although Polybius, perhaps from embarrassment, nowhere refers
to it by name.

In the first of these passages the rich leaders of the state, who are
the grandsons of the democratic founders, come to despise equality and
free speech and bankrupt themselves by bribing the people to give them
powers which they cannot secure on their own merits. This inspires the
people with an appetite for financial hand-outs, and when their original
corruptors no longer have enough wealth to continue providing these,
they fall for the blandishments of a leader who is bold and ambitious, but
poor. So they have recourse to violence, institute massacres, banishments,
plunder and division of the land and end up with a new master and a
monarch (δεσπότην καὶ μόναρχον). This new master is probably the

[53] vi.57.1.

poor, ambitious man who has led them on to this. He is, as Nicolet rightly observes, a Greek tyrant. For this picture is entirely Greek and draws on Polybius' own experience of similar seizures of power in the Greek political life of the third and second centuries. It bears no relation to Rome.

Chapter 57, on the other hand, deals with the eventual decline of the mixed constitution at Rome. Although this, towards the end, bears some similarity to the process described in 9.6–9, it diverges from it in several essentials. That is, indeed, what we should expect, since it is describing a decline from a mixed constitution, not one from democracy, as is the case in the regular constitutional cycle. Decline begins when after many perils a state achieves 'supremacy and uncontested sovereignty' (ὑπεροχὴν καὶ δυναστείαν ἀδήριτον).[54] – an obvious reference to Rome. For this is a new feature, peculiar to Rome, and indeed the central theme of Polybius' *Histories*. It leads to great prosperity, an extravagant life-style and growing fierceness in competition for office; and it is this that will initiate the decline. The responsibility for this decline will rest with the people who, flattered by those seeking office, and resentful of greedy politicians, against whom they conceive some grievance, will eventually refuse to obey or even accept equality with their rulers (τοῖς προεστῶσιν) but will demand the greater share for themselves; and this will end in mob-rule.

Where does all this come from? The answer is simple. It exactly matches the situation described by Polybius, in a later book, as existing at Rome after 168. In the course of a digression in Book XXXI he gives a character-sketch of Scipio || Aemilianus, his friend and patron, in which he contrasts his behaviour with that of his contemporaries. In this passage he asserts that it was precisely from that date that vicious and extravagant behaviour became widespread at Rome, because 'since the fall of the Macedonian kingdom it appeared that Rome enjoyed undisputed dominion and because after the riches of Macedonia had been brought to Rome, there was a great display of wealth, both public and private'.[55] Scipio was exceptional in spending his time hunting when the other young men were busy in the forum occupied with legal cases and morning *salutationes*, in an attempt to win popular favour.[56] There can be little doubt that Polybius' prognostication of Roman decline draws directly on his perception of this situation at Rome[57] and not on the

---

[54] vi.57.5.　　　[55] xxxi.25.6–7.

[56] xxxi.29.8–12; for a recent discussion of this passage see Dana (1993).

[57] Polybius had detected the beginnings of this even earlier in the land-legislation of Flaminius (ii.21.8).

Greek parallels so evident in the description of the comparable stage in the constitutional cycle.

In a recent review[58] of the *Festschrift* for Zvi Yavetz in the *Journal of Roman Studies* the Oxford scholar Andrew Lintott rightly pointed out that the divergent route back into the constitutional cycle, which Polybius postulates here, logically suggests a similar divergent route away from the cycle in its early stages, in order to arrive at the mixed constitution. As we have seen, his suggestion was not wholly original, since something like it was outlined in Taeger's study of 1922. But both were, I think, on the right track.

VIII

If we look forward to the first century, we can find there many aspects of Roman political life, which seem to correspond with Polybius' account of what is in store for Rome. The exploitation of popular grievances by tribunes, the breakdown of public order at the time of Milo and Clodius, culminating in the burning of the Senate House, and finally the resolution of several decades of disorder and civil war with the setting up of the principate – all this can be pressed into a pattern not unlike the one Polybius describes. But such a comparison would be superficial and misleading. Polybius' strength was not as a prophet. His monarchic conclusion to the cycle comes from Greek political theory, not from a subtle || analysis of the situation in second-century Rome. The merits of Book VI lie elsewhere.

As Taeger long ago observed, this remarkable book represents the first sketch in the history of political philosophy known to us from antiquity, in which an author with practical political experience attempts to investigate and set out, free from utopias, the development of a particular state in a historical context. But one can, I think, go further. Polybius was an intelligent Greek, caught up in a daunting exile, in which personal privilege and racial subordination were uneasily combined. He was, however, unusually resilient in turning his misfortune to direct advantage. Instead of repining in exile, he set out to understand and to elucidate, primarily for his own countrymen, the phenomenon of a new world power. Book VI deserves our especial attention because it is there that he has attempted to assess the real significance of Rome by interpreting its past, its present state and its probable future fate against the background of ideas

---

[58] Lintott (1996).

bequeathed to him from Greek political thought. In this direct response to the problems raised by the Roman empire he was the first of a long line of Greeks, including such figures as Panaetius, Poseidonius, Dionysius of Halicarnassus, Diodorus, Plutarch and Aristides. His interpretation suffers from some obvious failings; but that is a useful reminder of how far we are all limited, perhaps irretrievably, by the cultural presuppositions among which we are born and brought up.

Transmission of Polybius

19

Polybius, Mr Dryden, and the Glorious Revolution*

Retirement is well known to be a time for making excursions. And though indeed we all know that Wilhelmina Jashemski has not retired in any real sense of the word (nor is likely to do so), nevertheless, as my contribution to her *Festschrift* I invite her to tear herself away from Pompeii (and from the Garden Library at Dumbarton Oaks) and to accompany me on a brief voyage of exploration into late seventeenth-century England, where I shall try to expose the connections between Polybius' fortunes, the career of Mr John Dryden, and the Glorious Revolution of 1688.

I

Already by the fifteenth century Polybius was known in England, where a Latin translation of his work is mentioned among the books in John Shirwood's library in 1471–2. [1] But until well into the eighteenth century only three English translations of the historian had appeared. In the first two of these Polybius was not well served. In 1568, under Elizabeth I, Christopher Watson of St John's College, Cambridge, produced a self-indulgent volume[2] in which, after inveighing against 'tearing time and blinde ignorance, capital foes to vertue and good literature', he printed an indifferent rendering of Book I and, for no very good reason, filled out the rest of the volume with an account of 'the Victorious Actes of King Henry Fift'. Watson had a nice turn of phrase to render Polybian sentiments, for example: 'Time is tickle, Chaunce is fickle, Man is brickle!' But his book offered little more than a taste to anyone who wanted to

---

* [[R.I. Curtis (ed.) *Studia Pompeiana et Classica in Honor of Wilhelmina F. Jashemski* 2: *Classica* (New Rochelle, NY 1989) 255–71]]

[1] Cf. Weiss (1957) 152; Momigliano (1974b) 370.

[2] *The Hystories of the most famous and worthy Chronographer Polybius: Discoursing of the warres betwixt the Romanes and Carthaginienses a riche and goodly Worke, containing holsome counsels and wonderfull devices against the incombrances of fickle Fortune, Englished by C. W.* London 1568.

read Polybius in the vernacular; and the accompanying poem by R. W. is dismal stuff.[3] ||

The next English translation was that of Edward Grimeston,[4] of which two printings appeared in 1634 in the reign of Charles I. As well as Books I–V, this contained the collection of extracts which, following Schweighaeuser, we now call the *Excerpta antiqua*. In his book Grimeston also included an English version of the 'Epistle to the French Nobility' with which L. Maigret had prefaced his French translation of Polybius, published by order of Anne de Montmorency, the Constable of France, in 1543;[5] this seven-page effusion contained a short account of Polybius and a petulant explanation of why the translator had not carried his work beyond Book VIII: it was because of a 'quartan ague' and irritation at the printer for his 'obstinacy in using a small character, for the sparing of paper distasted me'. Grimeston did better than Maigret, including all the *Excerpta antiqua* down to Book XVIII. But he had the misfortune to be away from London during the proof-reading and in consequence, after a self-depreciatory reference to his 'harsh and unpolished stile', he requests the reader to 'pardon the errors committed at the presse during my absence'; that here he speaks no more than the truth is confirmed in a Note from the Printer requesting 'charitable censure' for 'having but a young Corrector which took too much upon him'.

The third English translation of Polybius, which is the subject of this chapter, was that of Sir H[enry] S[heeres][6] and was published in the late

---

[3] 'If famous factes / or worthee actes / rejoice thy daunted minde / Polybius reede / Whereas in deede / Goode Physike shalt thou finde', and so on for five verses more.

[4] *The Histories of Polybius the Megalopolitan: The five first Bookes entire with all the parcels of the subsequent Bookes unto the eighteenth according to the Greeke original. Also the manner of the Romans encamping, extracted from the discription of Polybius. Translated into English by Edward Grimeston, Sergeant at Armes.* London 1634.

[5] Momigliano (1974a) 8.

[6] *The History of Polybius the Megalopolitan containing a General Account of the Transactions of the World and Principally of the Roman People during the First and Second Punick Wars, etc. Translated by Sir H. S. to which is added, a Character of Polybius and his Writings: by Mr. Dryden.* London 1693. Despite the date printed here, references in Motteux's *Gentleman's Journal* show the book to have been published towards the end of 1692; cf. *The Critical and Miscellaneous Prose Writings of John Dryden*, ed. Ed. Malone, 4 vols. (London 1800), I, 221; III, 229. The author's name is variously spelt. According to Malone, ibid. I, 253, it was an eighteenth-century custom often to corrupt personal surnames by adding a superfluous final *s*. Sheeres signed himself 'H. Shere' and that is how Etherege referred to him. But Pepys, who knew him intimately, calls him 'Sheres'. A reprint of an Elizabethan pamphlet on resuscitating Dover harbour (below, n. 10) calls him 'Sheers'; and in the article by J. H. O. (the Rev. Canon Overton) in the *Dictionary of National Biography* (Rpt. Oxford 1963–4), s.v. Sheeres, hereinafter referred to as *DNB*, he is 'Sheeres', the form I have adopted. However spelt, 'Sheeres' is what most people called him (so Malone, above). See, correcting Malone from MS notes left by him in a copy of his own work now in the Bodleian Library, Oxford, J. M. Osborn, *John Dryden: Some Biographical Facts and Problems*[2] (New York 1965) 64.

months of 1692, in two volumes, by Samuel Briscoe, 'over against Wills Coffee-House, in Covent Garden'. It contained only Books I–V, though a second edition in 1698 included a third volume, in which the *Excerpta antiqua* from Books VI and VII were translated 'by another hand'. This was perhaps the fruit of Briscoe's enterprise and apparently Sheeres was not involved. Both editions contained, besides Sheeres' Preface, a 'Character' of Polybius by Mr Dryden, of which I shall say something shortly.[7]

II

First, however, a word about Sheeres himself. As Dryden points out, Sheeres should have been just the person to translate Polybius, for he was a man of whom the historian himself would have thoroughly approved.[8] A military engineer by profession, he had accompanied Edward Montague, the First Earl of Sandwich, to Spain in a diplomatic capacity in 1660. Between 1667 and 1669 he is to be found enjoying friendly social and professional relations with Samuel Pepys, who describes him as 'a good engenious man, but doth talk a little too much of his travels' – mainly about Spain, as Pepys several times later on remarks.[9] But very soon the excessively suspicious Pepys began to imagine that Sheeres was making too favourable an impression on || Mrs Pepys and the friendship cooled somewhat. In May 1669 Sheeres went out to an appointment in Tangiers, then under the British flag. It was not his first visit, for already in January of that year Pepys had paid him £100 for a drawing of the fortifications of the port. Sheeres was in Tangiers, off and on, from 1669 to 1683, when Pepys went out there in connection with the demolition of the mole (originally constructed by Sheeres) as a preliminary to evacuating the place, and in his Tangiers papers he

---

[7] Sheeres' two volumes are no. 138 (and the 1698 edition, no. 138b) in H. Macdonald, *John Dryden: a Bibliography of Early Editions and Drydeniana* (Oxford 1939). Dryden's 'Character' was reprinted by Ed. Malone in 1800 (above n.6, III, 229–68) and again in Dryden's *Collected Works*, ed. W. Scott, 18 vols. (London 1808; revised edition by G. Saintsbury, London 1893) XVIII, 21–53. Since the introductory section of Sheeres' own volume, containing the 'Character' and Sheeres' Preface, is unpaginated, I quote throughout from the Scott–Saintsbury reprint (hereafter Scott–Saintsbury).

[8] On Sheeres see E. I. Carlyle in the *DNB* (above n.6), Pepys' *Diary* between 1667 and 1669, Pepys' *The Tangiers Papers, Diary of 1683*, collected in *The Tangiers Papers of Samuel Pepys*, ed. Edwin Chappell (London 1935). For his conversation with Charles II see the essay quoted below, n.10.

[9] See extracts under 27 Sept. and 21 Dec. 1667 and 5 Apr. 1669. 'Ingenious' is the adjective which Dryden also uses of Sheeres, who informed him about the behaviour of bees about to swarm, when observed in a glass hive; see *The Works of Virgil containing his Pastoral, Georgics and Aeneis. Translated into English verse by Mr. Dryden* (London 1697) 627 (note on G. 4.27).

comments on Sheeres' efficiency compared with that of most of the personnel stationed there. Sheeres had not spent the fourteen years since 1669 uninterruptedly in Tangiers, for he records a conversation which he had had with Charles II in 1682,[10] in which he unsuccessfully advocated the development of the port of Dover. On his return from blowing up the mole at Tangiers, Sheeres joined Pepys in the successful defence of George Legge, Baron Dartmouth, who had been in command of the operation, against charges of peculation. The next year he took part in the resistance to Monmouth's rebellion at Sedgemoor, in recognition of which he was knighted and made surveyor of ordnance. We gain a glimpse of the circles in which he moved in a letter from the playwright Sir George Etherege, who had been sent by James II to pursue a scandalous career as English Plenipotentiary to Ratisbon (Regensburg), and who writes to John Dryden in 1686 or 1687: 'Pray tell Sir Henry Shere his honesty and good understanding have made me love him ever since I knew him: if we meet in England again, he may find the gravity of this place has fitted me for his Spanish humour.' Dryden's uncle, John Creed, was Secretary to the Tangiers Commission and Dartmouth, Etherege, Dryden and Sheeres were all linked together by their devotion to the Stuart cause. The Glorious Revolution of 1688 was, therefore, a disaster to all these men in varying degrees.

Sheeres adjusted to the new regime, but was twice arrested for conspiring in the interests of James II (in June 1690 and March 1695–6); and for some time his position was precarious. Like Dryden, whose career will occupy us shortly, he seems to have turned to his pen as a consolation in time of trouble – and as a possible source of income. Thus in 1690 he wrote a second prologue for Dryden's *Don Sebastian*; and in 1692 he published his translation of Polybius. It was his first substantial work and was followed by an *Essay on the certainty and causes of the earth's motion* (1698) and *A discourse on the Mediterranean Sea and the Streights of Gibraltar* (1703), while in 1700 and 1701 he reprinted two Elizabethan pamphlets containing proposals for the development of seaports in Kent. All these works were directly related to his military and naval experience (for before

---

[10] Sir Henry Sheers, *An essay on ways and means to maintain the Honour and Safety of England, to increase trade, merchandize, navigation . . . and seamen in war or peace: written by Sir W. Raleigh* (London 1701); this is a reprint of a memorial to Queen Elizabeth I advocating the development of Dover Harbour 'either by Sir W. Raleigh or Sir D. Diggs' (the catalogue in the Cambridge University Library states that the Memorial was actually written by T. Digges). Sheeres adds some 'useful remarks . . . on our ports and harbours, principally in Kent'; the account of his conversation with Charles II, rendered fruitless, he alleges, through the machinations of the French Ambassador (who, rather extraordinarily, eavesdropped on the conversation), is recorded on pages 9–15.

Pepys' great work at the Admiralty these two branches of the services were || not always clearly separated): they are precisely the kind of *opera minora* Polybius had himself written[11] and would have appreciated. Later Sheeres contributed to a translation of Lucian, for which Dryden wrote an introduction (published after Dryden's death in 1711), and in 1696 he had a poem prefixed to Southern's famous *Oroonoko*.

In the first part of the Preface to his translation of Polybius Sheeres accounts for his undertaking as having been prompted by a 'Great Man', his 'Friend', now dead after being driven from public life through slander and persecution. This must be Baron Dartmouth, who was in charge at Tangiers in 1683 and later commanded James II's fleet against William of Orange, for after the Revolution he had been deprived of his offices and sent to the Tower, where he had died in 1691, the year before Sheeres' translation of Polybius was published. Polybius' work was likely for many reasons to have commended itself to both Sheeres and Dartmouth; but a further point likely to enlist their sympathy was the coincidence that, like both of them, Polybius himself had suffered a severe blow from Fortune at the height of his career. After the reference to Dartmouth, the rest of Sheeres' Preface is devoted to a disingenuous apology for the shortcomings of his work[12] – this seems to have been a *communis locus* in such introductions[13] – balanced by a claim to be a 'Man of the World, of Business, Science and Conversation', the sort of man in short who alone possesses the qualities a translator needs, since the art of translation – especially the translation of a work like that of Polybius – lies outside the ability of 'mere Scholars and book-learned Men'. If, however (Sheeres continues), he should fail in his undertaking, he will have little cause of complaint, since it has been embarked on 'rather as a Diversion than a Task, helping me to while away a few long winter Hours'. Finally, after a reference to having spent 'near thirty Years in Publick Trusts; wherein I laboured and wasted my Youth and the Vigour of my Days, more to the Service of my Country and the impairment of my health than the improvement of my Fortune, having stood the mark of Envy, Slander

---

[11] Polybius wrote on *Tactics*, the *Numantine War*, and *On the habitability of the Equatorial Region*; but his *Histories* contain substantial digressions on the Bosphorus area (iv.39–85), on fire-signalling (x.43–7), on calculating the area of a city (ix.26a), or the height of a wall (ix.19.5–9) and on geographical matters generally (Book xxxiv). As an Arcadian his interests were of course military rather than naval.

[12] 'I frankly, first, confess that I had no warrant for my depth of learning, whereof to make Ostentation, and wherein indeed, he who most abounds, ever finds least cause of boasting.' This is of course an ambiguous disclaimer.

[13] See, for example, Grimeston's apology for his style (above, n.4), p. 2.

and hard Usage', he ends his remarks with a short lecture on Discipline which affords the reader little compensation for the complete absence of any information about what text he has used or any explanation of why, unlike Grimeston, he has translated only the first five books.

Sir Walter Scott[14] regarded Sheeres' translation as worthless, but this is over harsh. True, it misses many points, often important ones,[15] and it is frequently more of a paraphrase than a genuine translation. But it is well written, readable, and serviceable and no doubt fulfilled its purpose in introducing Polybius to the wider reading public which was beginning to appear in England in the last years of the || seventeenth century. To us, however, the main interest of his two volumes lies less in his text than in Dryden's 'Character of Polybius and his Writings' which introduced it, preceding Sheeres' own Preface.[16]

III

Neither Dryden nor Sheeres seems to have had a very clear idea of what the other was going to say in their respective introductions. Dryden[17] does not know whether the fragments of the books following V are to be translated in a later impression (as indeed was partly done, though not by Sheeres): 'He, I suppose, will acquaint you with his purpose in the prefix before *Polybius*'; this Sheeres did not do. And when Sheeres, having perhaps glanced at Casaubon,[18] is moved to a brief defence of Polybius against the charge of irreligion, he is clearly quite unaware that Dryden[19] is going to dismiss any such defence with the utmost severity. But whether the invitation to write the 'Character' came direct from Sheeres or (as seems perhaps more likely) was arranged by the publisher, Dryden had several good reasons for accepting.

[14] Scott–Saintsbury xviii, 21.

[15] For example, in i. 1.5 πῶς καὶ τίνι γένει πολιτείας is translated 'by what wonderful means and force of Conduct', thus missing the reference forward to Book VI; in 1.5.3 Sheeres completely misunderstands Polybius' statement that he must state the causes of the Roman crossing into Sicily without further comment, otherwise we shall become involved in a recession of cause leading to cause. And to take a matter in which Sheeres claimed special competence (i.73.2), where Polybius speaks of triremes, penteconters and *akontia*, Sheeres is content with 'their decay'd Ships': he does the same thing at i.20.14.

[16] Dryden had had Sheeres' translation in his hands for several months 'to review the English and Correct what I found amiss' (Scott–Saintsbury xviii, 23); there is no reason to question Dryden's statement that this task 'only cost me the dash of a pen in some few places, and those of very small importance'. Despite his reference to the 'care and diligence and exactness' of the translation, it seems likely that Dryden's main concern was with style rather than content.

[17] Scott–Saintsbury xviii, 50.   [18] See below, pp. 304–9.

[19] Scott–Saintsbury xviii, 47–8; below, p. 307.

In the first place there was his friendship with Sheeres, cemented by their common plight and partial disgrace following the triumph of William of Orange in 1688. Dryden's goodwill towards Sheeres is evident in the introduction to the translation of Lucian by various hands – though published after Dryden's death it was probably written in 1696[20] – in which he counts Sheeres (one of the translators) among 'the finer spirits of the age'. Then there was Dryden's genuine admiration for Polybius; for there seems no reason to question his statement[21] that he had read the historian 'with the pleasure of a boy before I was ten years of age; and even then had some dark notion of the prudence with which he conducted his design'.[22] Even at that early age Polybius' vivid power of description had impressed him; but it was only later that he came to a full appreciation of Polybius' political acumen. Since Dryden was ten years old in 1641, he evidently read Polybius in Grimeston's translation, which had appeared in 1634.

At this point we should note a curious coincidence. Only a few months before the appearance of Sheeres' translation, Dryden had produced a play entitled *Cleomenes*,[23] a romantic tragedy, set in Alexandria and based on the last months of Cleomenes III of Sparta, who was in exile there. This play dealt with events which are briefly touched on in Polybius, Book V; and when in his introduction he recounts the later fate of Ptolemy's mistress Agathoclea (in the play she is called Cassandra), basing his narrative on Polybius, Dryden mentions that 'this author is also made English and will shortly be published for the common benefit'.[24] Dryden's main source for the || *Cleomenes* was not, however, Polybius, but Plutarch's *Life* of that king, Creech's translation of which Dryden incorporated in the volume containing the published version of the play;[25]

---

[20] Scott–Saintsbury xviii, 78.   [21] Scott–Saintsbury xviii, 32.

[22] Dryden's remarks suggest an experience remarkably similar to that described by Gaetano De Sanctis, two and a half centuries later: 'trovai una traduzione di Polibio, e anche qui' (sc. after reading Thucydides) 'fermò la mia attenzione e m'indusse, per intendere e per giudicare, a sforzi superiori alla mia intelligenza di fanciullo la esposizione ragionata delle cause della seconda guerra punica, e m'impressionò poi incredibilmente il lucido e drammatico racconto dell'invasione d'Annibale'. (De Sanctis (1970) 31–2). [See below, ch.20, 310.]

[23] Scott–Saintsbury viii, 203–364. In this play, the last act of which was written by Southern, owing to Dryden's being ill, Agathoclea, the mistress of Ptolemy IV, has been changed into Cassandra, and Nicagoras, who contributed to Cleomenes' downfall, into Coenus, both for euphony.

[24] Scott–Saintsbury viii, 226–7. At the time Dryden still had Sheeres' manuscript in his possession. We read in Motteux's *Gentleman's Journal* (April 1692) that 'Mr. Dryden did me the favour to show [Polybius] to me in Manuscript.'

[25] The five volumes of Plutarch's *Lives* in English had been published by Jacob Tonson in 1683–6, with a dedicatory epistle by Dryden to the Duke of Ormond; various translators shared the task.

and in fact Polybius' account of Agathoclea's death was not contained in any of the books translated by Sheeres. Furthermore, in his introduction to the *Cleomenes* Dryden insists that he had planned it seven or eight years before it was actually produced, a statement which, it is true, must be treated with some suspicion since it has the palpable purpose of setting the origins of the play before the overthrow of James II in 1688. *Cleomenes* had run into trouble and its first performance had to be postponed from April 9th to around April 16th, when it appeared only as a result of the intercession of Rochester with the Lord Chamberlain. In fact, a play by a Stuart supporter,[26] which had as its theme the attempt of an exiled king to obtain foreign help to recover his throne, was likely to alarm the government and certainly upset Queen Mary (in the absence of William, her husband).[27] So Dryden had every reason to date the play's origins to a time when its theme could have had no political relevance. Nevertheless, Plutarch's *Life*, not Polybius, was undoubtedly the main source of the play; and though Dryden is known to have had Sheeres' manuscript in his hands for some time,[28] the production of the *Cleomenes* about the same time as the publication of Sheeres' translation of Polybius must be adjudged coincidental.

IV

Dryden's defence of his *Cleomenes* is, however, a pointer to a third and certainly no less important reason for his consenting to write the 'Character of Polybius' for Sheeres' book: to put it briefly, he was hard up. Like Sheeres, and other supporters of the Stuarts such as Etherege (who had accompanied James to Paris and died there)[29] and Lord Dartmouth, Dryden had found himself in disgrace on the accession of William and Mary. As a Catholic convert and a notable Tory pamphleteer, he had been deprived of his post as Poet Laureate and Historiographer-royal and of the £300 per annum which it brought him in (when indeed he received payment, which was not regularly).[30] His courageous and

---

[26] Dryden had already given offence by his prologue to *The Prophetess*.

[27] See Scott–Saintsbury VIII, 209.   [28] Above, nn. 16 and 24.

[29] The story that he had fallen down a staircase-well and killed himself while drunk at Ratisbon (so A. Beljame, *Men of Letters and the English Public in the Eighteenth Century, 1660–1744, Dryden, Addison, Pope*, ed. Bonamy Dobrée, tr. E. O. Lorimer [London 1948] 197, n.225) may be a 'fine text for a sermon' (Beljame), but appears to be without foundation. See Leslie Stephen, *DNB*, s.v. Etherege, Sir George (above, n.6). A plaque still marks the house in Regensburg, which was the scene of Etherege's escapades there.

[30] He still had some income from estates in Northamptonshire and Wiltshire; cf. G. R. Noyes in his introduction to Dryden's *Poetical Works*[2] (Boston 1950) lvii–lviii. See ibid p. 196 for a letter written by Dryden to the Treasury when his salary was four years in arrears!

eventually highly successful reaction to this *débâcle* was in fact to prove an important element in the writing of a new chapter in the social history of English literature. Down to 1688 creative writing depended ultimately on patronage. For a playwright the 'public' was the court; but published plays and other writings too were normally dedicated to some rich patron, who was expected to repay the compliment in a practical way. Had Sheeres embarked on his translation of Polybius under James II, there can be little doubt || that it would have been dedicated to Lord Dartmouth as his patron; but by 1692 Dartmouth was already dead and disgraced.[31] After 1688, moreover, such patronage was not easily available for men out of favour, and Dryden resolved to set his work on a new economic basis by turning to the general public for substantial sales. His first efforts took him up a blind alley. Between 1689 and 1693 he produced five plays, including the *Cleomenes*; but his type of play had fallen out of fashion and the financial results were meagre, and so he turned to another outlet – translations of the classics, to be published by his farsighted and enterprising publisher, Jacob Tonson. Already before the Revolution the two men had been concerned in a joint venture which pointed a possible way forward. In 1684 they had brought out what became known as 'Dryden's' or 'Tonson's' *Miscellany*, a collection of translations, and the sales had encouraged the production of a second volume in 1685 (*Silvae*). In the very year of the Revolution Tonson had produced on a subscription basis what was to be the first really popular edition of Milton's *Paradise Lost* and this edition proved a significant step towards catering for the growing reading public which was now beginning to emerge not only in London but also in the provincial towns of England. It was to this public that Dryden now turned. In close cooperation with Tonson he produced his Juvenal and Persius in 1692. In 1693 they brought out a third *Miscellany*, *Examen Poeticum*, containing selections from Ovid, Homer, and various other writers. And in 1697 there came his famous Virgil, financed (like the *Paradise Lost* of 1688) by subscription. The rewards created a sensation. Dryden is supposed to have netted £1400 from this enterprise – wealth which became almost proverbial. Thus Addison,[32] when he wished to emphasise the gains made by a famous astrologer, who merely put up a sign inscribed:

> Within this place
> Lives Dr. Case,

---

[31] Above, p. 299.
[32] *Tatler* (London 1822), no. 240 (21 Oct. 1710); quoted by Keith Thomas, *Religion and the Decline of Magic* (London 1971) 381.

remarked that 'he is said to have got more by this distich than Mr. Dryden did by all his works'.

But in 1692 this was all in the future. At that time Dryden was glad to earn £5 (later raised to £10) for writing a prologue to a play.[33] And the 'Character of Polybius' for Sheeres' translation was a much longer job than the writing of a prologue. It seems, indeed, not unlikely that the whole enterprise, with Sheeres' translation and Dryden's introduction, was set up on the initiative of Samuel Briscoe, perhaps taking a tip from the success of Jacob Tonson's publications. If so, Sheeres' unwillingness to do more than Books I–V may explain the third volume 'by another hand' in 1698 and Dryden's uncertainty on the matter. Briscoe's initiative would also account for the apparent || isolation in which Sheeres and Dryden wrote their respective Preface and 'Character'.

v

The 'Character' is a robust and lively essay: Dryden of course wrote excellently. But it does not contain much original work and he admits as much. As Saintsbury observed,[34] Dryden 'has incurred with his usual freedom and acknowledged with his usual frankness obligations to Latin and French predecessors'. The French creditor is the Abbé Pichon in his preface to the recently published Dauphin *Tacitus* (1682);[35] the Latin source is Casaubon, whose dedication to Henry IV of France in his edition of 1609 Dryden probably read in Gronovius' edition of Polybius (1670), in which it was reprinted.[36]

Dryden openly reproduces much of Casaubon's argument, frequently translating his Latin into graceful English *verbatim*, but using good judgement in omitting material likely to puzzle the English reader (and especially a reader who was only to be given Books I–V without the *Excerpta antiqua*). He has not always understood Casaubon fully and one has the impression of a skilful writer doing a rather slipshod job. For example, he confuses Lycortas, Polybius' father, with Lydiades, the former

---

[33] Beljame, *Men of Letters* (above, n. 29) 194.   [34] Scott–Saintsbury XVIII, 22.

[35] C.(sic!) *Cornelii Taciti Opera interpretatione perpetua et notis illustravit Julianus Pichon Abbas iussu Christianissimi Regis in usum Serenissimi Delphini.* 4. vols. Parisiis 1682–7.

[36] *Polybii Lycortae f. Megalopolitani Historiarum Libri qui supersunt.* rec. I. Gronovius. 3 vols. (Amsterdam 1670). Casaubon's dedication is in III, 3–69 (the pagination starts again after the index, which ends at p. 1816). It is also printed in Ernesti's edition Ἱστοριῶν τὰ σωζόμενα (Leipzig 1763–4) III, 603–65), from which I shall quote, as being more easily accessible than that of Gronovius. Casaubon had settled in England in 1610 as a virtual exile from Catholic France, once Henry IV was dead; but his edition of Polybius with a translation appeared the previous year. A fragmentary commentary appeared only posthumously in 1617.

tyrant of Megalopolis, who laid down his autocratic power to become an Achaean statesman;[37] and he believes Constantine VII Porphyrogenitus to be Constantine the Great, whom furthermore he regards as British – perhaps because his father Constantius died at York – and remarks: 'I congratulate my country that a Prince of our Extraction (as was *Constantine*) has the honour of obliging the Christian World, by these reminders of our great Historian.'[38] 'These reminders' were the *Excerpta de legationibus*, which formed two of the sections of the excerpts from a selection of Greek historians made on the instructions of Constantine VII, though scarcely (as Dryden following Casaubon asserts) 'on the consideration of Brutus' who had spent the eve of the battle of Pharsalus working on an epitome of Polybius.[39] The *Excerpta de legationibus* had been included in Casaubon's edition of 1609 and they were also printed in that of Gronovius; but Dryden can hardly have read them with care since he is under the strange delusion that they are an account of Polybius' own 'Negotiations, when he was sent Ambassador from his own Countrymen, the Commonwealth of the Achians, or afterwards was employed by the Romans, on their business with other Nations'.[40] This was a serious mistake; but Dryden may perhaps be forgiven for taking over Casaubon's romantic notion that Brutus' epitome formed the basis of the *Excerpta antiqua*.[41] There are other, similar, errors. For example, Dryden incorrectly attributes to Casaubon || the assertion (which is untrue) that Polybius' virtue led to his 'exaltation to greater Dignities than those which he had lost' (i.e. when he was exiled to Italy);[42] and makes Aratus Polybius' contemporary, though Casaubon knew and said that he had lived 'paullo ante huius aetatem'.[43]

Given the closeness with which Dryden follows Casaubon, it was perhaps inevitable that he should reckon Polybius' importance primarily in terms of diplomacy and military skill; as we have just seen, he believed the *Excerpta de legationibus* to be examples of Polybius' expertise in the former. And indeed, though the fragments of Book VI had been translated by Grimeston and were to be included in the third volume added to the Sheeres reprint of 1698, the emphasis on Polybius as a master of

---

37 Scott–Saintsbury xvIII, 29.   38 Scott–Saintsbury xvIII, 32.
39 Plut. *Brut.* 4.8; cf. Casaubon in Ernesti (above, n. 36) III, 622; Dryden in Scott–Saintsbury xvIII, 32.
40 Scott–Saintsbury xvIII, 28. The notion that the Romans employed Polybius as a *legatus* shows a remarkable failure to comprehend Roman diplomatic practice.
41 Scott–Saintsbury xvIII, 50; cf. Casaubon in Ernesti (above, n. 36), III, 631 (though he shows greater caution than Dryden).
42 Scott–Saintsbury xvIII, 34.
43 Scott–Saintsbury xvIII, 40; Casaubon in Ernesti (above, n. 36) III, 632.

political theory and on the mixed constitution was in the main a development of the early eighteenth century.[44] However, Dryden, here turning to Pichon,[45] goes beyond Casaubon in stressing Polybius' genius in predicting 'from Natural Causes those events, which must naturally proceed from them' and so foretelling the evolution of Rome towards monarchy – a clear reference to the *anacyclosis*, or cycle of constitutions, described in Book VI.[46] And for this development Dryden holds Scipio Aemilianus responsible, in that he obtained the consulship before the proper age, assembled in his own person the power of the Senate and then put it at the disposition of the soldiery. This reference to Scipio is not in Pichon, but appears to be Dryden's own addition – a perceptive, if somewhat exaggerated interpretation of Scipio's career, since although his 'company of Friends'[47] carried implications for the future, it had good republican precedents. Altogether it seems unjust to hold Aemilianus responsible for what is really a post-Marian phenomenon.[48]

The other subject on which Dryden goes his own way is one that was bound to arouse interest in the seventeeth century – Polybius' attitude to religion. In religion Dryden and Casaubon were poles apart. The latter, a Calvinist by upbringing, had gradually moved over to what one might call an Anglo-Catholic position – Catholicism without the Pope – so much so that on the death of Henry IV he had migrated permanently to England. Dryden, after defending the Anglican position in his *Religio Laici*, had incurred much criticism and raised many doubts as to his sincerity by going over to the Roman Catholic faith on the accession of James II. But the issue affecting Polybius was not one in which these doctrinal differences played any direct part. Here the question was, simply: was, or was not, Polybius a religious man? This was already a matter of learned dispute when Casaubon composed his dedication, for his defence of Polybius is directed against a charge of irreligion made by an unnamed predecessor whom he describes as 'male feriatus politicus et Theologaster || omnis humanitatis imperitissimus' ('an unseasonably idle politician and inflated theologian wholly devoid of all humanity'). Though supported with much rhetoric, Casaubon's arguments are feeble.[49] Polybius, he says, claimed piety as the chief glory of Arcadia;[50] he condemned the

---

[44] On this see Momigliano (1974b) 371.

[45] Pichon, *Taciti Opera* (above, n. 35); Pichon's preface is not paginated.

[46] Scott–Saintsbury XVIII, 48.

[47] Cf. App. *Hisp.* 84: ἴλη φίλων; see Astin (1967) 136, n. 2, on this unit.

[48] In terms of modern controversy Dryden's view of Scipio is closer to that of Astin ((1967) 242–4, 288–93) than that of Scullard ((1960) 59–74), who saw Scipio as a defender of the mixed constitution.

[49] Casaubon in Ernesti (above, n. 36) III, 639–40.   [50] Polyb. iv. 20.1

sacking of holy places as the worst form of outrage;[51] he praised the rebuilding of temples after a war was over;[52] and he regarded addiction to *deisidaimonia* as the foundation of Roman greatness.[53] But basically the argument is made to rest on a passage from the *Suda*,[54] which Casaubon interpreted to mean that Polybius gave his assent to the Christian view that God governs all the affairs of the world. In fact Büttner-Wobst rightly rejects this passage in the *Suda* as representing a fragment of Polybius; its final words, καὶ Πολύβιός φησι, do not mean 'and this is the view of Polybius too' (as Casaubon assumes), but simply 'and Polybius says', with the likelihood that they introduced a passage from Polybius, which has since dropped out of the text. That Polybius could have endorsed the view which precedes the mention of his name is highly unlikely, and nothing is to be built on this fragment from the *Suda*. Modern discussions of Polybius' religious views rightly ignore it.[55]

Dryden had little patience for Casaubon's naive and enthusiastic defence of Polybius as a proto-Christian. Polybius, he says, did not believe in Providence. When he speaks of Providence or of any Divine Admonition, he is as much in jest, as when he speaks of Fortune: 'tis all to the capacity of the Vulgar. Prudence was the only divinity which he worshipp'd; and the possession of Vertue the only end which he propos'd'.[56] And he dismisses Casaubon's rhetorical claims for Polybius with the down-to-earth argument that in any case 'to believe false Gods and to believe none, are Errors of the same importance'; lacking Revelation, Polybius had gone as far as he humanly could![57] This bluff reasoning, which would treat all who lived before the Christian era as being as near to atheists as made no difference, clearly oversimplifies a complex issue and certainly takes no account of Polybius' notion of *Tyche* as the power directing the rise of Rome to world domination. It also suggests that Dryden was more

---

[51] Polyb. iv.62.1, 67.3; v.9–12.   [52] Polyb. v.106.2.   [53] Polyb. vi.56.6.

[54] Polyb. fg. 83b Büttner-Wobst = *Suda* 1234 (Adler): Τύχη. οἱ δὲ χριστιανοὶ Θεὸν ὁμολογοῦμεν διοικεῖν τὰ πάντα. καὶ Πολύβιός φησι. Schweighaeuser (1789–95) v.99, fg. 131, followed by Bernhardy, *Suidas* II. 1853, believes the last three words to refer to Polyb. fg. 83 Büttner-Wobst = *Suda* 1232 (cf. 872) Adler = Schweighaeuser (1789–95) v.99, fg. 130, an extract from Polybius on the role of *Tyche*. This passage has been dubiously transmitted and both Hultsch and Büttner-Wobst offer emendations which are far from convincing. But, whatever the exact wording of fg. 83, it clearly opposes the attribution to *Tyche* of events for which men (οἱ χειρίζοντες τὰς πράξεις 'those controlling events') are responsible, and this has nothing to do with the argument in fg. 83b that God controls all that happens. Moreover, the words καὶ Πολύβιός φησι look more like the introduction of a fresh and different view (which has fallen out); they do not support Casaubon's translation 'idque etiam Polybius dicit' ('and Polybius too says this'), for the *Suda* has nothing in the Greek corresponding to the words *id* and *etiam*.

[55] See, for example, Alvarez de Miranda (1956); Pédech (1965); (1964) 397, n.296; Walbank (1972a) 28 n.143; 59–65.

[56] Scott-Saintsbury XVIII, 47.   [57] Scott-Saintsbury XVIII, 48.

critical of non-Christian superstitions than he in fact was. This is also apparent in another context.

Casaubon,[58] praising Polybius' rejection of all *paradoxologia*, asks the rhetorical question: 'Quis nescit, antiqua paganorum miracula meras ut plurimum fuisse daemonum illusiones et humanarum mentium ludibria?, ('Who is not aware that the ancient miracles of the pagans were usually nothing but devilish illusions and a mockery of human minds?') But Dryden goes further,[59] attacking miracles generally and drawing a contemporary parallel[60] between Livy's prodigies and 'our prognosticating Almanacks' which 'almost always fail in their Events'. From this one would assume that Dryden was a sceptic about astrology; but this is not so. In fact he remained a convinced believer in the pseudo-science throughout his life.[61] His expression of || contempt for the 'Almanacks' in this passage is, therefore, disingenuous or refers merely to the slapdash methods of those putting them out (or to their ignorance) and not to the 'science' on which they were supposed to be based. Neither Casaubon nor Dryden expressly mentions Christian miracles, though Casaubon's use of the word *paganorum* suggests that he would draw a distinction here – a distinction to which Dryden would of course have subscribed.

Finally, in taking up the traditional comparison of Polybius with Tacitus – it is in Pichon as well as in Casaubon – Dryden shows some originality, though indeed part of his criticism of Casaubon for denigrating the Roman historian in order to extol the Greek is also to be found in Pichon, who exclaims:[62] 'Nec audiendus, imo despiciendus vir ille, licet eximie doctus, qui amore et admiratione Polybii, quem Latine verterat, aestuans, longe infra despicit Tacitum nostrum, imo et vituperat; quia nempe non noverat satis.' ('We should not listen to, nay we should despise that man, uncommonly learned though he is, who through his passionate love and admiration for Polybius, whom he had translated, looks down on our Tacitus as far inferior and even disparages him – undoubtedly

[58] In Ernesti (above, n. 36) III, 635.   [59] Scott–Saintsbury XVIII, 43–4.

[60] Scott–Saintsbury XVIII, 44.

[61] See J. Aubrey, *Brief Lives*, ed. O. L. Dick (London 1938), introduction pp. civ-cv, where Dick quotes Malone for Dryden's belief in this pseudo-science. See also Scott–Saintsbury XVIII, 134, for a letter written by Dryden to his two sons at Rome in 1697: 'towards the latter end of this month Charles will begin to recover his perfect health, according to his nativity, which, casting it myself, I am sure is true; and all things hitherto have happened according to the very time I have predicted them'. This could, I suppose, be said simply to encourage the sick boy, but it certainly reads like the assertion of a man who believed what he was writing and carries far greater conviction than the comment published the very same year in the 'Life of Virgil' with which he prefaced his translation of the poet (above n. 9): 'if there be anything in that Art, which I can hardly believe' – a saving clause added to a context which suggests the opposite of disbelief.

[62] Pichon, *Taciti Opera* (above, n. 35), *praefatio*.

because he has an inadequate knowledge of him.') But Dryden does not simply reject Casaubon's putting down of Tacitus. He shows himself to be perceptive of Tacitus' real purpose as a writer expressing *indignatio* against tryanny and not merely as one furnishing deplorable examples for like-minded contemporary rulers to copy, as Casaubon had some-what insensitively suggested. However, the whole issue of Tacitus versus Polybius was really *crambe repetita* by Dryden's time and a hang-over from debates popular around the end of the sixteenth century.[63] After saying that he will not discuss the matter, Dryden in fact does so and ends his treatment with the rather flaccid conclusion that Tacitus was more useful to those living under a monarchy, Polybius to those in a republic.[64]

VI

Dryden's 'Character of Polybius' is not of great literary or historical im-portance and in his vast and prolific output it is easily overlooked. As we have seen, it is marred by errors of scholarship and hasty compo-sition. Clearly Dryden had read both Polybius and his own immediate sources somewhat cursorily. Nevertheless, his essay is of some interest. It provided the first extensive critique of Polybius in English and one con-sistently fuller and more serious than Maigret's introduction, reproduced in Grimeston. Its appearance so soon after what was for several figures in public life the *débâcle* of 1688 may connect with a certain sympathy which the fortunes of the Achaean exile inspired in such men as Sheeres and Dryden (not to mention Lord Dartmouth, who evidently read him in the Tower); for them the Revolution had brought comparable disaster. The conditions of its publication fit Sheeres' translation into the early phase of the new era in publishing, in which works were no longer to depend on noble || patronage, but looked rather to the new reading public to pay their way. This significant revision of the economic basis for publishing was not fully developed until the early eighteenth century, but its begin-nings were there, clear to see, in Dryden's translations and the speculative initiatives of Jacob Tonson. It is in the same context, I suggest, that we should place Sheeres' translation of Polybius; and if that is so, the new at-tention which came to Polybius from this translation and from Dryden's 'Character' which accompanied it must be accounted one of the indi-rect – and certainly unforeseen – benefits of the Glorious Revolution.

[63] Cf. Momigliano (1974b) 367.   [64] Scott–Saintsbury XVIII, 52.

20

Polybius through the eyes of Gaetano De Sanctis[1]

I

May I begin with a personal reminiscence? Fifty years ago, when I was just finishing my second year as a student at Cambridge, my teacher, B. L. Hallward, the author of the chapters on the Punic Wars in *The Cambridge Ancient History*, came to me and said: 'You have exactly two weeks free of work before the end of term. That will be enough to learn Italian. Then, next year, you can read De Sanctis.' As I soon discovered, he was too optimistic: two weeks is not enough to learn Italian! But I did learn sufficient to enable me (with the help of a dictionary) to read Volume III of the *Storia dei Romani*. It was a wonderful experience, which I have never forgotten. Through it I came to have a better understanding of Polybius, who has been a constant friend and companion ever since – as indeed he was clearly a constant companion (if not a friend) of De Sanctis himself.

As we know from his *Ricordi*,[2] he first encountered Polybius as a school-boy. After reading Thucydides, he tells us, 'I found a translation of Polybius, and here too my attention was arrested and I was led to make efforts beyond my childish understanding to comprehend and assess the reasoned exposition of the causes of the Second Punic War; and after that I was unbelievably impressed by the lucid and dramatic account of Hannibal's invasion.' The boy's enthusiasms were later confirmed by the judgement of the mature scholar who, in the third volume of the *Storia dei Romani*, concludes an accurate and balanced paragraph on Polybius' merits as a historian with the statement that 'by recalling events alongside their causes, by reducing them to their separate elements and by searching out the links between them with the aid of an intellect that was

---

[1] This is the original English text of a lecture delivered at the conference on 'Gaetano De Sanctis: learning and moral character', organised by the Istituto della Enciclopedia Italiana in Rome, 14–15 December, 1981, fifty years after his refusal to take the fascist oath. The Italian version was published in *Riv.Fil.* III (1983) 465–77. [The translations of passages from De Sanctis are my own.]

[2] De Sanctis (1970) 31–2.

neither wide-ranging nor yet scintillating, but was lucid, cool, cultured, sagacious and well-trained, Polybius has in his third book created one of the greatest historical works passed down to us from antiquity'.[3]

It was not in fact until Volume III that De Sanctis had to come to serious grips with Polybius as a historian; and the thirty pages in the first part of the volume which he devotes to a general assessment of Polybius' *Histories* and to the elucidation of the main problems which his work presents to the modern reader form a splendid example of his critical insight.[4] After sixty years it is remarkable how much of what is written there remains wholly valid. There are of course some arguments that date. But most of them have stood up extraordinarily well to the test of time. His reconstruction of the details of Polybius' life and journeys is essentially correct, as is his interpretation of Polybius' flexible chronological system; and he saw, sooner than most scholars, that the reason Polybius alleges for extending the final terminus of his *Histories* from 168 down to 145 'is introduced as it were obliquely and motivated in a not wholly clear or consistent manner following a reaffirmation of the original plan'.

II

De Sanctis' appreciation of Polybius' merits as a historian did not blind him to the historian's weaknesses; for he had little patience with Kahrstedt's '*polibiolatria*'.[5] Polybius was vain and pedantic and his style was intolerable. His geographical descriptions did not invariably fit exactly.[6] Nor was his work always as objective as he would have us believe. He was clearly biased in favour of Achaea, his remarks on Aratus and Philopoemen being 'apologetic, if not downright panegyrical'.[7] He failed to do justice to the Aetolians and their politicians; and both Philip V's Friends and Philip himself, when opposed to Achaea, get short shrift in his pages. But it was especially as the mouthpiece ('*portavoce*') of the Scipionic faction that De Sanctis felt that Polybius diverged most flagrantly from the path of truth.[8] This was evident not merely in his admiration for Africanus – though Polybius was far too much of a rationalist to understand fully the methods and motives of that unusual man[9] – but also in his artificial glorification of a mediocre general such as P. Scipio,

---

[3] De Sanctis (1917) 174–5.   [4] De Sanctis (1916) 201–30.   [5] De Sanctis (1917) 582.

[6] See, for example, De Sanctis (1916) 152 on Heirkte.   [7] De Sanctis (1935) 629.

[8] De Sanctis (1964) 89 n.23. Though published in 1964, this part of the *Storia* was already written substantially in 1919.

[9] De Sanctis (1917) 452 n.16.

the father of Africanus, in order to build him up into a counterweight to Hannibal. As De Sanctis points out,[10] Scipio's amazement at Hannibal's achievement in reaching Italy has to be balanced by Hannibal's quite imaginary surprise at the speed with which Scipio had doubled back to meet him in the Po valley; and at the Ticino, though caught unawares, Scipio has to be made to deliver a speech to his troops to match that of Hannibal. This prejudice in favour of the Scipios also led Polybius to disparage their political opponents[11] – for example, M. Claudius Marcellus' policy of pacification in Spain, which ran counter to the expansionist ambitions of Scipio Aemilianus, was attributed to cowardice. Worse still, in the speech which he has Africanus address to Hannibal on the eve of Zama certain clauses in the peace proposals which were bound to render them unacceptable to Hannibal are omitted. To De Sanctis the close of that war was a dire moment in the destinies of Rome, for it was then that Roman policy took the wrong turning; and perhaps for that reason this prevarication created a disproportionately bad impression on his mind, for he twice refers to it.[12]

III

It has frequently been remarked that the fourth volume of the *Storia dei Romani* displays a decided change in tone. There is an infusion of passion and a moralising note which seem to take their origin in a source other than the facts that are being related. The reader is constantly being made conscious of an ideal shape of Roman historical development, of what might or should have been, which contrasts starkly with what actually happened – 'la storia fuori della storia', the history outside history, as Ferrabino aptly described it. De Sanctis deplored the direction in Roman policy which sent the legions eastward – to make Rome mistress of the *oecumene* in just over fifty-three years, in Polybius' formulation. In reality the process was to continue down to 146 and beyond Polybius' own lifetime into the first century and was not to be completed until after the establishment of the principate. It was a process which De Sanctis saw as a kind of nemesis for the free republic.[13] The conquest of the eastern Mediterranean was something which he condemned partly because of the horrors that accompanied it but also because he saw these increasing as the victors found themselves in a more and more untenable situation.

---

[10] Ibid.171.   [11] De Sanctis (1923) 474.
[12] De Sanctis (1917) 536 n.142, 552 n.171.   [13] De Sanctis (1923) 367.

But even more he condemned it[14] as a diversion from what he regarded as Rome's manifest destiny, which was to conquer the west, to transform the vast spaces of Spain and Gaul into areas given over to a Roman civilisation which had inherited the best from Greece, thereby providing a firm bulwark against invasion by the German barbarians. 'Whoever rejects as unilateral both points of view [sc. those of both the Gauls and the Romans],' he declares, 'and ranges himself on the side of humanity and civilisation, is bound to recognise that the Roman conquest of Gaul also marked another notable stage in the history of progress . . . The historical justification of the Roman conquest lies in the Romans having secured with their own blood an immediate and effective recovery, driving Ariovistus across the Rhine, rather than clasping their hands and, while gazing on the uncertain future recovery of the Gauls, in the meantime allowing Germanisation to establish itself in the Gallic provinces, to the accompaniment of havoc and peril among the Gauls no less than among the Latins.'[15]

The concept of historical justification put forward here creates severe difficulties for anyone who does not share De Sanctis' deeply-held teleological view of history, since it apparently lays the emphasis not so much on the real motives which took the Romans into Spain, Gaul and Africa, but rather on the later consequences of a conquest achieved 'with their own blood', '*col proprio sangue*', and on its eventual cultural benefits, which manifestly had nothing to do with the objects of the Roman government in the second and first centuries BC and would have been incomprehensible to the legionaries whose blood was shed. His deep sense of humanity and hatred of injustice and oppression would have prevented De Sanctis from ever supposing that ends – whether regarded as aims or, retrospectively, as the results of the historical process – can justify means. But to talk of historical justification is to run the risk of seeing history in those terms; and when we speak of imperial conquest leading to the spread of humanity and civilisation, we should, I think, not forget – as De Sanctis did not forget – the cruel fate of Numantia and the severed hands of Uxellodunum.

I have digressed a little in order to show how De Sanctis' view of Roman imperialism contains a certain fundamental antinomy: for while he condemned Rome's eastern conquests in the light of what he regarded as Rome's true destiny, he gave his assent to Rome's imperial

---

[14] De Sanctis (1962) 1264. I quote this work, which originally appeared in *Atene e Roma* n.s.1 (1920) 3–14, 73–89, from the reprint in Treves (1962).
[15] De Sanctis (1962) 1275.

achievements viewed as a whole.[16] He concealed nothing of the horror of the destruction of Carthage, yet in a famous verdict, which did not go unchallenged, he claimed that 'only when liberated from this dead weight and opened up to classical culture could a romanised Africa begin to share in the civilised development of antiquity as the equal of Gaul and Spain and as an element in that development rich in hope and strength'.[17]

IV

Let us now return to Polybius. His personal career as a statesman and, later, his historical work both stand at the very centre of Roman imperial expansion in the east; and both were distinguished – some might say, were flawed – by ambiguities not unlike those which we have just seen present in De Sanctis' own thinking. There was much in Polybius which should have commended him to his successor, much that they shared in common; an expressed concern for truth, which, says Polybius,[18] is to history what its eyes are to a living creature, a passion for liberty – however much that over-worked slogan may have been distorted in reality – a hatred of barbarism (as revealed in the behaviour of the Carthaginian mercenaries or even, nearer home, in that of the *stasis*-ridden people of Arcadian Cynaetha). Polybius' devotion to Achaea, the unifier of the Peloponnese, was surely a trait to appeal to De Sanctis who, following Beloch, spoke frequently of 'national unity'.[19] Above all, it was Polybius who, though he championed the unity of the Achaean League, equated Roman history with universal history: 'As Leo aptly notes,' wrote De Sanctis,[20] 'it was precisely the synthesis of the concepts of Roman history and universal history that turned Polybius into a historian.' True, Polybius did not attain to the understanding of mankind as a single community, but at least he saw the greatness of the Roman achievement. Unfortunately, there was one – perhaps insurmountable – obstacle. It was the aberrant Rome, the Rome that had been diverted to the conquest of the Hellenistic east and, by reducing it to a fraction of the Roman empire, had turned Greeks into *graeculi*, that commanded Polybius' ultimate allegiance. This De Sanctis could not accept.

Both in Volume II of the *Storia dei Romani* and in a later article on *Polibio*, published in the *Enciclopedia Italiana* in 1935, he scarcely attempts to disguise his personal antipathy and even contempt for the Achaean

---

[16] De Sanctis (1962) 1275; (1964) 275.   [17] De Sanctis (1964) 37.   [18] Polyb. i.14.6.
[19] See for example De Sanctis (1964) 128.   [20] De Sanctis (1916) 216.

statesman caught up in what he admits was a 'tragic situation'. When Polybius seeks to defend Philopoemen's execution of political opponents at Sparta in 186, this is De Sanctis' comment: 'It is instructive to see how, according to Polybius, Philopoemen by condoning such a massacre as this found a way to reconcile καλόν and συμφέρον, a thing few succeed in doing.'[21] But it is in the events of the Third Macedonian War, in which Polybius was directly involved, that De Sanctis' hostility towards him emerges most clearly. It was no doubt an issue on which he had long pondered, for it is only in his article in the *Enciclopedia Italiana* that he sets out in full his mature thoughts. Already in part one of Volume IV he had warned his readers that Polybius' account of these events was 'tendentious and not to be accepted with one's eyes closed',[22] and he had pointed out that in his dealings with Rome as hipparch of the Achaean League Polybius, in contrast to his father Lycortas, 'although still motivated by genuine nationalist sentiments . . . possessed, far more than his father, a feeling for the new times and the capacity to adapt himself to these'.[23] In De Sanctis' eyes, needless to say, that was *not* a merit. However, in giving their support to the Romans, 'without helping them overmuch in their harsh need to conquer Macedonia', the moderates – including Polybius – were guilty of what was 'basically disguised treachery' and so failed after all to escape the anger of Rome.

The case for the prosecution is set out more fully in the *Enciclopedia*.[24] Polybius and Lycortas, he tells us there, supported Rome against Macedonia, although a Roman victory was bound to mean an end to Greek freedom; but to support Perseus would have played into the hands of 'the malcontents within the existing social order of proletarians and debtors, which the land-owning classes, supported by the Romans, had hitherto succeeded in holding in check'. By their policy Lycortas and Polybius avoided a conflict with Rome, but not a Roman victory; and since it was obvious that Achaea would never surrender her independence without a struggle, all they achieved was the postponement of that struggle to a time when it could not have the slightest hope of success – as was indeed the case when in 146 the league was disbanded and Corinth destroyed. This passage is fundamental to De Sanctis' judgement of Polybius and it deserves careful examination. There is, of course, an element of truth in the statement that the Romans gave their support and favour to the richer classes in Greece and that this was one reason why many statesmen such as Polybius became reconciled to Roman domination.

---

[21] De Sanctis (1923) 231 n.197.   [22] Ibid. 307–8 n.186.
[23] De Sanctis (1923) 300.   [24] De Sanctis (1935) 626.

But support of Perseus need not in itself have involved encouraging proletarians and debtors. To a man of Polybius' military experience a far stronger motive for not joining Perseus must have been the extreme unlikelihood of his succeeding where his father Philip V and Antiochus had failed. Nor was it as obvious as De Sanctis here assumes that in 170 everyone realised that a Roman victory would mean an end to Greek freedom. In a well-known passage of Book II,[25] which was certainly written after 168, Polybius explains that Achaea had achieved a growth of power and an internal political harmony which were altogether remarkable. This passage contains not the slightest suggestion that Greek freedom was already doomed following the Roman victory at Pydna: why then should that have been obvious in advance of that victory in 170? Achaea would never surrender without a fight, we are told. But it was by no means clear that Achaea would *need* to fight until the embassy of L. Aurelius Orestes in 147. The Achaean War blew up like a sudden squall: it certainly could not have been foreseen in 170 and any assessment of Polybius which assumes that it could is judging matters *ex eventu*.

In summer 169, advised by the consul Q. Marcius Philippus, Polybius took steps to prevent the Achaeans from having to send the help requested by App. Claudius Centho in Epirus. In Volume IV of the *Storia dei Romani* De Sanctis emphasises the service which he thereby rendered to the (so-called) 'national cause', but adds that 'he justifies himself with arguments distinguished by their shrewdness rather than their plausibility, putting the responsibility onto Marcius Philippus who, being dead at the time Polybius was writing, could not contradict him'.[26] Perhaps: but it is equally possible that Marcius *did* advise against sending the troops, either for personal reasons or to put the Achaeans in an invidious position. In the event the fate of Epirus was merely postponed; but after the ghastly terror perpetrated there by Aemilius Paullus – a terror excused by 'the noble Plutarch (here drawing on Polybius), who refers to the *senatus consultum*, which led Aemilius Paullus to act παρὰ τὴν αὐτοῦ φύσιν ἐπιεικῆ καὶ χρήστην οὖσαν, contrary to his mild and generous nature – those self-same *graeculi*, who could not find words strong enough to condemn the savagery of Philip of Macedon' – and here he must mean Polybius – 'hastened to shake the hand of the butcher of the Molossians and tried to find excuses for his deeds'.[27]

These are harsh words; and later, in 145 at Carthage, Polybius fares no better. His account of the fall of the city is 'full of lively colour and

[25] Polyb. ii.37.8. [26] De Sanctis (1923) 307–8 n.186. [27] De Sanctis (1923) 350–1 n.300.

rich in interesting detail, but full of hatred and contempt for the unfortunate Carthaginian general and so indubitably not impartial'.[28] This is indeed largely true and De Sanctis is quite right to point out that Hasdrubal's conduct in rejecting Scipio's proposed 'deal', which would have guaranteed freedom for himself and a small group of nominated friends, redounded to his credit. But admiration of Hasdrubal should perhaps have been tempered by the recollection of the horrible atrocities which the Punic general had inflicted on Roman prisoners on the walls of Carthage, a circumstance to which De Sanctis refers only as evidence that the Romans were already in possession of Hasdrubal's camp, yet one which makes Scipio's readiness to deal with him all the more shameful. De Sanctis' final comment is particularly significant for his attitude towards Polybius: 'Because he had surrendered when all was lost and the last of his fellow-citizens had laid down their arms, and when he had no alternative to surrender other than suicide in the company of a handful of soldiers who were not even his fellow-countrymen, we should not wish to treat him with the severity of the Greek officer who, having surrendered to the Romans without fighting, showed himself pitiless towards those who surrendered after fighting.'[29]

v

In this remark is the clue to De Sanctis' bitterness towards Polybius. He had surrendered to Rome – and without fighting. Unlike the rest of the Greek detainees he had become a turncoat, scarcely to be distinguished from his own *bête noire*, Callicrates; 'not only had he become a gutless admirer of Rome, but, having now defected openly from the national party, he had recognised no less than Callicrates the ineluctability of Roman rule ... And his was a conversion so complete that from now on, as is usually the case with apostates, he began to hate the heirs of the policy of Philopoemen and Lycortas, to atttribute to them the most shady intentions and, though from motives perhaps less base than those of Callicrates, or to be more correct less base than those Polybius attributed to Callicrates, to assume in opposition to them the same position that Callicrates had assumed in opposition to Arcon, Lycortas and Polybius himself.'[30] Later, in the *Enciclopedia*, De Sanctis went further, suggesting that Polybius was allowed to stay on in Rome as a reward for his unique apostasy; for he was alone among the detainees in going over to Rome.

[28] De Sanctis (1964) 71 n.101.   [29] Ibid. 74–5.   [30] Ibid. 128.

Both assertions are open to question. All our evidence suggests that it was as a friend of Aemilius Paullus and his household that Polybius was allowed to stay on in Rome, and that his continued presence there was assured when he became the tutor of the youthful Scipio Aemilianus. He would have to have experienced a conversion as sudden as that of St Paul for such a conversion to have been the cause of his exceptional treatment. As regards the other detainees, their attitude towards Rome has to be deduced mainly from probability. But that they all took the opposite view to that of Polybius is disproved by the behaviour of Stratius of Tritaea, the only one, to our knowledge, who resumed political activity after their release in 150 – his name had been linked with that of Polybius in the appeal of 160/59[31] – for he, far from following the intransigent line of Diaeus, urged the acceptance of the Roman proposals.[32] Perhaps he was the only one Polybius chose to mention. But it certainly looks as if De Sanctis adopted the least favourable interpretation of Polybius' 'conversion'.

Polybius' account of the events in Carthage, Macedonia and Achaea between 152 and 146 is undoubtedly slanted in the direction of Rome, even to the extent of suppressing facts and concealing stark realities under somewhat mealy-mouthed euphemisms. When he asserts that in 147 it was not the Roman intention to dissolve the Achaean League,[33] De Sanctis quite rightly points out[34] that this is not true; for there is no evidence at all that the Romans had withdrawn their ultimatum that Corinth, Argos, Arcadian Orchomenus and Heraclea in Trachis should be detached from the League. Gruen's recent attempt to defend Polybius on this point is unconvincing.[35] Polybius' reference to Mummius' massacre of a number of cavalrymen at Chalcis is also disconcerting: he called it 'a slight deviation from what was fitting' – ἐδόκει παρεωρακέναι τι τῶν καθηκόντων, and attributed this lapse to the bad advice of his friends.[36] 'Evidently,' says De Sanctis, 'we are dealing with a justification similar to those that friends of tyrants habitually adduce to excuse their cruelty.'[37] This just but bitter remark underlines the extent of his estrangement from the Greek historian. Even in commenting on Polybius' services in mitigating the severity of the treatment which the Romans accorded to the Achaeans in 146, his biting comment is that 'the Romans' (*not* the Greeks!) 'had the good fortune to find in Polybius of Megalopolis, who during the Achaean War had been detained below Carthage in the

---

[31] Polyb. xxxii.3.14.   [32] Polyb. xxxviii.17.4.   [33] Polyb. xxxviii.9.6.
[34] De Sanctis (1964) 140.   [35] Gruen (1976).   [36] Polyb. xxxix.6.4–5.
[37] De Sanctis (1964) 160.

camp of his friend Scipio, a man well qualified through his experience of the customs and laws of the Greeks and Romans to indicate the most opportune way to conciliate, and as far as possible avoid dissension between, victors and vanquished.'[38]

VI

It was not only the man who was at fault. Especially in the *Enciclopedia* article the historian too comes in for sharp reproof. He is given credit for his serious purpose, but this is outweighed by his disagreeable, prosaic manner and a spiritual aridity which wearies the reader and kills all traces of freshness and historical intuition. His moralising is verbose and banal. His miserable and wearisome vanity, deployed on every possible occasion to sing the praises of his own work and the harsh, quarrelsome and ungenerous way in which he attacks other historians, especially in Book XII, are all castigated in a general summing up which makes Polybius wholly unattractive. De Sanctis had said some of the same things in substance in Volume III, but more briefly and in far less offensive words.[39]

What then had gone wrong? I have, I think, quoted sufficient passages to show that De Sanctis' criticisms of Polybius, though nearly always substantially based, represent cumulatively a judgement rooted in deep emotions. The heart of the matter is to be found in his comment on the Punic general Hasdrubal. Having gone over to Rome without a struggle, Polybius, he there implies, would have done well to restrain his criticisms of those who went over *after* fighting. It is a fair point and would apply equally well to some of Polybius' harsh criticisms of Rhodians and others who, having chosen to back the wrong side, had then lacked the resolution to commit suicide. Whether De Sanctis was demanding – in retrospect – that Polybius should have done more than show forbearance, I am not wholly sure. But his assessment of the results of the policy of Lycortas and Polybius towards Rome seems to suggest that perhaps he was.[40] As I have explained, in his *Enciclopedia* article he characterised that policy as one that ensured that Achaea would ultimately have to fight – but without any hope of victory; and elsewhere he speaks of the gradual acceptance of slavery as a habit of mind which 'was encouraged by the conviction that was spreading among the most intelligent men, even among those who in the past had allowed themselves, like Polybius, to be

---

[38] Ibid. 177–8.   [39] De Sanctis (1917) 174.   [40] De Sanctis (1964) 79.

charmed into accepting the national idea, that the Roman people were politically superior and their rule inevitable'.[41] As a second reason for this defeatism he adds that by 170 the days of real freedom were a mere matter of hearsay, that 'the generation that had entered into public life before a more or less disguised predominance of Rome had asserted itself, that is before the Second Macedonian War, had by now, around 160–150, entirely yielded place to younger generations'.[42] Behind these words we catch the echo of another great historian: 'quotus quisque reliquus qui rem publicam vidisset!' – how few remained who had looked upon the republic.[43]

In this situation what ought Polybius to have done? Should he have tried to persuade the Achaeans to join Perseus against Rome? That surely would have been a fatal and catastrophic policy. But this is a question which by implication De Sanctis raises, but one which he never answers. In matters of conscience and of right and wrong it was of course not his way to think out all the pros and cons and to weigh them with an eye on expediency. Once he had decided on the proper course, the results of his action seemed of secondary importance. To him it was enough that Polybius had betrayed the 'national cause'.

There is a certain irony in the fact that the later careers of Polybius and De Sanctis were not without their resemblances. For reasons in a sense outside their control both were cut off at a vital moment from the exercise of their talents – the one as a statesman, the other as a teacher – through an arbitrary act of tyrannical power. Both found in the writing of history an alternative means of self-expression and both continued in that work after the original injustice had been in some degree removed. It was as a direct result of his own personal disaster that Polybius produced his great work. To De Sanctis writing on the same theme and necessarily in his constant debt, Polybius' *Histories*, for all their technical merits, clearly represented a monstrous act of submission, the record of Greek cowardice and failure and at the same time a piece of propaganda designed to encourage more of the same thing. Why exactly De Sanctis felt so strongly about this must be a matter of speculation. But I have the feeling that writing during and just after a European war of which he deeply disapproved and at a time when his own country was threatened with moral and political disaster, he saw the errors and the shame of his own times as to some degree reflected in the misfortunes and the betrayal of the 'Greek nation'. By coming to terms with oppression – with which

---

[41] Ibid.   [42] Ibid.   [43] Tac. *Ann.* i.3.

De Sanctis would have no truck – Polybius may have become a symbol in his mind for much of what he detested. The fact that he too, De Sanctis, was also convinced of the benefits ultimately conferred by the Roman empire and of its contribution to the civilised world perhaps complicated his feelings, but did nothing to mitigate his dislike of the Achaean.

Perhaps Polybius deserved it. Had he not given hostages to fortune when he wrote: 'Should either my contemporaries or future generations find me intentionally making false statements or neglecting the truth, I would urge them to censure me relentlessly!'[44] And when De Sanctis was put to the test, he did not fail. That is why we are here in Rome this week. Nevertheless, as we celebrate that great act of courage, we may, I suggest, experience a little sadness that the great man was unable to extend to his fellow-historian, who had faced equally hard decisions and in the end had deserved well of the Achaean people, a modicum of that charity to which, though he was not especially lavish in it himself, Polybius as a 'tragic figure' could surely lay some claim.

44 Polyb. xvi.20.8.

Bibliography

Aalders, G. J. D. (1968) *Die Theorie der gemischten Verfassung im Altertum*, Amsterdam
Aalders, G. J. D. (1987) 'Polybius en de Goden', *Lampas* 20: 119–30
Adams, W. L. (1986) 'Macedonian kingship and the right of petition', *Ancient Macedonia* 4: 43–52
Africa, T. W. (1961) *Phylarchus and the Spartan Revolution*, Berkeley–Los Angeles
Africa, T. W. (1982) 'Worms and the death of kings: a cautionary note on disease and history', *Class. Ant.* 1: 1–17
Ager, S. L. (1994) 'Hellenistic Crete and ΚΟΙΝΟΔΙΚΙΟΝ', *JHS* 104: 1–18
Akarca, A. (1959) *Les Monnaies grecques de Mylasa*, Paris
Alliot, M. (1951) 'La Thébaïde en lutte contre les rois d'Alexandrie sous Philopator et Epiphane (216–184)', *Rev. belge de phil. et d'hist.* 29: 421–43
Alliot, M. (1952) 'La fin de la résistance égyptienne dans le Sud sous Epiphane', *REA* 54: 18–26
Alonso-Nuñez, J. M. (1983) 'Die Abfolge der Weltreiche bei Polybios und Dionysios von Halikarnassos', *Historia* 33: 411–26
Alonso-Nuñez, J. M. (1986) 'The *anacyclosis* in Polybius', *Eranos* 84: 17–22
Alonso-Nuñez, J. M. (1990) 'The emergence of universal history from the 4th to the 2nd centuries BC', in Verdin, Schepens and De Keyser (eds.) (1990) 173–92
Applebaum, S. (1971) 'The Zealots: the case for revaluation', *JRS* 61: 155–70
Astin, A. (1967) *Scipio Aemilianus*, Oxford
Austin, M. (1986) 'Hellenistic kings, war and the economy', *CQ* 56: 450–66
Avenarius, G. (1956) *Lukians Schrift zur Geschichtsschreibung*, Meisenheim am Glan
Aymard, A. (1938a) *Les Assemblées de la confédération achaïenne*, Bordeaux–Paris
Aymard, A. (1938b) *Premiers Rapports de Rome et de la Confédération achaïenne*, Bordeaux
Aymard, A. (1967) *Etudes d'histoire ancienne*, Paris
Badian, E. B. (1980) 'Two Polybian treaties', in *Manni Miscellanea* (1980) 1, 159–69
Bagnall, R. G. (1976) *The Administration of the Ptolemaic Possessions outside Egypt*, Leiden
Bar-Kochva, B. (1976) *The Seleucid Army: Organization and Tactics in the Great Campaigns*, Cambridge
Bar-Kochva, B. (1989) *Judas Maccabaeus*, Cambridge

Baronowski, D. W. (1995) 'Polybius on the causes of the Third Punic War', *Class. Phil.* 90: 16–31

Beck, H. (1997) *Polis and Koinon* (*Historia* Einzelschrift 114), Stuttgart

Beister, H. (1995) 'Pragmatische Geschichtsschreibung und zeitliche Dimension', in Schubert and Brodersen (eds.) (1995) 329–49

Beloch, K. J. (1925) *Griechische Geschichte* IV 1, Berlin–Leipzig

Bengtson, H. (1952) *Die Strategie in der hellenistischen Zeit* III, Munich

Berger, H. (1880) *Die geographischen Fragmente des Eratosthenes*, Leipzig

Berger, P. (1992) 'Le portrait des Celtes dans les histoires de Polybe', *Ancient Society* 23: 105–26

Berger, P. (1995) 'La xénophobie de Polybe', *REA* 97: 517–25

Bernand, A. (1970) *Le Delta égyptien d'après les textes grecs* (MIFAO 91), 3 vols., Cairo

Bernhardt, R. (1984) *Polis und römische Herrschaft in der spätiken Republik, 149–31 v. Chr.*, Berlin

Bevan, E. R. (1927) *A History of Egypt under the Ptolemaic Dynasty*, London

Bikerman, E. (1938) *Institutions des Séleucides*, Paris

Blösel, W. (1998) 'Die Anakyklosistheorie und die Verfassung Roms im Spiegel des sechsten Buches bei Polybios und Ciceros *de re publica* Buch II', *Hermes* 126: 31–57

Boncquet, J. (1982–3) 'On the critical evaluation of historians', *Ancient Society* 13–14: 277–91

Bouché-Leclercq, A. (1903) *Histoire des Lagides* I, Paris

Bousquet, J. (1988) 'La Stèle des Kyténiens au Létoon de Xanthos', *REG* 101: 12–53

Brandstaeter, F. A. (1844) *Die Geschichten des ätolischen Landes, Volkes und Bundes, nebst einer historiographischen Abhandlung über Polybios*, Berlin

Braun, E. (1983) 'Die extreme Demokratie bei Polybios und bei Aristoteles', *JÖAI.* 54, Beiblatt 1–40

Braunert, H. (1960) Review of Koenen (1957), *Gnomon* 32: 531–3

Brink, C. O. (1971) *Horace on Poetry* II, Cambridge

Brink, C. O. and Walbank, F. W. (1954) 'The construction of the sixth book of Polybius', *CQ* 4: 97–122

Brown, T. S. (1958) *Timaeus of Tauromenium* (University of California Publications in History 35), Berkeley–Los Angeles

Brown, T. S. (1961) 'Apollophanes and Polybius, Book 5', *Phoenix* 15: 187–95

Brugsch, H. (1884) 'Der Apiskreis aus den Zeiten der Ptolemäer nach den hieroglyphischen und demotischen Weihinschriften des Serapeums von Memphis', *ZÄS* 22.1: 110–36

Brugsch, H. (1886) 'Der Apiskreis aus den Zeiten der Ptolemäer nach den hieroglyphischen und demotischen Weihinschriften des Serapeums von Memphis – Fortsetzung', *ZÄS* 24: 19–40

Brulé, P. (1978) *La Piraterie crétoise hellénistique*, Paris

Bruneau, Ph. (1970) *Recherches sur les cultes de Délos*, Paris

Brunt, P. A. (1971) *Italian Manpower 275 BC – AD 14*, Oxford

Brunt. P. A. (1977) 'Josephus on social conflicts in Roman Judaea', *Klio* 59: 149–53

Brunt, P. A. (1980) 'On historical fragments and epitomes', *CQ* 30: 477–94
Bulloch, A. W., Gruen, E. S., Long, A. A. and Stewart, A. (eds.) (1993) *Images and Ideologies: Self-Definition in the Hellenistic World*, Berkeley–Los Angeles–London
Bunge, J. G. (1974) ' "Theos Epiphanes": Zu den ersten fünf Regierungsjahren Antiochus' IV. Epiphanes', *Historia* 23: 57–85
Bunge, J. G. (1976) 'Die Feiern Antiochus' IV. Epiphanes in Daphne im Herbst 166 v. Chr.', *Chiron* 6: 53–71
Burck, E. (1934) *Die Erzählungskunst des T. Livius*, Berlin
Burr, V. (1955) *Tiberius Julius Alexander*, Bonn
Büttner-Wobst, T. (1901) *Beiträge zu Polybios*, Dresden
Calderone, S. (1980) 'Livio e il secondo trattato romano-punico di Polibio', *Manni Miscellanea* (1980) II, 363–75
Calderone, S. (1981) 'Polibio i.11.1ff.', edd. S. Calderone, I. Bitto, L. de Salvo, A. Pinzone, *Quaderni Urbinati di Cultura Classica* n.s. 7: 7–78
Canfora, L. (1993) 'La tipologia costituzionale', *Quaderni di Storia* 37: 19–27
Cartledge, P., Garnsey, P. and Gruen, E. (eds.) (1997) *Hellenistic Constructs: Essays in Culture, History and Historiography*, Berkeley–Los Angeles–London
Casson, L. (1973) *Ships and Seamanship in the Ancient World*, Princeton, NJ
Clarke, K. (1999a) *Between Geography and History: Hellenistic Reconstructions of the Roman World*, Oxford
Clarke, K. (1999b) 'Unusual perspectives in historiography', in C. S. Kraus, ed., *The Limits of Historiography: Genre and Narrative in Ancient Historical Texts* (Leiden–Boston–Cologne) 249–79
Clarysse, W. (1978) 'Hurgonaphor et Chaonnophris, les derniers pharaons indigènes', *Chron. d'Egypte* 53: 243–53
Cloché, P. (1936) 'Isocrate et la politique théraménienne', *Etudes Classiques* 5: 394ff.
Cohen, G. M. (1995) *The Hellenistic Settlements in Europe, the Islands and Asia Minor*, Berkeley–Los Angeles
Cohen, S. J. D. (1979) *Josephus in Galilee and Rome: his Vita and Development as a Historian*, Leiden
Cohen, S. J. D. (1980) 'Josephus, Jeremiah and Polybius', *History and Theory* 21: 366–81
Cole, T. (1964) 'The sources and composition of Polybius VI', *Historia* 13: 440–86
Cole, T. (1967) *Democritus and the Sources of Greek Anthropology* (American Philological Association), Boston, MA
Collatz, C. F., Helms, H. and Schäfer, M. (2000) *Polybios-Lexikon*, Band 1, Lieferung 1 (α–γ), 2nd edn, Berlin
Collingwood, R.G. (1946) *The Idea of History*, Oxford
Connolly, P. (1981) *Greece and Rome at War*, London
Courby, F. (1912) *Délos V: Le Portique d'Antigone ou du nord-est*, Paris
Crampa, J. (1969) *Labraunda: Swedish Excavations and Researches*, VIII, 1: *The Greek Inscriptions, Part I: 1–12 (period of Olympichus)*, Lund
Cuntz, O. (1902) *Polybius und sein Werk*, Leipzig

Dana, Y. (1993) 'Plutarch on political theory and praxis in the career of a Roman statesman in mid-second century BC', in I. Gallo and B. Scardigli, eds., *Teoria e prassi politica nelle opere di Plutarco* (Naples) 91–8

Daressy, G. (1911) 'Un décret de l'an XXIII de Ptolémée Epiphane', *Rec. trav.* 33: 1–8

Daressy, G. (1916–17) 'Un second exemplaire du décret de l'an XXIII de Ptolémée Epiphane', *Rec. trav.* 38: 175–9

Daux, G. (1936) *Delphes au IIe et au Ier siècle depuis l'abaissement d'Etolie jusqu' à la paix romaine*, Paris

Davidson, J. (1991) 'The gaze of Polybius' *Histories*', *JRS* 81: 10–24

Deininger, J. (1965) *Die Provinziallandtage der römischen Kaiserzeit von Augustus bis zum Ende des dritten Jahrhunderts n. Chr.* (Vestigia 6), Munich

Derow, P. S. (1979) 'Polybius, Rome and the East', *JRS* 69: 1–15

Derow, P. S. (1984) Review of Walbank, *Comm.* III, *JRS* 74: 231–5

Derow, P. S. (1989) 'Rome, the fall of Macedon and the sack of Corinth', *CAH* VIII, 2nd edn, 290–323

Derow, P. S. (1994) 'Historical explanation: Polybius and his predecessors', in Hornblower (ed.) (1994) 73–90

De Sanctis, G. (1907–64) *Storia dei Romani*, Turin–Florence

De Sanctis, G. (1916) *Storia dei Romani* III.1, Turin

De Sanctis, G. (1917) *Storia dei Romani* III.2, Turin

De Sanctis, G. (1923) *Storia dei Romani* IV.1, Turin

De Sanctis, G. (1935) 'Polibio' in *Enciclopedia Italiana*, Rome

De Sanctis, G. (1962) 'Dopoguerra antico', *Atene e Roma* n.s. 1 (1920) 3–14, 73–89; quoted here from the reprint in Treves (1962) 1247–82

De Sanctis, G. (1964) *Storia dei Romani* IV.3, Florence

De Sanctis, G. (1970) *Ricordi della mia vita*, ed. S. Accame, Florence

Develin, R. (1973) 'Mos Maiorum Mutatus: Tradition and the Basis of Change in the Roman Constitution, 287–201 BC', Dissertation Michigan

Devroye, I. and Kemp, L. (1956) *Over de historische methode van Polybios*, Brussels

D'Huys, V. (1987) 'How to describe violence in historical narrative: reflections of the ancient Greek historians and their ancient critics', *Anc. Soc.* 18: 209–50

D'Huys, V. (1990) 'Χρήσιμον καὶ τερπνόν in Polybios' Schlachtschilderungen. Einige literarische Topoi in seiner Darstellung der Schlacht bei Zama (15.9–16)', in Verdin, Schepens and De Keyser (eds.) (1990) 267–88 with discussion 301–12

Díaz Tejera, A. (1975) 'Análisis del libro VI de las Historias de Polibio respecto a la concepcion ciclica de las constituciones', *Habis* 6: 23–34

Díaz Tejera, A. (1985) 'Aportaciones del manuscrito *Vaticanus Gr. 1005(2)* a los libros II y III de las Historias de Polibio', *Habis* 14: 17–32

Dionisotti, A. C. (1983) 'Polybius and the royal professor', in E. Gabba, ed., *Tria corda. Scritti in onore di Arnaldo Momigliano* (Bibliotheca di Athenaeum 1) (Como) 179–99

Doering, K. (1978) 'Antike Theorien über die staatspolitische Notwendigkeit der Götterfurcht', *Antike und Abendland* 24: 119–30

Drexler, H. (1961–3) *Polybios' Geschichte*: Gesamtausgabe, eingeleitet und übertragen von H. Drexler, Zurich–Stuttgart

Droysen, H. (1875) 'Zu Polybius', *Rhein. Mus.* 30: 62–7

Dubois, M. (1891) 'Strabon et Polybe', *REG* 4: 343–56

Dubuisson, M. (1979) 'Procédés de la diplomatie romaine', *REL* 57: 114–25

Dubuisson, M. (1985) *Le Latin de Polybe. Les implications historiques d'un cas de bilingualisme* (Etudes et commentaires 96), Paris

Dubuisson, M. (1990) 'La vision polybienne de Rome' in Verdin, Schepens and De Keyser (eds.) (1990) 233–45

Dunand, F. (1981) 'Fête et propagande à Alexandrie sous les Lagides', in F. Dunand, ed., *La Fête, pratique et discours* (Paris) 13–40

Durrbach, F. (1921) *Choix d'inscriptions de Délos* i, Paris

Eckstein, A. M. (1980) 'Polybius on the role of the Senate in the crisis of 264 BC', *GRBS* 21: 175–90

Eckstein, A. M. (1984) 'Rome, Saguntum and the Ebro Treaty', *Emerita* 55: 51–68

Eckstein, A. M. (1985) 'Polybius, Syracuse and the policy of accommodation', *GRBS* 26: 265–82

Eckstein, A. M. (1987a) *Senate and General*, Berkeley–Los Angeles–London

Eckstein, A. M. (1987b) 'Polybius, Aristaenus and the fragment on traitors', *CQ* 37: 140–62

Eckstein, A. M. (1990) 'Josephus and Polybius: a reconsideration', *Class. Ant.* 9: 175–208

Eckstein, A. M. (1995) *Moral Vision in the Histories of Polybius* (Hellenistic Culture and Society 16), Berkeley–Los Angeles–London

Eckstein, A. M. (1997) '*Physis* and *nomos*: Polybius, the Romans and Cato the Elder', in Cartledge, Garnsey and Gruen (eds.) (1997) 175–98

Eddy, S. K. (1961) *The King is Dead*, Lincoln, Neb

Edlund, I. E. M. (1977) 'Invisible bonds: clients and patrons through the eyes of Polybius', *Klio* 59: 129–36

Edson, C. F. (1934) 'The Antigonids, Heracles, and Beroea', *Harv. Stud.* 45: 213–46

Edson, C. F. (1948) 'Philip V and Alcaeus of Messene', *CP* 43: 116–21

Ehrenberg, V. (1938) *Alexander and the Greeks*, Oxford

Eisen, K. F. (1966) *Polybiosinterpretationen: Beobachtungen zu Prinzipien griechischer und römischer Historiographie bei Polybios*, Heidelberg

Eisenberger, H. (1982) 'Die Natur und die römische Politeia im 6. Buch des Polybios', *Phil.* 126: 44–58

Erbse, H. (1957) 'Polybios-Interpretationen', *Phil.* 101: 269–97

Errington, R. M. (1969) *Philopoemen*, Oxford

Errington, R. M. (1971) 'The alleged Syro-Macedonian pact and the origins of the second Macedonian war', *Athenaeum* 49: 336–54

Errington, R. M. (1976) 'Alexander in the Hellenistic world', in E. Badian, ed., *Alexandre le Grand* (Entretiens Hardt 22) (Vandoeuvres–Geneva) 137–79

Errington, R. M. (1986) *Geschichte Makedoniens von den Anfängen bis zum Untergang des Königreichs*, Munich (English transl. *A History of Macedonia* (Hellenistic Culture and Society 5), Berkeley–Los Angeles–London, 1990)

Errington, R. M. (1989) 'Rome against Philip and Antiochus', *CAH* VIII, 2nd edn, 244–89

Erskine, A. (2000) 'Polybius and barbarian Rome', *Mediterraneo Antico* 3.1: 165–82

Ferrary, J.-L. (1988) *Philhellénisme et impérialisme: aspects idéologiques de la conquête romaine du monde hellénistique*, Paris–Rome

Finley, M. I. (1975) 'The ancient Greeks and their nation', in *The Use and Abuse of History* (London) 120–33. (Reprint Harmondsworth 1990)

Foertmeyer, V. (1988) 'The dating of the *pompe* of Ptolemy II Philadelphus', *Historia* 37: 90–104

Fornara, C. W. (1983) *The Nature of History in Ancient Greece and Rome* (Eidos: Studies in Classical Kinds), Berkeley–Los Angeles–London

Foucault, J. A. de (1972) *Recherches sur la langue et le style de Polybe*, Paris

Foulon, E. (1984) 'Polybe. x.10.20: la prise de Cartagine par Scipion', *Rev. Phil.* 63: 241–6

Fraser, P. M. (1954) 'Two Hellenistic inscriptions from Delphi', *BCH* 78: 49–67

Fraser, P. M. (1960) *Samothrace II, Part 1: The Inscriptions on Stone*, New York

Fraser, P. M. (1972) *Ptolemaic Alexandria*, 2 vols., Oxford

Frisch, P. (1975) *Die Inschriften von Ilion*, Bonn

Fritz, K. von (1954) *The Theory of the Mixed Constitution in Antiquity: a Critical Analysis of Polybius' Ideas*, New York

Fritz, K. von (1956) 'Die Bedeutung des Aristoteles für die Geschichts-schreibung', in *Histoire et Historiens dans l'antiquité* (Entretiens Hardt 4) (Vandoeuvres–Geneva) 83–145

Fritz, K. von (1967) *Die Griechische Geschichtsschreibung*, 2 vols., Berlin

Froidefond, C. (1971) *Le Mirage égyptien dans la littérature grecque d'Homère à Aristote*, Aix-en-Provence

Fuks, A. (1970) 'The Bellum Achaicum and its social aspect', *JHS* 90: 78–89 (= *Social Conflict in Ancient Greece* (Jerusalem–Leiden 1984) 270–81)

Funke, P. (1993) 'Stamm und Polis: Überlegungen zur Entstehung der griechis-chen Staatenwelt in den dunklen Jahrhunderten', in J. Bleicken, ed., *Colloquium aus Anlass des 80. Geburtstages von A. Heuss* (Frankfurter althistorische Studien 13) (Kallmünz) 29–48

Gabba, E. (1957) 'Studi su Filarco. Le biografie plutarchee di Agide e di Cleomene (Capp. I–IV)', *Athenaeum* 35: 3–55; continuaz. e fine 193–239

Gabba, E. (ed.) (1974) *Polybe* (Entretiens Hardt 20), Vandoeuvres–Geneva

Gabba, E. (1996) 'L'eredità classica nel pensiero di John Adams', *RSI* 108: 872–96

Gaertringen, F. Hiller von (1906) *Die Inschriften von Priene*, Berlin

Galili, E. (1976–7) 'Raphia 217 BCE revisited', *SCI* 3: 56–126

Garin, E. (1990) 'Polibio e Machiavelli', *Quad. di Storia* 16, no. 31, 5–22

Gawantka, W. (1985) *Die sogenannte Polis: Entstehung, Geschichte und Kritik der moder-nen althistorischen Begriffe, der griechische Staat, die griechische Staatsidee, die Polis*, Stuttgart

Geffcken, J. (1892) *Timaios' Geographie des Westens*, Berlin

Gelzer, M. (1912) *Die Nobilität der römischen Republik*, Leipzig–Berlin (= Gelzer (1962) 19–135)

Gelzer, M. (1962) *Kleine Schriften* I, edd. H. Strasburger and C. Meier, Wiesbaden

Gill, C. (1984) 'The *ethos/pathos* distinction in rhetorical and literary criticism', *CQ* 34: 149–66

Giovannini, A. (1969) 'Polybe et les assemblées achéennes', *Mus.Helv.* 26: 1–17

Giovannini, A. (1982) 'La clause territoriale de la paix d' Apamée', *Athenaeum* 60: 224–36

Glockmann, G. and Helms, H. (1998) *Polybios-Lexikon*, Band 1, Lieferung 1 (παγκρατιαστής–ποιέω), Berlin

Golan, D. (1989) 'Polybius and the Third Macedonian War', *Ant. Class.* 58: 112–27

Golan, D. (1995) *The Res Graeciae in Polybius: Four Studies* (Bibliotheca di Athenaeum 27), Como

Goodman, M. (1987) *The Ruling Class of Judaea: the Origin of the Jewish Revolt against Rome, AD 66–70*, Cambridge (paper-back reprint 1993)

Gray, V. (1987) 'Mimesis in Greek historical theory', *AJPh* 118: 467–86

Green, P. (1990) *Alexander to Actium: The Historical Evolution of the Hellenistic Age* (Hellenistic Culture and Society 1), revised edn 1993, Berkeley–Los Angeles–London

Green, P. (ed.) (1993) *Hellenistic History and Culture*, Berkeley–Los Angeles–London

Gruen, E. S. (1976) 'The origins of the Achaean War', *JHS* 96: 46–69

Gruen, E. S. (1984) *The Hellenistic World and the Coming of Rome*, 2 vols., Berkeley–Los Angeles–London

Gruen, E. S. (1992) *Culture and National Identity in Republican Rome*, London

Gschnitzer, F. (1955) 'Stammes- und Ortsgemeinden im alten Griechenland', *WS* 68: 120–44

Günther, L.-M. (1995) 'L. Aemilius Paullus und sein Pfeilerdenkmal in Delphi', in Schubert and Brodersen (eds.) (1995) 81–5

Habicht, C. (1957) 'Samische Volksbeschlüsse der hellenistischen Zeit', *Ath. Mitt.* 72: 233–41

Habicht, C. (1979) *Untersuchungen zur politischen Geschichte Athens im 3. Jahrhundert v. Chr.*, Munich

Habicht, C. (1989) 'The Seleucids and their rivals', *CAH* VIII, 2nd edn, 324–87

Hall, J. M. (1997) *Ethnic Identity in Greek Antiquity*, Cambridge

Halm, D. E. (1995) 'Polybius' applied political theory', in A. Laks and M. Schofield, eds., *Justice and Generosity: Studies in Hellenistic Social and Political Philosophy: Proceedings of the Sixth Symposium Hellenisticum*, Cambridge

Hammond, N. G. L. (1984) 'The battle of Pydna', *JHS* 104: 31–47 (= Hammond (1994a) 377–94)

Hammond, N. G. L. (1988) 'The campaign and battle of Cynoscephalae in 197', *JHS* 108: 60–82 (= Hammond (1994a) 351–75)

Hammond, N. G. L. (1994a) *Collected Studies* III, Amsterdam

Hammond, N. G. L. (1994b) *Philip of Macedon*, London

Hammond, N. G. L. (1994c) 'One or two passes on the Cilicia–Syria border?', *Ancient World* 25: 15–26 (=Hammond (1997) 193–204)

Hammond, N. G. L. (1997) *Collected Studies* IV, Amsterdam

Hammond, N. G. L. and Walbank, F. W. (1988) *A History of Macedonia* III: *336–167 BC*, Oxford

Hansen, E. (1947) *The Attalids of Pergamon*, Ithaca

Hansen, M. H. (1993) 'The battle-exhortation in ancient historiography: fact or fiction?', *Historia* 42: 161–80

Hansen, M. H. (ed.) (1996) *Introduction to an Inventory of* Poleis *in Archaic Greece* (CPCActs 3), Copenhagen

Harder, R. (1926) *'Ocellus Lucanus', Texte und Kommentar*, Berlin (Reprint Dublin–Zurich 1966)

Harris, W. (1979) *War and Imperialism in Republican Rome, 327–70 BC*, Oxford

Hatzopoulos, M. B. (1994) *Cultes et rites de passage en Macédoine* (Meletemata 19), Athens

Head, B. V. (1911) *Historia Numorum*, 2nd edn, Oxford

Heinen, H. (1972a) *Untersuchungen zur hellenistischen Geschichte des 3. Jahrhunderts*, Wiesbaden

Heinen, H. (1972b) 'Die politischen Beziehungen zwischen Rom und dem Ptolemäerreich von ihren Anfängen bis zum Tag von Eleusis (273–168 v. Chr.)', *ANRW* I.1, 631–59

Heinen, H. (1981) Review of Habicht (1979), *Götting. Anz.* 233: 175–207

Herman, G. (1987) *Ritualised Friendship and the Greek City*, Cambridge

Herrmann, P. (1965) 'Antiochus der Grosse und Teos', *Anadolu [Anatolia]* 9: 29–160

Hine, A. M. (1979) 'Hannibal's battle on the Tagus (Polyb. iii.14 and Livy xxi.5)', *Latomus* 38: 891–901

Hirzel, R. (1882) *Untersuchungen zu Ciceros philosophischen Schriften* II, Leipzig

Hofmann, W. (1942) *Livius und der zweite punische Krieg* (*Hermes* Einzelschrift 8), Berlin

Hölkeskamp, K.-J. H. (2000) 'The Roman republic: government of the people by the people, for the people?', *SCI* 19: 203–23

Holleaux, M. (1921) *Rome, la Grèce et les monarchies hellénistiques au IIIe siècle av. J.C. (273–205)*, Paris

Holleaux, M. (1942) *Etudes d'épigraphie et d'histoire grecques* III, Paris

Holleaux, M. (1952) ed. L. Robert, *Etudes d'épigraphie et d'histoire grecques* IV, Paris

Hooff, A. J. L. van (1977) 'Polybius' reason and religion: the relation between Polybius' causal thinking and his attitude towards religion in the *Studies of History*', *Klio* 59: 101–28

Hornblower, S. (ed.) (1994) *Greek Historiography*, Oxford

Hornyánszky, H. (1929) *Von Hippokrates bis Tacitus*, Pécs

Howald, E. (1944) *Vom Geist antiker Geschichtsschreibung*, Munich and Berlin

Hoyos, B. D. (1984a) 'Polybius' Roman οἱ πολλοί in 264 BC', *LCM* 9: 88–93

Hoyos, B. D. (1984b) 'The Roman–Punic pact of 279', *Historia* 33: 402–39

Huss, W. (1976) *Untersuchungen zur Aussenpolitik Ptolemaios' IV*, Munich

Huss, W. (1985) *Geschichte der Karthager* (Handbuch der Altertumswissenschaft III.8), Munich

Jacobsen, T. W. and Smith, P. M. (1968) 'Two Kimolian dikast decrees from Geraistos in Euboia', *Hesperia* 37: 184–99

Jardé, A. (1925) *Les céréales dans l'antiquité grecque*, Paris

Jones, A. H. M. (1940) *The Greek City from Alexander to Justinian*, Oxford

Jouguet, J. (1923) 'Les Lagides et les indigènes égyptiens', *Rev. belge de phil. et d'hist.* 2: 419–45

Kallet-Marx, R. (1995) *Hegemony to Empire*, Berkeley–Los Angeles–Oxford

Kapetanopoulos, E. (1999) 'Alexander's *patrius sermo* in the Philotas affair', *Ancient World* 30: 117–28

Kebric, R. B. (1977) *In The Shadow of Macedon: Duris of Samos* (*Historia* Einzelschrift. 29), Wiesbaden

Klatt, M. (1877) *Forschungen zur Geschichte des achäischen Bundes: Quellen und Chronologie des Kleomenischen Krieges*, Berlin

Klose, P. (1972) *Die völkerrechtliche Ordnung der hellenistischen Staatenwelt in der Zeit von 280–168 v. Chr. Ein Beitrag zur Geschichte des Völkerrechts* (Münch. Beitr. Papyr. 64), Munich

Koenen, L. (1957) *Eine ptolemäische Königsurkunde (P. Kroll)*, Wiesbaden

Koenen, L. (1962) 'Die "demotische Zivilprozessordnung" und die Philanthropa vom 9. Okt. 186 vor Chr.', *Arch. Pap.* 17: 11–16

Koenen, L. (1983) 'Die Adaptation aegyptischer Königsideologie am Ptolemäerhof', *Egypt and the Hellenistic World* (Studia Hellenistica 27) (Leuven) 143–90

Koenen, L. (1993) 'The Ptolemaic king as a religious figure', in A. Bulloch et al., eds., *Images and Ideologies: Self-definition in the Hellenistic World* (Berkeley–Los Angeles) 25–115

Koerner, R. (1974) 'Die staatliche Entwicklung in Alt-Achaia', *Klio* 56: 457–95

Kraay, C. (1976) *Archaic and Classical Greek Coins*, London

Kreissig, H. (1969) 'Die Landwirtschaftliche Situation in Palästina vor dem Judäischen Krieg', *Acta Antiqua* 17: 223–54

Kreissig, H. (1970) *Die sozialen Zusammenhänge des judäischen Krieges*, Berlin

Kromayer, J. (1912) *Antike Schlachtfelder*, III.1, Berlin

Kuhrt, A. and Sherwin-White, S. (eds.) (1987) *Hellenism in the East*, London

Kussmaul, P. (1978) 'Der Halbmond von Cannae', *Mus. Helv.* 35: 249–57

Labuske, H. (1984) 'Geschichtsschreibung im Hellenismus: Polybios und seine Konkurrenten', *Klio* 66: 479–87

Lacey, W. K. (1968) *The Family in Classical Greece*, London

Larsen, J. A. O. (1938) 'Roman Greece', in T. Frank, ed., *An Economic Survey of Ancient Rome* IV (Baltimore) 259–498. (Reprint New York, 1975)

Larsen, J. A. O. (1945) 'Representation and democracy in Hellenistic federalism', *Class. Phil.* 40: 65–97

Larsen, J. A. O. (1955) *Representative Government in Greek and Roman History*, Berkeley–Los Angeles

Larsen, J. A. O. (1972) 'A recent interpretation of the Achaean assemblies', *Class.Phil.* 67: 178–85

Launey, M. (1949) *Recherches sur les armées hellénistiques* I, Paris

Launey, M. (1950) *Recherches sur les armées hellénistiques* II, Paris

Le Bohec, S. (1993) *Antigone Dôsôn, roi de Macédoine*, Nancy

Lehmann, G. A. (1967) *Untersuchungen zur historischen Glaubwürdigkeit des Polybios*, Münster

Lehmann, G. A. (1974) 'Polybios und die zeitgenössische griechische Geschichts-schreibung' in Gabba (ed.) (1974) 145–205

Lehmann, G. A. (1989/90) 'The "ancient" Greek history of Polybius: tendencies and political objectives', *SCI* 10: 66–77

Lillo, A. and M. (1988) 'On Polybius x.10.12, the capture of New Carthage', *Historia* 37: 477–86

Lintott, A. (1972) 'Imperial expansion and moral decline in the Roman republic', *Historia* 21: 626–38

Lintott, A. (1996) Review of Malkin and Rubinsohn (eds.) (1995) in *JRS* 86: 193–4

Lintott, A. (1999) *The Constitution of the Roman Republic*, Oxford

Luce, T. J. (1989) 'Ancient views on the cause of bias in historical writing', *CP* 84: 16–31

McDonald, A. H. (1967) 'The Treaty of Apamea, 188 BC', *JRS* 57: 1–8

McDonald, A. H. and Walbank, F. W. (1969) 'The Treaty of Apamea (188 BC): the naval clauses', *JRS* 59: 30–9

McGing, B. C. (1997) 'Revolt Egyptian style: internal opposition to Ptolemaic rule', *Arch. Pap.* 43: 273–314

Mackay, P. (1970) 'The coinage of Macedonian republics 168–146 BC', *Ancient Macedonia* 256–64

Mahaffy, J. P. (1899) *A History of Egypt under the Ptolemaic Dynasty*, London

Malkin, I. and Rubinsohn, Z. W. (eds.) (1995) *Leaders and Masses in the Roman World: Studies in Honor of Zvi Yavetz* (*Mnemosyne* Supplement 139), Leiden

Manni Miscellanea (1980) Φιλίας χάριν: *Miscellanea di Studi Classici in onore di Eugenio Manni*, 6 vols., Rome

Marincola, J. (1997) *Authority and Tradition in Ancient Historiography*, Cambridge

Marsden, E. W. (1974) 'Polybius as a military historian', in Gabba (ed.) (1974) 267–95

Martínez Lacy, R. (1991) "Εθη καὶ νόμιμα: Polybius and his concept of culture', *Klio* 73: 83–92

Mattingly, H. (1997) 'Athens between Rome and the kings', in Cartledge, Garnsey and Gruen (eds.) (1997) 120–44

Mauersberger, A. (1956–) *Polybios-Lexikon*, Berlin

May, J. M. F. (1946) 'Macedonia and Illyria (217–167 BC)', *JRS* 36: 48–56

Meissner, B. (1986) 'Πραγματικὴ ἱστορία: Polybios über den Zweck pragmatis-cher Geschichtsschreibung', *Saeculum* 37: 313–51

Meister, K. (1967) *Die sizilische Geschichte bei Diodor von den Anfängen bis zum Tod des Agathokles* (Diss. Erlangen), Munich

Meister, K. (1975) *Historische Kritik bei Polybios* (Palingenesia, Monographien und Texte zur klassischen Altertumswissenschaft 9), Wiesbaden

Meister, K. (1989/90) 'The role of Timaeus in Greek historiography', *SCI* 10: 55–65

Meister, K. (1990) *Die griechische Geschichtsschreibung von den Anfängen bis zum Ende des Hellenismus*, Stuttgart–Berlin–Cologne

Mendels, D. (1981) 'The five empires: a note on a propagandist topic', *AJP* 102: 330–7 (= Mendels (1998) 314–23)

Mendels, D. (1992) *The Rise and Fall of Jewish Nationalism*, New York–London

Mendels, D. (1998) *Identity, Religion and Historiography: Studies in Hellenistic History*, Sheffield

Mette, H. J. (1936) *Sphairopoüa: Untersuchungen zur Kosmologie des Krates von Pergamon*, Munich

Meyer, Ed. (1937) *Geschichte des Altertums* III, 2nd edn, Stuttgart

Millar, F. (1984) 'The political character of the classical Roman republic, 200–151 BC', *JRS* 74: 1–19

Millar, F. (1986) 'Politics, persuasion and the people before the Social War (150–90 BC)', *JRS* 76: 1–11

Millar, F. (1987) 'Polybius between Greece and Rome', in J. M. T. Koumoulides and J. Brademas, eds., *Greek Connections: Essays on Culture and Diplomacy* (Notre Dame, Indiana) 1–18

Millar, F. (1989) 'Political power in mid-republican Rome: curia or comitium?', *JRS* 79: 138–50

Millar, F. (1993) *The Roman Near East 31 BC–AD 337*, Cambridge, MA

Millar, F. (1995) 'Popular politics at Rome in the late republic', in Malkin and Rubinsohn (eds.) (1995) 91–113

Millar, F. (1998) *The Crowd in Rome in the Late Republic* (Jerome Lectures 22), Ann Arbor, MI

Milne, J. G. (1939) 'Trade between Greece and Egypt before Alexander the Great', *JEA* 25: 177–83

Milne, M. (1989) 'Two humanistic translations of Polybius', *RPL* (Kansas) 12: 123–9

Miranda, A. Alvarez de (1956) 'La irreligiosidad de Polibio', *Emerita* 24: 27–65

Mohm, S. (1977) *Untersuchungen zu den historiographischen Anschauungen des Polybios*, Diss. Saarbrücken

Momigliano, A. (1934a) *Filippo il Macedone*, Florence

Momigliano, A. (1934b) 'Herod of Judaea', *CAH* X, 1st edn, 316–39 (with Note, pp. 884–7)

Momigliano, A. (1942) '"Terra Marique"', *JRS* 32: 53–64

Momigliano, A. (1944) Review of *CAH* X, 1st edn, 1934, *JRS* 34: 109–16

Momigliano, A. (1959) 'Atene nel III secolo A.C. a la scoperta di Roma nelle storie di Timeo di Tauromenio', *RSI* 71: 529–56 (= *Terzo contributo alla storia degli studi classici e del mondo antico* (Rome 1966) I, 23–53; published in English as 'Athens in the third century BC and the discovery of Rome in the histories of Timaeus', *Essays in Ancient and Modern Historiography* (Oxford–Middleton, Conn. 1977) 37–66)

Momigliano, A. (1963) 'An interim report on the origins of Rome', *JRS* 53: 95–121

Momigliano, A. (1969) *Quarto contributo alla storia degli studi classici e del mondo antico*, Rome

Momigliano, A. (1971) 'Popular religious beliefs and the late Roman historians', in *Studies in Church History* VIII (Cambridge) 1–18 (= *Quinto contributo alla storia degli studi classici e del mondo antico* I (Rome 1975) 74–92)

Momigliano, A. (1974a) *Polybius between the English and the Turks* (Seventh J. L. Myres Memorial Lecture), Oxford (= *Sesto Contributo* 125–41)

Momigliano, A. (1974b) 'Polybius' reappearance in Western Europe', in Gabba (ed.) (1974) 345–72 (= *Sesto Contr.* 103–23 = *Essays* 67–77)

Momigliano, A. (1975) *Alien Wisdom: The Limits of Hellenization*, Cambridge

Momigliano, A. (1980) 'Interpretazioni minime, IV; Polyb. iii.28', *Annali di Pisa* 10: 1221–3

Momigliano, A. (1981) 'Greek culture and the Jews', in M. I. Finley, ed., *The Legacy of Greece: a New Appraisal* (Oxford) 325–46

Momigliano, A. (1990) *The Classical Foundations of Modern Historiography*, Berkeley–Los Angeles–Oxford

Momigliano, A. and Fraser, P. (1950) 'A new date for the battle of Andros? A discussion', *CQ* 44: 107–18

Moore, J. M. (1965) *The Manuscript Tradition of Polybius*, Cambridge

Mooren, L. (1975) *The Aulic Titulature in Ptolemaic Egypt: Introduction and Prosopography*, Brussels

Moretti, L. (1953) *Iscrizioni agonistiche greche*, Rome

Moretti, L. (1967) *Iscrizioni storiche ellenistiche* I, Florence

Morgan, C. (1991) 'Ethnicity in early Greek states: historical and material perspectives', *PCPS* 37: 131–63

Morgan, C. and Hall, J. (1996) 'Achaian *poleis* and Achaian colonisation', in Hansen (ed.) (1996) 164–232

Morgan, M. G. (1990) 'Politics, religion and the games in Rome, 200–150 BC', *Phil.* 134: 14–36

Mørkholm, O. (1966) *Antiochus IV of Syria* (Classica et Mediaevalia Dissertations 8), Gyldendal

Müllenhoff, K. V. (1890) *Deutsche Altertumskunde* I, 2nd edn, Berlin

Müller, W. M. (1920) *Egyptological Researches: the Bilingual Decrees of Philae* (Carnegie Institution of Washington: Publication 53, Vol. III), Washington

Murray, O. and Price, S. (eds.) (1991) *The Greek City from Homer to Alexandria*, Oxford

Musti, D. (1966) 'Lo stato dei Seleucidi', *Studi classici e orientali* 15: 61–201

Musti, D. (1967) 'Polibio e la democrazia', *Annali della scuola normale superiore di Pisa* 36: 155–207

Musti, D. (1972) 'Polibio negli studi dell' ultimo ventennio (1950–1970)', *ANRW* 1.2, 1114–81

Musti, D. (1978) *Polibio e l'imperialismo romano*, Naples

Neils, J. (1992) *Goddess and Polis: The Panathenaic Festival in Ancient Athens*, Princeton, NJ

Neumann, K. J. (1886) 'Strabons Gesamturtheil über die Homerische Geographie', *Hermes* 21: 134–41

Nicolet, C. (1974) 'Polybe et les institutions romaines', in Gabba (ed.) (1974) 209–65

Nicolet, C. (1983a) *Demokratia et Aristokratia: A propos de Caius Gracchus: mots grecs et réalités romaines*, Paris

Nicolet, C. (1983b) 'Polybe et la "constitution" de Rome: aristocratie et démocratie', in Nicolet (ed.) (1983a) 15–35

Ninck, M. (1945) *Die Entdeckung Europas durch die Griechen*, Basle

Nippel, W. (1980) *Mischverfassungstheorie und Verfassungsrealität in Antike und früher Neuzeit* (Geschichte und Gesellschaft 21), Stuttgart

Nissen, H. (1863) *Kritische Untersuchungen über die Quellen der vierten und fünften Dekade des Livius*, Berlin

Nissen, H. (1871) 'Die Oekonomie der Geschichte des Polybius', *Rhein. Mus.* 26: 241–82

Nissen, H. (1902) *Italische Landeskunde*, Berlin

North, J. A. (1981) 'The development of Roman imperialism', *JRS* 71: 1–9

Nottmeyer, H. (1995) *Polybius und das Ende des Achaierbundes: Untersuchungen zu den römisch-achaiischen Beziehungen, ausgehend von der Mission des Kallikrates bis zur Zerstörung Korinths*, Munich

Oliva, P. (1971) *Sparta and her Social Problems*, Amsterdam–Prague

O'Neil, J. L. (1980) 'Who attended Achaian assemblies?', *Mus. Helv.* 37: 41–9

O'Neil, J. L. (1984–86) 'Political elites in the Achaian and Aitolian leagues', *Ancient Society* 15–17: 33–61

Ormerod, H. A. (1924) *Piracy in the Ancient World*, Liverpool and London

Pace, N. (1988) 'La traduzione di N. Perotti delle Historie di Polibio', in *RPL* (Kansas) 11: 221–34

Pace, N. (1989) 'La traduzione di N. Perotti delle Historie di Polibio II', in *RPL* (Kansas) 12: 145–54

Papastyliou-Philiou, Z. (1995) 'Polybe et la réforme de Cléomène III', Δωδώνη (Ioannina) 24: 5–13

Parker, R. (1998) *Cleomenes on the Acropolis*, Oxford

Pearson, L. (1987) *The Greek Historians of the West: Timaeus and his Predecessors* (Philological Monographs of the American Philological Association 35), Atlanta, GA

Pédech, P. (1961) *Polybe, Histoires Livre XII*, Paris

Pédech, P. (1964) *La Méthode historique de Polybe*, Paris

Pédech, P. (1965) 'Les idées religieuses de Polybe: Etude sur la religion de l'élite gréco-romaine au IIe siècle av. J.-C.', *RHR* 167: 35–68

Perdrizet, P. (1921) 'Miscellanea XIII: La Ligue Achéenne et les Lagides', *REA* 23: 281–3

Peremans, W. (1975) *Le Monde grec, pensée, littérature, histoire, documents: hommages à Claire Préaux*, Brussels

Peremans, W. and van 't Dack, E. (1950) *Prosopographia Ptolemaica* I (Studia Hellenistica 6), Louvain

Peremans, W. and van 't Dack, E. (1953) *Prosopographica* (Studia Hellenistica 9), Louvain

Perpillou-Thomas, F. (1993) *Fêtes d'Egypte ptolémaïque et romaine d'après la documentation papyrologique grecque* (Studia Hellenistica 31), Leuven

Pestman, P. W. (1965) 'Harmachis et Anchmachis, deux rois indigènes du temps des Ptolémées', *Chron. d'Egypte* 40: 157–70

Pestman, P. W. (1995) 'Haronnophris and Chaonnophris', in S. P. Vleeming, ed., *Hundred-Gated Thebes. Acts of a Colloquium on Thebes and the Theban Area in the Graeco-Roman Period (P.L. Bat 27)* (Leiden–New York–Cologne) 101–37

Petzold, K. E. (1969) *Studien zur Methode des Polybios und zu ihrer historischen Auswertung* (Vestigia 9), Munich

Petzold, K. E. (1977) '*Kyklos* und *Telos* im Geschichtsdenken des Polybios', *Saeculum* 28: 253–90

Pickard-Cambridge, A. W. (1914) *Demosthenes and the Last Days of Greek Freedom*, New York–London

Podes, S. (1991a) 'Polybios' Anakyklosislehre, diskrete Zustandssyteme und das Problem der Mischverfassung', *Klio* 73: 382–90

Podes. S. (1991b) 'Polybius and his theory of anacyclosis: problems of not just ancient theory', *HPTh* 12: 577–87

Pohlenz, M. (1920) 'Die Anfänge der griechischen Poetik', *Nachrichten von der Gesellschaft der Wissenschaften zu Göttingen*, 143–78

Pöhlmann, R. (1889) *Hellenische Anschauungen über den Zusammenhang zwischen Natur und Geschichte*, Leipzig

Pollitt, J. J. (1986) *Art in the Hellenistic Age*, Cambridge

Pöschl, V. (1936) *Römischer Staat und griechisches Staatsdenken bei Cicero*, Berlin

Préaux, C. (1936) 'Esquisse d'une histoire des révolutions égyptiennes sous les Lagides', *Chron. d'Egypte* 25: 522–52

Préaux, C. (1965) 'Polybe et Ptolémée Philopator', *Chron. d'Egypte* 40: 364–75

Préaux, C. (1978) *Le Monde hellénistique: la Grèce et l'Orient (323–146 av. J.-C.)*, 2 vols., Paris

Price, M. (1974) *Coins of the Macedonians*, London

Pritchett, W. K. (1965) *Studies in Ancient Greek Topography, Part I*, Berkeley–Los Angeles

Pritchett, W. K. (1969) *Studies in Ancient Greek Topography, Part II (Battlefields)*, Berkeley–Los Angeles

Pritchett, W. K. (1984) 'The polis of Sellasia', in K. Rigsby, ed., *Studies Presented to Sterling Dow on his 80th Birthday* (*GRBS* Supplement 10), 251–4

Pritchett, W. K. (1989) *Studies in Ancient Greek Topography, Part VI*, Berkeley–Los Angeles–London

Pritchett, W. K. (1991) *Studies in Ancient Greek Topography, Part VII*, Amsterdam

Pritchett, W. K. (1992) *Studies in Ancient Greek Topography, Part VIII*, Amsterdam

Proctor, D. (1971) *Hannibal's Pass in History*, Cambridge

Radt, S. L. (1990) 'Polybiana', *Mnemosyne* 43: 73–85

Rahe, P. A. (1992) *Republics Ancient and Modern: Classical Republicanism and the American Constitution*, Chapel Hill–London

Rajak, T. (1983) *Josephus; the Historian and his Society*, London

Raphael, F. (1977) 'Esquisse d'une sociologie de la fête', *Contrepoint* 24: 109–30

Revillout, E. (1883) 'Association de Ptolémée Epiphane à la couronne et quelques autres associations royales', *Rev. Egypt.* 3: 1–8

Reynolds, J. (1966) 'Roman epigraphy, 1961–65', *JRS* 56: 116–21

Rice, E. E. (1983) *The Grand Procession of Ptolemy Philadelphus*, Oxford

Rich, J. and Wallace-Hadrill, A. (eds.) (1991) *City and Country in the Ancient World*, London

Rizakis, A. D. (1990) 'La politeia dans les cités de la confédération achéenne', *Tyche* 5: 109–34

Rizakis, A. D. (1995) *Achaie I, sources textuelles et histoire régionale* (Meletemata 20), Athens

Rizzo, F. P. (1968–9) 'Problemi costituzionali sicelioti', *Kokalos* 14–15: 365–96

Robert, L. (1936) 'Smyrne et les Sôtéria de Delphes', *REA* 38: 1–23

Robert, L. (1960) 'Sur un décret des Korésiens au musée de Smyrne', *Hellenica* 11–12: 132–76

Robert. L. (1966) 'Sur un décret d'Ilion et sur un papyrus concernant des cultes royaux', *American Studies in Papyrology* 1: 175–211

Romilly, J. de (1958) 'L'Utilité d'histoire selon Thucydide', in *Histoire et historiens dans l'antiquité* (Entretiens Hardt 4) (Vandoeuvres–Geneva) 39–82

Rostovtzeff, M. (1941) *The Social and Economic History of the Hellenistic World*, 3 vols., Oxford

Rostovtzeff, M. and Welles, C. B. (1940) 'A note on the new inscription from Samothrace', *AJP* 61: 207–8

Roussel, P. (1932) 'Delphes et l'Amphictionie après la Guerre d'Aitolie', *BCH* 56: 1–36

Roux, M. (1993) 'Recherches sur les aspects militaires de la conquête du monde gréco-hellénistique par Rome au iie siècle av. J.-C.', *REA* 95: 443–57

Roveri, A. (1964) *Studi su Polibio*, Bologna

Ryffel, H. (1949) Μεταβολή πολιτειῶν: *der Wandel der Staatsverfassungen*, Bern

Sabin, P. (2000) 'The face of Roman battle', *JRS* 90: 1–17

Sacks, K. (1981) *Polybius on the Writing of History* (University of California Classical Studies 24), Berkeley–Los Angeles–London

Sakellariou, M. B. (1989) *The Polis-State: Definition and Origin* (Meletemata 4), Athens

Scala, R. von (1890) *Die Studien des Polybios*, Stuttgart

Scardigli, B. (1991) *I trattati romano-cartaginesi*, Pisa

Schepens, G. (1974) 'The bipartite and tripartite division of history in Polybius xii.25e and 27', *Ancient Society* 5: 277–87

Schepens, G. (1975) "Ἔμφασις und ἐνάργεια in Polybios' Geschichtstheorie', *Riv. stor. ant*, 5: 185–200

Schepens, G. (1978) 'Polybius on Timaeus' account of Phalaris' bull: a case of *deisidaimonia*', *Ancient Society* 9: 117–48

Schepens, G. (1990) 'Polemic and methodology in Polybius, Book XII', in Verdin, Schepens and De Keyser (eds.) (1990) 39–61

Schmitt, H. H. (1964) *Untersuchungen zur Geschichte Antiochos' des Grossen und seiner Zeit*, Wiesbaden

Schmitt, H. H. (1974) 'Polybios und das Gleichgewicht der Mächte', in Gabba (ed.) (1974) 65–102

Schmitthenner, W. (1968) 'Über eine Formveränderung der Monarchie seit Alexander dem Grossen', *Saeculum* 19: 31–46

Schubert, C. (1995) 'Mischverfassung und Gleichgewichtssystem: Polybios und seine Vorläufer', in Schubert and Brodersen (eds.) (1995) 225–35

Schubert, C. and Brodersen, K. (eds.) (1995) *Rom und der griechische Osten: Festschrift für Hatto H. Schmitt zum 65. Geburtstag,* Stuttgart

Schulten, A. (1911) 'Polybius und Posidonius über Iberien und die iberischen Kriege', *Hermes* 46: 568–607

Schwarte, K.-H. (1993) 'Roms Griff nach Sardinien: Quellenkritisches zur Historizität der Darstellung des Polybios', in *Festschrift A. Lippold: Klassiches Altertum, Spätantike und frühes Christentum* (Würzburg) 107–46

Schweighaeuser, J. (1789–95) *Polybii Megalopolitani historiarum quidquid superest,* 8 vols, Leipzig

Scott-Kilvert, I. (1979) ed. *Polybius: The Rise of the Roman Empire,* Harmondsworth

Scullard, H. H. (1930) *Scipio Africanus in the Second Punic War,* Cambridge

Scullard, H. H. (1960) 'Scipio Aemilianus and Roman politics', *JRS* 50: 59–74

Scullard, H. H. (1973) *Roman Politics, 220–150 BC,* 2nd edn, Oxford

Segre, M. (1952) *Tituli Calymnii,* Bergamo

Seibert, J. (1993) *Hannibal,* Darmstadt

Sethe, K. (1904) *Urkunden des aegyptischen Altertums, II (Hieroglyphische Urkunden der griechisch-römischen Welt),* Leipzig

Sethe, K. (1917) 'Die historische Bedeutung des 2. Philä-Dekrets aus der Zeit des Ptolemaios Epiphanes', *ZÄS* 53: 35–49

Sherwin-White, A. N. (1964) Review of A. Prova, *L'Iscrizione di Ponzio Pilato a Cesarea* (Milan, 1961), *JRS* 54: 258–9

Sherwin-White, S. and Kuhrt, A. (1993) *From Samarkhand to Sardis: A New Approach to the Seleucid Empire,* London

Shimron, B. (1972) *Late Sparta: The Spartan Revolution 243–146 BC* (Arethusa Monographs 3), Buffalo

Shimron, B. (1979/80) 'Polybius and Rome: a new examination of the evidence', *SCI* 5: 94–117

Shipley, G. (2000) *The Greek World after Alexander, 323–146 BC,* London–New York

Skeat, T. C. (1954) *The Reigns of the Ptolemies,* Munich

Skutsch, O. (1985) *The Annals of Ennius,* Oxford

Smyly, J. G. (1921) *Greek Papyri from Gurob,* Dublin

Snodgrass, A. M. (1991) 'Archaeology and the Greek city', in Rich and Wallace-Hadrill (eds.) (1991) 1–23

Sommella, P. (1971–2) 'Heroon di Enea a Lavinium: recenti scavi a Pratica di Mare', *Rend. Acc. Pont.* 44: 47ff.

Souza, P. de (1999) *Piracy in the Graeco-Roman World,* Cambridge

Stählin, G. (1974) 'Das Schicksal im Neuen Testament und bei Josephus', in *Josephus-Studien: Festschrift O. Michel* (Göttingen) 335–43

Stier, H. E. (1945) *Grundlagen und Sinn der griechischen Geschichte,* Stuttgart

Stiewe, K. and Holzberg, N. (eds.) (1982) *Polybios* (Wege der Forschung 347), Darmstadt

Strachan-Davidson, J. L. (1888) *Selections from Polybius*, Oxford
Swain, J. W. (1940) 'The theory of the four monarchies: opposition history under the Roman empire', *CP* 35: 1–21
Taeger, F. (1922) *Die Archäologie des Polybios*, Stuttgart
Tarn, W. W. (1910) 'The dedicated ship of Antigonos Gonatas', *JHS* 30: 218–21
Tarn, W. W. (1913) *Antigonos Gonatas*, Oxford
Tarn, W. W. (1928) 'The struggle of Egypt against Syria and Macedonia', *CAH* VII, 1st edn, 699–731 (with Chronological Note, p. 862)
Tarn, W. W. (1929) 'Queen Ptolemais and Apamea', *CQ* 23: 138–41
Tarn, W. W. (1933) 'Two notes on Ptolemaic history', *JHS* 53: 57–68
Tarn, W. W. (1941) Review of Walbank (1940), *JRS* 31: 173
Thiel, J. H. (1946) *Studies on the History of Roman Sea-power in Republican Times*, Amsterdam
Thompson, D. J. (1988) *Memphis under the Ptolemies*, Princeton, NJ
Thompson, D. J. (1992) 'Literacy and the administration in early Ptolemaic Egypt', in J. H. Johnson, ed., *Life in a Multi-cultural Society: Egypt from Cambyses to Constantine and Beyond* (Studies in Ancient Oriental Civilization 51) (Chicago) 323–6
Thompson, D. J. (2000) 'Philadelphus' procession: dynastic power in a Mediterranean context', in L. Mooren, ed., *Politics, Administration and Society in the Hellenistic and Roman World* (Studia Hellenistica 36) (Leuven) 365–88
Thompson, W. E. (1971) 'Philip V and the Islanders', *TAPA* 102: 616–20
Thompson, W. E. (1985) 'Fragments of the preserved historians – especially Polybius', in *The Greek Historians. Literature and History. Papers Presented to A. E. Raubitschek* (with a preface by M. H. Jameson) (Saratoga, CA) 119–39
Thompson, W. E. (1986) 'The battle of the Bagradas', *Hermes* 64: 111–17
Tipps, G. (1985) 'The battle of Ecnomus', *Historia* 34: 432–65
Torelli, M. (1984) *Lavinio e Roma*, Rome
Tränkle, H. (1978) *Livius und Polybius*, Basle–Stuttgart
Treves, P. (1962) *Lo studio dell'antichità classica nell'ottocento*, Milan–Naples
Treves, P. (1970) 'Balance of power politics in classical antiquity', *Thirteenth International Congress of Historical Sciences: Proceedings*, Moscow
Troiani, L. (1979) 'Il funzionamento dello stato ellenistico e dello stato romano nel v e nel vi libro delle *Storie* di Polibio', in *Ricerche di storiografia greca di età romana* (Pisa), 9–19
Trompf, G. W. (1979) *The Idea of Historical Renewal in Western Thought*, Berkeley–Los Angeles–London
Trüdinger, K. (1918) *Studien zur Geschichte der griechisch-römischen Ethnographie*, Dissertation Basel.
Uhden, R. (1933) 'Das Erdbild in der Tetrabiblos des Ptolemaios', *Philol.* 88: 302–25.
Ungern-Sternberg, J. von (1975) *Capua im zweiten punischen Krieg*, Munich
Urban, R. (1991) 'Die Kelten in Italien und in Gallien bei Polybios', in J. Seibert, ed., *Hellenistische Studien: Gedenkschrift für Hermann Bengtson* (Münchener Arbeiten zur Alten Geschichte 5) (Munich) 137–57

Vaahtera, J. E. (2000) 'Roman religion and the Roman *politeia*', in C. Bruun, ed., *The Roman Middle Republic: Politics, Religion and Historiography, 400–133 BC* (Acta Instituti Romani Finlandiae 23) (Rome) 251–64

Vercruysse, M. (1984) *Het thema van de waarheidsverdraaiing in de Griekse geschiedschrijving. Een onderzoek van Polybius en zijn voorgangers*, Brussels

Vercruysse, M. (1990) 'A la recherche du mensonge et de la vérité: la fonction des passages méthodologiques chez Polybe', in Verdin, Schepens and De Keyser (eds.) (1990) 17–38

Verdin, H. (1990) 'Agatharchide de Cnide et les fictions des poètes', in Verdin, Schepens and De Keyser (eds.) (1990) 1–15, with discussion 63–71

Verdin, H., Schepens, G. and De Keyser, E. (eds.) (1990) *Purposes of History: Studies in Greek Historiography from the 4th to the 2nd Centuries BC, Proceedings of the International Colloquium, Louvain 24–26 May 1988*, Leuven

Veyne, P. (1976) *Le Pain et le cirque: sociologie historique d'un pluralisme politique*, Paris

Vidal-Naquet, P. (1977) 'Flavius Josephus ou du bon usage de la trahison', preface to *Josephus, De Bello Gallico*, tr. P. Savinel, Paris

Walbank, F. W. (1936) 'The accession of Ptolemy Epiphanes', *JEA* 22: 20–34 (= Walbank (1985a) 38–56)

Walbank, F. W. (1938) 'Φίλιππος τραγῳδούμενος: A Polybian experiment', *JHS* 58: 55–68 (= Walbank (1985a) 210–23 = Stiewe and Holzberg (eds.) (1982) 1–23)

Walbank, F. W. (1940) *Philip V of Macedon*, Cambridge

Walbank, F. W. (1942) 'Alcaeus of Messene, Philip V and Rome, Part I', *CQ* 36: 134–45

Walbank, F. W. (1943a) 'Alcaeus of Messene, Philip V and Rome, Part II', *CQ* 37: 1–13

Walbank, F. W. (1943b) 'Polybius and the Roman constitution', *CQ* 37: 73–89

Walbank, F. W. (1944) 'Alcaeus of Messene, Philip V and Rome: a footnote', *CQ* 38: 87–8

Walbank, F. W. (1951) 'The problem of Greek nationality', *Phoenix* 5: 41–60 (= Walbank (1985a) 1–19)

Walbank, F. W. (1954) 'The construction of the sixth book of Polybius', *CQ* n.s. 4: 97–122 (in conjunction with C. O. Brink)

Walbank, F. W. (1960) 'History and tragedy', *Historia* 9: 216–34 (= Walbank (1985a) 224–41)

Walbank, F. W. (1962) 'Polemic in Polybius', *JRS* 52: 1–12 (= Walbank (1985a) 262–79)

Walbank, F. W. (1963) 'Polybius and Rome's eastern policy', *JRS* 53: 1–13 (= Walbank (1985a) 138–56)

Walbank, F. W. (1965a) *Speeches in Greek Historians* (Third Myres Memorial Lecture), Oxford (= Walbank (1985a) 242–61)

Walbank, F. W. (1965b) 'Political morality and the friends of Scipio', *JRS* 55: 1–16 (= Walbank (1985a) 157–80)

Walbank, F. W. (1966) 'The Spartan ancestral constitution in Polybius', in E. Badian, ed., *Ancient Society: Studies Presented to Victor Ehrenberg on his 75th Birthday* (Oxford) 303–12

Walbank, F. W. (1968–9) 'The historians of Greek Sicily', *Kokalos* 14–15: 476–98

Walbank, F. W. (1970) 'The Achaean assemblies again', *Mus.Helv.* 27: 129–43

Walbank, F. W. (1972a) *Polybius* (Sather Classical Lectures 43), Berkeley–Los Angeles–London (paper-back reprint 1990)

Walbank, F. W. (1972b) 'Nationality as a factor in Roman history' *Harv. Stud.* 76: 145–68 (= Walbank (1985a) 57–76)

Walbank, F. W. (1974) 'Polybius between Greece and Rome', in E. Gabba, ed., *Polybe* (Entretiens Hardt) (Vandoeuvres–Geneva) 1–31 (= Walbank (1985a) 280–97)

Walbank, F. W. (1975) '*Symploke*: its role in Polybius' Histories', *YCS* 24: 197–212 (= Walbank (1985a) 313–24)

Walbank, F. W. (1976/7) 'Were there Greek federal states?', *SCI* 3: 27–51 (= Walbank (1985a) 20–37)

Walbank, F. W. (1977) 'Polybius' last ten books', in *Historiographia Antiqua: Commentationes Lovanienses in honorem W. Peremans septuagenarii editae* (Leuven) 139–62 (= Walbank (1985a) 325–43)

Walbank, F. W. (1981) *The Hellenistic World* (Fontana History of the Ancient World), London

Walbank, F. W. (1981/2) 'Il giudizio di Polibio su Roma', *Atti dell' Istituto Veneto di Scienze, Lettere ed Arti* 140: *Classe di scienze morali, lettere ed arti*, 237–56

Walbank, F. W. (1983) 'Polybius and the *aitiai* of the Second Punic War', *LCM* 8: 62–3

Walbank, F. W. (1984a) 'Monarchies and monarchic ideas' *CAH* 2nd edn, VII.1, 62–100

Walbank, F. W. (1984b) Review of Rice (1983), *LCM* 9: 50–4

Walbank, F. W. (1985a) *Selected Papers: Studies in Greek and Roman History and Historiography*, Cambridge

Walbank, F. W. (1985b) 'Two misplaced Polybian passages from the *Suda* (xvi.29.1 and xvi.38)', in *Xenia: Scritti in onore di Piero Treves* (Venice) 227–34

Walbank, F. W. (1985c) Review of Fornara (1983), *JHS* 105: 211

Walbank, F. W. (1989) 'Antigonus Doson's attack on Cytinium (*REG* 101 (1988), 12–53)', *ZPE* 76: 184–92

Walbank, F. W. (2000) 'Athenaeus and Polybius', in D. Braund and J. Wilkins, eds., *Athenaeus and his World* (Exeter) 161–70

Wallinga, H. T. (1986) 'Een aardrijkskundeles van Polybius', *Lampas* 19: 208–19

Wallis Budge, E. A. (1929) *The Rosetta Stone and the Decipherment of Egyptian Hieroglyphics*, London

Walsh, P. G. (1999) *Titi Livi ab urbe condita*, VI, *Libri XXXVI–XL*, Oxford

Weber, G. (1995) 'Herrscher, Hof und Dichter: Aspekte der Legitimierung und Repräsentation hellenistischer Könige am Beispiel der ersten drei Antigoniden', *Historia* 44: 283–316

Wehrli, F. (1967) *Die Schule des Aristoteles: Texte und Kommentar* I, *Dikaiarchos*, 2nd edn, Basle

Weil, R. (1977) *Polybe, Histoires Livre vi*, Paris

Weil, R. (1988) 'La Composition de l'histoire de Polybe', *Journ. Sav.* 185–206

Weiss, R. (1957) *Humanism in England*, 2nd edn, Oxford

Welles, C. B. (1934) *Royal Correspondence in the Hellenistic Period: A Study in Greek Epigraphy*, New Haven, Conn.

Welwei, K.-W. (1963) *Könige und Königtum im Urteil des Polybios*, Herbede, Ruhr

Wiedemann, T. (1990) 'Rhetoric in Polybius', in Verdin, Schepens and De Keyser (eds.) (1990) 289–300

Wiegand, Th. (1914) *Milet: Ergebnisse der Ausgrabungen und Untersuchungen seit dem Jahre 1899* I, Berlin

Wiemer, H.-U. (2001) *Rhodische Traditionem in der hellenistischen Historiographie*, Frankfurt

Will, E. (1966–7) *Histoire politique du monde hellénistique (323–30 av. J.-C.)*, 1st edn, 2 vols., Nancy

Will, E. (1979) *Histoire politique du monde hellénistique (323–30 av. J.-C.)*, 2nd edn, I, Nancy

Will, E. (1982) *Histoire politique du monde hellénistique (323–30 av. J.-C.)*, 2nd edn, II, Nancy

Winnicki, J. K. (1989) 'Das ptolemäische und das hellenistische Heerwesen', in L. Criscuolo and G. Geraci, eds., *Egitto e storia antica dall' ellenismo all' età araba: bilancio di un confronto* (Bologna) 213–30

Wooten, C. (1974) 'The speeches in Polybius: an insight into the nature of Hellenistic oratory', *AJP* 95: 235–51

Wunderer, C. (1901) *Polybios-Forschungen* II, Leipzig

Yakobson, A. (1999) *Elections and Electioneering in Rome: a Study in the Political System of the Late Republic* (*Historia* Einzelschrift 128), Stuttgart

Indexes

II AUTHORS AND PASSAGES

III INSCRIPTIONS, COINS AND PAPYRI

IV GREEK WORDS